FOUNDATIONS OF
MULTICULTURAL
PSYCHOLOGY

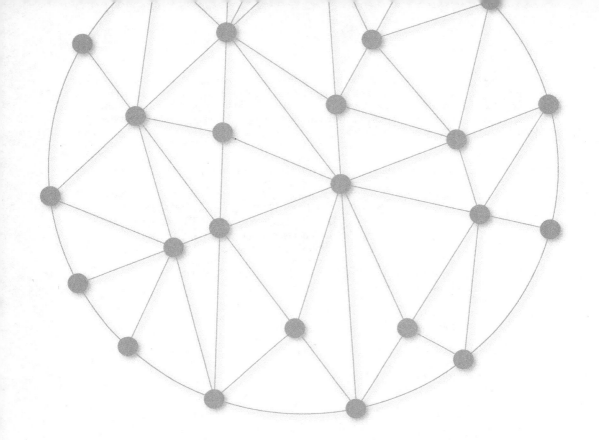

FOUNDATIONS OF
MULTICULTURAL
PSYCHOLOGY

RESEARCH TO INFORM
EFFECTIVE PRACTICE

TIMOTHY B. SMITH and JOSEPH E. TRIMBLE

American Psychological Association • Washington, DC

Published by
American Psychological Association
750 First Street, NE
Washington, DC 20002
www.apa.org

To order
APA Order Department
P.O. Box 92984
Washington, DC 20090-2984
Tel: (800) 374-2721; Direct: (202) 336-5510
Fax: (202) 336-5502; TDD/TTY: (202) 336-6123
Online: www.apa.org/pubs/books
E-mail: order@apa.org

In the U.K., Europe, Africa, and the Middle East, copies may be ordered from
American Psychological Association
3 Henrietta Street
Covent Garden, London
WC2E 8LU England

Typeset in Goudy by Circle Graphics, Inc., Columbia, MD

Printer: Bang Printing, Brainerd, MN
Cover Designer: Naylor Design, Washington, DC

The opinions and statements published are the responsibility of the authors, and such opinions and statements do not necessarily represent the policies of the American Psychological Association.

Library of Congress Cataloging-in-Publication Data

Smith, Timothy B.
  Foundations of multicultural psychology : research to inform effective practice / Timothy B. Smith and Joseph E. Trimble.
    pages cm
  Includes bibliographical references and index.
  ISBN 978-1-4338-2057-1 — ISBN 1-4338-2057-9 1. Multiculturalism—Psychological aspects. 2. Clinical psychology. 3. Counseling psychology. I. Trimble, Joseph E. II. Title.
  HM1271.S6295 2016
  305.8—dc23
                                        2015011087

British Library Cataloguing-in-Publication Data

A CIP record is available from the British Library.

Printed in the United States of America
First Edition

http://dx.doi.org/10.1037/14733-000

CONTENTS

Acknowledgments .... *vii*

Chapter 1.   Introduction: Multiculturalism in Psychology
              and Mental Health Services... 3

**I. Synthesis of Multicultural Research
   on Therapist Characteristics** **19**

Chapter 2.   Multicultural Education/Training and Experience:
              A Meta-Analysis of Surveys and Outcome Studies 21

Chapter 3.   Therapist Multicultural Competence: A Meta-Analysis
              of Client Experiences in Treatment.................................. 49

**II. Synthesis of Research on the Experiences of People
    of Color With Mental Health Services** **65**

Chapter 4.   Mental Health Service Utilization Across Race:
              A Meta-Analysis of Surveys and Archival Studies........ 67

Chapter 5.   Participation of Clients of Color in Mental
              Health Services: A Meta-Analysis of Treatment
              Attendance and Treatment Completion/Attrition 95

Chapter 6.   Matching Clients With Therapists on the
              Basis of Race or Ethnicity: A Meta-Analysis
              of Clients' Level of Participation in Treatment 115

Chapter 7.   Culturally Adapted Mental Health Services:
              An Updated Meta-Analysis of Client Outcomes 129

Chapter 8.   Acculturation Level and Perceptions of Mental
              Health Services Among People of Color:
              A Meta-Analysis 145

III. Synthesis of Research on the Experiences
     and Well-Being of People of Color 165

Chapter 9.   The Association of Received Racism With
              the Well-Being of People of Color:
              A Meta-Analytic Review 167

Chapter 10.   Ethnic Identity and Well-Being of People of Color:
              An Updated Meta-Analysis 181

IV. Foundations for the Future 207

Chapter 11.   Philosophical Considerations for the Foundation
              of Multicultural Psychology 209

Chapter 12.   Firming up the Foundation for an Evidenced-Based
              Multicultural Psychology 235

Appendix: General Methods of the Meta-Analyses (Chapters 2–10)........ 249

References 253

Index 297

About the Authors 307

ACKNOWLEDGMENTS

In the late 19th century, Lone Man (*isna la wican*), a Lakota spiritual leader, is thought to have said, "I have seen that in any great undertaking it is not enough for a man to depend upon himself." The conceptualization, preparation, and writing of this book depended on the research conducted by hundreds of scholars from a variety of academic disciplines whose work we synthesized. This book also depended on the monumental efforts of many students who searched for the research and coded the manuscripts. Several friends and colleagues provided thoughtful guidance, criticism, and commentary along the way. We express our profound gratitude to all those kindred spirits and others who guided us without our awareness. To paraphrase Lone Man, we could not have completed this undertaking without them.

Cindy Smith and Molly Trimble shared the ebb and flow of our frustrations and enthusiasm for the book from the moment we decided to embark on our venture. Their loving spiritual encouragement and wisdom enable us in all ways.

We acknowledge the imperfections of this book, including the long delays between the data analyses and the publication of this volume. Our aim to conduct multiple meta-analyses proved overly ambitious, given personal circumstances and other professional obligations. We now depend on our colleagues to use what we have offered to continue to improve the field, the great undertaking of infusing multiculturalism in the mental health professions.

FOUNDATIONS OF
MULTICULTURAL
PSYCHOLOGY

1

INTRODUCTION: MULTICULTURALISM IN PSYCHOLOGY AND MENTAL HEALTH SERVICES

> Recognizing that all behavior is learned and displayed in a cultural context makes possible accurate assessment, meaningful understanding, and appropriate intervention relative to that cultural context. Interpreting behavior out of context is likely to result in misattribution.
>
> —Paul Pedersen (2008, p. 15)

Imagine the work of a mental health professional who accepts a new position in a close-knit community with cultural lifestyles very different from mainstream society. The therapist was born and raised far from that community but had been successful elsewhere. Although the therapist uses the same approach and techniques that had previously worked well, most clients fail to return after the first or second session. The few clients who remain in therapy seem to understand the therapist's intentions and respond to treatment, but reluctantly, the therapist begins to face the fact that the approaches taken in therapy do not align with the experiences and worldviews of most of the new clients. The clients perceive situations in ways unanticipated by the therapist. The clients' explanations about emotional events seem peculiar to the therapist, who realizes that trying to interpret the clients' behavior, feelings, and thoughts often results in misattributions. Desiring to better understand local lifeways and thoughtways and to acquire the skills necessary to implement that understanding, the therapist searches for evidenced-based guidelines

http://dx.doi.org/10.1037/14733-001

Foundations of Multicultural Psychology: Research to Inform Effective Practice, by T. B. Smith and J. E. Trimble

and resources in the professional mental health literature (G. C. N. Hall & Yee, 2014). Where to begin?

MULTICULTURAL PSYCHOLOGY AND COUNSELING: AN OVERVIEW

Multicultural psychology and counseling is an emerging discipline with the potential to inform therapists of cultural considerations relevant to mental health (Paniagua & Yamada, 2013). It is based on the premise that the ethical provision of mental health services should include an accurate accounting of clients' cultural lifeways and thoughtways (Leong, Comas-Díaz, Hall, McLoyd, & Trimble, 2014; Pedersen, 1999). As an emerging discipline, it has developed guidelines for therapists seeking to be more effective in their work (American Psychological Association [APA], 2003; G. C. N. Hall & Yee, 2014; Leong et al., 2014; D. W. Sue & Sue, 2013), and it has become increasingly influential across the mental health professions, most recently in the revised standards for psychology graduate programs and internships (APA, 2014). Although exceptions persist, multicultural perspectives are becoming increasingly normative among mental health professionals.

But to what extent are the tenets and guidelines for practice that have arisen from multicultural perspectives based on research evidence? Psychologists and other mental health professionals understand the benefits of using data to inform practice and policy (APA 2005 Presidential Task Force on Evidence-Based Practice, 2006), but to what extent has that occurred? A solid research foundation is essential to the credibility and long-term effectiveness of multicultural guidelines for practitioners.

A primary purpose of this volume is to summarize research data to inform mental health practices relevant to client race and ethnicity, two delimited aspects of multiculturalism. Using meta-analytic methods to summarize data in Chapters 2 to 10, the book addresses questions that are fundamental to the discipline. For instance, how large are racial discrepancies in mental health service utilization and client retention, and what factors predict those racial discrepancies? To what degree are perceptions of racism and ethnic identity associated with psychological well-being? To what extent can therapists' training in multicultural issues and their level of multicultural competence benefit diverse clients? These are among the key questions relevant not only to the therapist described at the beginning of this chapter but also to every therapist who works in a multicultural world.

Practitioners improve the effectiveness of their work when they understand and apply research data (APA 2005 Presidential Task Force on Evidence-Based Practice, 2006; G. C. N. Hall & Yee, 2014). The meta-analyses in

Chapters 2 through 10 of this book contain interpretations useful for practitioners, students, and researchers. Practitioners and students need not be experts in meta-analytic methods to understand the implications of the findings, summarized at the end of each chapter. This book emphasizes research findings, but that should benefit, not deter, mental health professionals seeking answers. One need not be a researcher to benefit from research. The divide between practitioners and researchers can be bridged. This book attempts to construct a foundation for that bridge, but the reality is that research and practice necessarily inform one another and have been doing so for decades.

Brief Historical Overview of Multiculturalism in Mental Health Services

Topics of culture, race, ethnicity, gender, religion and spirituality, sexual orientation, and so forth were rarely covered in social science theories and research until the second half of the 20th century. Mental health practitioners and scholars often presumed that theories and research findings could be applied to everyone, so they sought to establish "universal validity" (Dawson, 1971, p. 291). Although they acknowledged that different cultures exist around the world, most concerned themselves almost exclusively with the majority population in their own narrow segment of the global society. And they often reasoned that cultural influences were insufficiently strong to merit serious consideration, let alone merit the time required to gain in-depth familiarity and proficiency across cultures. Culture was seen as a nuance, with the substance of theories and research presumed universal, enduring across circumstances.

The rise of multicultural psychology and counseling in North America came following the expansion of civil rights to historically oppressed populations and paralleled the diversification of the population in the final decades of the last century. Mental health professionals began to realize that although much of human experience is universal (e.g., we desire companionship and grieve at its loss), interpretations of experience are informed by circumstances, values, and worldviews that differ from culture to culture. "It is by no means self-evident that a concept embodied in a theory that has its origins within a particular culture can necessarily be operationalized into a conceptual equivalent in a different culture" (Jahoda, 1979, p. 143). For instance, child rearing is universally essential to human survival irrespective of culture, but child-rearing practices differ dramatically from one culture to another (Whiting, 1963). Psychology that had ignored cultural differences was "guilty of *suggestio falsi* [because] textbooks and articles commonly implied universality without seeking to provide any grounds for their implicit claims" (Jahoda, 1988, p. 93). Multiple factors influence emotional well-being and mental health, and the field gradually began to account for those contextual variables.

Inclusion of multicultural perspectives began to spread during the 1970s when increased numbers of women and individuals from diverse backgrounds received graduate degrees in the mental health professions and joined together to form professional associations on multicultural issues. In 1972, for example, a group of psychologists from different countries convened in Hong Kong to critically examine and discuss culture's influence on the human experience (Lonner, 2000). The meeting led to the founding of the International Association for Cross-Cultural Psychology. Two years earlier, the well-established and distinguished *Journal of Cross-Cultural Psychology* was launched (Berry, Poortinga, Segall, & Dasen, 1992). Many other organizations with an emphasis on multicultural issues also established research journals because mainstream publications did not represent those considerations. In 1974 the first issue of the *Journal of Black Psychology* appeared. In 1978, the *White Cloud Journal of American Indian/ Alaska Native Mental Health* was founded (and was renamed *American Indian and Alaska Native Mental Health Research, the Journal of the National Center* in 1987). The *Hispanic Journal of Behavioral Sciences* and the *Asian American Journal of Psychology* were first published in 1979. With publication outlets available, opportunities for scholarship broadened.

During the 1980s and 1990s, the amount of research focusing on multicultural issues increased markedly. Professional conferences such as the Winter Roundtable at Teachers College, Columbia University, strengthened networks and collaborations. Scholarly books began to appear with regularity. The APA began publishing a series of annotated bibliographies to help cohere the accumulated research findings. The series' topics include African Americans (Evans & Whitfield, 1988; Keita & Petersen, 1996), Hispanic/Latino(a) Americans (Olmedo & Walker, 1990), Asian Americans (Leong & Whitfield, 1992), and North American Indians (Trimble & Bagwell, 1995). By the end of the 1990s APA's Division 45 journal *Cultural Diversity and Ethnic Minority Psychology* had appeared (previously titled *Cultural Diversity and Mental Health*), and three APA divisions sponsored the first National Multicultural Conference and Summit. It had taken several decades, but multicultural perspectives had achieved professional recognition (D. W. Sue, Bingham, Porché-Burke, & Vasquez, 1999).

Brief Overview of Contemporary Contexts

Infusion of multiculturalism into mental health practices, training programs, and policies is underway. Mental health professionals increasingly understand "that all behavior is learned and displayed in a cultural context" and that accounting for clients' cultures "makes possible accurate assessment, meaningful understanding, and appropriate intervention relative to that cultural context" (Pedersen, 2008, p. 15). Over the past 4 decades mental health services delivered to ethnic minority populations in the United States and Canada has grown dramatically in terms of general availability as well as in the range of care offered. This growth can be attributed to a number of factors, notably changes in national public health policies, increasing community resources and expertise, and community demands for more comprehensive and culturally relevant care.

The rapid expansion of mental health services to diverse populations has frequently preceded careful consideration of several critical components of such care, specifically the delivery structure itself, treatment processes, program evaluation, epidemiological data, and preventive strategies. Clarity is lacking, and mainstream journals and professional publications persist in inadequately addressing multicultural issues (Henrich, Heine, & Norenzayan, 2010). The relevance and applicability of general psychological knowledge across diverse populations remain uncertain (e.g., Leong, Holliday, Trimble, Padilla, & McCubbin, 2012; S. Sue, 1999). Multiculturalism too often remains separated from mainstream discussions about mental health services (Wendt, Gone, & Nagata, 2014). To better integrate multicultural considerations into mainstream practices, government agencies are implementing more culturally sensitive mental health programs along with more accurate research and reporting. For example, under the directive of health disparities research national agencies have developed initiatives to promote preventive intervention efforts in ethnic minority communities. These interests and the initiatives are positive steps and have potential for improvement of mental health conditions among historically oppressed populations.

Looking to the future, multicultural psychology and counseling must now establish a solid foundation of research to better meet pressing needs in a pluralistic society. North America is increasingly culturally diverse (Statistics Canada, 2011; U.S. Census Bureau, 2010). Individuals with ancestry from Africa, Asia, and Central and South America, along with peoples indigenous to North America and the Pacific Islands, will eventually constitute the majority of the population (U.S. Census Bureau, 2010). Accounting for cultural differences can no longer be the concern of professionals chiefly working in urban ethnic enclaves or isolated rural communities. Demographic realities signal that mental health services must account for cultural differences to meet the needs of the majority of clients seeking services. Whereas a therapist like the one described at the beginning of this chapter would be struck by the cultural contrasts evident in an unfamiliar environment, therapists working in familiar settings may only occasionally realize the realities of diversity and take action accordingly.

The field now needs a translational pathway from practice to research and back to training, driven by demographic realities and clients' needs. New priorities for research, teaching, and practice must be developed so that current knowledge and new knowledge in psychology becomes relevant and applicable across diverse contexts. Demographic changes will inevitably move the field toward the full consideration of diversity in ways that are inclusive and representative. How soon and with what tools?

FOUNDATIONAL MULTICULTURAL ISSUES IN THE MENTAL HEALTH PROFESSIONS

Multicultural scholarship in the mental health professions is so broad, encompassing global diversity in all its varieties, that it can appear fragmented and diffuse—and thus hamper the credibility and effectiveness of the field. To overcome this limitation, multicultural scholarship should articulate a core set of principles and address major challenges to those principles to facilitate genuine improvements in mental health practices. This volume provides a partial remedy by articulating some principles and addressing their major challenges empirically.

One key principle is that therapists must remain focused on the fundamental issues impacting the mental health of historically oppressed populations. Such fundamental issues pertinent to race and ethnicity include (a) the degree of client access and involvement in mental health treatment as a function of race or ethnicity; (b) the degree to which the experiences of clients of color in therapy are associated with their level of acculturation and the racial and ethnic background of the therapist; (c) the influence of cultural experiences, particularly racism and ethnic identity, on client well-being; and (d) the effectiveness of treatment as a function of therapist multicultural competence, therapist training in multicultural competence, and cultural adaptations and culture-specific approaches to treatment. Although other critical issues merit consideration, this volume focuses on and evaluates data relevant to these four particular topics because they are central; they address the interaction between treatment and the cultural experiences of clients seeking treatment.

Client Access to and Involvement in Mental Health Services

Although in an optimal world mental health services would be accessible to and used by people of all backgrounds, racial discrepancies were identified by the U.S. Surgeon General in mental health service utilization (U.S. Department of Health and Human Services, 2001). The ideal of universal access to mental health services in many urban ethnic enclaves and in most rural communities falls short, but to what degree are people of color systematically disadvantaged? And when people of color enter treatment, how likely are they to complete it? As depicted in the scenario at the start of this chapter, cultural factors unaccounted for by universalistic treatment approaches can result in premature client discontinuation. Mental health professionals must constructively confront racial and ethnic discrepancies in service utilization and retention, if those discrepancies currently persist more than a decade after the report of the U.S. Surgeon General. Research can ascertain the nature and extent of racial disparities, factors contributing to the discrepancies, and solutions.

Association of Client Acculturation and Therapist Race and Ethnicity With Client Experiences in Mental Health Treatment

Despite the findings of the Human Genome Project that ethnic and especially racial distinctions have no biological basis (Bonham, Warshauer-Baker, & Collins, 2005), these constructs remain integral aspects of our social fabric (Gómez & López, 2013). Racial and ethnic categories align with political and social structures that continue to influence individuals and communities. In part because of they are so integral to sociopolitical contexts, it is often difficult to separate race and ethnicity from socioeconomic status and experiences of migration, acculturation, and discrimination. At times, categorical race and ethnicity may serve as a proxy for those variables (e.g., individuals' ethnic self-identifications vary as a function of acculturation). Given this complexity and the multiple problems inherent in approaches that perpetuate ethnic gloss[1] (Trimble, 1990, 1995; Trimble & Bhadra, 2013), should scholars move beyond simplistic categories of race and ethnicity and develop constructs that account for the reality of multivariate convergence in these categories? Among many other factors, the answer to this question depends on whether the individual or group experience differs substantially in terms of acculturation style and assimilation to mainstream North American society (which strongly overlap with race and ethnicity). In mental health settings, does client acculturation style predict experiences and outcomes in treatment? Alternatively, are race and ethnicity so important to clients that the categorical race or ethnicity of the therapist affects the client's willingness to engage in treatment?

---

[1]*Ethnic gloss* is an overgeneralization stemming from simplistic labeling of ethnocultural groups, such as Native American Indians (consisting of over 500 tribes), that ignores differences between and within groups. An ethnic gloss presents the illusion of homogeneity where none exists and therefore may be considered a superficial, almost vacuous, classification that further separates groups from one another (Trimble & Bhadra, 2013).

Association of Racism and Ethnic Identity With Well-Being

The multicultural literature has long emphasized that therapists must be keenly aware of clients' cultural experiences and lifestyles (N. B. Miller, 1982). Understanding clients' experiences with racism, for instance, would be important for a therapist because those experiences could be relevant to clients' presenting problems or at the very least could exacerbate distress. Hence, therapist efforts to ascertain not only clients' experiences of racism but also the degree to which those experiences affect client well-being should inform treatment approaches otherwise ignorant of that particular distress. Similarly, knowing a client's strength of ethnic identification could at the very least inform a therapist's understanding of client self-perceptions, and if the therapist also understood how the client's ethnic identity was associated with psychological coping mechanisms, emotional support from community members, and other resources relevant to well-being, therapy would be further strengthened. Clients' cultural supports, resources, and sources of distress are clearly relevant to therapy, but to what degree? To what extent are level of ethnic identity and experiences of racism associated with individuals' emotional well-being and distress?

Therapist Multicultural Competencies, Multicultural Training, and Cultural Adaptations and Culture-Specific Approaches to Treatment

Therapist abilities useful for working with diverse clients have been termed *multicultural competencies*, commonly broken down into components of knowledge, skills, and awareness (Arredondo et al., 1996). Multicultural competencies articulate ways of enhancing the therapeutic alliance and meeting client needs through strategies and approaches that explicitly account for cultural contexts. For instance, work with culturally diverse clients can be enhanced when mental health professionals account for (a) their own cultural worldview, (b) the client's cultural worldview, (c) the interaction between their own worldviews and those of the client, including assumptions related to therapy processes, and (d) the culture of the environment in which the therapy occurs (Pedersen, Draguns, Lonner, & Trimble, 2008). Combining these possible conditions, therapists could find themselves, in a rather extreme case, "working with a client from another culture, on a problem relating to a third culture, in the environment of a fourth culture where each participating culture presents its own demands" (Pedersen, Draguns, & Lonner, 1976, p. vii). Scholars have asserted that the cultural complexities associated with providing mental health services necessitate multicultural competencies distinct from general therapy skills (e.g., Arredondo et al.,

1996), but to what extent do clients' outcomes benefit from therapist multi-cultural competence? To what degree do training programs facilitate therapist multicultural competence?

An important component of multicultural competence is flexible adaptation to clients' cultural experiences and worldviews, with resulting cultural adaptations to treatment protocols, and procedures that extend beyond conventional practice (G. Bernal & Domenech Rodríguez, 2012). Although it seems obvious that treatment should account for clients' experiences and worldviews, a tension can arise between the benefits of aligning treatment with individual clients and the benefits of systematic implementation of traditional forms of therapy with fidelity to the intervention model (Castro, Barrera, & Holleran Steiker, 2010). To what degree do cultural adaptations to traditional treatments improve client outcomes or hamper them because they diverge from established evidence-based practices? The answer to this question has profound implications for the future of the profession. If adapting treatments to align with clients' worldviews is more effective than standardized approaches, then the field has only begun to account for the breadth and depth of individuality contextualized within multiple systems. If culturally adaptations prove to be equivalent in effectiveness to established, standardized approaches, then multiculturalism can remain relegated to a secondary consideration within the broader profession, useful in circumstances when treatment as usual no longer seems to work, as in the scenario described at the start of the chapter. Stated differently (and in direct opposition to the presumed universalism characteristic of the past), to what extent must individuals' worldviews and experiences, embedded in cultural, familial, environmental, and economic circumstances, permeate mental health treatments?

BUILDING UP THE FOUNDATION FOR MULTICULTURAL PSYCHOLOGY AND COUNSELING

Multicultural psychology and counseling is at a key juncture in terms of its influence on the mental health professions. Following decades of incremental growth, scholarship inclusive of multicultural issues has reached a proverbial "tipping point" (Gladwell, 2006), with the potential to now pervade all aspects of the professions, as has been envisioned (Pedersen, 1999). An analysis of 40 years of citations cataloged in PsycINFO shows a remarkable increase in the number of citations that reference racial and ethnic groups: About 2% of scholarly manuscripts referred to racial or ethnic groups in the 1960s, which doubled to about 4% in the 1980s, and doubled again to about 8% in the 2000s. Citations making references to Africans and African Americans increased from about 2,000 across the entire decade of the 1960s to over 5,000 in the single year of 2014. References to Asians and Asian Americans increased from about 1,000 citations across the decade of the 1960s to over 8,000 in the single year of 2014. In 2014, over 4,000 manuscripts mentioned Hispanic/Latinos(as) and over 500 mentioned First Nations peoples, Native American Indians, or Alaska Natives. Overall, more than 23,000 manuscripts in PsycINFO mentioned concepts of race, ethnicity, or culture in 2014 alone. Whereas in previous decades scholars urged the "vigorous expansion" (M. E. Bernal & Castro, 1994, p. 797) of research on multicultural topics, the clear and present need is now for a distillation and synthesis of this rapidly expanding literature.

Need for Literature Syntheses Using Meta-Analytic Methods

Multicultural psychology no longer lacks numbers of interested scholars; it instead lacks a coordinated approach to scholarship, informed by data instead of opinion. Supporters of multicultural psychology can sometimes press forward, unwittingly advocating measures and approaches that go beyond the data of what has been confirmed by research evidence. As a consequence, skeptics of multicultural psychology continue to point to overgeneralized statements about multicultural issues and to scattered and contradictory research findings (e.g., O'Donohue & Benuto, 2010). This lack of clarity helps no one.

With tens of thousands of manuscripts now appearing every year on issues relevant to race or ethnicity, a massive amount of information is available, but traditional narrative review methods would clearly be inadequate to accurately summarize so much data. A solution is available: *Meta-analysis*, the quantitative "study of studies."

> Meta-analysis . . . [is] the statistical analysis of a large collection of analysis results from individual studies for the purpose of integrating the findings. It connotes a rigorous alternative to the casual, narrative discussions of research studies which typify our attempts to make sense of the rapidly expanding research literature. (Glass, 1976, p. 3)

Meta-analysis aggregates quantitative data to provide a descriptive summary of the results. Statistical models combine data across many individual manuscripts to estimate the overall strength of the effect or the relationship, the averaged effect size. Meta-analyses have become normative in scientific journals, and scholars rely heavily on their results.

Meta-analytic methods offer multiple advantages over impressionistic summaries of research findings. When research findings are inconsistent, which is certainly the case in multicultural psychology (and thus only broad, tentative conclusions are possible in narrative literature reviews), meta-analysis can identify sources of variation across studies; for example, meta-analysis can ascertain the degree to which findings differ across participant characteristics (e.g., age, gender) and study characteristics (e.g., research design, measurement used). Knowing an average effect size and, even more important, the conditions under which effect sizes vary benefits both practitioners who use evidenced-based practices and scholars who seek to build on current findings when designing new research questions and new treatments. Whereas narrative literature reviews provide information based on expert opinion, meta-analyses summarize research data.

Reliance on aggregated data can improve the mental health professions (APA 2005 Presidential Task Force on Evidence-Based Practice, 2006). A failure to examine aggregated data in multicultural psychology would pose a significant roadblock to the field, particularly if decisions about the content of graduate training and about reimbursements for professional services become restricted to empirically supported treatments (ESTs) and evidence-based practices (EBPs; see also G. C. N. Hall & Yee, 2014). Although rigid and narrow decision making about ESTs and EBPs can bestow empirical data with a false aura of truth (Slife & Williams, 1995), meta-analytic methods should inform consequential decisions so long as data interpretation includes contextual factors. Chapters 2 through 10 in this book use meta-analytic methods to examine the existing literature, identify gaps in present understanding, and suggest areas for future inquiry. Chapter 11 covers issues pertinent to data interpretations.

Limitations of Meta-Analyses and This Book

Limitations characterize every scholarly undertaking. The approaches taken in this book are necessarily qualified by limitations associated with meta-analytic methodology and by the focus of our work, delimited to selected topics relevant to race and ethnicity.

Meta-analyses describe research findings, and those descriptions necessarily depend on the research available. When research data are limited, the conclusions of a meta-analysis must remain tentative. And when research data differ as a function of research design, those factors must also be considered. Poor quality research can yield unreliable results, even in the aggregate ("garbage in, garbage out"). Nevertheless, removing studies a priori from meta-analytic reviews can restrict the generalizability of the findings: The tighter the methodological controls within studies, the more likely those studies represent solely the conditions in which the study was undertaken. Meta-analyses involve trade-offs between internal and external validity. In most of the chapters of this book, our meta-analytic approach erred on the side of inclusion of research manuscripts, maximizing external validity, rather than excluding research manuscripts based on methodological considerations. However, we also accounted for factors relevant to internal validity by analyzing differences in findings across methods (e.g., convenience sampling vs. random selection of participants). Thus we attempted to address both internal and external validity. This approach was warranted when prior meta-analyses were unavailable and primary sources of variation in data were largely unknown: It was preferable to examine all research findings and then evaluate the degree to which findings vary as a function of methodology rather than to exclude studies based on hypothetical variation. When previous meta-analyses had been conducted in a given topic area (e.g., cultural adaptations of mental health services, multicultural education and training), we restricted our analyses to experimental and quasi-experimental research designs, with our data extraction from manuscripts accounting for differences in methods (e.g., comparison groups using bona fide treatments vs. wait-list controls). Although we attended to considerations relevant to both internal and external validity, ultimately meta-analyses remain descriptive: They portray the state of current practice in aggregate form, which does not necessarily represent the experiences of any individual client or therapist.

Another limitation of the approach taken in this book is its delimited focus. We address multicultural counseling competence and a few selected topics relevant to race and ethnicity. Although a targeted focus has several advantages, including the fact that a broader coverage of human diversity using meta-analytic methods would be virtually impossible in a single book, there are several disadvantages that deserve mentioning. First, emphasis on any particular variable to the exclusion of others obscures the holistic realities of human experience. An individual can never be understood solely in terms of race and ethnicity, no matter how important those particular sources of identity may be to the person or to the society in which the person resides. Second, race and ethnicity are often conceptualized in terms of discrete categories, yet people vary substantially in terms of their experiences, attributes, and degrees of identification. Variability within purportedly homogeneous racial and ethnic groups is many times larger and often more complex than variability between groups (Trimble, 2007; Trimble & Dickson, 2005). Moreover, the processes of racial and ethnic identity development can be complex enough for individuals with a clearly defined racial and or ethnic heritage, let alone for biracial and multiracial individuals, individuals adopted by parents not of their same racial or ethnic heritage, and so forth. Third, racial and ethnic categorizations perpetuate stereotypes. No research finding presented in this volume will be completely accurate for a particular client or therapist, so research findings specific to racial and ethnic groups can be considered tentative possibilities for exploration. Thus, although this book provides useful information for mental health professionals, the information retains its benefit only to the degree that the reader uses it along with all other sources of information available. In that sense, the content of this volume provides the reader with an opportunity to use a key professional skill: Learn from data and improve therapeutic practices accordingly, but always remain focused on the individual client's needs and experiences. Students and practitioners uninterested in the data tables can still benefit from the interpretations of the findings provided at the end of each chapter. The gap between research and practice is only as wide as our ability to bridge it.

Research Data Versus Expert Opinion

Some practitioners may question our emphasis on research and meta-analytic findings as the foundation for effective multicultural mental health services. Why so much insistence on evidence? A parallel from the history of health care may prove persuasive to readers doubtful of this emphasis. Prior to rigorous research becoming the norm in the medical profession, expert opinion was the primary foundation for practices, yet death rates for individuals in medical treatment were excessively high, even after common sources of infections were understood and antibiotics had become available in the 20th century (Bynum & Porter, 2013). Replacing reliance on expert opinion with reliance on high quality research made the difference. Systematic lines of research identified risk factors and causal mechanisms and improved treatment effectiveness for a broad range of health conditions, not merely infectious diseases. A pervasive reliance on research data prevents illness and saves lives (Watkins & Portney, 2009).

Social scientists and mental health professionals understand that all empirical research, including medical research, is fraught with problems (Slife & Williams, 1995). Nevertheless, the benefits of relying on research evidence outweigh both the many disadvantages and the advantages of alternatives. Expert opinion is no substitute for evidence. And the reality is that mental health professionals in general (with some notable exceptions) have not subjected their explanations and treatments to scrutiny as intense and as systematic as is necessary to clearly distinguish information from opinion.

Like related disciplines, multicultural psychology and counseling could be accurately described as having been more reliant on expert opinion than on data. One purpose of this volume is to shift the conversations in the mental health professions toward greater inclusion of contextual factors, particularly culture, race, and ethnicity. But an equally important objective is to have those conversations become more reliant on data than opinion.

OVERVIEW OF BOOK CONTENT

Foundational questions about mental health and mental health services across racial and ethnic groups involve multiple considerations, including client experiences with treatment, factors that influence client well-being, and therapist characteristics. This book addresses each of those broad topic areas for an audience of practitioners, students, and researchers in mental health professions.

The first section of the book attends to the therapist characteristics of multicultural competence and multicultural training. Chapter 2 investigates the degree to which therapists' training in and experiences with multicultural issues relates to their work with clients of color. Training in multicultural issues is mandatory for graduate students in accredited programs, but how effective is that training? Chapter 3 deals with the topic of therapist multicultural competence. To what extent do therapists' purported knowledge, awareness, and skills relevant to multicultural considerations affect clients' experiences in treatment?

The second section of the book focuses on client experiences with treatment as a function of race and ethnicity. Chapter 4 addresses the issue of utilization: How large are racial and ethnic discrepancies in mental health service utilization? This question is among the most important for mental health providers to address. If people of color who are in need of mental health services are not receiving them, the field needs to rectify systematic inequities.

Chapter 5 responds to a related question: How large are racial and ethnic discrepancies in mental health treatment participation? Clients discontinue treatment for a variety of reasons, but the extent to which clients of color prematurely discontinue treatment due factors related to race and ethnicity requires serious attention. Pursuing this same line of inquiry, Chapter 6 evaluates the extent to which clients remain in mental health services as a function of the race of the therapist.

Chapter 7 discusses the degree to which the outcomes of clients of color can be improved when adapting treatment to align with the client's cultural background. Previous research has shown that culturally adapted treatments are more effective than treatments not explicitly accounting for client culture, and this chapter provides an updated review of that literature.

An associated issue of client level of acculturation receives attention in Chapter 8. Clients' attitudes about and experiences with mental health treatments could vary substantially based on the degree of their acculturation to North American cultural mores.

The third section of the book addresses two topics relevant to psychological well-being. Chapter 9 investigates the degree to which experiences of racism among people of color are associated with their well-being. Chapter 10 provides an updated review on the association between the ethnic identity of people of color and their reports of well-being.

The fourth section of the book reflects on the overall state of the field. Diverging sharply from the preceding data-focused chapters, Chapter 11 encourages the reader to consider the underlying assumptions and popular beliefs characterizing contemporary multicultural psychology and counseling research. Purposefully distinct in tone and content, this chapter invites the reader to take the crucial steps of asking hard questions and engaging in critical analysis. Improvement of mental health services for multicultural populations depends on what kinds of questions are being asked in research, how concepts are operationalized in research, and many other factors requiring careful consideration. Chapter 12 summarizes the findings of the meta-analyses reported in Chapters 2 through 10 and provides some recommendations for the future.

Overall, this book covers several topics relevant to race and ethnicity that can affect mental health and mental health treatment. The book addresses client access to and involvement in mental health treatment, conditions that affect client experiences in treatment, experiences that influence individuals' well-being, and factors that influence the effectiveness of treatment. Although many more topics deserve consideration, the focus of this book on research data and its invitation for critical analysis provide a foundation for the work of students, scholars, and practitioners invested in the well-being of all people.

CHAPTER SUMMARY

For decades the mental health professions have been selective in the study and characterization of people. Most of the early research occurred in a monocultural vacuum involving restricted classes of research participants from Europe and North America. These populations most often studied in social science research have been referred to as WEIRD (Western, educated, industrialized, rich, and democratic; Henrich et al., 2010). Among other sources, Robert Guthrie's (1976) book, *Even the Rat Was White*, documented systematic historical racial biases in psychological research and practice.

Although many racial and ethnic groups remain underrepresented in the mental health literature, representation has increasingly been achieved (e.g., Case & Smith, 2000). Mental health professionals are beginning to understand that multicultural considerations are central to the experiences of many clients and that therefore these considerations should be central to their work with these clients (Leong et al., 2014). Mental health professionals increasingly seek information about how to better account for cultural contexts in their work (Pedersen, 1999). They also strive to improve mental health service utilization and retention rates among historically underserved populations. They are interested in the multitude of ways in which the ethnic identity of clients of color and their experiences with racism affect their emotional well-being. They wonder whether cultural adaptations to existing mental health treatments are justified and whether culture specific approaches are warranted.

They seek confirmation that multicultural education and the acquisition of certain skills, referred to as *multicultural competencies*, will genuinely benefit diverse clients seeking their services. They have many questions about the complexity of cultural realities, and they seek answers.

This book responds to several key questions by summarizing available research data via meta-analysis. Many books on multicultural psychology have been published, and expert opinions on multicultural considerations in mental health treatment have been widely circulated. But which of the many recommendations and practices are based on evidence? A synthesis of research findings should assist in supporting or refuting opinions, popular or not. Although far from yielding definitive answers, research findings present the most solid foundation on which a field of multicultural inquiry could be built. And multicultural issues are so important to mental health practices that no other foundation should suffice.

In sum, mental health professionals cannot fully understand the human condition without viewing it through a lens informed by multiculturalism. Even with the aid of this lens, the complexity of individual variations embedded within multiple systems poses enough challenges to make multicultural understanding a lifelong quest (T. B. Smith, Richards, Granley, & Obiakor, 2004). Avoiding the complexities of the human condition, including but not limited to race and ethnicity, is not a sustainable option for purported experts in human behavior, mental health professionals. Minimizing that complexity or rationalizing it away through universalistic assertions has been the norm in the past, but the harmful consequences of such minimizations become easily apparent when working with diverse clientele whose experiences and worldviews do not fit supposedly universal conceptualizations (D. W. Sue, 2015a). Moreover, mental health services, circumscribed and confined to European and North American academic notions about treatment modalities and well-being, remain restricted in their scope and in their potential for ongoing refinement that could instead be expanded by the holistic, multifaceted conceptualizations of multiculturalism. Multiculturalism is not merely a perspective to adopt when meeting someone perceived to be "different." Multiculturalism seeks to convey knowledge of factors that are part and parcel of the human condition. The sooner mental health professionals account for and embrace the facts of human diversity, the better they will be able to serve the next client who seeks their services. Whether that audacious claim is brash rhetoric (aka expert opinion) or is an invitation justified by research evidence remains to be seen in the data.

I

SYNTHESIS OF MULTICULTURAL RESEARCH ON THERAPIST CHARACTERISTICS

2

MULTICULTURAL EDUCATION/ TRAINING AND EXPERIENCE: A META-ANALYSIS OF SURVEYS AND OUTCOME STUDIES

Mental health professionals have a moral and ethical responsibility to facilitate client well-being. In a pluralistic society, this responsibility includes working in ways congruent with clients' cultural backgrounds, commonly referred to as *multicultural counseling competencies*. Descriptions of multicultural competence have provided essential guidance for mental health professionals for over 40 years (D. W. Sue et al., 1982). For 3 decades, the American Psychological Association (APA; 1986) has required accredited programs to address multicultural issues in the curricula. APA guidelines (1994, 2003) have clarified the importance of multicultural education for psychologists, with other mental health professional associations having similar requirements and guidelines. Multicultural education has become a primary strategy for improving therapists' abilities to serve diverse clients effectively (Abreu, Gim Chung, & Atkinson, 2000). "The critical importance of training psychologists and

A complete list of references for the studies included in this chapter's meta-analysis is posted online. Readers can consult it at http://pubs.apa.org/books/supp/smith

http://dx.doi.org/10.1037/14733-002

mental health professionals for work in an increasing multicultural society is now unquestioned" (Ponterotto & Austin, 2005, p. 19).

The entire discipline of multicultural psychology and counseling has been based on the assumption that multicultural awareness, knowledge, and skills can be taught and learned (Abreu et al., 2000; Rogers & O'Bryon, 2014). Although multicultural counseling competencies overlap with general counseling competencies (Sheu & Lent, 2007), they require specialized instruction (Cates, Schaefle, Smaby, Maddux, & LeBeauf, 2007; Yutrzenka, 1995). Evaluating that specialized instruction can verify its effectiveness (does it actually work?) and suggest ways for enhancing the abilities of therapists to meet the needs of diverse clients, the aim of the discipline.

This chapter provides a brief overview of relevant considerations and previous research on multicultural education, followed by a quantitative summary of research findings using meta-analytic methods. Implications of the results of the meta-analysis conclude the chapter.

NARRATIVE REVIEW OF THE LITERATURE

The objective of multicultural education should be to enhance multicultural competency (Abreu et al., 2000). To what degree is it meeting that objective? Does multicultural education improve therapists' abilities to effectively serve diverse clients?

Relevant Theory

The tripartite model of multicultural competence (D. W. Sue et al., 1982) provided the initial blueprint for multicultural education in psychology and counseling. Standards subsequently derived from this model provided additional guidance (D. W. Sue, Arredondo, & McDavis, 1992b). Later operationalization of the competencies provided even more specific objectives (Arredondo et al., 1996). Most subsequent scholarship in multicultural education has aligned with the general paradigm of multicultural competence. For instance, Ponterotto (1997, 1998; Ponterotto & Austin, 2005) has identified exemplary practices, proposed a model, and identified characteristics of effective multicultural trainers and mentors, multicultural trainees, and multicultural training environments. A cross-cultural triad training model and related content were developed and refined by Pedersen (2000), who also generated an extensive list of training activities and resources (2004). Brislin and colleagues have produced many volumes on intercultural training that can easily be applied to mental health practitioners (e.g., Landis & Brislin, 2013). Ridley and colleagues have provided a nearly comprehensive model for multicultural program development (Ridley, Mendoza, & Kanitz, 1994), specific guidelines for developing multicultural coursework (Ridley, Espelage, & Rubinstein, 1997), and a model of general counseling competence that explicitly integrates culture (Ridley, Mollen, & Kelly, 2011a). These models provide valuable conceptual foundations for instruction designed to enhance competence in general and multicultural counseling. Instructors should use these and similar foundational resources.

Narrative Review of Previous Research

Just as there is no single "psychotherapy," there is no single type of multicultural education. The content, format, duration, intensity, and techniques vary substantively among programs (Ponterotto & Austin, 2005). Most of the published literature has addressed university classes in graduate programs, although ongoing professional development for practicing clinicians is also essential (Rogers-Sirin, 2008). The limited literature investigating multicultural education provided at predoctoral internship sites indicates variability in the extent and effectiveness of training (R. M. Lee et al., 1999), which consists mostly of brief seminars or workshops typical for clinical settings, with a few notable exceptions (e.g., Sevig & Etzkorn, 2001).

Although seminars and workshops for interns and clinicians can be delimited to a specific topic (e.g., family therapy with Cuban Americans), semester-long graduate classes devoted to multicultural psychology typically attempt to cover a broad range of topics using a wide variety of methods and techniques. Two separate reviews of syllabi from graduate classes across the United States (Pieterse, Evans, Risner-Butner, Collins, & Mason, 2009; Priester et al., 2008) found coverage of broad topics—notably race, culture, gender, sexual orientation, age, and physical and cognitive abilities—but treatment was also given to specific subgroups, such as Amish and Appalachians. This remarkable breadth of coverage impedes depth of coverage, and scholars have requested greater clarity in what content should be taught (Newell et al., 2010). This book, hence this chapter, focuses on race and ethnicity; nevertheless, guidelines regarding structure, design, instructional strategies, and training philosophy are available in the literature (Ridley et al., 1994, 1997).

The philosophical assumptions underlying multicultural education differ considerably across programs, from universal approaches that emphasize shared humanity to culture-specific and race-based approaches (Carter & Qureshi, 1995). Although a broad range of approaches allows flexibility for instructors, "the lack of a unifying framework often results in confusion and the tendency for trainers and educators to use a hodgepodge approach to facilitating students' multicultural competence" (Ancis & Ali, 2005, p. 95).

Although most instructors indicate that multicultural competencies provide the foundation for their teaching (Reynolds, 2011), multicultural education has typically been delimited to instruction designed to enhance multicultural knowledge and self-awareness, failing to foster the development of multicultural skills. A survey of 169 instructors found that the vast majority emphasized multicultural awareness and sensitivity (93%) and knowledge and content (82%), but only half (49%) addressed multicultural skill development (Reynolds, 2011).

Perhaps more accurate estimates than those based on instructor self-report come from two content analyses of syllabi collected from graduate classes across the nation. The first of these (Priester et al., 2008) indicated that only nine of 64 syllabi (12%) required substantive evaluations of students' skills, whereas 84% based evaluation on their knowledge. The authors concluded that multicultural courses "almost completely ignore the development of skills" (p. 29). A second review of 54 multicultural course syllabi from across the nation (Pieterse et al., 2009) found that only 40% mentioned relevant counseling interventions, with a limited 19% covering culture-specific interventions. Evaluation of participant counseling skills occurred only 7% of the time. Participant self-reported multicultural competence was evaluated 13% of the time. The author found it "disconcerting that multicultural courses seem deficient in specific skill-based instruction" (Pieterse, 2009, p. 109). Thus, the field appears to be engaged in providing content-oriented instruction, rather than facilitating genuine shifts in abilities and worldviews (Reynolds, 1997). Improvement is obviously needed.

Multicultural competencies appear to be used as general guidelines for content rather than standards for evaluation of mastery. The two reviews of syllabi from multicultural education classes consistently found assignments indirectly assessing multicultural knowledge and self-awareness, including journal writing (56%); a cultural self-examination paper (42%); reaction papers to art, literature, or film (12%–34%); attendance at cultural events (34%); a class presentation (33%); and an interview of a member of a different cultural group (31%; Priester et al., 2008). Infrequently used (thus innovative) assignments fostering and evaluating skill development included designing a culturally appropriate intervention, reviewing videotaped clinical sessions with cross-cultural dyads, conducting role plays, presenting clinical cases, and working with local communities or organizations to help underserved populations (service-learning).

An unfortunate by-product of content-oriented instruction in multicultural education is inadequate focus on the needs of individual students "who differ in terms of their multicultural competence" (Ancis & Ali, 2005, p. 95). Scholars have observed that "present multicultural training tends to emphasize helping White trainees improve their counseling of clients of color" (Chao, Wei, Good, & Flores, 2011, p. 80), finding that such training "significantly enhanced Whites' multicultural awareness, but did not enhance racial/ethnic minority trainees' awareness" (p. 72). Students from historically oppressed groups come to a multicultural workshop or class with experiences and abilities perhaps underutilized and underdeveloped by generic instruction (Coleman, 2006; Rooney, Flores, & Mercier, 1998). Multicultural education can strengthen multicultural competencies independent of strength of racial and ethnic identity (Chao & Nath, 2011), such that all participants should be able to improve. Multicultural psychology is so vast as to require "a lifelong journey toward the goal of increasing multicultural competence" (Dickson, Argus-Calvo, & Tafoya, 2010, p. 262).

Although some participants resist multicultural education, openness to multiculturalism is increasing over time: A national survey found that only 5% of instructors reported primarily negative responses among participants (Reynolds, 2011). Nevertheless, individuals who engage in racial color blindness (universalizing human experiences rather than acknowledging racial differences) are less likely to acquire multicultural knowledge through multicultural education (Chao et al., 2011). Acquiring multicultural awareness can entail intense emotional reactions such as defensiveness, guilt, pain, and tears (Tummala-Narra, 2009). Hence confrontation must be constantly balanced with a climate conducive to emotional safety and support (Kiselica, 1998; Reynolds, 2011; Sevig & Etzkorn, 2001). As with most clinical skills, acquiring multicultural competence requires genuine personal involvement and, ultimately, personal stretching beyond comfort zones in gaining the competence to enhance the therapeutic alliance with clients from every walk of life.

Trends in Recent Research on Multicultural Education

Research on multicultural education in psychology attracted widespread interest after APA (1986) required that multicultural issues be addressed in accredited graduate programs. Initially, this scholarship attempted to justify the requirement of multicultural education (Yutrzenka, 1995). However, the focus has shifted over time: "After decades of deliberating, studying, and even debating the role of multicultural training . . . scholars are moving from studying whether trainees should take a multicultural training course to examining the effectiveness of training" (Chao et al., 2011, p. 81).

Substantial research evidence has accumulated on multicultural education. A meta-analytic review located 82 studies with empirical data published before 2003 (T. B. Smith, Constantine, Dunn, Dinehart, & Montoya, 2006).

The authors of the review identified 45 surveys of participants' previous exposure to multicultural education and 37 studies of the effectiveness of a particular multicultural education program. The results of these two sets of analyses were discussed using a hypothetical scenario of an employer desiring to hire a therapist with multicultural competence:

> [The first analysis, including 45 surveys,] was similar to an employer asking "What is the difference between an average applicant who has had multicultural education and one who has not?" . . . In answer to the hypothetical employer's question, an applicant who has completed multicultural education will report moderately higher multicultural competence [Cohen's $d = .49$] than an individual who has not. [The second analysis, including 37 outcome studies,] answered a different question, similar to an employer asking "How much did the average employee change during the multicultural training we provided?" . . . In answer to the employer's second hypothetical question, the average participant completing a particular multicultural education intervention will report large increases [Cohen's $d = .92$] in multicultural competence. (T. B. Smith et al., 2006, p. 139–140)

The cumulative research evidence has established the effectiveness of multicultural education in the mental health professions.

Many research studies have appeared since 2003. Some of these recent studies have sought to improve on the limitations of previous work, which have been "(a) [the] small and fairly homogeneous samples, (b) the tendency to examine students' experiences in only one course, and (c) the use of simple methods of examining teaching methods" (M. N. Coleman, 2006, p. 180). A few studies have moved beyond simplistic evaluations to more complex designs, such as hierarchical regression considering environmental factors such as training environment (Dickson & Jepsen, 2007), structural equation models testing mediation of variables between multicultural education and multicultural competence (Spanierman, Poteat, Wang, & Oh, 2008), and other analyses of moderating and mediating factors (Chao & Nath, 2011; Chao et al., 2011). The effectiveness of multicultural education is an area that has continued to attract scholarship, which necessitates periodic synthesis: "Multicultural education initiatives and the construct of multicultural competence must undergo ongoing and rigorous scrutiny if they are to continue receiving widespread support from mental health professions" (T. B. Smith et al., 2006, p. 142). We therefore evaluated the cumulative research evidence in an updated meta-analysis to verify the effectiveness of multicultural education in mental health professions and to estimate the degree to which study and participant characteristics moderate the overall findings. Readers seeking a summary may skip to that section.

QUANTITATIVE SYNTHESIS OF RESEARCH DATA

Our updated meta-analysis evaluated research studies conducted in the United States or Canada that took place in professional mental health settings (university coursework, professional conference workshop, or workplace seminar). Each study in the meta-analysis considered a pertinent dependent variable: therapist multicultural counseling competencies (self-reported multicultural knowledge, awareness, and skills), therapist racial attitudes or biases (e.g., ratings of comfort levels working with clients of a given race), trained observers' evaluations of therapists (e.g., ratings of therapists' congruence with the client), clients' ratings of therapists (e.g., rating of therapists' empathy), client retention rates (e.g., premature dropouts vs. treatment completers), and client outcomes in therapy (e.g., changes in symptoms over time). We planned to ascertain any differences among these dependent variables.

If studies simultaneously evaluated the influence of individuals' multicultural experience (i.e., number or percentage of clients of color) on those same outcome variables, we extracted those estimates for a separate analysis. Regarding attitudinal measures, we extracted effect sizes only for measures specific to race or ethnicity (i.e., racial prejudice), not considering other forms of prejudice (e.g., sexist or homophobic beliefs) because multicultural education inconsistently addresses issues of gender, sexual orientation, and so forth, but consistently addresses issues of race and culture (Pieterse et al., 2009). Statistical estimates within manuscripts were converted to Cohen's *d* using meta-analytic software.

Outcomes of multicultural education delivered as part of a study were analyzed separately from retrospective surveys that considered participants' previous levels of multicultural training and/or experience. The effect sizes for these two classes of studies have distinct meanings: Outcome studies estimate the effectiveness of a specific intervention, whereas retrospective studies evaluate participants' level of exposure to multicultural education. Furthermore, retrospective studies confound the issue of effectiveness with such factors as the accuracy of participants' memories, their interest in multicultural topics, and their desire to appear experienced in multicultural issues. Thus, we analyzed these two sets of studies separately.

We further disaggregated the data by the research design used in the outcome studies to reflect the different meaning of effect sizes generated from distinct research designs: (a) pre- to posttest changes for a single group of participants (e.g., university students measured at the beginning and end of a class) and (b) comparisons of gains across groups that differed in form of multicultural education (e.g., students taking a multicultural class compared with students taking a class without multicultural content). The data for these two types of research designs have distinct interpretations. Effect sizes generated from single group pre- to posttest designs estimate the degree of change participants experienced during the time of the multicultural education, without considering extraneous factors. In contrast, comparative, quasi-experimental, and experimental designs provide an estimate of the relative improvement made by participants receiving multicultural education, while also controlling for several possible confounding factors. Positive values for Cohen's *d* effect sizes from these outcome studies indicated the degree of effectiveness of the particular multicultural education program or class provided in the study, whereas positive values for effect sizes from the retrospective studies represented the degree to which exposure to multicultural education (or multicultural experience) was associated with favorable ratings on dependent variables (i.e., multicultural counseling competence and/or racial attitudes). The methods of the meta-analysis are reported in the Appendix of this book.

Description of Analyzed Research Literature

Our literature search yielded a total of 47 outcome studies that reported data on 2,665 individuals' changes as a function of multicultural education. Of these studies, 24 evaluated pre- to posttest changes within a single group as a function of multicultural education (i.e., differences over time for participants completing a class), and 23 evaluated relative gains compared with a control group using static group comparison, quasi-experimental, or experimental designs. The 47 outcome studies typically involved a particular multicultural education class or workshop conducted at a university or clinic studying the people available in those settings (convenience sampling), with an average of only 57 participants, most often involving White graduate students, with females represented more than males (see Table 2.1). Thus, these studies evaluated the effectiveness of actual multicultural workshops or university classes.

We also located 68 retrospective studies that evaluated the previous multicultural education of 9,596 total participants. These studies typically involved one-time surveys administered to a convenience sample of about 141 participants, with the surveys measuring the number of multicultural education courses or workshops that participants had completed, along with a pertinent dependent variable (e.g., multicultural competence, racial attitudes). Of these studies, 16 also obtained data regarding participants' levels of experience working with culturally diverse clients. These retrospective studies typically involved White trainees or clinicians, with females represented more than males (Table 2.1). Only one retrospective study controlled for social desirability, and none controlled for possible confounds such as degree of commitment to multiculturalism. Thus, the results of these

TABLE 2.1
Characteristics of 47 Outcome Studies of Multicultural Education and
68 Retrospective Studies of Participants' Prior Multicultural Education

	Outcome studies			Retrospective studies		
Characteristic	M	No. of studies (k)	%	M	No. of studies (k)	%
Year of report	1996			2002		
Before 1980		3	6		0	0
1980–1989		5	11		0	0
1990–1999		17	36		15	22
2000–2008		22	47		53	78
Publication status						
Published		30	64		35	52
Unpublished dissertations		17	36		33	49
Sampling procedure						
Convenience		46	98		47	69
Representative (random selection)		1	2		21	31
Research design						
Cross-sectional (survey)					57	84
Longitudinal					1	1
Comparison groups		3	6		1	1
Quasi-experimental/ experimental		20	43			
Pre- to posttest change, 1 group		24	51			
Other (e.g., analogue, archival)					9	14
Population sampled						
Practicing clinicians		9	19		24	38
Clinical trainees		34	74		36	53
Both clinicians and trainees		3	7		6	9
Sample size	57			141		
<50		27	57		10	15
50–99		15	32		17	25
100–199		3	6		28	41
200–399		2	4		12	18
400–999		0	0		1	1
>1000		0	0		0	0
Age of participants[a]	32			35		
Young adults (19–29 years)		22	51		16	24
Middle-aged adults (30–55 years)		21	49		52	76
Gender (% female)	74			72		
Race of participants[b] (%)						
African American	10			7		
Asian American	5			3		
Hispanic/Latino(a) American	2			4		
Native American	0			0		
White/European American	78			82		
Other	4			4		

Note. Not all variables sum to the total number of studies because of missing data; not all percentages sum to 100 because of accumulated rounding errors.
[a]Although this category represents the average age category of participants in studies, not all participants in the study would necessarily be in the category listed. [b]The racial composition of participants across all studies was calculated by multiplying the number of participants within studies by the percentage of participants from each racial group and dividing that product by the total number of participants.

retrospective studies represent the degree to which individuals who self-report their level of multicultural education (and multicultural experience) make statements reflecting favorable dispositions. The associated effect sizes represent correlational, not causal, estimates of the degree to which exposure to multicultural education may relate to individuals' perceptions about working with diverse clients.

Overall Research Findings

Outcome Studies Using Comparison Groups (Static Group Comparison, Quasi-Experimental, or Experimental Designs)

Across 23 studies that compared groups differing in their exposure to multicultural education, the random effects weighted effect size was $d = .67$ ($SE = .114$, 95% CI = [.44, .89], $p < .0001$). Thus, participants in multicultural education tended to report moderately large gains relative to control groups on measures. The heterogeneity of the findings was large ($I^2 = 75.4$, 95% CI = [63, 84]; $Q_{(22)} = 89.4$, $p < .0001$; $\tau^2 = .21$), meaning that the results were inconsistent across studies.

Outcome Studies Measuring Pre- to Posttest Changes for a Single Group of Participants

We found 24 studies evaluating pre- to posttest changes among participants receiving a particular multicultural education class or program. The average random effects weighted effect size was $d = .95$ ($SE = .154$, 95% CI = [.65, 1.25], $p < .0001$), indicating that on average participants reported large improvements from pre- to posttest. The heterogeneity of the findings was very large ($I^2 = 86.1$, 95% CI = [81, 91]; $Q_{(23)} = 165.7$, $p < .00001$; $\tau^2 = .44$); the results varied substantially across the 24 studies, suggesting inconsistency in effectiveness.

Retrospective Studies

With the retrospective studies, the amount of multicultural education (e.g., number of multicultural classes completed) was reported separately from the amount of multicultural experience (e.g., caseload percentage of culturally diverse clients). We therefore conducted a multivariate meta-analysis (Becker, 2000) on those data to simultaneously account for the two different types of effect sizes in those studies (specifying the within-study effect size correlation to the obtained value of $r = .41$). The overall model was statistically significant when the 68 studies were examined (Wald $X^2 = 149.1$, $p < .0001$). The random effects weighted average effect sizes were $d = .41$ ($SE = .034$, 95% CI = [.34, .47]) for multicultural education and

$d = .29$ ($SE = .066$, 95% CI = [.16, .42]) for multicultural experience. The difference between these two types of effect sizes did not reach statistical significance ($p > .05$). Because only 16 studies contained effect sizes specific to multicultural experience, subsequent analyses were delimited to the effect sizes pertaining to multicultural education in all 68 studies. For those data, the heterogeneity of the findings was in the moderate range ($I^2 = 59.2$, 95% CI = [47, 69]; $Q_{(67)} = 164.1$, $p < .0001$), meaning that the results were fairly inconsistent across studies.

Influence of Study and Participant Characteristics on the Findings

Study Characteristics Among the 47 Outcome Studies

Studies differed in the type of dependent variables measured (self-reported multicultural competence, self-reported racial attitudes, observer/client ratings), so the results had to be analyzed across these different measures. These analyses did reveal statistically significant differences in effect size across the type of dependent variable measured (see Table 2.2). Among the 24 studies involving pre- to posttest changes in a single group of participants, the average effect size was higher for studies using participant-rated measures of multicultural competence (e.g., the Multicultural Competence Inventory) than for those using measures of racial attitudes or observer/client ratings of the therapist. Among the 23 comparison group studies, the effect sizes were highest on observer/client ratings of therapists and much lower on self-rated measures of multicultural competence or racial attitudes. Thus, although participants in the 24 studies measuring pre- to posttest changes of a single group tended to self-report strong gains over time in their multicultural competence, the 23 studies using comparison group designs showed the effectiveness of multicultural education to be more pronounced when observer/client ratings were used.

Studies also differed in the authors' descriptions of how they developed the multicultural education provided in the study. Most authors explicitly described the theoretical foundation for the multicultural education, but 20 of the 47 outcome studies lacked that information. In the 23 comparison group studies, multicultural education that was explicitly based on models of multicultural competence or relevant theories was three times as effective as that provided in studies containing no information about how the multicultural education was developed (Table 2.2). The majority cited models of multicultural competence (e.g., D. W. Sue et al., 1982) as the theoretical foundation, with relevant models such as Paul Pedersen's (2000) triad training model.

The kind of multicultural education provided differed among studies, so we evaluated the results across the average duration of the education provided

TABLE 2.2
Weighted Mean Effect Sizes (*d*) Across Characteristics of 24 Single Group (Pre- to Posttest Changes) and 23 Comparison Group Studies of Multicultural Education

Characteristic	Single group studies				Comparison studies			
	Q_b	k	d_+	95% CI	Q_b	k	d_+	95% CI
Data source	0.7				6.5*			
Published		17	1.03	[.68, 1.38]		13	.89	[.62, 1.15]
Unpublished		7	.76	[.24, 1.28]		10	.37	[.08, .67]
Assignment to groups[a]					1.5			
Convenience/self-selected						15	.57	[.31, .83]
Random assignment						8	.86	[.48, 1.25]
Population sampled[b]	0.4				0.1			
Clinicians		5	.78	[.06, 1.50]		4	.56	[.09, 1.04]
Trainees		17	1.06	[.63, 1.51]		17	.61	[.38, .84]
Required training[c]	0.2				0.5			
Required		12	1.09	[.70, 1.49]		7	.62	[.19, 1.04]
Optional		5	.95	[.37, 1.53]		13	.81	[.47, 1.15]
Theory-based training	1.3				12.9**			
Yes		14	1.09	[.72, 1.47]		13	.97	[.72, 1.22]
Not reported		10	.77	[.37, 1.17]		10	.32	[.07, .57]
Dependent variable[d]	8.9*				7.6*			
Self-ratings, competencies		16	1.18	[.87, 1.49]		18	.58	[.36, .81]
Self-ratings, racial attitudes		9	.48	[.08, .87]		4	.47	[.00, .95]
Observer/client ratings		5	.56	[.03, 1.09]		5	1.23	[.80, 1.67]

Note. d_+ = random effects weighted effect size; k = number of studies; Q_b = Q-value for variance between groups; CI = confidence interval.
[a]This analysis contrasted studies using static group comparison and quasi-experimental designs with those using true experimental designs. [b]Studies including both trainees and clinicians were excluded from these analyses. [c]Studies not reporting whether the training was required or not were excluded from these analyses. [d]Each type of measurement occurring in studies was represented in this analysis, so it was possible for some studies to contribute more than one effect size.
$*p < .05. **p < .01.$

and on whether the education was required or voluntary. We also sought to contrast the findings from studies that assigned participants randomly to conditions, because true experimental designs are less susceptible to threats to internal validity. However, these analyses did not identify any statistically significant differences in the results obtained across studies (Table 2.2).

Participant Characteristics in the 47 Outcome Studies

Studies included a wide variety of participants, so we sought to determine whether systematic differences in findings could be attributable to several participant characteristics: gender (operationalized as percentage of females in the study), average age, estimated age cohort (year of study minus average age of participants), education level, professional status (clinicians vs. trainees), and racial diversity (operationalized as percentage of people of color in the study). Only the latter variable reached statistical significance for the 23 comparison group studies, with the percentage of people of color included in the sample strongly associated with the magnitude of the effect sizes ($r = .55, p = .003$). Comparison group studies with relatively more participants of color tended to have larger effect sizes, indicating greater effectiveness of training, than those with almost all White/European American participants.

Study Characteristics Among the 68 Retrospective Studies

Most of the studies evaluated participants' self-reported multicultural competence (69%), with some measuring racial attitudes (16%) or a combination of the two. The averaged results were consistent across these dependent variables ($Q = 0.4, p > .10$). The type of participant sampling (convenience vs. random) did not consistently influence the findings ($Q = 0.1, p > .10$), and the magnitude of the effect sizes did not differ significantly as a function of the year of publication of the study ($r = -0.16, p > .10$). Thus, these three study characteristics did not moderate the overall findings of the 68 retrospective studies.

Participant Characteristics in the 68 Retrospective Studies

No differences in the findings of the retrospective studies were observed across any of the participant characteristics analyzed: participant gender composition (operationalized as percentage of females in the study), participants' average age, estimated participants' age cohort (year of study minus average age of participants), participants' average years of education, participants' professional status (trainee or clinician), or participants' racial diversity (operationalized as percentage of people of color in the study). The association between participants' prior multicultural education and their current self-reported multicultural competence and/or racial attitudes appeared to be independent of the characteristics of participants across studies.

Likelihood of Publication Bias Adversely Influencing the Results

Among the 47 outcome studies, possible publication bias appears to have influenced the magnitude of the overall findings reported previously. Although one statistical method (Duval & Tweedie, 2000) did not identify any "missing" studies for either the 24 single group (pre- to posttest changes) or 23 comparison group studies, visual inspection of the contour-enhanced funnel graphs indicated a disproportionate number of studies reporting statistically significant results relative to the standard errors (combined 47 studies depicted in Figure 2.1). Moreover, Egger's regression test (an estimate of asymmetry of effect sizes that would indicate possible "missing" studies) was statistically significant for both of these types of studies ($p < .01$), suggesting likely publication bias. Across the 23 comparison group studies, those that had been published had larger effect sizes than doctoral dissertations that had remained unpublished (Table 2.2), so it is almost certain that unpublished studies not included in the meta-analysis would have lowered the average effect sizes reported previously.

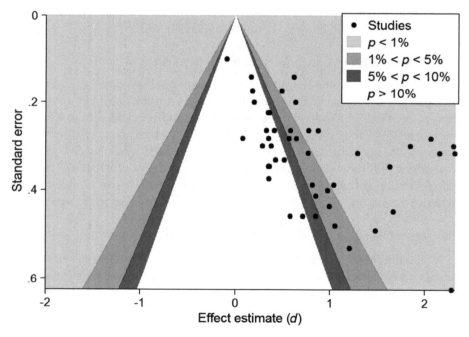

Figure 2.1. Contour-enhanced funnel plot of effect sizes (Cohen's *d*) by standard error for 47 outcome studies of multicultural education. Normally, data portrayed in this manner should be distributed in the shape of a pyramid, but the lack of studies in the lower left of the other data points suggests "missing" studies, those with small numbers of participants and nonsignificant results that may have failed to be published or were never submitted for publication.

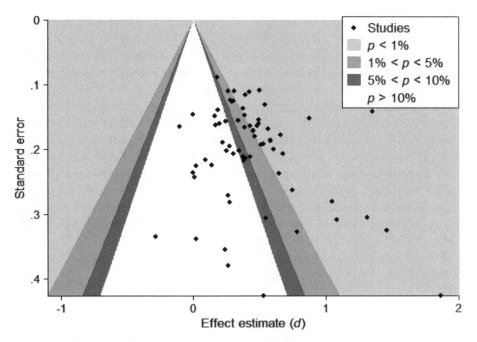

Figure 2.2. Contour-enhanced funnel plot of effect sizes (Cohen's *d*) by standard error for 68 retrospective studies of multicultural education.

The data for the 68 retrospective studies (see Figure 2.2) were more evenly distributed around their numeric average than the 47 outcome studies (Figure 2.1). Although the trim and fill method using random effects weighted estimates did not identify any "missing" studies, Egger's regression test was statistically significant ($p < .05$). Thus, publication bias may have mildly inflated the results of the 68 retrospective studies, although not nearly as conspicuously as in the 47 outcome studies.

DISCUSSION AND INTERPRETATION OF THE FINDINGS

Multicultural education is effective for mental health professionals. Therapists' and trainees' self-reported abilities, self-reported racial attitudes, and observer/client reported clinical performance have all been shown to improve through multicultural education. On average, participants receiving multicultural education improved about one standard deviation ($d = .95$) over their initial scores on those indicators or about two thirds of a standard deviation ($d = .67$) more than people who had not received multicultural education during the same time frame. These findings confirmed the results of the previous meta-analysis, which evaluated fewer studies (T. B. Smith et al., 2006).

Separate analyses of retrospective studies estimated the cumulative effect of multicultural education and multicultural experience. In general, the more multicultural education individuals received, the more likely they were to report multicultural competence and positive racial attitudes ($d = .41$). Furthermore, individuals' level of experience working with culturally diverse clients was positively but mildly related to their self-reported multicultural competence and racial attitudes ($d = .29$). These two findings were based on correlational designs, so personal commitment to multiculturalism and other likely confounds cannot be ruled out. Moreover, the findings were of smaller magnitude than would be expected; other factors (not measured) must better account for individuals' level of multicultural competence in providing mental health service.

Implications From the Secondary Analyses

Analyses of the influence of study and participant characteristics suggest five qualifications to the foregoing overall conclusions. First and foremost is the likelihood that the statistical estimates of the effectiveness of multicultural education may be inflated due to publication bias, which occurs when nonsignificant research findings remain unpublished or otherwise inaccessible to researchers conducting meta-analyses (Rosenthal, 1991). The apparent absence of some negative or nonsignificant findings likely resulted in excessively high estimates of the effectiveness of multicultural education. Thus, the overall effect size values reported earlier are liberal estimates of the effectiveness of multicultural education in improving participants' multicultural competence.

A second qualification concerns the differences in results across outcome measures. Participants in multicultural education tended to rate themselves as substantially improved in multicultural competence from pre- to posttest, but those "gains" were much lower when treatment participants were compared with control groups ($d = 1.18$ compared with $d = .58$; see Table 2.2). About one half of the apparent effectiveness of multicultural education in improving participants' self-reported multicultural competence is attributable to study invalidity: failing to account for participants' explicit expectations for improvement to have occurred, sensitization invoked through the initial measurement. Thus, it may be preferable to ignore the statistical estimates generated from the 24 studies measuring pre- to posttest changes and rely exclusively on the estimates provided by the 23 studies using control groups.

This concern relevant to study internal validity is somewhat mitigated by the finding that the effectiveness of multicultural education was more pronounced in the 23 comparison group studies when trained observers or clients rated the study participants. Observer ratings are presumably less susceptible to bias than self-reports, assuming that the raters are blind to the participants' level of multicultural education (e.g., Constantine & Ladany, 2000). So it remains impressive that trained observers or clients themselves rated participants who had received multicultural education much higher than participants who had not received multicultural education. Unfortunately, only 10 estimates involved observer or client ratings (Table 2.2), so these results may be unreliable. At least the overall estimates from the 23 comparison group studies indicate moderate effectiveness.

A third qualification of the results concerns the inconsistency in results of the outcome studies (Figure 2.1): ranging from no improvement to substantial gains. As mentioned early in this chapter, multicultural education varies remarkably in method, intensity, content, format, and so forth. Clearly and obviously, multicultural education varies remarkably in its effectiveness.

A fourth qualification helps account for the high degree of variability in effectiveness. Although 57% of the authors of outcome studies described the theoretical and research foundations for the multicultural education that participants received, primarily the tripartite model of multicultural competence (e.g., D. W. Sue et al., 1982), 20 reports did not include any conceptual basis or rationale for the multicultural education provided. And the findings from the experimental and quasi-experimental studies differed accordingly: Studies containing details about the theoretical basis of the intervention (i.e., multicultural competencies) were three times as effective as those not containing this information (Table 2.2). Three times as effective! Although the failure of authors to describe the conceptual basis of the multicultural education provided could reflect other nuisance variables (e.g., precision in conducting research), it seems likely that the programs not explicitly based on the multicultural competencies or relevant models were of poorer quality than those based on a particular model. These differences, apparently attributable to quality, cannot be overemphasized. So the previous qualification regarding the "moderate" effectiveness of multicultural education should be counterbalanced with a qualification about quality: Multicultural education explicitly based on principles relevant to multicultural competence is very effective; multicultural education not explicitly based on principles relevant to multicultural competence is only mildly effective.

A fifth qualification of the findings concerns the racial composition of the participants. Across the 23 comparison group studies, the effectiveness of multicultural education was strongly associated ($r = .55$) with the percentage of participants who were people of color. On average, the more people of color participating, the more effective the multicultural education. Many scholars had previously called attention to this possibility (e.g., Dickson et al., 2010), but the trend is only now being confirmed. Nevertheless, we cannot yet ascertain the degree to which this finding results from one or more of the following conditions: (a) greater racial diversity of participants allows for enhanced learning opportunities about multiculturalism for all participants; (b) greater interest in (and less resistance toward) multiculturalism occurs among people of color, who improve more than Whites as a result of the education provided; and/or (c) multicultural education is of higher quality when provided by institutions composed of greater numbers of people of color (i.e., the institutional environment being more conducive to multicultural competence, such as higher expectations by instructors for student growth). Whatever the specific causality, participant racial composition does matter when comparing gains of treatment with control groups.

Other than those five qualifications, the data did not systematically differ across multiple study and participant characteristics, a consistency worthy of note. For instance, the effectiveness of multicultural education did not differ when it was required or voluntary, even though some would assume that people voluntarily taking a multicultural workshop might be more motivated to improve than people required to take a university class. The fact that the data did not differ between voluntary and mandated settings provides indirect support for the stance taken by APA and other professional organizations to require multicultural education in accredited graduate programs. Similarly, results did not differ when the participants were trainees or working professionals: Multicultural education equally benefitted both.

Recommendations for Practitioners

Practicing psychologists can enhance their abilities to serve diverse clients by participating in multicultural education. For their benefit, many professional conferences now offer specific training in multicultural issues. It is in professionals' best interest to seek out additional learning and experience (Ponterotto, 1998). Practitioners should approach multicultural education selectively, however. Some programs are clearly more effective than others (Figure 2.1). Programs that are based on the principles of multicultural competence or relevant theory offer training best suited to personal skill development and client melioration (Rogers-Sirin, 2008). Practitioners additionally benefit from programs with a balance between awareness, knowledge, and skill development. Too many programs focus on awareness and knowledge without adequate attention to skills (Pieterse et al., 2009). Ultimately, the best type of multicultural education is a program that fills gaps in personal skills. A self-evaluation of multicultural competence (Arredondo et al., 1996; D. W. Sue et al., 1992a) can help identify areas in which an individual needs improvement.

Considerations for Future Research

Our meta-analytic review included 115 studies containing quantitative data, an indication that researchers have been fairly interested in evaluating multicultural education. Although our comments in this section are based on those quantitative studies, "we need a balance of quantitative and qualitative approaches to multicultural training research" (Ponterotto, 1998, p. 64). With that caveat stated, we offer the following questions and suggestions for scholars to consider in future research (see Exhibit 2.1).

Real-World Applications

Meta-analyses evaluate "effect sizes," but the interpretation of an effect size is not straightforward. Improvements reported in this chapter in terms of standard deviation units (Cohen's d) are not at all the same as individuals actually achieving adequate multicultural competence. Consider the following example. A national survey evaluating multicultural competence (Vereen, Hill, & McNeal, 2008) obtained mediocre average subscale scores of about 55 (possible range of 20 to 80) and standard deviations of about 6 on the Multicultural Awareness/Knowledge/Skills Survey (D'Andrea, Daniels, & Heck, 1991). Assuming the average effect size from studies using comparison group designs ($d = .67$), these scores would represent an absolute gain (relative to controls) of one point on the rating scale (e.g., improving from *agree* to *strongly agree*) on four of 20 items of each subscale, equating to an average 7% improvement on the subscale scores (relative to controls). Is that change meaningful? Do these results indicate that participants are truly more effective as a result of multicultural education? In terms of the scaling used in this particular example, the participants from the national survey would still rate themselves between *disagree* and *agree* in their multicultural competence, even after the hypothetical gains. Do we remain satisfied with

EXHIBIT 2.1
Recommendations for Researchers

- Examine practical/clinical significance: clients' experiences, improvement, and retention as a function of therapist multicultural education, experience, and competence.
- Use research designs that will answer research questions with minimal likelihood of bias.
- Incorporate concepts and resources from related disciplines.
- Recruit as many participants as possible to minimize sampling error.
- Control for or examine the influence of responses attributable to social desirability.
- Develop measures focused on skills and behaviors associated with multicultural competence.

mediocre abilities because they are better than incompetence? What level of abilities sufficiently enhances clients' experiences in therapy? Future research will benefit from considering issues of practical significance and real-world applications, not merely issues of statistical "improvement."

Client Perspectives

We doubt that anyone seeking treatment for a medical condition would be impressed by a research study in which medical students rated their own improvement on their ability to perform that treatment. A prospective medical patient would want to know whether current and potential physicians who had received training specific to that treatment were able to perform it effectively to improve patient outcomes. The same principle applies to mental health practices: "The ultimate purpose of counseling competence is therapeutic change. All other aims and activities of psychologists and counselors . . . are subordinate to this raison d'être" (Mollen, Kelly, & Ridley, 2011, p. 919–920). However, the vast majority of studies identified in this meta-analytic review used participants' self-reports on variables indirectly relevant to therapy. We identified only two outcome studies and one retrospective study in which clients provided the ratings. The field does not need more research measuring therapists' self-reported changes; it desperately needs research on clients' experiences, improvement, and retention.

Clinical Settings

If researchers attended more to clients' experiences, a related gap in the current literature would be corrected: assessment of multicultural education provided in the workplace. Although some research has evaluated clinic-based programs and work environments, the primary emphasis has been on graduate school programs.

Evaluations Versus Retrospective Surveys

Surveys can be used for a wide variety of research purposes. For example, surveys about current opinions or practices provide needed information about specific topics, such as what percentage of programs evaluate participants' multicultural skills: 12% according to Priester et al. (2008) and 7% according to Pieterse (2009). Similarly, retrospective surveys can help in estimating general relationships of variables when experimental or quasi-experimental research designs are impossible.

Our review located 68 surveys that attempted to evaluate therapists' and/or trainees' multicultural education and experience retrospectively (e.g., correlating the number of multicultural classes taken with self-reported multicultural competence or racial attitudes). These kinds of surveys cannot accurately evaluate questions regarding effectiveness, efficacy, usefulness, and so forth, and they are characterized by all kinds of threats to internal validity, such as participant self-selection bias (i.e., likelihood of people interested in multicultural issues choosing to complete the survey). If conducted at all, such surveys should control for confounding factors, such as preexisting multicultural interest and motivation and topic social desirability (Castillo, Brossart, Reyes, Conoley, & Phoummarath, 2007; Constantine & Ladany, 2000). After summarizing the results of 47 outcome studies, we anticipate little if any benefit from conducting a 69th retrospective survey. Retrospective surveys are easy to conduct, so dissertation committees will be tempted to approve such projects. We urge constructiveness over convenience.

Seeking Out Best Practices From Related Disciplines

Any organization tends to seek solutions internally, and this practice certainly characterizes the literature that we reviewed; most authors cited exclusively other psychologists and/or counselor educators. Yet, it can be useful to learn from the successes (and failures) of other disciplines (Baca et al., 2007). For instance, the profession of teacher education and the National Association for Multicultural Education have a rich literature on the same issues and problems so frequently cited in the mental health professions. The fields of social work and international business have multiple and varied resources that can help individuals work effectively across cultures. Cross-fertilization of ideas may improve similar abilities among mental health service providers.

Procedures for Correcting Publication Bias

Negative and nonsignificant research findings are typically inaccessible (not submitted for publication or presentation), so we encourage researchers to archive such findings online (e.g., submitting results to databases such as ERIC). Another way to diminish the likelihood of publication bias is for researchers to substantially increase the number of study participants, which would both reduce sampling errors and increase the likelihood that the results will achieve statistical significance, even if effect size remains minimal.

Recommendations for Instructors and Program Directors

Multicultural education is required for every professionally accredited graduate program. Hundreds of instructors, thousands of students, and millions of clients stand to benefit from improvements in multicultural education.

EXHIBIT 2.2
Recommendations for Instructors and Clinical Directors

- Provide specific, concrete, tangible illustrations of multicultural competencies.
- Demonstrate the overlap between multicultural and general counseling competencies.
- Focus instruction on and provide models of multicultural competencies.
- Integrate multicultural issues across the curriculum, particularly in practica.
- Maintain high expectations for multicultural competence.
- Identify and meet individual students' needs.
- Promote mastery of skills through practice.
- Evaluate student skills regularly.
- Evaluate the multicultural education provided.
- Foster effective learning environments.
- Implement published guidelines:
  - Teaching counseling based on competence (Ridley, Mollen, & Kelly, 2011b)
  - Multicultural program development model (Ridley, Mendoza, & Kanitz, 1994)
  - Multicultural course development model (Ridley, Espelage, & Rubinstein, 1997)
  - Multicultural competency model of training (Ponterotto, 1997, 1998)
  - Characteristics of effective instructors, students, and programs (Ponterotto, 1998)

Several recommendations should help promote that improvement (see Exhibit 2.2).

Keep the Focus of Instruction on Multicultural Competence

The objective of multicultural education is multicultural competence (Abreu et al., 2000). Anything that does not promote multicultural competence can be dropped, no matter how interesting the facts, engaging the activities, enlightening the self-scrutiny, and so forth. Knowing about a cultural group becomes valuable in therapy only when that knowledge facilitates worldview congruence with a particular client. The objective for gaining cultural knowledge is to be able to apply it in a therapeutic relationship (e.g., Ridley, Mollen, & Kelly, 2011b). As the data show (Figure 2.1), entire groups of people may fail to improve after months in a multicultural psychology class.

Every activity, every bit of information provided in multicultural education should enhance participants' motivation and abilities to provide effective therapy (e.g., Mollen et al., 2011). Although some individuals may experience discouragement when they become more aware of their incompetence (and thus rate themselves low at posttest), the realistic appraisal provided by effective instruction contributes to skill enhancement. Activities commonly used to promote self-awareness (such as cultural autobiographies) should be made explicitly relevant to therapy or replaced with activities that promote skills simultaneously with self-awareness, such as those suggested by Pedersen

(2000). We hope that within a few years, research reviews of multicultural course syllabi will show a balance of all aspects of multicultural competence, which will necessitate a substantial and sustained increase in skill development (Pieterse, 2009).

Integration of Multicultural Issues Across the Curriculum, Particularly Practica

For decades scholars have called for integration of multicultural issues across the curricula of professional graduate programs (Abreu et al., 2000; Ponterotto, 1998; Vereen et al., 2008). Research confirms that such integration fosters a cultural learning environment that predicts multicultural competence (Dickson & Jepsen, 2007); students in programs with strong support for multiculturalism gain most from multicultural education (M. N. Coleman, 2006). The literature emphasizes particularly the benefits of integrating practicum supervision with a multicultural focus (Vereen et al., 2008). Explicit integration with clinical practice is necessary if multiculturalism is to be taken seriously, learned, and applied (Abreu et al., 2000; Pieterse et al., 2009). The topic of multicultural supervision is receiving increased attention in the literature (e.g., Constantine, 2001; Lassiter, Napolitano, Culbreth, & Ng, 2008; Ober, Granello, & Henfield, 2009), providing guidance to graduate programs, internship sites, and mental health clinics. Programs should also facilitate opportunities for trainees to work with underserved populations (Toporek & Vaughn, 2010; Vereen et al., 2008).

Model the Processes Essential to Multicultural Competence

People learn by observing. If participants observe how an instructor maintains an open learning environment (López et al., 1989), they will understand a foundational principle of multiculturalism: Mutual benefits come through sharing power (Toporek & Vaughn, 2010). If they observe how an instructor facilitates mutual understanding during inevitable participant value conflicts, they will have learned an essential clinical skill seldom witnessed in the real world: genuine dialogue. Participants do not need self-analysis or motivational gimmicks as much as they need to observe multiculturalism applied. If instructors respect differences among the participants, the resulting emotional safety will facilitate participants' growth (M. N. Coleman, 2006; Reynolds, 2011). Participants learn how to work with personal vulnerabilities as the instructor invites genuine engagement by modeling genuine attitudes and behavior.

Maintain High Expectations for Multicultural Competence

People rise to expectations. If therapists and trainees realize that clients expect their therapist to understand their worldview, make them feel comfortable, and promote well-being in ways congruent with their values, these professionals may focus on improvement more than if the training is perceived as just a workshop for credit or a class for a grade.

Identify and Meet Individual Participants' Specific Needs

Participants in a multicultural education program are diverse in interests and experiences; a generic training program will not meet everyone's needs (Chao et al., 2011; Dickson et al., 2010; Ridley et al., 2011a). As suggested by the finding reported previously that greater racial diversity among participants is associated with enhanced effectiveness of multicultural education, differences in experiences of White/European Americans and people of color may require attention from instructors of racially mixed groups (Rooney et al., 1998) as they attempt to make the experience meaningful for people at all levels of multicultural competence. One useful procedure involves four steps: (a) require participants to self-evaluate their own limitations and competencies (which vary with the individual), (b) bolster motivation to improve on the identified areas of needed growth, (c) show examples of replacement behaviors and worldviews, and (d) provide opportunities to practice and solidify the newly adopted procedures and perspectives.

The instructor teaches principles underlying multicultural competencies and then provides examples of how those principles apply to particular cases. Important principles include promoting recovery from experiences of cultural incongruence, maintaining a multicultural perspective, verifying cultural meaning, practicing flexibility in meeting client needs, and so forth. The participants remain responsible for applying those principles. Participants benefit from setting specific self-motivating goals and being accountable to report their progress. The efforts of any instructor are multiplied when participants actively self-instruct—instituting for themselves the individualization necessary to improve despite different experiences and abilities.

Support Participants in Mastering Challenges That Engage Them on Many Levels

Workshops and classes are time-limited. After preliminary instruction and modeling, participants may tend to learn best by engaging in learning activities that provide opportunities to practice the principles described. Certain activities and experiences, such as conducting an interview focused on issues of race or culture, can simultaneously facilitate awareness of self, knowledge of others, and skills for counseling. "Identifying which activity engages students on many levels (e.g., cognitive, affective, and behavioral) seems crucial to promoting the development of professionals who can effectively work with diverse populations" (Ancis & Ali, 2005, p. 96–97). As instructors help students analyze complex clinical vignettes, consult with cultural informants, reevaluate their own cultural assumptions reflected in role plays or simulations, practice skills demonstrated on videotapes, and so forth, they both enhance participants' self-confidence and develop essential skills (Pieterse, 2009).

Conduct Multiple Performance Evaluations

Many scholars have encouraged relevant performance evaluations: "In the future more programs will hold students to a competence standard in classes that are designed to teach them about racial-cultural issues, especially since the cultural competence standards have been in existence for more than [30] years" (Carter, 2003, p. 30). Learners absorb as much as they are required to demonstrate. If participants in multicultural education know they will soon need to demonstrate a particular skill, they tend to pay attention. For instance, an instructor of a 3-hour workshop could invite culturally diverse surrogates to engage participants in role plays at the end of the session, providing feedback on participants' application of principles. Or at the end of each clinical placement, supervisors could observe videotaped sessions of their students, using a rubric of multicultural competencies to provide formal evaluations (Fouad & Arredondo, 2007; Sevig & Etzkorn, 2001). Clinicians could be told that their employers will be tracking client retention data across race. Performance improves when people remain accountable.

Perform Internal Evaluations of the Multicultural Education Provided

Improvement requires self-scrutiny. Program directors, clinical supervisors, and instructors can regularly evaluate the quality of the multicultural education they provide, using external metrics and guidelines created for multiculturally competent programs (Fouad & Arredondo, 2007; Ponterotto & Austin, 2005; Utsey, Grange, & Allyne, 2006). They may conduct evaluations of the multicultural competence of instructors (Spanierman et al., 2011), use narrative descriptions of exemplary programs as models (Fouad, 2006; Ponterotto & Austin, 2005), and consult faculty members from those exemplary programs. Also essential is ongoing personal professional development—training the trainer (Newell et al., 2010; Ponterotto, 1998; Toporek & Vaughn, 2010). The whole enterprise of multicultural education assumes that instructors understand the literature of multicultural psychology. An effective curriculum necessitates this familiarity. Programs should never have to scramble to find an adjunct instructor for a multicultural class. Not every faculty member has the required preparation to teach a class on forensic psychology; similarly, not every instructor has the genuine experience with multicultural psychology that should be prerequisite to teaching it (see characteristics listed by Ponterotto, 1998).

Apply the General Factors of Effective Psychotherapy
to the Learning Environment

Limited research has evaluated the effectiveness of different methods, formats, and approaches to multicultural education (Ancis & Ali, 2005). Although it may be tempting to compare the effectiveness of those approaches, findings from psychotherapy research emphasize the importance of general factors over specific techniques. Thus, it may be wiser to transfer and promote those same general factors in multicultural education (e.g., enhancing the alliance of instructors with students, raising student expectations for self-improvement) than to scrutinize the nuances of unproven methods and techniques (Priester et al., 2008).

Incorporate Recommendations Provided in the Literature

Recommendations for improving multicultural education regularly appear in professional publications. Excellent guidelines have been provided by Ponterotto (1997, 1998; Ponterotto & Austin, 2005) and Ridley et al. (1994, 1997), among others. Beyond information in those foundational sources, recent specific recommendations for improvement include the following:

- Address international perspectives and global psychology (Ægisdóttir & Gerstein, 2010).
- Cover indigenous healing practices and perspectives on mental health (Bojuwoye & Sodi, 2010).
- Facilitate "service learning" by having participants practice essential multicultural skills while meeting needs of local communities (Tomlinson-Clarke & Clarke, 2010), collaborating with families and community organizations (Newell et al., 2010).
- Use technology and Internet resources to enhance students' learning (Ancis, 2003).
- Provide instruction regarding spiritual and religious diversity (Crook-Lyon et al., 2012).
- Ensure that students understand the principles of contextualization and the intersections of diversity, rather than teaching one content area at a time as if the distinct topics existed in isolation (Pieterse et al., 2009).
- Provide direct and indirect supervision of participants' activities designed to promote multicultural competence (Newell et al., 2010; Vereen et al., 2008).

Instructors and program directors are intensely busy, but time spent in the literature will not only prevent serious mistakes but also promote maximal benefit from the time already invested in providing multicultural education.

CONCLUSION

Mental health professionals would benefit from receiving instruction in multicultural issues as part of their graduate degree requirements and across their careers through professional development programs and workshops. Although multicultural education results in moderate improvements in self-ratings, its quality is highly variable. The most effective training programs focus on participants' acquisition of multicultural competencies. Openly talking about historically oppressed groups and gaining insight into personal feelings about those groups is important for the development of a therapist (López et al., 1989), but dialogue and insight alone do not necessarily enhance therapists' abilities to work effectively with clients from those groups. Education, in the true sense of the word, is functional. It is past time for the field to focus more on skill development (Pieterse, 2009); it is time to demonstrate that skill acquisition results in improved client outcomes.

To increase the focus on skill development, multicultural issues must be integrated across other aspects of professional training, particularly clinical supervision (e.g., Ober et al., 2009). This need for systematic integration of multicultural issues has been repeatedly emphasized (Dickson et al., 2010; Fouad & Arredondo, 2007; Toporek & Vaughn, 2010). Acquiring and maintaining multicultural competence in mental health services is more likely when the institution or clinic supports it (Dickson & Jepsen, 2007; Utsey et al., 2006). Sporadic workshops and a single university class are better than nothing at all, but genuine multicultural education entails "a lifelong journey toward the goal of increasing multicultural competence" (Dickson et al., 2010, p. 262).

This chapter has provided specific recommendations for improving multicultural education for practitioners, program directors, researchers, and instructors. We have much to improve. A question to guide the actions of all parties was suggested by Rogers-Sirin (2008): "How does training relate to improvements in [client] use of services, client satisfaction, client retention?" (p. 318). If we collectively redesign and then implement multicultural education with that question as our primary consideration, it seems likely that the statistical estimates reported in this chapter will appear small by comparison with what we will achieve in the future.

3

THERAPIST MULTICULTURAL COMPETENCE: A META-ANALYSIS OF CLIENT EXPERIENCES IN TREATMENT

Mental health professionals have an ethical responsibility to facilitate effective psychotherapeutic interventions for all clients; this necessarily entails accounting for and being sensitive to human diversity (Arredondo & Toporek, 2004; S. Sue, 1998). Although mental health professionals would not intentionally mistreat clients from diverse multicultural backgrounds, inadequate cultural knowledge or awareness may result in unintentional harm to the client (Pope-Davis, Liu, Toporek, & Brittan-Powell, 2001; S. Sue, 1988). For example, when a clinician misunderstands a client's cultural worldviews, lifestyles, and experiences, the mental health needs of the client may remain unrecognized and unmet (S. Sue & Zane, 1987). To prevent this type of situation, scholars have suggested that therapists

Alberto Soto and Derek Griner of Brigham Young University contributed to the writing of this chapter.

A complete list of references for the studies included in this chapter's meta-analysis is posted online. Readers can consult it at http://pubs.apa.org/books/supp/smith

develop multicultural competencies (Arredondo et al., 1996; Arredondo & Tovar-Blank, 2014) that will enable them to adjust their practices to meet the needs of culturally diverse populations (American Psychological Association, 2009).

The broad concept of multicultural counseling competence (MCC) has been operationalized in terms of *multicultural counseling competencies* (MCCs), which are most often described as therapists' awareness, knowledge, and skills in working with diverse clients (Constantine, 2002; D. W. Sue, Arredondo, & McDavis, 1992a; D. W. Sue et al., 1982). The potential benefits to diverse clients of having therapists who are aware, knowledgeable, and skillful in handling multicultural issues may be so obvious that perhaps some scholars immersed in multicultural psychology have taken them for granted. Despite wide acknowledgement of MCCs and attempts to evaluate them across more than three decades, scholars in multicultural psychology actually have limited data about how these competencies affect clients' perspectives and experiences in therapy (D'Andrea & Heckman, 2008; Huey, Tilley, Jones, & Smith, 2014).

Some of the difficulties associated with evaluating MCCs may be due in part to the methods traditionally used to measure these constructs (e.g., Constantine & Ladany, 2001; Hoyt, Warbasse, & Chu, 2006). Self-report measures have long been used to determine clinicians' multicultural case conceptualization abilities, but self-report measures overestimate abilities compared with expert ratings (Cartwright, Daniels, & Zhang, 2008). The inherent confounds associated with self-evaluation raise serious questions about the validity of self-report measures of MCCs (e.g., overconfidence, social desirability). For example, Constantine and Ladany (2001) found a positive correlation between MCC self-report measures and a general index of social desirability: After the researchers had controlled for social desirability, none of the self-report scales were significantly related to a clinician's MCC conceptualization ability. Thus, many research questions should be asked about therapists MCC (Ridley & Shaw-Ridley, 2011; Worthington & Dillon, 2011). Most notably, to what degree do MCCs increase the effectiveness of therapeutic services provided to culturally diverse clients, reduce clients' premature discontinuation of therapy, and enhance clients' experiences in therapy?

It would not be an exaggeration to say that the MCC construct is the most fundamental concept in applied multicultural psychology, which is based on the premise that therapeutic services received by culturally diverse clients are more effective when therapists skillfully attend to specific cultural variables (Arredondo et al., 1996; Arredondo & Tovar-Blank, 2014; S. Sue, 1998, 2003). Without the concept of MCC, multicultural psychology informs mental health treatment but does not prescribe specific actions.

REVIEW OF THE LITERATURE

Relevant Theory

The seminal paper written for *The Counseling Psychologist* by D. W. Sue and his colleagues (1982) established the foundational tripartite conceptualization of MCC as comprising therapists' cultural knowledge, awareness, and skills. The authors also presented a detailed listing of specific MCCs, later operationalized by Arredondo and colleagues (1996). Subsequent scholarship regarding MCC has continued to build and expand on the foundational tripartite model, with occasional calls for more objective data that include clients' perceptions of the multicultural competency of their therapist (Constantine, 2002; Imel et al., 2011; Pope-Davis et al., 2001; Worthington & Dillon, 2011). Although elaboration on the various conceptualizations and multiple lists of MCCs published in the literature is beyond the scope of this chapter, we describe briefly the components of the tripartite model.

Awareness

Therapists who are keenly aware of their own cultural values, beliefs, and worldviews should be able to more accurately discern and interpret the cultural values, beliefs, and worldviews of their clients than those who are not. Therapists lacking cultural awareness risk misunderstanding clients' actions and comments, perhaps assuming that their clients' values are the same as their own. Or they may fail to account for their own implicit biases (A. D. Katz & Hoyt, 2014). For instance, a middle-class male therapist who fails to account for his own insecurity over his socioeconomic status may falsely conclude that because his affluent female client was "born into money," she does not appreciate the value of work. This preconceived notion could subtly (or perhaps not so subtly) affect the approach of the therapist and the relationship between the therapist and client. The following are brief examples of multicultural awareness (Arredondo et al., 1996):

- awareness of one's own limits in multicultural competency;
- awareness of how one's own background shapes personal values, assumptions, and biases; and
- awareness of how different methods of treatment (including theoretical orientations and their sociopolitical contexts) can affect work with people from culturally diverse backgrounds.

Knowledge

Therapists with cultural knowledge can ascertain both differences and similarities across various domains, such as race and ethnicity, gender, sexual orientation, and religion. They are able to put into context and accurately interpret the meaning of the actions and perceptions of others. For instance, a psychologist familiar with the traditional Latin American value of *familismo* ("family first") may welcome a client's request that family be included in the therapy process, rather than interpreting this request as a form of enmeshment. Examples of multicultural knowledge include the following (Arredondo et al., 1996):

- knowledge of the impact that culture and history have had on psychological theory, inquiry methods, and professional practice;
- knowledge of specific contexts of oppression, discrimination, and prejudice that many culturally diverse clients have encountered and experienced; and
- knowledge of cultural attitudes about mental health and mental health services.

Skills

Multiculturally skilled therapists apply their awareness and knowledge to engage effectively with others and to use culturally appropriate strategies in therapy (Arredondo et al., 1996). They avoid overgeneralizing or over-individualizing treatment (S. Sue, 1998) by accounting for cultural contexts as they meet the needs of the client. For instance, a therapist who learns of an African immigrant's strong beliefs regarding gender roles (knowledge) that differ from those of the therapist (awareness) will appropriately seek common ground with the client in other areas to strengthen the therapeutic alliance (skills) before exploring how gender roles relate to the client's presenting concern. The following are examples of multicultural skills (Arredondo et al., 1996):

- ability to look beyond color, culture, religion, sexual orientation, accent, and so forth, and see individuals in a holistic way, thus viewing the client in the context of his or her historical, sociopolitical, and economic background;
- initiative to seek out educational and consultative experiences to increase the therapist's own effectiveness in working across cultural differences; and
- ability to modify assessment and treatment methods to better match the needs of multicultural clientele.

MCCs have strongly influenced formal guidelines adopted by the American Psychological Association (2003) and other professional organizations. Applied psychology practice needs specific guidelines that stipulate what therapists must do to improve the effectiveness of their work (Kaslow et al., 2007), including their work with diverse clientele. Some research has shown that the abilities of therapists to understand and attend to cultural variables in treatment influence therapeutic processes (Imel et al., 2011). Evaluating the degree to which therapists' MCCs affect treatment processes and outcomes will ultimately improve the delivery of services to a broad range of clients. Therapists who develop MCCs increase their effectiveness in working with culturally diverse clients. Therapists who do not may cause harm to clients or provide therapy that is culturally incongruent and therefore less effective (D. W. Sue & Sue, 2013).

Narrative Review of Previous Research

During the 3 decades since D. W. Sue and colleagues (1982) published their conceptualization of MCC, scholars have examined both conceptual and empirical components of multicultural competence (e.g., Arredondo, Rosen, Rice, Perez, & Tovar-Gamero, 2005; Drinane, Owen, Adelson, & Rodolfa, 2014; Dunn, Smith, & Montoya, 2006; Owen, Leach, Wampold, & Rodolfa, 2011a). Unfortunately, empirical research focused specifically on the validity of MCC (Pope-Davis, Coleman, Liu, & Toporek, 2003) has remained limited, with little attention to its effect on client outcomes (D'Andrea & Heckman, 2008).

Several researchers have conducted content analyses to identify themes in the MCC literature (Arredondo et al., 2005; Ponterotto, Fuertes, & Chen, 2000; Pope-Davis et al., 2001). Ponterotto and his colleagues (2000) conducted a comprehensive review of MCC models, considering both therapists' acquisition of MCCs and clients' ratings of their therapists' MCCs. They concluded that although indirect support for MCCs was available, outcome research with actual clients was needed. They also recommended that MCC research move away from self-report measures toward evaluation of the abilities of therapists to conceptualize cases from multicultural perspectives.

In a content analysis of research spanning 20 years, Worthington, Soth-McNett, and Moreno (2007) examined empirically based studies of MCCs published between 1986 and 2005. Across the 81 studies reviewed, 56 (72.7%) reported findings from descriptive field surveys and 19 (24.7%) used some form of analogue research. The vast majority involved therapists' self-reported levels of MCCs, with only nine studies (11%) using an assessment of MCCs completed by someone other than the therapist. Of the studies that included clients' ratings of therapists' MCCs, the clear majority (82%) involved volunteers rather than actual clients, which raises questions about the generalizability to clinical settings.

The dearth of client outcome research evaluating therapists' MCC has been openly lamented (D'Andrea & Heckman, 2008). Critics have questioned the utility of the construct, arguing that therapists who claim to have obtained such competence may gain a false sense of effectiveness (Weinrach & Thomas, 2002, 2004). Other scholars, however, have contested these criticisms while still acknowledging the need for increased empirical research of MCC (Arredondo & Toporek, 2004; Arredondo & Tovar-Blank, 2014; H. L. K. Coleman, 2004; Owen, Leach, Wampold, & Rodolfa, 2011b). Increased research evaluation of MCC is clearly needed (McCutcheon & Imel, 2009; Worthington et al., 2007).

The historical trend to discuss rather than investigate MCC is beginning to reverse (Worthington et al., 2007). For example, several studies have examined the correlation of clients' ratings of their therapists' MCCs and their satisfaction with psychotherapy (Constantine, 2002, 2007; Fuertes et al., 2006; Owen et al., 2011a; Owen, Tao, Leach, & Rodolfa, 2011). This increasing attention to research indicates that the field will benefit from a current systematic evaluation of recent research findings to support widespread implementation of the MCCs (Pope-Davis et al., 2003; Worthington et al., 2007). We therefore conducted a meta-analysis to determine the degree to which therapists' multicultural competence is associated with clients' experiences in therapy, including their perceptions of the therapist, their participation levels in treatment, and their clinical outcomes. The following section describes the data, and a subsequent section summarizes the findings.

QUANTITATIVE SYNTHESIS OF RESEARCH DATA

Our meta-analysis evaluated studies with a quantitative measure of therapist multicultural competence that was statistically associated with at least one quantitative measure of client experiences in mental health services with that therapist in three broad categories: (a) client perceptions of the therapist and treatment (e.g., client evaluations of therapists' skills, client satisfaction with the treatment received), (b) client level of participation in treatment (e.g., premature termination vs. completion of treatment), and (c) and client clinical outcomes (e.g., symptom reduction). In most cases, the manuscripts reported associations in terms of Pearson's r, with other types of statistics converted to that metric. Positive correlations indicated positive client experiences in therapy associated with higher levels of therapist multicultural competence, and negative correlations indicated positive client experiences in therapy associated with lower levels of therapist multicultural competence. Additional information regarding the methods of the meta-analysis is presented in the Appendix of this book.

Description of the Existing Research Literature

We identified a total of 16 studies that reported data on 2,025 clients' experiences in mental health treatments as a function of their therapists' level of multicultural competence. Ten studies (67%) involved clients receiving individual psychotherapy. One study involved an outdoor adventure program for at-risk youth, another consisted of volunteer clients who attended five sessions of counseling in an experimental design, and four studies evaluated clients participating in several modalities (individual and group mental health treatments). The previously mentioned three aspects of client treatment were considered: (a) client perceptions of therapists and treatments, (b) client participation in treatment, and (c) client outcomes (i.e., symptom reduction). Two studies evaluated both the participation of the client and the client perceptions of the therapist; those distinct areas were evaluated separately in our analyses.

Table 3.1 contains breakdowns of several study and participant characteristics. The majority of studies have appeared since the year 2000, including several unpublished doctoral dissertations. All studies used convenience samples, with more than half involving university study clients. Studies averaged 127 clients, with only two studies having sample sizes greater than 200. Most often clients were either African Americans or Hispanic/Latino(a) Americans, with limited research investigating other racial or ethnic groups. Only one study involved clients with relatively low levels of acculturation to Western society (Li & Kim, 2004); this was also the only one that explicitly adapted the treatment to client culture. The typical study involved cross-sectional (correlational) data, with only four studies evaluating changes in client symptoms over time.

Overall Research Findings

Across 10 studies that evaluated client perceptions of therapists, the random effects weighted correlation with therapist multicultural competence was $r = 0.50$ (95% CI = [.31, .65], $p < .0001$). Across four studies that evaluated the level of client participation in treatment, the value was $r = 0.26$ (95% CI = [.05, .44], $p = .02$). Finally, across four studies that evaluated client outcomes, the value was $r = 0.16$ (95% CI = [.03, .28], $p = .01$). The differences among these three types of outcomes reached statistical significance ($Q = 7.6, p = .02$).

The heterogeneity of the findings was very high for studies evaluating client perceptions of therapists ($I^2 = 86.3$, 95% CI = [77, 92]; $Q_{(9)} = 65.7$, $p < .001$) and for those evaluating client participation in treatment ($I^2 = 80.9$, 95% CI = [50, 93]; $Q_{(3)} = 15.7, p = .001$). Heterogeneity was moderately high

TABLE 3.1

Characteristics of 16 Studies of the Association Between
Therapist Multicultural Competence and Client Experiences
in Mental Health Treatments

Characteristic	M	No. of studies (k)	%
Year of report	2005		
Before 1990		0	0
1990–1999		2	12
2000–2011		14	88
Publication status			
Published		9	56
Unpublished		7	44
Sampling procedure used			
Convenience		16	100
Representative (random selection)		0	0
Research design			
Cross-sectional		12	75
Longitudinal		4	25
Population sampled			
Outpatient mental health clients		5	31
University/college student clients		9	56
At-risk group members		2	13
Sample size	126.6		
<50		5	31
50–99		3	19
100–199		6	38
200–399		1	6
400–999		1	6
Age of participants[a]	28.2		
Children (<13 years)		1	6
Adolescents (13–18 years)		2	13
Young adults (19–29 years)		5	31
Middle-aged adults (30–55 years)		6	37
Senior adults (>55 years)		0	0
Not reported		2	13
Gender of participants (% female)	64.1		
Race of clients[b] (%)			
African American	46		
Asian American	9		
Hispanic/Latino(a) American	33		
Native American Indian	1		
Other ethnic minority	4		

[a]Average age category of participants in studies. Not all participants in the study would necessarily be in the category listed. [b]The racial composition of clients across all studies, calculated by multiplying the number of clients in studies by the percentage of clients from each racial group and dividing that product by the total number of clients across all studies. Three studies included White/European American participants, whose data were accounted for in statistical models.

for the four studies evaluating client outcomes ($I^2 = 67.3$, 95% CI = [5, 89]; $Q_{(3)} = 9.2$, $p = .03$). In the 16 research studies identified, the observed correlations prior to aggregation ranged from –0.25 to 0.83. Inconsistent findings characterized this meta-analysis, with the association between therapist multicultural competence and client experiences in treatment so varied across studies that it was difficult to interpret the averages reported earlier. We therefore sought explanations for the variability we observed.

Factors Influencing the Association

As shown in Figure 3.1, the effect sizes in all types of studies were very unevenly distributed. Specifically, studies tended either to cluster around $r = 0$ (indicative of no effect) or to be statistically significant (located beyond the shaded regions to the right in Figure 3.1), without studies filling in the space between those two extremes. We therefore examined the data for

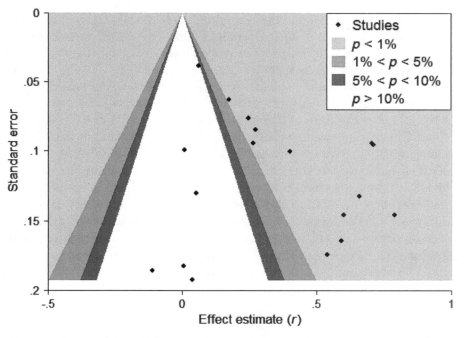

Figure 3.1. Contour-enhanced funnel plot of effect sizes (Pearson r) by standard error. This graph depicts the correlation coefficients between therapists' multicultural competence and clients' experiences in therapy as a function of the number of participants in the study (operationalized as standard error). The results are highly scattered. Particularly, the six studies in the region of statistical nonsignificance (white background) were disconnected from the other studies, which were all statistically significant at $p < .01$. This discrepancy was found to be attributable to study characteristics.

systematic differences that could account for this unusual distribution. We found that the 11 studies with the largest effect sizes all involved the same method of evaluating client perceptions of therapist multicultural competence by using the same measure, the Cross-Cultural Counseling Inventory—Revised (CCCI–R; LaFromboise, Coleman, & Hernandez, 1991). Thus, the larger effect sizes obtained in these studies likely reflected shared rater variance (clients completing all measures) and/or shared measurement variance (the content of CCCI–R items having similar meaning to the content of items on the measures of clients' perceptions of therapists; see Drinane et al., 2014). The 11 effect sizes from studies measuring client perceptions of therapists' multicultural competence averaged $r = 0.54$, whereas the seven effect sizes from studies using a measure of multicultural competence completed by the therapist averaged $r = .05$. The difference reached statistical significance in a random effects weighted regression model that controlled for the type of outcome evaluated and explained a remarkable 71% of the variance in effect sizes ($Q = 36.3$, $p < .00001$). Thus, this model accounted for the disparate findings shown in Figure 3.1. All of the nonsignificant studies in the center of the graph involved therapist self-reported multicultural competence, and all but one of the statistically significant findings (to the right of the shaded lines) involved client ratings of therapist multicultural competence.

Thus, shared rater variance explained the findings obtained within studies, even after accounting for the three different types of outcomes measured (client perceptions of therapists, client participation in treatment, and client clinical outcomes), with the added possible confound of shared measurement variance (similar content between the CCCI–R and clients' ratings of other therapists' attributes; see Drinane et al., 2014) likely influencing the findings of the studies measuring client perceptions of therapists. Across those studies of client perceptions of therapists, the random effects weighted correlation was $r = .64$ in seven studies in which ratings of therapists' multicultural competence were completed by clients, compared with $r = -.02$ in three studies in which the therapists rated their own multicultural competence.

We also examined the unusual distribution of effect sizes (Figure 3.1) for the possibility of publication bias influencing the results. Publication bias occurs when studies with insignificant or even negative effect sizes are not located in a literature search (typically because those studies remain unpublished). In the case of this meta-analysis, the notable gap between statistically significant studies (on the right) and nonsignificant studies (in the center) suggested several "missing" studies (i.e., studies conducted but unpublished with values that would fill in the missing spaces in the existing distribution). Nevertheless, when we controlled for the type of outcome evaluated by studies located in this meta-analysis, published studies yielded results of about the same magnitude as unpublished studies ($p = .17$ when testing for differences), suggesting that the results of the meta-analysis were not attributable to publication status. Furthermore, one statistical method (Duval & Tweedie, 2000) failed to identify any "missing" studies when conducted on the overall data and applied separately for each of the three types of study outcomes, the findings of which also contradict the hypothesis that publication bias influenced the reported data. Thus, we concluded that the unusual distribution of data (Figure 3.1) was accounted for in the regression model reported previously (type of outcome and source of data) and was not attributable to publication bias.

DISCUSSION AND INTERPRETATION OF THE FINDINGS

Overall Findings

We located only 16 studies that considered how therapist MCCs related to the experiences of culturally diverse clients in therapy, with only four of those studies evaluating client outcomes in treatment. Those small numbers restrict our degree of confidence in interpreting the findings of the meta-analysis; also, the high variability in the findings is problematic. Thus, we presently have a very unreliable estimate of the association between therapist MCC and client experiences in therapy, given the limited data available. Nevertheless, even preliminary interpretations of the available data are preferable to unsupported rhetoric.

Overall, MCCs are positively associated with clients' experiences in therapy. However, the findings clearly depend on the type of dependent variable evaluated. Clients' perceptions of therapists' characteristics (expertness, warmth, trustworthiness, etc.) and clients' satisfaction with the therapist were strongly related ($r = .50$) to clients' perceptions of the therapists' multicultural competence. Clients' level of participation in treatment (i.e., premature termination vs. completion) was moderately positively associated with clients' perceptions of therapists' multicultural competence ($r = .26$), but clients' outcomes in treatment were only mildly associated with ratings of therapists' multicultural competence ($r = .16$).

The pattern of these findings is understandable, given that therapist attributes typically explain a much smaller percentage of variance in client clinical outcomes than do other factors (Norcross & Lambert, 2011). If client outcomes typically vary about 12% on the basis of therapeutic alliance and 7% on the basis of therapist attributes, the total amount of variance in client outcomes possibly attributable to MCCs is already quite small. The average correlation of $r = .16$ obtained across four studies suggests that about 2.6% of the variance in outcomes for culturally diverse clients could possibly be attributable to therapist MCCs. That value corresponds with about 13.7% of the variance possibly attributable to therapists and the therapeutic alliance ($7 + 12 = 19\%$ and $2.6/19 = 13.7\%$, assuming an unlikely situation of no overlap with other therapist attributes). Thus, MCCs do positively influence client outcomes to a small degree, along with many other relevant factors. Given the small percentage of the variance in client outcomes explained by therapist competence in general (Webb, DeRubeis, & Barber, 2010), therapist MCCs deserve consideration. Nevertheless, the small number of studies and the wide variability in the findings prohibit any conclusive interpretation of the data.

Other Factors Influencing the Findings

Secondary analyses confirmed the presence of a major confound in research on MCCs: the source of the evaluations of therapist MCCs. When therapists rated their own MCCs, those evaluations consistently explained less than 1% of the variance in the therapy experiences of diverse clientele, irrespective of the outcome measured. When culturally diverse clients rated their therapists' level of multicultural competence using the CCCI–R, however, those ratings explained 61% of the variance in clients' perceptions of the therapist, 44% of the variance in clients' participation in treatment, and 16% of the variance in clients' clinical outcomes (i.e., symptom reduction). That latter value of 16% accounts for the vast majority of variance possibly attributable to therapist attributes and the therapeutic relationship ($16/19 = 84\%$, still assuming the unlikely scenario of MCCs being independent of other therapist attributes).

Therapist MCCs may not matter much if we rely on therapist judgment, but therapist MCCs may be critical from the perspective of the client. As already stated, these findings are based on few studies, but the contrast is so remarkable as to deserve substantial attention in the future: The method for evaluating therapist multicultural competence clearly influences the data. In fact, the method for evaluating therapist MCCs is more consequential than any other factor in this line of research.

Considerations for Future Research

For decades scholars have been calling for increased research on therapists' MCC, yet few studies have been conducted from the perspectives of clients. Much of the early scholarship on MCC was necessarily conceptual, and subsequent scholarship was appropriately concerned with measurement and psychometric considerations. After these earlier phases, dozens of correlational studies appeared. Despite the slowly increasing variety in approaches, researchers have persistently avoided working with clinical data.

We offer an analogy for consideration. If a health care breakthrough were proposed, widely advocated, and required as knowledge for professional licensure, would it be relegated to fewer than five clinical trials during the following 30 years? This would never happen in the practice of health care, but it has happened with the construct of multicultural competence in the profession of psychology.

Simply stated, fundamental topics deserve the highest priority, not only to firmly establish their importance but also to promote and support progress in the field. Despite the innate interest of other topics in multicultural psychology or the popularity of certain lines of inquiry, multicultural psychology applied to counseling and psychotherapy has little reason for existing without the concept of therapist multicultural competence. A stronger research foundation must be established to support the weight MCC carries in the field.

The highest priority for scholars in applied multicultural psychology must be to thoroughly evaluate therapist multicultural competence in terms of its real world benefits. Therapist multicultural competence was and continues to be a breakthrough idea in mental health treatment, but it is also a professional skill set, not merely popular jargon used to maintain an image of cosmopolitan therapy. The MCCs must be operationalized with sufficient specificity to measure their influence—not merely to document their importance (now affirmed for over 30 years) but also to systematically improve their application among clinicians who work with people in need of professional assistance. It is essential to better promote applied research that evaluates the outcomes that matter most: clients' experiences.

The meta-analytic review also suggested that study quality requires attention. Experimental designs should be used, randomly assigning participants to therapists with clearly demonstrable MCCs or to "treatment as usual." This line of research will also benefit from larger samples and random selection of participants (D'Andrea & Heckman, 2008), optimally from mental health clinics rather than from the overrepresented college student clientele. As study quality improves, the publication rate of research on MCCs should also improve beyond the current estimate of 56%.

Given the discrepancies in the findings of research studies across the MCCs evaluation sources (therapist self-report vs. client report), researchers must separate out their findings accordingly. Data reported by clients tend to yield very high correlations with clients' experiences in therapy (on average $r = .64$), but therapists' self-reported data on their MCC are not related at all to clients' experiences (on average $r = -.02$). For instance, in one study that measured both therapist and client ratings of therapist multicultural competence (Fuertes et al., 2006), the MCCs ratings completed by clients correlated $r = .65$ with measures of clients' perceptions of therapists, but the self-reported MCC ratings completed by therapists only correlated $r = .06$

with the measures of clients' perceptions. In the same study, the correlation between the MCCs ratings by clients and the MCCs ratings by therapists themselves averaged $r = -.03$, indicating no meaningful relationship. Such data should inspire a wave of new inquiry into the operationalization and evaluation of MCCs.

Specifically, future research will need to sort out at least two likely problems in this line of inquiry. First, which MCCs do clients distinguish from general counseling skills (Drinane et al., 2014)? As currently operationalized, MCCs may be difficult for clients to distinguish from other therapeutic alliance constructs such as connectedness, empathy, and so forth. Although many MCCs differ conceptually from general counseling competence, in reality they overlap; therapists who demonstrate MCCs would likely demonstrate general counseling competencies as well. Thus, some research might involve trainees whose general counseling skills and MCCs involve a broader range than those of more experienced clinicians. Measures of MCCs involving observation and client ratings must be carefully evaluated for content and revised for major overlap with general counseling competencies. Detailed operationalization of specific behaviors and microskills relevant to MCC may help make MCCs measurement less abstract and thus less likely to correlate so highly with other constructs rated by the client.

Second, the field should consider the degree to which self-rated MCCs evaluations are valid. Therapists' evaluations of their own abilities may involve abstractions and generalities difficult for a conscientious self-evaluator to rate with precision. Previous research has already shown that self-ratings of MCCs differ markedly from expert evaluations of MCC (Cartwright et al., 2008), but as undesirable as that may be, the results of the present meta-analysis depict an even more dire problem: Therapists' self-ratings of MCCs are not at all related to clients' experiences in treatment. A future meta-analysis specific to MCCs measurement could inform this controversy, but the issue is highly complex. Some seasoned therapists may insist that they have much more to learn about multicultural issues (and thus score themselves only moderately high on measures of MCCs), yet other therapists with relatively limited experience with diverse clientele would insist they are adequately informed to treat a broad range of clients equitably (and thus score moderately high on self-reported MCCs). Scholars should undertake the important work of improving evaluations of therapist MCC (Ridley & Shaw-Ridley, 2011; Worthington & Dillon, 2011), perhaps starting with evaluations of client outcomes across race of therapist and race of client (Owen et al., 2011a, 2011b).

Until adequate data suggest consensus on best practices, we recommend considering existing measures involving either therapist self-ratings or client ratings as problematic in clinical research, albeit for very different reasons. Past research is suspect unless procedures were in place to address the two likely confounds just described. Of course the alternative of observational measurement entails a different set of problems, certainly in terms of the human resources required. Yet until MCCs measurements are validated against clearly defined practices in therapy that account for client experiences, the field will lack the data needed to improve clinical practice with multicultural clientele. As a temporary measure until such definitions and measurements receive support, researchers can administer multiple measures of therapist MCCs (i.e., completed by clients and by trained observers; see also the approach recommended by Worthington & Dillon, 2011) or evaluate client outcomes by race within and across therapists (Owen et al., 2011a, 2011b). Using only one type of traditional measurement of MCCs (particularly therapist self-reports) in research with clients without accounting for likely confounds will yield misleading results.

Suggestions for Practitioners

All individuals, therapists included, are subject to a variety of preconceived biases and personal limitations. We may underestimate, or more likely, overestimate our competencies and skills, which could possibly be damaging to clients if our own certainty prevents us from accurately understanding client characteristics and needs. In the present meta-analysis the essential message for practitioners is to continue to be humble, acknowledge our limitations, and seek to learn from every single client. A culturally competent therapist is a continual student, reexamining beliefs and enhancing skills, benefitting from ongoing clinical supervision and peer feedback (e.g., Soheilian, Inman, Klinger, Isenberg, & Kulp, 2014). Clinicians also gain valuable insights from clients. It would therefore be wise to solicit and respond to explicit client feedback (both verbal and data-based; Lambert, 2010), rather than rely on our own impressions of multicultural competence. In fact, the contrast between client- and self-reported data suggests that therapists should continually work toward increasing multicultural competencies rather than assuming competence can be fully achieved. The knowledge required to understand how cultural worldviews interact with aspects of the human experience is highly complex, so of course all therapists, regardless of experience, will benefit from systematic learning over time—perhaps a lifetime.

Overall, practitioners should continue to have faith in the construct of therapist MCC (Owen et al., 2011b), even though several problems require attention (Ridley & Shaw-Ridley, 2011; Worthington & Dillon, 2011). Although this chapter has highlighted major deficiencies in the research, the results of the meta-analysis in no way detract from the centrality or the utility of the underlying construct of MCC. MCC enhances the effectiveness of therapy. In fact, when relying on clients' evaluations (arguably the most important perspective to consider), the data showed that therapist MCCs are associated with clients' perceptions of the therapist. Clients are much more likely to complete treatment and experience positive outcomes when therapists demonstrate MCCs.

CONCLUSION

The available data affirm that therapist multicultural competence is favorably associated with the experiences of culturally diverse clients in treatment. The data are imprecise, necessitating caution in deciding how much can be extrapolated to therapeutic practice, but the data obtained from clients (rather than therapist self-reports) develop a striking picture. Diverse clients tend to see therapist multicultural competence as highly related to, yet distinct from, other positive counselor attributes. In addition, culturally diverse clients are moderately more likely to prematurely discontinue treatment when their therapists do not demonstrate multicultural competence. Client outcomes improve when their therapists are able to competently attend to and value the varying experiences of culturally diverse clients.

Our review located only 16 studies that considered the association of therapist MCC with client experiences in therapy. The research on this topic has been increasing in recent years; thus, future reviews will be needed as the field continues to advance. We emphasize that although the limitation of available data should not be twisted to undercut the utility of therapist multicultural competence, our review represents a direct challenge to researchers to focus more attention on the MCC construct. Other variables that have been fiercely calling for research attention must be temporarily put on hold until researchers have squarely dealt with the most fundamental variable in applied multicultural psychology: the multicultural competencies of therapists.

II

SYNTHESIS OF RESEARCH ON THE EXPERIENCES OF PEOPLE OF COLOR WITH MENTAL HEALTH SERVICES

4

MENTAL HEALTH SERVICE UTILIZATION ACROSS RACE: A META-ANALYSIS OF SURVEYS AND ARCHIVAL STUDIES

This chapter reviews data regarding racial discrepancies in mental health service utilization (see also Snowden & Yamada, 2005). Historically, racial discrimination has restricted access to mental health services by people of color in North America (Richards, 2012). In previous centuries, inadequate access to quality mental health services was simply one of countless forms of systemic discrimination. Over many decades, as individuals, then social organizations, then finally the government gradually recognized and then slowly enforced civil rights, the racial desegregation of civic institutions, then health institutions, and then finally mental health institutions became increasingly normative. Attention was given to equity. Clinic doors opened to multicultural America.

Now, many decades after the civil rights movement, we have to ask whether we have achieved racial equity in mental health service utilization, with all racial groups accessing mental health services at the same rate as

A complete list of references for the studies included in this chapter's meta-analysis is posted online. Readers can consult it at http://pubs.apa.org/books/supp/smith

http://dx.doi.org/10.1037/14733-004
Foundations of Multicultural Psychology: Research to Inform Effective Practice, by T. B. Smith and J. E. Trimble
Copyright © 2016 by the American Psychological Association. All rights reserved.

White/European Americans. If utilization rates are now equal across race, multicultural psychology has overcome a major consequence of systemic racial discrimination. However, if contemporary mental health services continue to be underutilized by persons from groups that have been historically oppressed, we of the present generation must work with policymakers to remove the entrenched racial inequities (McGuire & Miranda, 2008; Meyer & Takeuchi, 2014; Valentine, DeAngelo, Alegría, & Cook, 2014).

Following a review of relevant theory and an overview of relevant research, this chapter describes the results of a meta-analysis of studies examining mental health service utilization across race. Implications of the results of the meta-analysis for practitioners and researchers are presented. The term *utilization* in this chapter refers to the receipt of mental health services; it does not include referrals for services or retention and dropout during services.

NARRATIVE REVIEW OF THE LITERATURE

Relevant Theory

Why do some individuals in need of professional mental health services not obtain them? Scholars commonly provide at least three types of explanation (Meyer & Takeuchi, 2014). First, individual and social factors include perceived susceptibility to future distress, external and social cues to take action, and extent to which professional services are perceived to be beneficial (Rosenstock, 1966). Second, poverty and related socioeconomic factors decrease access and utilization (Dressler, Oths, & Gravlee, 2005; Lo, Cheng, & Howell, 2014). Third, system and delivery factors include the number of clinicians available in the client's area, location of and distance to services, length of services, prerequisite conditions for services, and nature of services (Andersen & Newman, 1973; Cook, Doksum, Chen, Carle, & Alegría, 2013). These three classes of factors interact with race to exacerbate racial discrepancies (e.g., Snowden & Yamada, 2005). Specifics are provided in Exhibit 4.1 and in the sections that follow.

Individual and Social Factors

Cultures conceptualize well-being and mental illness differently (Kleinman, Eisenberg, & Good, 1978). For instance, in some Asian cultures only chronic or violent conditions may be considered to be mental illness requiring professional treatment, whereas anxiety and depression may be seen as problematic conditions requiring informal, not formal, intervention (S. Chen, Sullivan, Lu, & Shibusawa, 2003). Some people perceive emotional difficulties to be caused by imbalances in forces of nature

EXHIBIT 4.1
Common Explanations for Racial Discrepancies
in Mental Health Service Utilization

Individual/social factors
- Perceptions of mental health and self-care/desire to obtain professional mental health treatment
  - Conceptualization of mental illness and its causes
  - Cultural values and social norms regarding treatment for mental illness
- Unfamiliarity with professional services/options
- Use of informal/family networks (rather than professionals) to cope with mental illness
- Negative stigma about seeking professional treatment for mental illness
- Mistrust of mental health services
- Possible racial differences in levels of need for mental health services
- Individual/social characteristics that systematically differ across racial groups (age, education, English language fluency, religious beliefs, acculturation to Western society)

Socioeconomic factors
- Incidence and prognosis of mental illness associated with poverty
- Social/family instability associated with poverty
- Lack of access to quality professional services associated with poverty
- Lack of insurance coverage for mental illness (until only recently)
- Legal or undocumented immigrant status

Systems/delivery factors
- Lack of mental health services located in areas where people of color reside
- Poorer quality of mental health services located in areas where people of color reside
- Greater likelihood of involuntary mental health treatments for people of color
- Bias/racism in assessment and service delivery

or supernatural causes (Alvidrez, 1999) irrelevant to Western methods of professional treatment. Alternatively, mental health may be conceptualized in terms of physical health, such that individuals seek treatment from physicians rather than mental health specialists (e.g., Neighbors et al., 2007). Still other cultural beliefs suggest that emotional difficulties result from a lack of motivation or willpower (Alvidrez, 1999) and that individuals should be strong enough to handle difficulties alone (Alegría et al., 2002; Cachelin & Striegel-Moore, 2006). Thus, we cannot assume that individuals with cultural origins outside of Europe would seek out Western professional mental health services (Bosworth et al., 2000). They may not perceive such services to be helpful, or they may be unfamiliar with professional service options and availability (Broman, 1987; Cachelin & Striegel-Moore, 2006). Even when people of color perceive professional services to be helpful, they may still underutilize those services (Diala et al., 2000).

When individuals from non-Western cultures need mental health treatment, they may rely on familiar informal networks for assistance (Golding & Wells, 1990). In particular, they may feel that mental health issues are best addressed within the family (Alvidrez, 1999). Individuals with strong family support experience several benefits that promote well-being (Berkman, Glass, Brissette, & Seeman, 2000), and some cultures implicitly or explicitly discourage taking personal difficulties outside the family (M. Yeh et al., 2005). Thus, some cultures prefer to seek mental health assistance from sources other than psychotherapy (Broman, 1987).

Many of these individual and social considerations interact with negative stigmata associated with professional mental health services (Alvidrez, 1999; Corrigan, 2004). People of color who are contemplating using mental health services may experience guilt or shame that prevents them from entering therapy (Cachelin & Striegel-Moore, 2006), but treatment decisions are not so simple (Alvidrez, Snowden, & Patel, 2010). The common assumption that negative stigmata about mental illness and use of mental health treatment may affect people of color more intensely than Whites may or may not be justified, with only limited research directly confirming that hypothesis (Conner, Koeske, & Brown, 2009).

Related to, yet distinct from, negative stigma is outright mistrust of professional mental health services. The psychology literature has long recognized mistrust stemming from past racial oppression and associated mistreatment of people of color by institutions historically serving the needs of Whites (e.g., Triandis, 1976). For instance, several years ago Blacks considering mental health services feared being involuntarily hospitalized (Sussman, Robins, & Earls, 1987). Contemporary mistrust of professional mental health services may still influence differences across race (Henderson et al., 2014).

Racial differences in utilization rates could also reflect differences in mental illness rates (Lo et al., 2014). Racial groups may differ in their level of psychological distress (e.g., Broman, 1987), and obviously "need for treatment . . . is a strong and consistent predictor of use of outpatient mental health services" (Swartz et al., 1998, p. 141). Despite the unequivocal impact of need for treatment on service utilization, most community-based studies of racial differences conducted in previous decades did not control for this factor. More recent research has begun to adjust for factors such as symptom severity and duration, an important step toward understanding the nature of racial differences in mental health service utilization.

A variety of other individual and social factors thought to influence utilization rates across race have been mentioned in the literature. These include age and gender (e.g., Neighbors et al., 2007; Swartz et al., 1998), but variables more likely to differ across race include English language fluency (Alegría et al., 2002), religious beliefs (Alvidrez, 1999), level of acculturation to Western society (e.g., Cachelin, Veisel, Barzegarnazari, & Striegel-Moore, 2000), and level of education (Cachelin & Striegel-Moore, 2006). Of course, level of education is also highly related to socioeconomic status, the next area to be considered.

Socioeconomic Factors

Socioeconomic differences persist across racial groups (U.S. Census Bureau, 2011) and confound racial differences in mental health service utilization. "Generally speaking, socioeconomic status not only affects the onset, development, and prognosis of mental illnesses, but also has an effect on help seeking and service receiving" (S. Chen et al., 2003, p. 27).

Poverty is clearly associated with multiple risk factors for mental illness, including social and family instability, which could contribute to under-utilization of mental health services. "Neighborhoods with high concentrations of poor people . . . tend to have high rates of unemployment, homelessness, crime, and substance abuse. There is high residential turnover and little opportunity for the development of . . . community services." (Chow, Jaffee, & Snowden, 2003, p. 792). Given these multiple considerations, the emphasis on socioeconomic factors in the research literature has become so strong that some authors have suggested that reported findings of no racial differences in mental health service utilization are due to failure to control for socioeconomic differences (Bosworth et al., 2000).

Related to socioeconomic status is mental health insurance coverage. Until recent decades low-income individuals and families not qualifying for public assistance (e.g., Medicaid) typically lacked mental health coverage either because they could not afford insurance or because mental health treatments were excluded from coverage in low-cost health insurance plans. Some scholars have even described the relationship between insurance coverage and mental health service utilization as causal: "Lack of insurance may cause underrepresentation in services" (Garland et al., 2000, p. 135).

Despite the strong emphasis on socioeconomic factors and insurance coverage shown by the recent literature, research data have been mixed. Although some research findings substantiate commonly held assumptions about the strong influence of socioeconomic factors explaining the racial discrepancies in utilization, the results of several studies were unaffected by socioeconomic variables (e.g., Neighbors et al., 2007; Padgett, Patrick, Burns, & Schlesinger, 1994). One author concluded that among people of color "research indicates that availability of health insurance does not necessarily promote greater contact with mental health services" (Cachelin & Striegel-Moore, 2006, p. 159), which suggests that racial differences in utilization are not solely economic. Discrepancies cannot be explained by any single set of variables. Socioeconomic, intrapersonal, interpersonal, and racial–cultural variables interact. For example, immigration status is associated not only with cultural beliefs but also with socioeconomic status, access to mental health insurance, and familiarity with systems.

Systems and Delivery Factors

Scholars repeatedly mention restricted access to mental health services as an explanation for racial discrepancies in utilization (e.g., Alegría et al., 2002). Many mental health clinics are located in suburbs that are predominantly White; fewer are located in urban areas with higher concentrations of people of color. Underutilization also occurs in rural areas where few clinics are available (e.g., Angold et al., 2002). Thus, likelihood of mental health service utilization is a function of density of mental health service providers (Cook et al., 2013). "Availability and accessibility of mental health services are clearly factors in ethnic differences in utilization" (Alvidrez, 1999, p. 515).

Mental health clinics in inner-city and rural areas tend to be public institutions, which are likely to provide different kinds of services than those in suburban facilities, which are commonly private institutions. Systematic differences in quality of care, range of services, office procedures, and general accessibility could account for racial differences in utilization rates (e.g., Cook et al., 2013).

Quality of care may also differ systematically across client race. For instance, traditional mental health services are less effective with clients of color than culturally adapted services (see Chapter 7, this volume), so people of color receiving traditional mental health services are at a comparative disadvantage, whereas those receiving culturally congruent services may be more likely to refer others to treatment and thus perpetuate positive cycles of service utilization within a community.

Differential treatment of clients across race can be indirectly evaluated by such variables as involuntary versus voluntary utilization. Research has shown that people of color are more likely than Whites to use emergency mental health services (which are not necessarily voluntary) and that people in impoverished areas tend to receive services that are "more coercive and less volitional" (Chow et al., 2003, p. 796). Macro-level dynamics that maintain racism in professional mental health services include denial of or selective attention to race, marginalization of the experiences of people of color and normalization of the experiences of Whites, and minimization of discrepancies across race (Thompson & Neville, 1999). To the extent that those dynamics continue in contemporary mental health practices, discrepancies in utilization rates across race remain possible.

Narrative Review of Previous Research

In the middle of the previous century community mental health services were promoted as a means to overcome common barriers to mental health treatment. However, the lofty ambitions of early community psychology remained unachieved (Sarason, 1974). In the 1970s, research documentation of continued racial discrepancies in the utilization of community mental health services, despite egalitarian ideals, brought national attention to the issue of race in psychology (S. Sue, 1977). The evidence failed to confirm aspirations. If utilization discrepancies across race continued, even after years of effort, the entire system warranted reconsideration. Clearly, additional effort was needed to achieve equity, but increasing evidence showed that the effort would have to come from an entirely different direction. Revising the existing mental health system would not suffice. New perspectives would be needed—multicultural perspectives. The ground had been cleared for the rise of multicultural scholarship in the 1980s.

Awareness of racial discrepancies in mental health utilization became widespread in 1999 when the first report of the U.S. Surgeon General specific to mental health highlighted those inequities. The topic received even more attention through a follow-up government report, *Mental Health: Culture, Race, and Ethnicity in 2001*. Among other points, the report strongly encouraged several means for increasing equal access to services and reducing racial barriers to services, such as those listed in Exhibit 4.1. A recent special section of *American Psychologist* provided updated perspectives (López, Barrio, Kopelowicz, & Vega, 2012; Snowden, 2012; S. Sue, Cheng, Saad, & Chu, 2012). Of all the topics in multicultural psychology, utilization discrepancies have received the broadest public attention.

Notwithstanding the attention given to racial discrepancies, it is plausible that racial discrepancies have diminished over time. Mental health services have become more commonly accepted in the general population and mental health providers increasingly receive training in multicultural competence, such that the results of contemporary research may differ from findings of earlier studies.

It is also possible that differences in utilization attributed to race may be more attributable to socioeconomic factors (or other factors). To address the interactions of the multiple explanations for utilization discrepancies (Exhibit 4.1) with race, researchers increasingly use statistical models that include factors such as differences in socioeconomic status and symptom severity (Alegría et al., 2002; McGuire, Alegría, Cook, Wells, & Zaslavsky, 2006; Snowden & Yamada, 2005).

Among other contributions to the literature, a meta-analysis of research findings would be able to identify whether research findings have changed over time and would help to clarify whether race or other factors account for the utilization discrepancies. Our objective in conducting a meta-analysis was to contrast the reported number of actual clients with estimates of the total number of individuals available in the area (non-clients) across race to (a) determine the relative degree to which people of color in the United States and Canada utilize mental health services and (b) estimate the degree to which study and participant characteristics moderated any racial discrepancies in mental health service utilization. That is, we sought to determine the size of the racial discrepancies and to identify factors that could account for them.

The methods and results of the meta-analysis are described in the following section. Individuals uninterested in the details of meta-analytic methodology may find the details cumbersome and the tables difficult to interpret, but a subsequent section summarizes the findings (see "Discussion and Interpretation of the Findings").

QUANTITATIVE SYNTHESIS OF RESEARCH DATA

To estimate the degree to which people of color have utilized mental health services, we carried out a meta-analysis of research conducted in the United States or Canada that evaluated individuals' use of mental health services across race. Data typically came from two sources: (a) studies of individuals' current and past mental health utilization broken down by race (i.e., a survey of whether participants had ever used mental health services, with responses to that question analyzed by race) and (b) utilization figures in clinics compared with estimates of the available population by race (i.e., the racial percentages represented by clients at a clinic compared with census estimates of the racial composition of the city and vicinity in which the clinic is located). We necessarily excluded studies containing only information about clients' racial composition that could not be contrasted with a pool of potential clients (individuals who should have had access to the same clinic) because the relevant effect size statistic requires that baseline information.

Almost all studies reported data from White/European Americans and Canadians, so we used that population as the contrast group when calculating effect sizes because no other racial group was consistently represented in the literature. Having made that determination based on the need for a consistent comparison group,[1] we excluded the few studies that did not evaluate that group.

After gathering manuscripts, we reviewed data reported in studies to identify truly independent estimates. Two manuscripts included the results of more than one completely distinct study and database, which we treated as distinct studies when coding effect sizes. We also found multiple instances of duplicated findings involving the same database, such as the Epidemiological

---

[1]We oppose the assumption that Whites are a normative reference group. The experiences of other racial groups do not need to be compared with Whites to be understood or valued. Our decision to contrast the utilization rates of people of color with Whites in this chapter was based on our preference to include as many studies in our analyses as possible, and no other racial group was represented as consistently in the literature. Moreover, having a consistent contrast group allowed for contrasts involving every group. Our strategy therefore maximized the number of studies we could include in the meta-analysis while also enabling comparisons to be made involving every group.

Catchment Area Study and county mental health databases in California. Inclusion of multiple manuscripts with the same participants would have violated the assumption of statistical independence; therefore, we retained only manuscripts that did not overlap substantially with the data in other manuscripts (<20% of the same participants or over 7 years between estimates with the same participants). When the data in manuscripts did overlap substantially, we retained the manuscript with the largest number of participants; when the number of participants was identical across manuscripts, we retained only the manuscript that statistically controlled for participant mental health status. In all, we eliminated 26 manuscripts located in our literature search because of duplication of data publication.

Different rates of use of mental health services across race were commonly reported in the metric of an odds ratio. An odds ratio of 0.50 would indicate that people of color were 50% less likely than Whites to utilize mental health services, given their representation in the population. Odds ratio values cannot be meaningfully combined using simple averages: An odds ratio of 2.0 (meaning *twice as likely*, a 2:1 ratio) and an odds ratio of 0.50 (meaning *half as likely*, a 1:2 ratio) average to 1.0 (meaning *equally likely*, a 1:1 ratio). To account for that difficulty and thus enable analyses, we transformed the data to the natural log of the odds ratio.

Statistical estimates derived from other metrics were converted to log odds ratios using meta-analytic software and subsequently converted back to odds ratios to enable interpretation. If studies contained both unadjusted and adjusted effect sizes, we coded those that had been adjusted for possible confounds (e.g., mental health status, socioeconomic status) as long as the adjusted values pertained to the entire sample, not to a restricted subsample. We tracked whether estimates were based on unadjusted or adjusted data in order to subsequently analyze possible differences in those types of effect sizes. The general methods of the meta-analysis are reported in the Appendix to this book.

Description of the Existing Research Literature

We located 130 independent studies that met inclusion criteria. Typically, this research has involved one of two approaches: (a) obtaining responses on surveys about individuals' prior mental health service use and subsequently analyzing the data by race, or (b) reviewing archived records of mental health agencies and comparing the percentages of actual clients by race with census estimates of the available clientele. The effect sizes therefore represent the degree to which individuals of different races report having used mental health services or having actually used services relative to comparable individuals who would have been potential clients. In 60% of the studies these comparisons were made with general community members, but several studies conducted comparisons with groups at risk of mental health challenges (e.g., medical patients) or groups known to have symptoms of mental illness (e.g., screened for clinical conditions; see Table 4.1).

The total number of clients identified in studies exceeded 4,771,472. (Ten studies not included in this total reported only the total number of participants, not the number of clients.) Large databases containing over 1,000 mental health clients (i.e., county or state records or nationwide surveys) were used in 40% of the studies. The extremely large average number of clients per study reported in Table 4.1 was based on a positively skewed distribution; the median number of clients was 603. The large number of participants in many studies resulted in a cluster of studies with small standard error values (those at the top of Figure 4.1).

African American clients were evaluated in 94 studies, Hispanic/ Latino(a) American clients in 66 studies, and Asian Americans in 31 studies. Only 13 studies contained estimates specific to Native American Indians, so those results were grouped with 35 studies that did not specify the race of the "ethnic minority" participants or contained estimates for "other" ethnic groups.

Overall, the data appeared to be characterized by strong external validity. Studies contained large numbers of participants, data were collected from every major population center and many rural areas in North America, and multiple age groups were represented.

Overall Research Findings

We examined racial differences in mental health service utilization by conducting a multivariate meta-analysis (accounting for the observed value of $r = 0.42$ for within-study correlations). The overall model reached statistical significance (Wald $X^2(4) = 77.9$, $p < .0001$), with the results by race reported in Table 4.2. African Americans, Asian Americans, and Hispanic/Latino(a) Americans all statistically differed from White/European Americans in their use of mental health services ($p < .001$), but participants from unspecified/other racial groups did not ($p = .10$). Odds ratios can be interpreted in terms of likelihood, with an odds ratio of 0.67 equating to a 33% difference in likelihood of service utilization ($1.0 - 0.67 = 0.33$), which value J. Cohen (1988) characterized as a "small" effect size (a 60% difference in likelihood being a "moderate" effect size according to J. Cohen). Thus, African Americans were only 21% ($1.0 - 0.79 = 0.21$) less likely (meaning *slightly less likely*) than White/European Americans to use mental health services; Asian Americans were 51% less likely, and Hispanic/Latino(a) Americans were 25% less likely than Whites to use mental health services.

The confidence intervals in Table 4.2 can be used to compare findings among all groups. Asian Americans were less likely to use mental health

TABLE 4.1
Characteristics of 130 Studies of Utilization of Mental Health
Services Across Race

Characteristic	M	No. of studies (k)	%
Year of report	1996		
Before 1980		12	9
1980–1989		23	18
1990–1999		32	25
2000–2008		63	49
Publication status			
Published		112	86
Unpublished dissertations		18	14
Research design			
Cross-sectional		67	51
Longitudinal		12	9
Archival		50	39
Mixed (more than one of the above)		1	1
Population sampled			
General community members (former clients)		87	67
Clinical populations (currently in treatment)		43	33
Comparison group			
General community members (non-clients)		78	60
At-risk group members		23	18
Diagnosable populations (in need of treatment)		29	22
Sample size (number of clients)	40,087		
<50		8	7
50–99		11	9
102–199		18	15
200–399		11	9
400–999		23	19
>1000		48	40
Age of participants[a]	30.7		
Children (<13 years)		17	15
Adolescents (13–18 years)		12	11
Young Adults (19–29 years)		19	17
Middle-aged Adults (30–55 years)		58	52
Senior Adults (>56 years)		6	5
Gender of participants (% female)	55.8		
Race of clients[b] (%)			
African American	5		
Asian American	<1		
Hispanic/Latino(a) American	3		
Native American Indian	<1		
Unspecified/other ethnic minority	12		
White/European American	76		

Note. Not all variables sum to the total number of studies because of missing data.
[a]Average age category of participants in the studies is given; however, not all participants in the study would necessarily be in the category listed. [b]The racial composition of mental health clients across all studies was calculated by multiplying the number of clients within studies by the percentage of clients from each racial group and dividing that product by the total number of clients.

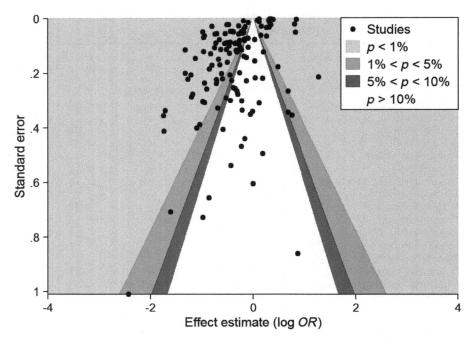

Figure 4.1. Contour-enhanced funnel plot of effect sizes (natural log odds ratios) by standard error for 130 studies of utilization of mental health services across race. This graph shows the distribution of effect sizes as a function of the number of participants in the study (operationalized as standard error). In this case, the overall average is slightly to the left of 0, indicating a small racial discrepancy in utilization of mental health services, but the results are scattered, with that variability weakening the interpretability of the numerical average.

TABLE 4.2
Weighted Mean Effect Sizes (Odds Ratios) Across Participant Race

Group	k	OR_+	SE	95% CI
African Americans	94	.79[a]	.064	[.69, .89]
Asian Americans	31	.49	.099	[.41, .60]
Hispanic/Latino(a) Americans	66	.75[a]	.051	[.68, .83]
Unspecified/other ethnic minorities	48	.86[a]	.092	[.72, 1.03]
All groups combined	130	.74	.027	[.70, .78]

Note. Effect sizes were derived from contrasts of mental health utilization rates with those of White/European Americans; nevertheless, all groups can be contrasted within the table. CI = confidence interval; k = number of studies; OR_+ = random effects weighted effect size (odds ratio), a value of 1.0 indicating no difference, a 1:1 ratio of utilization; SE = standard error.
[a]Statistically significantly different from Asian Americans ($p \le .0001$).

services than any other group, but groups did not differ statistically from one another. Specifically, Asian Americans were 37% less likely to use mental health services than African Americans, 34% less likely to use mental health services than Hispanic/Latino(a) Americans, and 43% less likely to use mental health services than unspecified/other people of color. We emphasize that although these numbers may appear impressive, they are of small magnitude according to J. Cohen's (1988) interpretation guidelines.

Given difficulties in interpreting odds ratios, we found it useful to present the data in terms of averaged within-study utilization rates. Across studies, Whites within samples tended to use mental health services 24% of the time, African Americans 19% of the time, Hispanic/Latino(a) Americans 17% of the time, and Asian Americans 12% of the time. Overall, two trends were clearly shown in the data: White/European Americans tended to use mental health services most often, and Asian Americans used mental health services least often.

Across all 130 studies, the random effects weighted effect size was $OR = 0.739$ (95% CI = [0.70, 0.78], $p < .0001$). The heterogeneity of the findings was extremely large ($I^2 = 99.7$, 95% CI = [99.6, 99.7]; $Q_{(129)} = 43,324.1$, $p < .00001$), meaning that the results were very inconsistent across studies. This variability of the overall findings was so large that we decided to conduct all subsequent analyses within racial groups. Race-specific analyses would reduce the amount of variability and be easier to interpret than conglomerate results.

Likelihood of Publication Bias Adversely Influencing the Results

Publication bias occurs when the data obtained in a meta-analysis fail to represent the entire universe of studies due to the increased probability of nonsignificant results remaining unpublished (and therefore less accessible for meta-analytic reviews). As seen in Figure 4.1, the data in this meta-analysis appeared somewhat imbalanced toward the left line, which indicates statistical significance; the distribution of the data was dense on the left side but sparse on the right, which is the area of nonsignificance. This distribution normally suggests that some nonsignificant studies were missing in the meta-analysis. Both Egger's regression test and an alternative to that test recommended for odds ratio data (Peters, Sutton, Jones, Abrams, & Rushton, 2006) reached statistical significance ($p < .01$), which suggested possible publication bias. One statistical method (Duval & Tweedie, 2000) estimated 26 "missing" studies, and when these were accounted for, the resulting overall effect size was $OR = 0.85$ (95% CI = [0.81, 0.88]), a value closer to 1.0 (no difference) than the overall finding of $OR = 0.74$ reported earlier. It thus seemed likely that the effect sizes reported in Table 4.2 overestimate discrepancies in mental health service utilization across race.

Before reaching the conclusion of overestimated discrepancies, however, we sought to rule out an alternative explanation for the suspicious distribution of the data in Figure 4.1. In coding the data we had observed that most of the studies at the top of Figure 4.1 had involved census records and other large databases (e.g., health department records), so it was possible that the results of the studies at the top of Figure 4.1 differed from the others as a function of methodology. We evaluated that possibility as part of a comprehensive evaluation of study characteristics, as discussed in the following section.

Influence of Study and Participant Characteristics on the Findings

Study Characteristics

We examined differences in effect sizes as a function of research design, statistical adjustment of data, type of comparison group, and year of data collection. Statistically significant differences were found across all study characteristics for every group except Asian Americans (see Tables 4.3 and 4.4). Three findings were consistent across African American, Hispanic/Latino(a) American, and unspecified/other people of color. First, studies surveying participants regarding past mental health utilization yielded much larger effect sizes than studies using archival designs involving institutional databases (which yielded no discrepancy in mental health service utilization across racial groups except Asian Americans). Second, studies using institutional databases or surveys found utilization rates of people of color significantly lower than those of Whites, but studies using census estimates (of potentially available clients) found utilization rates equivalent to or higher than those of Whites. Third, statistical estimates that controlled for potential confounds (e.g., principally mental health status as an indicator of need for services but also socioeconomic status, age, gender, insurance status) were associated with larger effect sizes than those based on unadjusted values.

Because the 130 studies had been conducted over many decades, it was essential to also ascertain whether racial discrepancies had changed over time. As suggested previously, we considered it possible that racial discrepancies in mental health service utilization have decreased over decades. However, initial analyses indicated the opposite: Studies in recent years demonstrated greater racial inequities in mental health service utilization than studies conducted in previous decades ($r = -0.27$, $p < .0001$). This finding was so surprising that we doubted its validity. When coding manuscripts, we had found that study quality had improved over time, with many of the recent studies statistically adjusting for possible confounds (uncommon among earlier studies) such that methodological differences could possibly account for the results opposite of those expected. We therefore conducted random effects weighted regression models to evaluate the simultaneous relationship among all study characteristics.

TABLE 4.3
Weighted Mean Effect Sizes (Odds Ratios) for African Americans and
Asian Americans Across Study and Participant Characteristics

Characteristic	African Americans				Asian Americans			
	Q_b	k	OR_+	95% CI	Q_b	k	OR_+	95% CI
Study characteristics								
Data source	0.6				2.0			
Published		82	.73	[.67, .79]		25	.48	[.41, .56]
Unpublished		12	.80	[.64, .99]		6	.62	[.45, .85]
dissertations								
Research design	37.8***				1.6			
Cross-sectional survey		61	.61	[.56, .67]		14	.45	[.36, .56]
Archival		32	.99	[.87, 1.11]		17	.54	[.45, .66]
Comparison data source[a]	119.8***				0.9			
Census/population		16	1.46	[1.27, 1.67]		10	.46	[.36, .58]
Institution database		13	.63	[.54, .74]		7	.52	[.39, .71]
Sample surveyed		65	.61	[.57, .67]		14	.53	[.43, .66]
Statistical controls[b]	21.3***				1.7			
Unadjusted effect size		65	.82	[.76, .89]		25	.52	[.44, .60]
Adjusted effect size		25	.56	[.49, .65]		5	.39	[.27, .57]
Participant characteristics								
Client population[c]	33.6***				2.1			
Former clients (retrospective)		66	.64	[.58, .70]		19	.55	[.46, .65]
Clients at a clinic		28	1.00	[.88, 1.13]		12	.45	[.36, .55]
Comparison group[d]	18.3***				0.6			
Community members		53	.86	[.79, .95]		24	.51	[.44, .60]
Clinical populations		22	.58	[.50, .68]		6	.45	[.33, .61]
Acculturation level[e]					5.3*			
Low						6	.41	[.34, .51]
High						6	.59	[.47, .74]
Payment method	27.6***				0.2			
Not specified		27	.59	[.49, .70]		9	.48	[.36, .63]
Public		24	1.09	[.91, 1.30]		10	.51	[.40, .64]
Private and mixed public/private		43	.65	[.57, .75]		12	.52	[.41, .65]

Note. CI = confidence interval; k = number of studies; OR_+ = random effects weighted odds ratio; Q_b = Q-value for variance between groups.
[a]This variable overlapped with study research design. Studies either compared clinic records with census data or institutional databases (archival designs) or compared survey responses of utilizers with nonutilizers. [b]This variable contrasted effect sizes computed from raw data with those statistically adjusted for participants' mental health status and other variables. The few studies that adjusted for variables unrelated to mental health status were omitted to make the contrast as clean as possible. [c]This variable contrasted studies evaluating retrospective recall of mental health service utilization with actual client records maintained by a mental health agency. [d]This variable contrasted studies in which the non-client comparisons were general community samples or individuals identified as being in need of mental health services. [e]Studies not containing adequate information relevant to acculturation were excluded. This variable was calculated only for Asian Americans and Hispanic/Latino(a) Americans because those are the groups most likely to be recent immigrants to North America.
*$p < .05$. **$p < .01$. ***$p < .001$.

TABLE 4.4
Weighted Mean Effect Sizes (Odds Ratios) for Hispanic/Latino(a) Americans and Unspecified/Other Ethnic Minorities Across Study and Participant Characteristics

Characteristic	Hispanic/Latino(a) Americans				Unspecified/other			
	Q_b	k	OR_+	95% CI	Q_b	k	OR_+	95% CI
Study characteristics								
Data source	12.1***				1.6			
Published		58	.68	[.63, .73]		44	.90	[.85, .96]
Unpublished dissertations		13	.92	[.79, 1.08]		4	1.03	[.85, 1.25]
Research design	10.1**				65.1***			
Cross-sectional survey		40	.66	[.61, .71]		27	.69	[.63, .75]
Archival		26	.79	[.73, .86]		21	1.12	[1.04, 1.21]
Comparison data source[a]	17.5***				129.6***			
Census/population		16	.88	[.78, .99]		16	1.33	[1.23, 1.45]
Institution database		10	.69	[.59, .81]		5	.67	[.57, .78]
Sample surveyed		40	.65	[.59, .70]		27	.71	[.65, .77]
Statistical controls[b]	6.5*				25.5***			
Unadjusted effect size		47	.75	[.70, .81]		33	1.00	[.94, 1.07]
Adjusted effect size		15	.62	[.54, .71]		12	.68	[.60, .78]
Participant characteristics								
Population sampled[c]	18.8***				0.9			
Former clients (retrospective)		43	.64	[.59, .69]		31	.87	[.79, .95]
Clients at a clinic		23	.85	[.77, .94]		17	.94	[.83, 1.05]
Comparison group[d]	3.7				2.9			
Community members		43	.75	[.70, .81]		27	1.00	[.91, 1.09]
Clinical populations		15	.65	[.57, .74]		13	.87	[.73, 1.00]
Level of acculturation[e]	0.1							
Low		11	.84	[.63, 1.11]				
High		5	.81	[.55, 1.19]				
Method of payment	12.5**				24.4***			
Not specified		18	.61	[.52, .71]		13	.71	[.60, .85]
Public		21	.83	[.74, .93]		12	1.24	[1.05, 1.47]
Private and mixed public/private		27	.68	[.62, .75]		23	.81	[.71, .91]

Note. CI = confidence interval; k = number of studies; OR_+ = random effects weighted odds ratio; Q_b = Q-value for variance between groups.
[a]This variable overlapped with study research design. Studies either compared clinic records with census data or institutional databases (archival designs) or compared survey responses of utilizers with nonutilizers. [b]This variable contrasted effect sizes computed from raw data with those statistically adjusted for participants' mental health status and other variables. The few studies that adjusted for variables unrelated to mental health status were omitted to make the contrast as clean as possible. [c]This variable contrasted studies evaluating retrospective recall of mental health service utilization with actual client records maintained by a mental health agency. [d]This variable contrasted studies in which the non-client comparisons were general community samples or individuals identified as being in need of mental health services. [e]Studies not containing adequate information relevant to acculturation were excluded. This variable was calculated only for Asian Americans and Hispanic/Latino(a) Americans because those are the groups most likely to be recent immigrants to North America.
*p < .05. **p < .01. ***p < .001.

The regression models by race included all study characteristics, including the recommended estimate of publication bias (Peters et al., 2006). Thus, the models would differentiate not only between the effects of time and study quality but also between study quality and possible publication bias, as mentioned in the previous section.

The five variables in the model explained 44.2% of the variance in effect sizes with data from African American participants (see Table 4.5). Two predictors reached statistical significance: research design and type of contrast. Specifically, studies using archival data tended to have less discrepancy across race than studies in which data had been collected using surveys (standardized beta = .16), and studies that compared the racial composition of clients with local census estimates showed much higher rates of mental health service

TABLE 4.5
Random Effects Regression Weights for Study Characteristics
Associated With Effect Sizes

Group/variable	R^2	SE	p	β
African Americans (k = 93)	44.2***			
Year of data collection		.005	.63	−.03
Archival research[a]		.040	.02	.16
Census comparison[b]		.104	<.001	.53
Statistical controls[c]		.082	.38	−.06
Publication bias estimate[d]		26.3	.63	−.03
Asian Americans (k = 31)	17.2			
Year of data collection		.013	.91	.03
Archival research[a]		.142	.46	.20
Census comparison[b]		.254	.11	−.37
Statistical controls[c]		.296	.37	−.19
Publication bias estimate[d]		167	.17	−.30
Hispanic/Latino(a) Americans (k = 66)	10.8***			
Year of data collection		.004	.04	.14
Archival research[a]		.031	.26	.08
Census comparison[b]		.071	<.001	.26
Statistical controls[c]		.064	.10	−.10
Publication bias estimate[d]		24.3	.26	−.07
Unspecified/Other (k = 48)	24.7***			
Year of data collection		.004	.07	.13
Archival research[a]		.045	.03	.15
Census comparison[b]		.092	<.001	.47
Statistical controls[c]		.087	.99	.01
Publication bias estimate[d]		30.6	.50	−.03

Note. k = number of studies; SE = standard error. [a]This variable contrasted archival designs with cross-sectional surveys. [b]This variable contrasted studies that used relevant census estimates as the comparison for non-clients with studies that used non-clients identified in surveys or databases. [c]This variable contrasted studies that statistically controlled for potential confounds (primarily mental health status but also variables such as age, gender, socioeconomic status, and insurance coverage) with studies that used unadjusted data. [d]Estimate of publication bias recommended by Peters and colleagues (2006) for data in OR format.
***p < .001.

utilization among African Americans than the studies that used surveys or institutional databases (standardized beta = .53). The other variables in the model failed to reach statistical significance. Thus, the trend for the findings of studies to have changed over time was accounted for by study methodology. Similarly, publication bias seemed an unlikely threat to the findings when considered simultaneously with study methodology.

The model with data from Asian Americans failed to reach statistical significance (Table 4.5). The variables entered in the model for that racial group did not account for systematic differences in the results. Nevertheless, the results of the model with data from unspecified/other ethnic minorities were very similar to the results obtained with African Americans (Table 4.5). The model with data from Hispanic/Latino(a) Americans was also similar, except that year of data collection did achieve statistical significance. Notably, the direction of the association had reversed from that reported for the bivariate correlation; whereas the association had been negative, it was positive (the expected direction) in the regression model. After controlling for study characteristics, we found racial discrepancies somewhat less likely to occur in recent years than in previous years (standardized beta = .14).

In the other models, year of data collection failed to reach statistical significance; thus, after accounting for other factors, racial discrepancies in mental health service utilization appear to have changed very little over the past 3 decades. The estimate of possible publication bias did not reach statistical significance in any model, indicating that the univariate data and the unusual pattern of data in Figure 4.1 can be accounted for by study methodological characteristics. We therefore concluded that publication bias had not adversely affected the overall findings.

Participant Characteristics

Studies involved participants with a variety of backgrounds and characteristics. We therefore sought to determine whether results systematically differed as a function of participant age, approximate age cohort (year of the data collection minus the average age of participants), sample gender composition (operationalized as percentage female), sample racial heterogeneity (estimated by the percentage of White participants involved in the study), type of client (former client retrospectively recalling service utilization or current client in a specific clinic), type of comparison group member (community member or individual identified as needing mental health services), participant level of acculturation (estimated for Asian Americans and Hispanic/Latino(a) Americans on the basis of descriptions of the sample within studies), and client form of payment for the mental health services. The categorical variables were analyzed using random effects weighted analyses of variance, and the continuous variables were analyzed using random effects weighted correlations, with statistically significant variables included in subsequent random effects weighted regression models, also conducted by race.

Participants' age, estimated age cohort, and gender were not statistically significantly associated with effect size magnitude for any of the four racial groups analyzed. However, the racial heterogeneity of the samples was associated with effect sizes in the analyses involving African Americans ($r = .21$, $p = .002$), Asian Americans ($r = .48$, $p < .0001$), unspecified/other people of color ($r = .37$, $p < .0001$), but not Hispanic/Latino(a) Americans ($r = .09$, $p = .22$). Thus, for the three former groups the studies conducted in settings with relatively fewer White participants were more likely to yield rates of mental health service utilization discrepant from that of Whites. Stated differently, people of color used mental health services relatively less often when the total research sample had greater representation of people of color. Given that some community mental health centers specifically serve communities with large percentages of people of color, this unexpected finding should receive particular scrutiny in the future.

Tables 4.3 and 4.4 portray the results of the random effects weighted analyses of variance with the categorical variables. The first analysis evaluated whether any differences were found when the clients participating in studies had recalled past mental health utilization or were identified with a particular clinic at the time of the study. Among studies involving African American and Hispanic/Latino(a) American participants, individuals providing retrospective information were relatively less likely to report using mental health services than individuals who had access to a particular clinic. Thus, people from those groups tended to report using mental health services more frequently when they were actually using the services than when asked generically about their past experiences with services.

A second analysis involved the contrast groups (non-clients), which consisted either of general community samples (ostensibly with low rates of mental illness) or of individuals identified as being in need of mental health treatment (those in the clinical range on a screening instrument). In the data from African American participants, statistically larger racial discrepancies in service utilization were found when contrasting utilization rates with those of clinical populations than when contrasting them with rates of general community members. Thus, African Americans who needed mental health services were at greater risk of underutilizing those services (Lo et al., 2014). This finding did not occur with the three other racial groups evaluated.

We considered it possible that level of acculturation to Western society could be related to mental health service utilization (e.g., Cachelin et al., 2000). This information was only available in studies of Asian Americans and Hispanic/Latino(a) Americans, and what was found was limited. Analyses indicated that the difference between participants of high versus low levels of acculturation reached statistical significance only in the data involving Asian American participants. Asian Americans low in acculturation to Western society were less likely to use mental health services than those who appeared to be highly acculturated.

As noted earlier in the review of relevant theory, previous researchers have strongly suggested that utilization discrepancies across race have been a function of socioeconomic status, particularly insurance status and method of payment for services (e.g., S. Chen et al., 2003; Garland et al., 2000). Although we could not directly evaluate socioeconomic status of participants because studies commonly omitted relevant information, we did analyze differences in the type of payment arrangement for clients in the studies. Very few studies explicitly limited data collection to clinics or practices that did not accept public payment for services, so we combined those few studies involving such clinics with the more common category involving clinics that accepted either public or private payment. That contrast revealed statistically significant differences across all groups except Asian Americans. Participants who received public mental health services were relatively more likely to use those services than participants in studies that had failed to report any information regarding payment or those in studies of clinics that accepted mixed private and public payment or solely private payment. Public mental health services negated racial discrepancies for all groups except Asian Americans.

Recognizing that participant characteristics could interact with one another, we conducted a random effects weighted regression model for each racial group to ascertain which participants remained statistically significant in the presence of one another. The results of these four models are presented in Table 4.6.

In the data involving African American participants, all four of the variables that had been statistically significant at the univariate level remained statistically significant in the regression model. Thus, African Americans were less likely to use mental health services in studies when there were relatively fewer White participants, when individuals retrospectively recalled mental health service use, when participants not using mental health services needed those services, and when clients attended anything other than exclusively public agencies.

In the regression model with Asian American participants, the only predictor variable to remain statistically significant was the percentage of White participants in the study. Asian Americans had relatively higher utilization rates in studies with greater percentages of White participants. The other variables in the model did not reach statistical significance, although the magnitude of the standardized coefficients was moderate in some cases.

The regression model involving Hispanic/Latino(a) American participants explained only 11% of the variance in effect sizes, and the only predictor

TABLE 4.6
Random Effects Regression Weights for Participant Characteristics
Associated With Effect Sizes

Group/Variable	R^2	SE	p	β
African Americans (k = 92)	32.8***			
% of White participants[a]		.002	.006	.21
Clients at a clinic[b]		.104	.01	.22
Public payment of services[c]		.108	<.001	.34
Clinical population comparison[d]		.105	.007	−.21
Asian Americans (k = 31)	16.0***			
% of White participants[a]		.004	.002	.44
Clients at a clinic[b]		.154	.30	−.15
Public payment of services[c]		.152	.88	.02
Clinical population comparison[d]		.186	.29	−.15
Low acculturation[e]		.180	.10	−.23
Hispanic/Latino(a) Americans (k = 64)	11.0***			
% of White participants[a]		.002	.29	.07
Clients at a clinic[b]		.079	.004	.23
Public payment of services[c]		.082	.14	.12
Clinical population comparison[d]		.083	.63	−.03
Low acculturation[e]		.100	.60	.04
Unspecified/Other (k = 46)	21.4***			
% of White participants[a]		.285	<.001	.36
Clients at a clinic[b]		.124	.70	−.03
Public payment of services[c]		.131	<.001	.32
Clinical population comparison[d]		.139	.78	.02

Note. k = number of studies; SE = standard error.
[a]Studies not reporting this information were excluded from the analysis. [b]This variable contrasted studies evaluating retrospective recall of mental health service utilization with actual client records maintained by a mental health agency. [c]This variable contrasted studies in which payment for mental health services was provided by public or other means with studies not reporting method of payment and reporting private or mixed methods of payment. [d]This variable contrasted studies in which the non-client comparisons were general community samples or individuals identified as being in need of mental health services. [e]This variable was calculated only for Asian Americans and Hispanic/Latino(a) Americans; it contrasted studies estimated to involved participants with low levels of acculturation to Western society (recent immigrants) with all other studies.
***p < .001.

variable to reach statistical significance was the type of clients within studies. Studies in which former clients retrospectively recalled their service utilization found lower relative mental health use compared with studies in which participants were clients at a particular clinic involved in the study.

The two predictor variables in the regression model involving unspecified/other people of color that reached statistical significance were the percentage of White clients in the study and the type of payment made for services. Studies with greater percentages of White clients and with public payment tended to find greater relative utilization of mental health services for the unspecified/other people of color in the study. Thus, these variables remained statistically significant, even when considered simultaneously with the other two variables in the model.

DISCUSSION AND INTERPRETATION OF THE FINDINGS

People in North America use mental health services at rates that differ by race. Asian Americans are the least likely of any group evaluated to use mental health services. The differences observed among racial groups (Table 4.2) fall in the range of "small" magnitude, according to J. Cohen's (1988) benchmark value, equivalent to $OR = 0.67$ (a 33% reduced likelihood of service utilization), but we here provide some contextualization to J. Cohen's generic guidelines for interpretation.

Issues of Interpretation

Admittedly, odds ratios can be difficult to interpret.[2] Illustrating the findings in terms of human lives can facilitate interpretation of the odds ratios in Table 4.2.

Consider a hypothetical research study of 1,000 participants exactly representative of the 2010 U.S. census populations by race (i.e., 122 African American participants to correspond with the census estimate of 12.2% of the total population), with an average within-study mental health service utilization rate of 24% among White participants (the average utilization rate found across all studies in the meta-analysis), and with the same statistical estimates as those presented in Table 4.2. Given those parameters, the hypothetical study would have identified 19 people of color (1.9% of the study's total participants and 5.2% of the participants of color) who would have failed to receive mental health services had those services been equitable with White/European Americans. Of those 19, there would have been five African Americans, eight Hispanic/Latino(a) Americans, five Asian Americans, and one "other" ethnic minority individual.

Thus, the overall percentage of inequity is very small (with the racial inequity negatively affecting 19 of about 363 people of color). However, that interpretation would be no consolation to the 19 untreated individuals and their family members. Moreover, when multiplying the findings of the present meta-analysis by the total U.S. population, the figures would suggest that tens of thousands of people of color may fail to receive needed mental health services if those services remain inequitable across race.

---

[2]For individuals familiar with the common statistic R^2, the overall differences in race accounted for 0.7% of the variance in the relative likelihood of mental health service utilization across the 130 studies. The greatest contrast observed in the meta-analysis occurred between Whites and Asian Americans, a difference which explained about 3.7% of the variance in the results of 31 studies with Asian American participants.

Implications From the Secondary Analyses

The overall findings differed across several study and participant characteristics. These differences help illuminate the meaning of the overall estimates. Five major themes emerged from the secondary analyses, detailed next.

Contrasts Involving Census Estimates

Initially, publication bias was identified as a threat to the interpretation of the overall results of the meta-analysis, but the results of subsequent analyses suggested that studies using different research methods yielded different results—and those different methods accounted for the nonsymmetric data distribution (Figure 4.1). Specifically, studies involving census estimates of the population typically included very large numbers of people, so the effect sizes extracted from those studies tended to have very small standard error values (resulting in the cluster of studies at the top of Figure 4.1). Except for studies involving Asian Americans, when researchers contrasted client utilization rates by race with relevant census estimates of the population's racial composition, relatively greater mental health service utilization was observed among people of color. In fact, studies involving African Americans and unspecified/other people of color that used census estimates actually found higher rates of mental health service utilization for these groups than for Whites, a finding completely opposite from the direction of the overall results.

Two possible explanations could account for this finding. Censuses of ethnic neighborhoods may have underrepresented people of color; however, the small degree of error in census data would make this explanation untenable. A more plausible explanation stems from the fact that studies using census estimates had to have at least one mental health clinic in the vicinity (that is why the researchers conducted the study in that location), whereas general surveys likely involved some participants who had no easy access to a mental health facility: Proximity of mental health services could possibly account for the differences in the findings. This same explanation could account for the differences observed between cross-sectional surveys and archival research, the latter design necessarily entailing clinic accessibility.

Racial Heterogeneity of Clients

Across studies of all racial groups except Hispanic/Latino(a) Americans, the greater the percentage of White clients, the greater the relative utilization rates shown for clients of color. This finding is not attributable to a statistical artifact (odds ratios are based on the relative utilization rates and are not affected by the percentages of clients within racial groups). However, this finding could be attributable to either clinic accessibility and/or individuals' level of acculturation. If mental health services are disproportionately more available in neighborhoods with predominantly White/European Americans, people of color living elsewhere may have relatively decreased access to clinics (e.g., Cook et al., 2013). Another congruent possibility is that people of color who attend a clinic with a large percentage of White clients could be more acculturated to White culture than those who attend a clinic with lower percentages of Whites.

Retrospective Reporting of Mental Health Utilization

In studies with African Americans and Hispanic/Latino(a) Americans, less frequent mental health utilization rates were found in retrospective reports by participants (i.e., responding to a survey) compared with data derived from actual clients at a clinic. This finding could be attributable to inaccurate reporting by survey participants, who may have felt disinclined to report past mental health service use because of an internalized negative stigma about seeking these services, despite apparent confidentiality. Whatever the cause of inaccuracy, the data from actual clinic records would likely be more dependable than estimates obtained from participant retrospective recall.

Public Payment of Services

In studies with African Americans and unspecified/other people of color, public payment of mental health services was associated with utilization rates equitable with those of Whites. Thus, in those instances, racial inequities appeared to be related to economic factors. Public payment of services did not significantly affect the utilization rates of Asian American or Hispanic/Latino(a) American clients, which suggests that for those populations cultural views or other factors such as immigration or legal status are more relevant to mental health service utilization than economic matters. Overall, these findings deserve future attention. For instance, there is a need to rule out the possibility of sampling bias, given that individuals who apply for public assistance may differ from those who could benefit from public assistance but do not apply (e.g., clients with chronic mental health conditions and minimal support networks).

Mental Health Status of the Comparison Group

Although most studies used the general population as the comparison group of non-clients, some studies involved participants who had been identified by clinical screening instruments or recent clinical records as in need of mental health services. Comparisons using the general population sought to answer the question "To what degree do individuals of different races avail themselves of mental health services?" Comparisons involving at-risk or diagnosable populations asked, "To what degree do individuals of different races use mental health services that are needed?" The answer to these questions proved to be similar for all populations except for African Americans, for whom mental health service utilization was lower when the individuals were in need of services. If African Americans needing services are less likely to receive them, the finding is troubling. Negative stigmata or racial biases may or may not explain the finding (Alvidrez et al., 2010), but the precise causes must be identified and corrected.

Considerations for Future Research

For several decades scholars have been aware of multiple factors plausibly resulting in utilization discrepancies across race (Exhibit 4.1; McGuire et al., 2006; Snowden & Yamada, 2005). Of course, researchers could not possibly evaluate or control for all of these factors simultaneously in any given research study. Thus, in most studies we located, scholars (particularly those who found minimal differences across race) hedged their interpretations with the reality that they did not account for all possible factors—and they listed unmeasured variables that could have possibly influenced the results (see Exhibit 4.1). A typical discussion section might read, "We did not find large racial discrepancies, but this finding could be accounted for by X, Y, or Z that we did not measure." This understandable qualification in data interpretation, characteristic of many research reports, has led to an undesirable trend: repetition of the same plausible confounds and explanations (Exhibit 4.1) without strong confidence in the overall results and without much evidence regarding the relative contribution of the various explanations for the discrepancies.

In that context, the present meta-analysis contributed substantially to the literature by evaluating findings across studies that controlled for a variety of factors, particularly socioeconomic status. Meta-analytic aggregation of data involving different sets of statistical controls provides less methodological control than would be desirable, but it provides an estimate of a hypothetical general condition with multiple variables controlled within many studies. And the findings indicated that the combined data remained of low magnitude, whether or not the studies controlled for potential confounds. Those findings contrast with the general tone of discussions in the literature about utilization discrepancies across race: Small racial discrepancies are not necessarily qualified by multiple confounds. Some unknown deficiency of the meta-analysis may yet qualify the findings, but the meta-analytic results are highly unlikely to have been influenced by any single confound, let alone some improbable combination of variables that happened to diminish the magnitude of the findings across 130 studies, making the racial discrepancies appear less strong than they are in reality. Thus, we can be fairly certain that the small differences in utilization across race were racial differences.

The meta-analysis was also a useful step forward for researchers seeking to identify the relative contributions of some of the causal and confounding factors mentioned in the literature (Exhibit 4.1). Among the factors evaluated consistently within studies, results sometimes differed as a function of the five conditions detailed in the previous section: contrasts involving census estimates, racial heterogeneity of clients, retrospective reporting of mental health utilization, public payment of services, and mental health status of the comparison group. In some cases, these factors remained explanatory even in the presence of one another. Thus, future research can continue to investigate these particular variables with confidence. However, the data were not moderated by gender, age, or age cohort, so those particular variables should not require sustained attention when considering utilization discrepancies across race.

Indirectly, the data showing differences between studies using census estimates and those using surveys seemed to indicate that proximity and access to mental health services may account for racial discrepancies. Underlying differences in access to care across race remain problematic (Cook et al., 2013). We therefore encourage research evaluating proximity to mental health services through geospatial analysis (e.g., de Smith, Goodchild, & Longley, 2007), a method perfectly suited to address that important topic.

A major limitation to the research findings would have occurred if the underlying rates or severity of mental illness differed across race (e.g., Lo et al., 2014). However, most of the recent research studies controlled for symptom incidence or severity. Systematic differences in the rates or the severity of mental illness across race may occur but seem unlikely explanations for underutilization of mental health services by people of color (e.g., Alegría et al., 2002).

Many scholars have emphasized the influence of socioeconomic factors on utilization discrepancies across race. Our finding that public payment of services minimized racial discrepancies involving African American participants and unspecified/other people of color certainly lends support to that prevalent conclusion (Thomas & Snowden, 2001). Nevertheless, this finding did not characterize the data from Asian American and Hispanic/Latino(a) American clients. The fact that in some cases

> socioeconomic factors cannot explain ethnic differences in use points to a need to go beyond conventional wisdom that liberalizing health benefits will be sufficient to address the health and mental health needs of ethnic minority groups. Thus changes in health policies designed to reduce economic barriers to care are necessary but not sufficient to close the gap in unmet need for these groups. (Padgett et al., 1994, p. 358)

Cultural explanations cannot be overridden by socioeconomic explanations; both must be considered simultaneously (see Exhibit 4.1).

Suggestions for Practitioners and Agencies

The tenets of multicultural psychology can inform practitioners seeking to increase mental health service utilization among people of color. A key principle of multicultural psychology is to make the services provided congruent with the cultural worldviews and experiences of the clients. When clients perceive services to be helpful, they are more likely to utilize them and recommend them to others; when they have negative experiences in treatment, the opposite occurs: "Underuse of mental health services . . . [may not be due] to intrinsic negative attitudes, but to problems in the health services delivery systems that have a negative impact on those attitudes following the use of mental health services" (Diala et al., 2000, p. 462). Practitioners should understand clients' cultural worldviews, including the stigma attached to receiving mental health services, and they should work in ways that alleviate rather than exacerbate incongruence between therapist and client expectations.

Despite the importance of therapist multicultural competence during therapy, therapist expertise alone does not attract new clients in large numbers. Community awareness initiatives and outreach programs may be necessary if people of color are to seek mental health services when needed (Neighbors et al., 2007), particularly among Asian Americans, who are least likely to utilize mental health services. "Better outreach and public education of mental health care workers are essential to improve [client] access" (Chow et al., 2003, p. 796).

Practitioners can also influence local referral networks. In most communities, a variety of agencies (health, legal, employment, youth, religious, community development, etc.) tend to work frequently with culturally diverse clientele. Regular communication and consultation with those agencies would likely increase referrals. Moreover, because people of color tend to be more likely to use emergency services than outpatient clinics (Chow et al., 2003), practitioners providing outpatient services can maintain close ties with emergency service professionals to enhance efforts aimed at prevention and long-term recovery. In addition, practitioners can invite current clients and community leaders sympathetic to professional mental health services to pass along information to people they believe would consider those services. These and similar methods for working with local referral networks should greatly enhance utilization by individuals otherwise unlikely to consider mental health care.

Practitioners should also keep in mind the multiple barriers to treatment (Exhibit 4.1) and recognize that financial considerations do not necessarily trump cultural considerations. "Changes in health policies designed to reduce economic barriers to care are necessary but not sufficient to close the gap in unmet need for [people of color]" (Padgett et al., 1994, p. 358). Practitioners can consider reduced or sliding fees, but ultimately, they will need to find out and address multiple concerns of the potential clients in their locale. The concerns about mental health services among Native American Indian military veterans residing in Sioux Falls, South Dakota, likely diverge from those of African American high school students in Asheville, North Carolina, and from those of immigrant families in Calexico, California. Practitioners can identify the issues and concerns of local clientele by consulting with community members or conducting a focus group at a public health center. With that essential local information, they can find local solutions to facilitate individuals' engagement in treatment when needed.

CONCLUSION

In North America, individuals of Asian descent are the least likely to use professional mental health services, but other people of color are still less likely to use mental health services than Whites. Nevertheless, the magnitude of inequity is lower than has been commonly assumed, and racial discrepancies decreased over time for all groups except Asian Americans in studies with census data. Truly, "little progress has been made to eliminate the disparities in mental health service access for Asian American populations" (S. Sue et al., 2012, p. 540).

We felt grateful that the racial inequities were smaller than we had imagined them to be, but like most people receiving news too good to be true, we could not help questioning the data. In the end, we could not dismiss the facts that the data came from many research studies, most of them by recognized advocates of multicultural psychology, with participants totaling in the millions, conducted in rural and urban settings across multiple geographic regions. If a meta-analysis has been conducted in multicultural psychology that could claim stronger external validity, we have not yet found it. And the meta-analytic data indicate that race accounts for small differences in mental health service utilization, except in the case of Asian Americans.

Multicultural psychology attracted national attention when research documented racial discrepancies in mental health service utilization (e.g., S. Sue, 1977). We are grateful that the inequities were shown to be smaller than long presumed. We are keenly aware that inequities persist. And we recognize that access to services is not the same as access to high quality services. We join others in urging policy makers and mental health providers to take additional steps necessary to eradicate all inequity and to promote high quality services for all populations (López et al., 2012; McGuire & Miranda, 2008; Meyer & Takeuchi, 2014; Snowden, 2012; S. Sue et al., 2012; Valentine et al., 2014). We have offered specific recommendations that can increase accessibility of mental health services to all cultural and racial groups.

5

PARTICIPATION OF CLIENTS OF COLOR IN MENTAL HEALTH SERVICES: A META-ANALYSIS OF TREATMENT ATTENDANCE AND TREATMENT COMPLETION/ATTRITION

After an individual has decided to utilize mental health services and has entered treatment, multiple concerns can arise with every session: Is therapy as helpful as anticipated? How much trust, effort, emotional discomfort, money, and time away from work and family should be invested and for how long? What if an employer or an acquaintance finds out? Other considerations include, but are not limited to, preexisting level of distress and motivation for change, external and environmental contingencies, social norms and peer support, interactions with the therapist, and expectations for and beliefs about therapy. A client's decision to enter treatment is an extremely important step, but it is among the first in a complex process.

The complexity increases for clients of color, whose experiences and worldviews may not be understood or supported by their community or therapist. Clinicians must be skilled in adapting traditional therapeutic methods to

A complete list of references for the studies included in this chapter's meta-analysis is posted online. Readers can consult it at http://pubs.apa.org/books/supp/smith

http://dx.doi.org/10.1037/14733-005
Foundations of Multicultural Psychology: Research to Inform Effective Practice, by T. B. Smith and J. E. Trimble
Copyright © 2016 by the American Psychological Association. All rights reserved.

meet the needs of diverse clientele (e.g., a recent immigrant from Bangladesh or a first-year college student who is Hopi). Cultural factors clearly influence not only a client's perceptions and experiences in therapy but also the therapist's perceptions and skills in working with diverse clients (e.g., Hayes, Owen, & Bieschke, 2015). In addition to the multiple retention factors common to most clients' experience, continuation in treatment for clients of color also depends on a therapist's multicultural competence (Gaztambide, 2012; Langer, 1999). Multiculturally competent therapists may be more likely to recognize the concerns of culturally diverse clients and address those concerns in a sensitive manner that will encourage continued participation in treatment.

For decades researchers have reported that clients of color discontinue mental health services more frequently and earlier in treatment than White/ European Americans (e.g., S. Sue, 1977). However, the magnitude of that discrepancy has remained unspecified. Mental health providers advocating for the needs of clients of color would be in a better position to help serve those needs if they had accurate data regarding the extent of inequities. How great are racial and ethnic differences in treatment participation? Are those differences affected if participation is considered in terms of attendance (number of sessions) versus treatment completion? Do socioeconomic differences account for participation differences across racial and ethnic groups? The answers to these and similar questions would facilitate the work of both scholars and therapists concerned with providing culturally competent mental health services.

REVIEW OF THE LITERATURE

Improved client functioning and well-being are among the principal goals of mental health services, but achieving them is contingent on client participation in treatment. When rates of client participation and discontinuation differ across race or ethnicity, the most logical explanation seems to be that the services inadequately accounted for cultural values, expectations, and worldviews (e.g., failing to understand that a Japanese American client might prefer directive counseling methods to open-ended exploration). The field of multicultural psychology seeks to help practitioners meet diverse clients' mental health needs through participation in treatment that is appropriately aligned with those needs (La Roche & Lustig, 2013).

Relevant Theory

Clients' therapy experiences vary not only according to their circumstances but also in terms of their expectations, so social psychological theories regarding expectations provide a framework to conceptualize client participation (e.g., Swift & Callahan, 2011). At the most basic level, unmet expectations lead to discontinuation of treatment, but the associations are more complex: Expectations affect every aspect of treatment, including the roles that clients take in therapy, their interpretations of the recommendations provided in therapy, and the perceived racial, ethnic, and gender compatibility between the client and therapist. Client expectations are related to their attitudes and subjective norms, which are components of the theory of reasoned action (Ajzen & Fishbein, 1977). Seen through that theoretical lens, client participation in treatment is a function of both beliefs/attitudes about therapy and interpretations about what constitutes normative behavior. So a client whose culture values self-sufficiency over interactivity may be suspicious of treatments that magnify misalignments with the therapist.

Narrative Review of Previous Research

In practice, client participation in therapy can be conceptualized several ways. The broadest categories are client treatment attendance (number of sessions completed, percentage of appointments kept, and number of days in treatment) and client treatment completion/attrition (also referred to as *retention*, *dropout*, or *premature termination/discontinuation*; Alegría et al., 2008). The latter variable, completion/attrition, can be operationalized in at least five ways: (a) completion of a prespecified number or percentage of sessions, (b) completion of a treatment protocol or manual, (c) unilateral termination (client missing a scheduled appointment without subsequently rescheduling or contacting the therapist), (d) discontinuation prior to clinically significant or reliable improvement in presenting symptoms, and (e) therapist judgment of whether discontinuance of therapy was warranted (see Swift & Greenberg, 2012). The latter method, therapist judgment, accounts for contexts known to the therapist and not otherwise measurable, but this method results in the largest rates of attrition compared with the others (Swift & Greenberg, 2012), although it does not accurately correspond with client symptom reduction (Swift, Callahan, & Levine, 2009). This inaccuracy may result from therapists' self-serving biases that can prevent them from accurately evaluating client termination (Murdock, Edwards, & Murdock, 2010). Of the five methods, the fourth (symptom reduction trajectory), which would logically be the most clinically useful indicator, has accumulated research support (e.g., Swift et al., 2009), but few research studies evaluate client mental health symptoms frequently enough to calculate symptom trajectories. Overall, the research literature is inconsistent in how completion/attrition is operationalized (Kazdin, 1996; Swift & Greenberg, 2012).

Irrespective of how client treatment completion/attrition is operationalized, research in this area deserves high priority status among clinicians and researchers. Clients frequently discontinue treatment prior to adequate symptom reduction and/or without therapist foreknowledge. Widely cited estimates of premature or unilateral termination have ranged from 20% to 60%, with a previous meta-analysis estimating the number at 47% (Wierzbicki & Pekarik, 1993) and a recent meta-analysis specific to adult clients yielding an estimate of 20% (Swift & Greenberg, 2012), although client attrition may be higher in clinics not explicitly tracking client progress. Unfortunately, the modal number of therapy sessions most commonly reported in the literature is one (e.g., Connolly Gibbons et al., 2011).

The fact that so many clients discontinue treatment is extremely problematic. Clients who discontinue treatment prior to symptom improvement may experience minimal or no benefit, which occurs much more often than therapists realize (Lambert, 2010). Some experience symptom exacerbation. Client attrition also affects the quality of care provided to others in clinical settings; missed appointments reduce the availability of services for other clients and increase the length of waiting lists, sometimes resulting in negative client perceptions about the agency (Barrett, Chua, Crits-Christoph, Gibbons, & Thompson, 2008). As financial losses to the agency may result, "the problem of attrition is particularly acute in agencies that provide mental health services to those who are economically disadvantaged" (Barrett et al., 2008, p. 248).

Commonly Cited Reasons for Treatment Completion/Attrition

Some of the reasons clients of color choose to discontinue therapy prior to adequate improvement are outside the control of client or therapist. However, many impediments to clients' active consistent engagement in treatment are psychological and social and thus potentially amenable to change in the therapeutic relationship (e.g., reframing, empowering; see Alegría et al., 2008). Two commonly referenced factors amenable to therapist intervention are (a) client expectations about the nature and duration of treatment and (b) the therapeutic alliance (Piselli, Halgin, & MacEwan, 2011; Reis & Brown, 1999). Clients entering therapy may expect rapid improvement but have little prior experience using therapy techniques. When therapists clarify treatment expectations with clients (e.g., Swift & Callahan, 2011) and establish strong relationships with their clients (Sharf, Primavera, & Diener, 2010), particularly culturally congruent relationships (La Roche & Lustig, 2013), clients are much less likely to discontinue treatment before symptom improvement.

Although client expectations and the client–therapist alliance have received much attention in the literature, previous research has identified multiple risk factors for premature discontinuation of treatment in the general population (e.g., Kazdin, 1996; Reis & Brown, 1999). Exhibit 5.1 lists the

EXHIBIT 5.1
General Factors Associated With Client Premature/Unilateral Discontinuation of Mental Health Treatment

Client factors supported by research findings

- Perceived need for services and level of psychological functioning and symptom severity, including comorbidity and physical illness
- Outcome and role expectations, including the length and purpose of therapy
- Dissatisfaction with therapist; strength of therapeutic alliance
- Socioeconomic factors, including level of education, time constraints, and residential stability
- Parent or caregiver support and influence for child and adolescent clients
- Age (older clients being slightly more likely than younger clients to remain in therapy)
- Life circumstances (e.g., crises, family needs, workplace demands, documentation status)

Other factors supported by research findings

- Setting (settings being equivalent with exception of university-based clinics, which have higher attrition rates)
- Time limits (lower attrition in time-constrained therapy)
- Operationalization of completion/attrition (higher attrition observed when based on therapist judgment alone)
- Experience level of therapist (trainees having higher rates of client attrition than experienced therapists)
- Availability of equivalent services elsewhere; physical distance to services
- Changes in treatment procedures during treatment
- Session availability; length of waiting list

---

risk factors most commonly mentioned in the literature and indicates the factors that are likely to interact. For instance, symptom severity and treatment expectations are associated with socioeconomic factors, which are associated with physical distance to viable treatment and the quality of treatment, and so on. Even when a single factor may explain why a particular client discontinued early, consideration of multiple risk factors is preferable to focusing on single factors when looking at aggregate data. The inadequacy of evaluating a single risk factor in isolation from others becomes readily apparent when considering the research on differences in treatment participation across race or ethnicity.

Racial and Ethnic Discrepancies

Racial and ethnic discrepancies in client treatment attendance and treatment completion/attrition have been widely reported in the research literature. A 1993 meta-analysis (Wierzbicki & Pekarik) concluded that ethnic minority clients were more likely to discontinue treatment than White clients, and subsequent narrative literature reviews reached the same conclusion (Barrett et al., 2008; Reis & Brown, 1999). The professional literature commonly asserts racial and ethnic discrepancies, often referring to them in passing as if they are common knowledge.

However, a recent meta-analysis found small racial and ethnic differences in the rate of premature discontinuation across 11 studies reporting data by race (not statistically significant at $p = .06$) and found no correlation between the percentage of clients of color and the rate of premature client discontinuation in 243 studies (Swift & Greenberg, 2012). These recent findings suggest the possibility that racial and ethnic discrepancies in client treatment completion/attendance have decreased over time. Such a decrease may suggest improved multicultural competence among mental health professionals, increased exposure to and understanding of mental health treatments among clients of color, or influence from a factor not yet identified. Unfortunately, previous research has failed to identify specific predictors of racial and ethnic discrepancies in client treatment participation. Authors commonly list race and ethnicity among several factors that have been found to be associated with participation (Table 5.1), but few authors address the interactions of race and ethnicity with those other factors—and even fewer examine underlying causes for the discrepancies across race and ethnicity.

Sometimes cultural explanations are given for racial and ethnic differences in treatment participation. For instance, clients from some cultures prefer to avoid confrontation or assume passive roles with clinicians (Alegría et al., 2008) and may discontinue treatment rather than openly raise concerns. Lack of familiarity with mental health treatments or communication difficulties may account for lower participation among some clients of color, particularly recent immigrants. Other authors emphasize that client participation depends on the therapist's multicultural competence (e.g., Langer, 1999). Research confirms that client unilateral termination varies across therapist characteristics, with some therapists having greater retention of clients of color than others (Owen, Imel, Adelson, & Rodolfa, 2012). Thus, therapists should facilitate attunement and alliance across cultural differences (Gaztambide, 2012).

Although cultural explanations for client completion/attrition are certainly reasonable, research has yet to confirm the associated assumptions. Evidence of potential causes for racial discrepancies and research designs that establish causality are presently limited. The vast majority of research has been either descriptive (means and percentages) or correlational:

> Research on attrition from treatment is frequently less well executed than would be desirable. The literature reflects an extensive yet mainly atheoretical search for correlates of attrition, which thus far has provided little firm direction for understanding why clients leave treatment. (P. M. Harris, 1998, p. 302)

Our literature search located no studies of racial and ethnic discrepancies that involved causal modeling or even such obviously appropriate statistical methods as survival analysis (Corning & Malofeeva, 2004). We did locate a handful of studies involving path analysis or fixed/random effects models, but in our review we found that most researchers simply collected demographic data at intake and then evaluated subsequent differences in attendance or completion/attrition, without accounting for treatment processes, symptom levels, cultural values and expectations, or other likely explanations for racial and ethnic differences.

Despite the methodological limitations of the available research on racial and ethnic discrepancies in client treatment participation, extensive research has been completed using descriptive and correlational designs. This evidence can and should be synthesized to inform future inquiry. As far as we can determine, our summary in this chapter of the extant findings is the first specific to racial and ethnic differences; previous meta-analyses have treated a contrast of White/European Americans with people of color as one of several variables, without specifically searching for manuscripts contrasting findings across race or ethnicity (Swift & Greenberg, 2012; Wierzbicki & Pekarik, 1993). We undertook this meta-analysis to generate estimates of racial and ethnic differences in client treatment attendance and client treatment completion/attrition and to estimate the degree to which study and participant characteristics moderated the findings. A summary of the findings can be found in the next section (Discussion and Interpretation of Findings).

QUANTITATIVE SYNTHESIS OF RESEARCH DATA

We conducted a meta-analysis of the available research literature. To evaluate individuals' degree of participation (attendance or completion/attrition or both) in mental health services across race or ethnicity, we had to calculate an effect size that was conceptually consistent across studies by comparison with a single racial group. Because almost all studies we located reported data for White/European American clients, we selected that group as the contrast.[1] We used Cohen's d as the effect size metric, with positive values indicating greater participation rates (higher attendance or completion, lower attrition) than the contrast group and negative values indicating

---

[1]We oppose the assumption that Whites are a normative reference group; the experiences of other racial and ethnic groups do not need to be compared with Whites to be understood or valued. Our decision to contrast the participation rates of people of color with Whites in this chapter was based on our desire to include as many studies in our analyses as possible, and no other racial or ethnic group was represented as consistently in the literature. Moreover, having a consistent contrast group allowed for contrasts between every group.

lower participation rates than those of the contrast group. General methods of the meta-analysis are reported in the Appendix to this book.

Description of the Existing Research Literature

We located 67 studies that compared client participation (attendance and/or completion/attrition) in a mental health treatment by race. As may be seen in Table 5.1, the majority of studies involved archival data, retrieving information regarding client attendance or completion/attrition, and then comparing those data across racial groups. With so many studies involving archival data, the number of participants tended to be large (overall median of 423 clients per study with 275,037 total clients). Most studies were conducted in outpatient treatment facilities (e.g., community mental health clinics), but some involved treatment programs for youth or college counseling centers. Only five evaluated inpatient/residential treatments.

Adolescents and senior adult clients were underrepresented. African Americans tended to be evaluated most frequently, but Asian Americans and Hispanic/Latino(a) Americans were also frequently studied. Only three studies reported data specific to Native American Indian clients, and 14 studies collapsed participants of color into a catchall "ethnic minority" group.

Research studies operationalized client participation both as treatment attendance (number of sessions attended, return to treatment after an initial session, and number of days in treatment) and as treatment completion/ attrition (finishing a prescribed protocol or number of sessions or being judged by a therapist as either having completed necessary treatment or having prematurely discontinued treatment), with 12 studies using both methods of evaluation. The effect sizes represent simple comparisons of these data across race, with no causality inferred.

The 48 effect sizes based on client attendance data averaged $d = -0.06$, whereas the 31 effect sizes based on client completion/attrition data averaged $d = -0.15$; this difference reached statistical significance ($Q = 4.3$, $p < .05$). Evaluation of client participation based on measures of treatment completion/ attrition consistently resulted in greater discrepancies with White/European American clients than that based on measures of client attendance. We therefore report analyses of data for client attendance and for client completion/ attrition separately.

Findings Across Measures of Client Attendance

Differences in client attendance (e.g., number of sessions completed) by race were examined through a multivariate meta-analysis, in which effect sizes specific to each racial group were examined simultaneously (accounting

TABLE 5.1
Characteristics of 67 Studies of the Participation of Clients
in Mental Health Services Across Race

Characteristic	M	No. of studies (k)	%
Year of report	1993		
Before 1980		7	10
1980–1989		17	26
1990–1999		25	37
2000–2008		18	27
Publication status			
Published		41	61
Unpublished dissertations		26	39
Research design			
Archival		43	64
Comparison groups		16	24
Longitudinal		8	12
Clinical setting			
Outpatient treatment		38	57
Day treatment program		7	10
College counseling center		7	10
Inpatient/residential treatment		5	8
Mixed settings		10	15
Sample size	4,105		
<50		2	3
50–99		7	11
100–199		13	19
200–399		9	14
400–999		13	19
>1,000		23	34
Age of participants[a]	30.3		
Children (<13 years)		10	17
Adolescents (13–18 years)		4	7
Young adults (19–29 years)		6	11
Middle-aged adults (30–55 years)		36	63
Senior adults (>56 years)		1	2
Gender of participants (% female)	48.5		
Race of participants[b] (%)			
White/European American	53		
African American	22		
Asian American	10		
Hispanic/Latino(a) American	14		
Native American Indian	0		
Other	1		

Note. Not all variables sum to the total number of studies because of missing data.
[a]Average age category of participants within studies, though not all participants within the study would necessarily be in the category listed. [b]The racial composition of participants across all studies was calculated by multiplying the number of participants within studies by the percentage of participants from each racial group and dividing that product by the total number of participants.

for the observed value of $r = .00$ for the results of different racial groups within studies). The overall model reached statistical significance (Wald $X^2(4) = 43.2, p < .0001$); the results by race are reported in Table 5.2. Asian American clients had higher average attendance rates than all other groups, including White/European Americans. African American clients had lower average attendance rates than all other groups. Although most of the differences between groups reached statistical significance, they were all of very small magnitude. Across all 48 studies examining client attendance, the random effects weighted effect size was $d = -.06$ ($SE = .011$, 95% CI = [$-.08, -.04$], $p < .0001$). The heterogeneity of the findings was moderate ($I^2 = 64.3$, 95% CI = [51, 74]; $Q_{(47)} = 131.6, p < .00001$), meaning that the results tended to be inconsistent across studies (see Figure 5.1).

Effects of Study and Participant Characteristics

Studies involved a wide variety of participants and procedures, so we evaluated differences across participant age and gender (percentage of females in the study), year of study publication, estimated age cohort (year of study publication minus average age of participants), and racial diversity of the setting (percentage of people of color in the study). None of these correlations reached statistical significance. Thus, the variables coded were unrelated to

TABLE 5.2
Weighted Mean Effect Sizes (Cohen's *d*) Across Participant Race

Group	k	d	SE	95 % CI
Client attendance discrepancies				
African Americans	33	−.11[a,b]	.02	[−.15, −.07]
Asian Americans	14	.08[b,c]	.03	[.02, .13]
Hispanic/Latino(a) Americans	30	−.06[a]	.01	[−.09, −.04]
Unspecified/other ethnic minorities	7	−.07[a,c]	.05	[−.17, .03]
All groups combined	48	−.06[a,c]	.01	[−.08, −.04]
Client completion/attrition discrepancies				
African Americans	17	−.23[a,b]	.05	[−.33, −.13]
Asian Americans	8	−.13[c]	.09	[−.31, .05]
Hispanic/Latino(a) Americans	15	−.04[c]	.04	[−.12, .05]
Unspecified/other ethnic minorities	12	−.15[b]	.07	[−.29, −.02]
All groups combined	31	−.15[b]	.04	[−.24, −.06]

Note. Effect sizes were derived from contrasts of participation data with White/European Americans; nevertheless, all groups can be contrasted within the table. CI = confidence interval; *d* = random effects weighted effect size; *k* = number of studies. [a]Statistically significantly different from Asian Americans ($p \le .05$). [b]Statistically significantly different from Hispanic/Latino(a) Americans ($p \le .05$). [c]Statistically significantly different from African Americans ($p \le .05$).

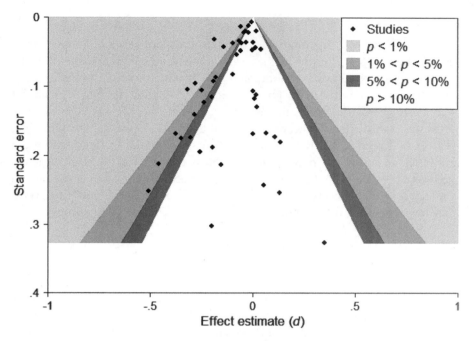

Figure 5.1. Contour-enhanced funnel plot of effect sizes (Cohen's *d*) by standard error for 48 studies of client treatment attendance across racial groups. This graph shows the distribution of effect sizes as a function of the number of participants in the study (operationalized as standard error). The studies at the top of the graph are those with many participants (and small standard error values), which studies yielded results that clustered very slightly to the left of zero (evenly distributed around the overall average, *d* = –0.06). By contrast, inconsistent results were obtained when studies involved few participants, as seen by the scattered data points toward the middle and bottom of the graph. This kind of pyramid-shaped distribution is expected in meta-analyses.

racial discrepancies in client attendance, although the small number of studies restricted the statistical power of these analyses, which diminished the likelihood of obtaining statistically significant results.

Given that 14 of the 48 effect sizes were adjusted for potential confounds, including client socioeconomic status (in 10 of the 48 studies) and client mental health status or severity of symptoms (in 13 of the 48 studies), it was important to ascertain whether the results differed when they were adjusted versus unadjusted. Nevertheless, the average effect size values were essentially the same (*d* = –0.05 for adjusted values and *d* = –0.07 for unadjusted values, *p* > .05). Thus, the results across studies did not consistently differ with the inclusion of covariates.

Influence of Publication Bias

When research manuscripts with nonsignificant results remain unpublished, they are less likely to be located in a literature search and thus bias the findings of a meta-analysis. Publication bias appeared to have influenced the overall findings reported in the previous section. Although the data in Figure 5.1 were fairly symmetric, Egger's regression test (an estimate of asymmetry of effect sizes) was statistically significant ($p < .001$). In addition, one statistical method (Duval & Tweedie, 2000) identified six "missing" studies in the distribution. However, when those hypothetical data were accounted for, the resulting effect size was $d = -0.05$ (95% CI = [-0.08, $-.03$]), essentially the same as the overall value of $d = -0.06$ reported earlier (Table 5.2). Thus, although publication bias may have occurred, its effect on the results appears to have been minimal.

Findings Across Measures of Client Treatment Completion/Attrition

We next examined racial differences in client treatment completion and attrition patterns (e.g., either finishing a prescribed protocol or prematurely discontinuing treatment) through multivariate meta-analysis, with effect sizes specific to each racial and ethnic group examined simultaneously. The overall model reached statistical significance (Wald $X^2(4) = 27.8, p < .0001$); results by race are reported in Table 5.1. African American clients had the lowest levels of treatment completion (highest levels of attrition), followed by unspecified/other ethnic minorities and Asian American clients. Hispanic/Latino(a) American clients had almost the same average completion/attrition rates as White/European American clients.

Across all 31 studies examining client completion and attrition patterns, the random effects weighted effect size was $d = -.15$ ($SE = .044$, 95% CI = [$-.24$, $-.06$], $p < .0001$). The heterogeneity of the findings was very large ($I^2 = 85.4$, 95% CI = [80, 89]; $Q_{(30)} = 205.8, p < .0001$), meaning that the results were highly inconsistent across studies (see Figure 5.2).

Influence of Study and Participant Characteristics

As in previous analyses, we correlated effect sizes with participant age and gender composition, year of study publication, estimated age cohort, and racial diversity of setting. The random effects weighted correlations of these variables with study effect sizes did not reach statistical significance. Thus, the racial discrepancies in treatment completion and attrition patterns were unrelated to the characteristics analyzed, but the small number of studies restricted the statistical power of the analyses.

The minimal differences between the effect sizes of studies using statistical controls ($d = -0.17$) versus not using them ($d = -0.14$) did not reach

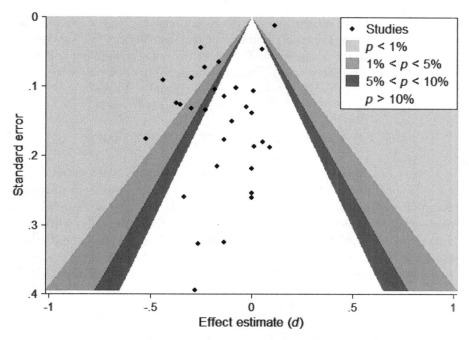

Figure 5.2. Contour-enhanced funnel plot of effect sizes (Cohen's *d*) by standard error for 31 studies of client treatment completion/attrition across racial groups. In this case the overall average is also slightly to the left of 0, but the results are widely scattered, with high variability even among studies with a larger number of participants (and lower standard errors) depicted at the top of the graph. This inconsistent distribution limits the interpretability of the overall average.

statistical significance in a random effects weighted analysis of variance. Effect sizes remained of similar magnitude whether or not the data had been statistically adjusted for potential confounds.

Effects of Publication Bias

The data in Figure 5.2 were asymmetric, shifted toward negative effect size values (indicating less participation of clients of color). This unbalanced distribution suggested possible missing studies with data indicating greater participation of clients of color. Egger's regression test, an estimate of asymmetry of effect sizes, was statistically significant ($p < .001$), but one statistical method (Duval & Tweedie, 2000) failed to identify any "missing" studies in the distribution. This contradictory information seemed to have occurred because the study with the smallest standard error (at the top of Figure 5.2) fell on the right side of the distribution, the side where missing data would have been expected. To evaluate the possible impact on the findings if a few studies were actually missing, we temporarily inserted six hypothetical values where gaps appeared on the right side of the distribution. This procedure resulted in an overall mean of $d = -0.09$, a value that was small but still statistically different from 0 ($p < .01$). Thus, although publication bias was possible in the data, the results appear to have been minimally affected.

DISCUSSION AND INTERPRETATION OF FINDINGS

Notable differences were found between estimates based on metrics of attendance (number of sessions completed) and metrics based on treatment completion/attrition (as evaluated by the therapist or by a set number or percentage of sessions); thus, separate analyses were conducted with those distinct classes of data. The differences observed between racial and ethnic groups in these analyses ranged from almost nonexistent to small, according to commonly used guidelines for interpreting Cohen's d (J. Cohen, 1988). On average, racial and ethnic groups participated similarly in treatment. However, results may be enhanced by considering the meaning of the effect size (Cohen's d) in real-world terms: number of sessions completed (for studies reporting attendance data) and percentages of clients completing treatment (for studies reporting completion/attrition data).

To conceptualize the meaning of Cohen's d in terms of therapy attendance, we suggest a hypothetical scenario in which an average of 15 therapy sessions are expected, with substantial variability in the actual number of sessions completed ($SD = 9$). Given those parameters and the Cohen's d values for attendance data found in Table 5.2, African American clients complete on average 14 sessions, one less than expected (transforming $d = -0.11$). Using those same parameters and attendance data transformed from Cohen's d values in Table 5.2, Asian Americans would attend an average of 15.7 sessions, and Hispanic/Latino(a) Americans would attend an average of 14.5 sessions. Typically, 14 or more total sessions are required for the majority of clients to demonstrate clinically significant change, and the number of total sessions is very weakly correlated with client outcome (Lambert, 2007), so missing on average of one session of therapy would not likely have a meaningful impact on therapy effectiveness. Average racial and ethnic differences in therapy attendance appear to have minimal real-world consequences unless very few sessions are provided.

The effect size Cohen's d takes on a different meaning when transformed into the metric of percentages of clients completing treatment. Across 41 studies that reported absolute completion rates, about 61% of all clients completed treatment. Using that baseline estimate of 61%, the racial discrepancy corresponding with J. Cohen's (1988) description of a "small" effect size ($d = 0.20$) would be about 10%, which would mean that one out of every 10 clients discontinued therapy on the basis of reasons apparently related to race and ethnicity. To reach the value for a "medium" effect size ($d = 0.50$), the racial discrepancy would have to be about 24%: one out of every four clients discontinuing therapy on the basis of reasons apparently related to race. In the real world, a racial discrepancy of 24% would be unconscionable. Mental health professions would come under scathing attack and legal action—well deserved—if racial and ethnic inequities were that obvious. Even the "small" discrepancy of 10% seems truly problematic when multiplied by the number of clients seeking mental health services. Thus, interpretations of the data in terms of the real-world metric of percentages of treatment completion appear preferable to the standard guidelines given for values of Cohen's d.

Using the observed average baseline participation rate of 61%, transformation of the treatment "criterion and completion" data for African Americans in Table 5.2 ($d = -0.23$) indicates that African American clients remained in treatment on average 11.5% less often than White/European American clients. Using those estimates, for every five African American clients who completed therapy, an additional individual should have completed therapy if race had not been a factor in treatment participation. Calculated differently, for every nine African American clients who walked into a clinic, one would have failed to complete treatment for reasons associated with race. Asian Americans, who we found in previous analyses to be more likely to attend therapy than White/European Americans, are nevertheless 6.5% less likely to complete treatment (transformation of $d = -0.13$ in Table 5.2). One out of every 15 Asian Americans who walk into a clinic would fail to complete treatment for reasons related to race. Hispanic/Latino(a) American clients completed treatment 2% less often than White/European Americans but 9.5% more often than African Americans. For every 50 Hispanic/Latino(a) American clients who walked into a clinic, one would have failed to complete treatment for reasons related to race or ethnicity. Whereas one out of 50 clients is extremely small in real-world terms, one out of nine clients is a consequential number, a true racial discrepancy deserving serious attention. By comparison, one out of 15 clients seems much less egregious but certainly far from optimal.

Nonetheless, the statistical estimates of racial and ethnic discrepancies in client participation may be mildly inflated due to publication bias, which occurs when nonsignificant or counterintuitive research findings remain unpublished or otherwise inaccessible to researchers conducting meta-analyses (Rosenthal, 1991). Thus, the effect size values just interpreted (and reported in Table 5.2) may represent liberal estimates of racial discrepancies.

The analyses also indicated that averaged participant characteristics of age, age cohort, and gender were unrelated to the degree of racial and ethnic discrepancies in client participation. And the results across studies were essentially the same whether or not participants' characteristics (commonly including those variables but also including mental health functioning and socioeconomic status) were statistically controlled. These findings suggest that commonly measured demographic variables are on average unrelated to racial and ethnic discrepancies in client attendance or client treatment completion/attrition.

Recommendations for Future Research

Researchers must consistently evaluate mental health treatments to ensure that clients are receiving the best services available. On the basis of research specific to client participation in therapy, the results of this meta-analysis strongly suggest that the dependent variables of client (a) attendance and (b) completion/attrition patterns must be kept completely distinct. "Attendance and retention differ both conceptually and empirically" (Alegría et al., 2008, p. 248). Unless very few sessions are planned, measures of client attendance are less consequential than measures of client treatment completion. Further studies of client attendance rates may not contribute much to the body of literature already accumulated; future research should focus on treatment completion/attrition and the other recommendations listed in Exhibit 5.2.

To identify why African American, Asian American, and unspecified clients of color are at risk of therapy attrition, scholars should conduct both

EXHIBIT 5.2
Recommendations for Researchers for Improving the Study of Racial Discrepancies in Treatment Completion

- Statistically control for preexisting symptom severity and length of treatment.
- Use optimal statistical methods: survival analysis, including proportional hazards regression.
- Use proximal cultural characteristics, not race only, in models that account for multiple likely predictors of treatment completion (see Exhibit 5.1).
- Optimally evaluate client termination in terms of symptom reduction or reduction trajectory. Examine clinical significance of outcomes.
- Contact clients who discontinued treatment to ascertain their reasons, rather than assume that discontinuation was unwarranted; also deepen qualitative inquiry into client experiences of termination.
- Report absolute and adjusted rates of treatment completion/attrition.
- Evaluate possible differences across treatment settings that are currently under-represented in the literature, particularly inpatient and residential (controlling for whether treatment was voluntary).
- Evaluate the alignment of the treatment provided with client expectations and worldviews.

qualitative inquiry and psychotherapy process research. Scholars should also make efforts to locate former clients who discontinued therapy and learn about those clients' experiences in therapy and their rationale for discontinuing it. Too little of this kind of scholarship presently exists (Knox et al., 2011).

Qualitative and quantitative differences in the reasons for client discontinuation of treatment can inform refinement of dependent variables, which include operationalization of treatment completion/attrition. Therapists' evaluations of client dispositions may be problematic (e.g., Murdock et al., 2010; Swift et al., 2009). Other commonly used methods, such as predetermined cutoff values for number of sessions completed and dichotomous conceptualizations of treatment completion, fail to account for underlying reasons for discontinuation. For instance, in one study "clients who were better adjusted initially tended to withdraw from treatment; clients receiving particularly severe diagnoses tended either to finish or to drop out" (Snowden, Storey, & Clancy, 1989, p. 116). In another study, clients who successfully completed treatment averaged 40 sessions, whereas those who discontinued "early" in treatment averaged 10 sessions, and those who discontinued "late" in treatment averaged 47 sessions (Talebi, 2006). If a client attended 47 sessions and discontinued because her or his symptoms remained unimproved, certainly researchers should not categorize that client alongside another client who failed to schedule a return appointment following intake. We concur with Kazdin's observation (1996):

> The variables that are selected for investigation to predict dropping out often appear to be "variables of convenience," that is, measures that are readily available on clinic intake forms. . . . It is [more] useful to conceptualize the process of dropping out and then to place these (and other variables) in the context of that conceptualization. (p. 138)

We believe that the evaluation of client completion and attrition patterns should include clients' symptom trajectories (Swift et al., 2009) and underlying motives (Knox et al., 2011). Using precise dependent variables informed by clients' reasons for treatment discontinuation and their rate of symptom improvement should enhance the interpretability of future research findings.

Finally, scholars conducting future research on client participation should identify and control for probable confounds, not merely demographic variables. Only 19% of the 67 studies in the meta-analysis statistically controlled for client socioeconomic variables, yet economic constraints undoubtedly influence treatment participation rates. Furthermore, the most likely confound, client symptom severity, was controlled in only 24% of the studies. Although our analyses with this limited number of studies did not find evidence that change in statistical controls altered averaged results across studies, results did change within studies when statistical controls were used (e.g., Snowden et al., 1989). Logically, it seems essential to account for likely confounds when attempting to examine differences across race and ethnicity: for example, to account for the overall length of time in treatment, not merely measure the percentage of expected sessions completed. How can researchers speak with any confidence about racial and ethnic differences if we fail to systematically evaluate likely confounds? Future research must control for preexisting symptom severity and should optimally use statistical methods such as survival analysis (Corning & Malofeeva, 2004) and proportional hazards regression (M. H. Katz & Hauck, 1993), rather than simply reporting percentages and means. "The phenomenon of attrition from treatment requires more rigorous attention" (P. M. Harris, 1998, p. 293) and more rigorous methodology to distinguish what differences are attributable to race and ethnicity.

Suggestions for Practitioners

Previous research has shown that therapists can facilitate completion of therapy for clients of color by implementing culturally competent practices (e.g., Alegría et al., 2008). The multicultural psychology literature contains a myriad of suggestions for appropriately engaging diverse clients (e.g., Gaztambide, 2012; Ponterotto, Casas, Suzuki, & Alexander, 2010; T. B. Smith, 2010). Practitioners can also keep in mind that several macro-level factors influence client continuation in treatment. For instance, most of the factors thought to adversely affect mental health service utilization (see Chapter 4, this volume, Exhibit 4.1) are likely to adversely affect client continuation in treatment. If a clinic is located in a suburban area consisting of predominantly White/European Americans, clients of color might find it more difficult to repeatedly travel to the clinic. Although the publicly available data do not identify which specific factors are most influential, all levels of explanation for discrepancies (Exhibit 5.1) can be considered by practitioners to identify the particular factors most likely to affect racial and ethnic discrepancies at their particular clinic and to change procedures and practices to better facilitate client engagement in and completion of needed mental health services.

In adopting practices that will increase client engagement in therapy (see Exhibit 5.3), practitioners must also take a broad perspective on the reasons for client premature discontinuation. Our meta-analysis indicated that an average of 61% of clients completed therapy across 41 of 67 studies reporting those data. The fact that so many clients prematurely discontinue treatment (Swift & Greenberg, 2012; Wierzbicki & Pekarik, 1993) is the proverbial "elephant in the room" that mental health professionals typically minimize or avoid. The discontinuance average of four out of 10 clients shown by our analyses is far

EXHIBIT 5.3
General Recommendations for Practitioners
in Increasing Client Treatment Completion

- Help clients clearly/precisely articulate their reasons for desiring treatment.
- Establish agreement regarding the focus of treatment; verify that the content and process of therapy align with clients' values and goals, including readiness for change.
- Empower clients by facilitating opportunities to ask questions, seek information, and involve themselves in treatment decisions.
- Strengthen the therapeutic alliance, and take immediate corrective action when client–therapist misalignments occur.
- Explicitly solicit client expectations regarding the duration of treatment, then align treatment to match client expectations and/or provide clients with specific reasons why treatment of a different (longer) duration would be beneficial, and finally revisit client expectations.
- Openly discuss the pros and cons of therapy from the client's perspective.
- Identify and correct misalignments in understanding.
- Involve client support networks/family in treatment to the extent helpful.
- Facilitate client imagery of systematic improvement over time.
- Limit treatment to an attainable duration (rather than leave treatment open-ended).

too many failures, even before accounting for racial and ethnic discrepancies. Eliminating racial and ethnic discrepancies in treatment completion should occur alongside efforts to raise overall percentages of clients who complete treatment. Thus, the findings from this meta-analysis align with ample extant data that "suggest the need for providers and service managers to give high priority to keeping patients in treatment longer" (Lambert, 2007, p. 4).

Of the common recommendations for increasing client engagement in and completion of therapy (Exhibit 5.3), research strongly supports working with client expectations about the nature and duration of treatment and the roles of the client in therapy (e.g., Swift & Callahan, 2011). Although some authors describe didactic methods of client induction and orientation that implicitly maintain power imbalances favoring the clinician, a method specifically designed to empower multicultural clients focuses on activation—facilitating clients in formulating questions, seeking information, and managing their own mental health care decisions and processes (Alegría et al., 2008). This activation approach also strengthens the quality of client–therapist interaction, a critical factor in client completion of treatment (Sharf et al., 2010).

CONCLUSION

In our perusal of the relevant research literature, we identified two distinct qualitative tones taken by authors when referring to racial and ethnic discrepancies in mental health treatment participation. Some authors openly lamented the discrepancies, voicing alarm that current mental health practices are extremely problematic for clients of color. Many others referred to the racial and ethnic discrepancies in passing, as one of several variables associated with treatment participation, without considering underlying dynamics—as if nothing could be done to rectify the situation. Neither of these tones accurately captures the available data. Our analyses of the research data raise concern about racial and ethnic differences, but we found those differences much less severe than we had supposed. Treatment attendance differs minimally across race and ethnicity, but on average treatment completion and attrition patterns and differences have adverse effects on African American clients, with a smaller but still notable impact on Asian American clients. Our interpretation of the completion and attrition data demonstrated that even small statistical differences have real-world consequences.

We believe that it is now time for scholars and practitioners to rectify these differences through identifying and addressing the underlying causes. For instance, although most therapists oppose racist beliefs, therapists vary in their effectiveness in cross-cultural therapy (Hayes et al., 2015). It is not difficult to imagine that the behavior of one out of nine therapists might influence the one out of nine African American clients (or the one out of 15 Asian American clients) who discontinue therapy for reasons apparently related to race. This particular interpretation exceeds the bounds of our data; we did not evaluate therapist racism, and although therapists account for some of client treatment completion and attrition patterns (Owen et al., 2012; Piselli et al., 2011), many other concomitant factors also contribute to racial discrepancies (Exhibit 5.1).

Racial discrepancies in client treatment completion may occur relatively infrequently, but the fact that racial discrepancies exist at all deserves remediation, not resignation. If a client discontinues therapy for reasons apparently related to her or his race or ethnicity, the profession should take steps to remove those reasons.

6

MATCHING CLIENTS WITH THERAPISTS ON THE BASIS OF RACE OR ETHNICITY: A META-ANALYSIS OF CLIENTS' LEVEL OF PARTICIPATION IN TREATMENT

Mental illness occurs across all races and ethnicities, but not all races and ethnicities receive equivalent mental health treatment. People of color in North America may receive an inferior quality of care (Alegría et al., 2008; Gone & Trimble, 2012; Shin et al., 2005; S. Sue, 1988), and they tend to report greater dissatisfaction with mental health services than White/European Americans (Garroutte, Kunovich, Jacobsen, & Goldberg, 2004; S. Sue & Zane, 1987). To help improve the quality of care provided to people of color, scholars have emphasized the need to adapt treatments culturally and to establish cultural congruence between clients and therapists (Griner & Smith, 2006; La Roche & Lustig, 2013; S. Sue, 1998). Although not the same as adapting treatments, matching clients with therapists according

Racquel R. Cabral provided the foundational work for this chapter, including data collection and cleaning. Derek Griner and Alberto Soto of Brigham Young University contributed to the writing of this chapter.

A complete list of references for the studies included in this chapter's meta-analysis is posted online. Readers can consult it at http://pubs.apa.org/books/supp/smith

http://dx.doi.org/10.1037/14733-006
Foundations of Multicultural Psychology: Research to Inform Effective Practice, by T. B. Smith and J. E. Trimble

to race or ethnicity has received consistent attention over the past several decades as one way to foster cultural congruence (Presnell, Harris, & Scogin, 2012; S. Sue, Fujino, Hu, Takeuchi, & Zane, 1991).

This matching approach assumes that therapeutic outcomes may improve because clients and therapists share similar worldviews and values (Kelly & Strupp, 1992). In addition to a preference for a therapist who shares their racial or ethnic background, some clients may experience a stronger therapeutic alliance and greater levels of participation in treatment when matched on race or ethnicity (S. Sue, 1977; S. Sue et al., 1991). Shared race and ethnicity may also attenuate factors that often preclude clients of color from seeking professional mental health services—for example, mistrust of cultural differences, unfavorable views of mental health professionals (Whaley, 2001), lack of culturally congruent services, and institutional barriers (D. W. Sue et al., 2007; S. Sue, 2003). Cultural barriers may be so prominent that some clients of color may feel a sense of relief when they see a mental health professional who phenotypically appears to share their racial or ethnic background.

Shared race or ethnicity, however, cannot be presumed to align with the more precise, proximal variables of shared values and worldviews (Helms, Jernigan, & Mascher, 2005). People are remarkably different within as well as across cultures (see Trimble & Bhadra, 2013). For instance, Hispanic/Latino(a) Americans include individuals from dozens of ethnic groups, but even if working with only one delimited group, such as the Runakuna of Peru, a wide variety of attributes and worldviews should still be expected. Moreover, perceived similarity based on visible attributes, such as race, can mask actual differences in values and worldviews. So matching mental health clients with therapists of the same race or ethnicity only accounts for some aspects of human experience, albeit important ones. It should therefore come as no surprise that the effects of matching clients with therapists of the same race or ethnicity are mixed and likely to vary on the basis of the type of evaluation conducted (e.g., preferences, dropout, outcome; Cabral & Smith, 2011; H. L. K. Coleman, Wampold, & Casali, 1995; Flaskerud & Liu, 1990).

A question that has not yet been resolved in the research literature is the degree to which clients participate in treatment (i.e., attendance and completion/attrition) as a function of the racial or ethnic match with the therapist. Research has found that clients prefer therapists of their own race and perceive therapists of their own race somewhat more positively than other therapists (Cabral & Smith, 2011). Therefore, clients may be more likely to remain in treatment when they are matched with therapists of their same race or ethnicity.

REVIEW OF THE LITERATURE

Relevant Theory

The idea that client engagement in treatment could be improved by matching clients and therapists according to race or ethnicity is loosely based on social psychology. Oversimplified, several theories indicate that individuals tend to have greater affiliation with people perceived to be similar to themselves (e.g., D. E. Byrne, 1971). Social scientists refer to greater preference for similarity as *homophily* (McPherson, Smith-Lovin, & Cook, 2001), which is frequently observed in behavioral tendencies. Our choices tend to be homogenous. Race and ethnicity influence the strongest divides in our personal environments, with age, religion, education, occupation, and gender following in roughly that order (McPherson et al., 2001).

On the basis of such principles, clients and therapists of the same race or ethnicity should experience a stronger working relationship than client–therapist dyads with dissimilar backgrounds (e.g., Simons, Berkowitz, & Moyer, 1970). Nevertheless, such similarity could become problematic if differences are overlooked. And differences in perspective can be beneficial when they facilitate insight, create dialogue, and promote change. The degree to which racial or ethnic matching actually benefits clients, therefore, deserves investigation.

Narrative Review of Previous Research

Research on the effects of matching clients with therapists on the basis of race or ethnicity has accumulated over many decades (Cabral & Smith, 2011; H. L. K. Coleman et al., 1995; Flaskerud & Liu, 1990; Shin et al., 2005). This research has addressed a variety of relevant variables, including (a) client preferences for therapist race or ethnicity, (b) client perceptions of therapists across race or ethnicity, and (c) client outcomes as a function of therapist race or ethnicity. Because negative biases can adversely affect people of color and these experiences can be difficult to discuss (D. W. Sue, 2015; D. W. Sue et al., 2007), having a therapist of one's own race or ethnicity can decrease discomfort. Previous research has suggested that Hispanic/Latino(a) Americans and African Americans generally prefer that arrangement (Flicker, Waldron, Turner, Brody, & Hops, 2008), although there is great variability in research findings, and generalization of findings can be problematic (Dumas, Moreland, Gitter, Pearl, & Nordstrom, 2008). Overall, when given the option, culturally diverse individuals tend to have a moderately strong preference for therapists from their own racial or ethnic background, with a recent meta-analysis reporting a $d = .63$ across 52 studies (Cabral & Smith, 2011).

Client preferences for therapists of their own race or ethnicity may lead to the assumption that clients could also perceive those therapists more positively than therapists from other cultural backgrounds, expecting them to be more competent in addressing cultural issues (Knox, Burkard, Johnson, Suzuki, & Ponterotto, 2003). Overall, research supports the notion that clients view therapists of their own race or ethnicity somewhat more positively than those of other races, with a reported $d = .32$ across 81 studies (Cabral & Smith, 2011).

Given the relevance of racial or ethnic matching to client preferences and perceptions of therapists, to what degree does matching improve client outcomes? Overall, research has found little evidence to support the hypothesis that therapeutic outcomes improve as a result of racial or ethnic matching (Maramba & Nagayama Hall, 2002; Presnell et al., 2012; Shin et al., 2005), although in some instances improvements have been noted (Ruglass et al., 2014). Across 53 studies, therapy outcomes were only slightly more positive ($d = .09$) for clients who were matched with therapists on race or ethnicity (Cabral & Smith, 2011), although the effect was more notable among African American clients ($d = .19$). Ethnic or racial matching does not necessarily improve client–therapist communication (Zane & Ku, 2014), and generally client outcomes are not greatly affected by the race or ethnicity of the therapist.

The finding that client preferences and perceptions relevant to therapist match do not necessarily translate into improved outcomes requires explanation. One possible explanation is that clients with higher levels of discomfort related to racial or ethnic differences may be less likely to initiate and attend therapy if unmatched with a therapist of their own race or ethnicity. In addition, clients may be more likely to drop out of treatment if they feel misunderstood by a therapist of a different race or ethnicity. Thus, the results of the client outcome research could be confounded by client attrition: Clients who are uncomfortable with unmatched conditions could be less likely to complete the research, such that research findings without those participants would be biased in the direction of no effect. Examining client levels of participation in therapy as a function of racial or ethnic match is therefore essential (Cabral & Smith, 2011).

One meta-analysis specific to African American clients reported a very minor effect of racial match on dropout and number of sessions attended (Shin et al., 2005), but some research indicates that ethnic or racial match decreases premature treatment dropout (Ibaraki & Hall, 2014). The field will now benefit from investigation of differential rates of client participation in therapy across other groups using updated research reports available in the literature. The objectives of our meta-analytic review were to generate estimates of differences in client participation in mental health treatments across racial or ethnic match with therapists and to estimate the degree to which study and participant characteristics moderate the overall findings. A summary of the findings is presented in the subsequent section.

QUANTITATIVE SYNTHESIS OF RESEARCH DATA

We conducted a meta-analysis of the research literature in the United States and Canada that evaluated individuals' degree of participation (attendance or completion/attrition) in mental health services as a function of whether the client and therapist were of the same race or ethnicity. Statistical estimates in the studies were converted to Cohen's *d*. Positive values for effect sizes indicated greater participation rates (higher attendance or completion, lower attrition) among the clients who were matched with a therapist of their same race or ethnicity, and negative values indicated lower participation rates for the matched clients. General methods of the meta-analysis are described in the Appendix to this book.

Description of the Existing Research Literature

We located 53 studies that reported comparisons of client participation (measured by session attendance and/or treatment completion/attrition) as a function of client racial or ethnic match with the therapist. As shown in Table 6.1, studies typically selected participants among those conveniently available and rarely randomized clients to matched versus unmatched conditions. Data tended to either be culled from clinic databases or gathered across clients available in a clinic, with differences between matched and unmatched conditions described rather than experimentally tested. Although only one study involved senior adults, clients of a variety of ages were represented in the literature. The fact that 56% of studies involved middle-aged adults reflected the fact that data were most often collected in community mental health clinics. Treatment involved outpatient mental health services of various types and modalities.

Native American Indians and Alaska Natives were not examined in any of the studies we found, but other racial groups were represented. Clients of a single race (e.g., African American clients with either African American therapists or therapists of another race) were examined in 24 studies, clients of multiple races with therapists of a single race (e.g., White/European American therapists with clients of color contrasted with White/European American clients) were involved with 15 studies, and a combination of therapist and client races evaluated in a binary matrix, matched versus unmatched, was the subject of 14 studies. Overall, the 53 studies contained data from 62,434 individual clients, with a median number of 250 clients per study.

TABLE 6.1
Characteristics of 53 Studies of the Participation of Clients in Mental Health Services as a Function of Racial or Ethnic Match With the Therapist

Characteristic	M	No. of studies (k)	%
Year of report	1997		
Before 1980		2	4
1980–1989		5	9
1990–1999		28	53
2000–2013		18	34
Publication status			
Published		32	60
Unpublished dissertations		21	40
Research design			
Archival		22	41
Comparison groups		30	57
Retrospective survey		1	2
Participant selection			
Random		7	13
Convenience		46	87
Assignment to therapist			
Random		6	11
Convenience		47	89
Treatment modality			
Individual therapy		32	61
Group or family therapy		5	9
Mixed, individual and group/family		16	30
Sample size	1,178		
<50		3	6
50–99		11	21
103–199		10	19
200–399		8	15
400–999		6	11
> 1,000		15	28
Participant age[a]	31.0		
Children (< 13 years)		8	15
Adolescents (13–18 years)		6	11
Young adults (19–29 years)		6	11
Middle-aged adults (30–55 years)		30	56
Senior adults (> 56 years)		1	2
Participant gender (% female)	57.3		
Participant[b] race (%)			
African American	21		
Asian American	29		
Hispanic/Latino(a) American	19		
Native American Indian	0		
White/European American	30		
Other	0		

Note. Not all variables sum to the total number of studies because of missing data.
[a]Average age category of participants in studies, although not all study participants would necessarily be in the category listed. Three studies did not report information about client age. [b]The racial composition of participants across all studies was calculated by multiplying the number of participants in studies by the percentage of participants from each racial group and dividing that product by the total number of participants.

Research studies operationalized client participation both as (a) treatment attendance (number of sessions attended, return for additional treatment after an initial session, and number of days in treatment) and (b) treatment completion/attrition (completion of a proscribed protocol or certain number of sessions or judged by a therapist as having completed necessary treatment vs. premature treatment discontinuation). The effect sizes represent simple comparisons of these data across conditions of client–therapist match based on race or ethnicity.

Research Findings Across Racial Groups

Racial and ethnic differences in client attendance were first examined through a multivariate meta-analysis in which effect sizes specific to each racial or ethnic group were examined simultaneously (accounting for the observed value of $r = .07$ for within-study correlation of effect sizes). The overall model reached statistical significance, Wald X^2 (5) = 85.7, $p < .0001$, with the results by race as reported in Table 6.2. Asian American clients were moderately more likely to continue participating in mental health treatment when they were matched with a therapist of their own race, and they were much more likely than any other group to have increased participation in mental health treatment when matched with a therapist of their own race. Hispanic/Latino(a) Americans and African Americans were somewhat more likely to participate when they were matched, but the effect of matching on client participation was minimal for unspecified/other ethnic minorities. The participation level of White/European American clients was influenced very minimally by the therapist's race or ethnicity.

Across all 53 studies examining client attendance, the random effects weighted effect size was $d = .22$, a value that obscures the differences found across client race. The heterogeneity of the overall findings was very high,

TABLE 6.2
Weighted Mean Effect Sizes (Cohen's *d*) Across Participant Race

	k	d	SE	95% CI
African Americans	16	.19[a]	.08	[.04, .34]
Asian Americans	16	.46[b]	.07	[.31, .60]
Hispanic/Latino(a) Americans	15	.22[a, c]	.06	[.10, .33]
Unspecified/other ethnic minorities	22	.13[a]	.02	[.08, .18]
White/European Americans	8	.09	.06	[−.02, .20]
All groups combined	53	.22[a, c]	.03	[.16, .28]

Note. CI = confidence interval; k = number of studies; d = random effects weighted effect size; SE = standard error.
[a]Statistically significantly different from Asian Americans ($p < .001$). [b]Statistically significantly different from all other groups ($p < .001$). [c]Statistically significantly different from White/European Americans ($p \le .05$).

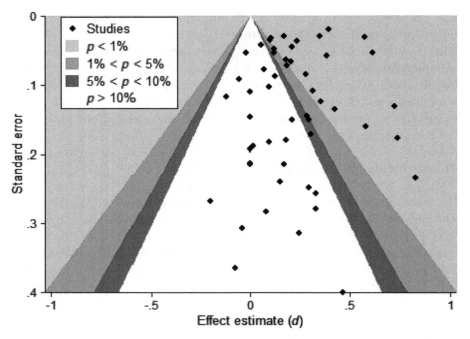

Figure 6.1. Contour-enhanced funnel plot of effect sizes (Cohen's *d*) by standard error for 53 studies of client participation in treatment as a function of racial or ethnic match with the therapist. In this graph the overall average is to the right of 0, but the results are widely scattered, with high variability even among studies with a large number of participants (and lower standard errors) depicted at the top of the graph. This inconsistent distribution restricts the interpretability of the overall average. Analyses were conducted by client race to reduce variability.

$I^2 = 87.7, 95\%$ CI $= [85, 90], Q_{(52)} = 428.9, p < .0001$, meaning that the overall results were very inconsistent across studies (see Figure 6.1).

Study and Participant Characteristics Influencing the Results

Studies involved a wide variety of participants and procedures, so we sought to determine if systematic differences in findings could be attributable to participant or study characteristics. Specifically, we conducted random effects weighted correlations with continuous level variables and random effects weighted analyses of variance with categorical level variables and with the study effect size as the dependent variable. Overall, no differences were found across client gender (operationalized as percent female), average age, education level, or socioeconomic status, and no differences were found across type of research design, including whether participants were or were not randomly selected and/or randomly assigned to matched versus unmatched conditions.

We observed a strong decline over time in the benefits of ethnic and racial matching on client participation in treatment, with the year of study publication correlating $-.48$ ($p < .001$) with effect sizes. Studies published before 1990 averaged $d = .42$, studies published in the 1990s averaged $d = .23$, and studies published since the year 2000 averaged $d = .14$.

The benefits of ethnic or racial matching were stronger when client participation was operationalized in terms of treatment completion ($d = .27$) rather than treatment attendance ($d = .15$, $p = .03$). The 33 studies that matched on the basis of race tended to show smaller benefits from the match than did the 20 studies that operationalized the match by ethnicity (e.g., Mexican American clients matched with Mexican American therapists; $d = .17$ and .28, respectively, $p = .03$). The 27 studies reporting the race of therapists showed a negative correlation ($r = -.39$, $p = .03$) between the percentage of White/European American therapists in the study and the effect size; thus, studies with predominantly White/European American therapists tended to find less benefit from racial or ethnic matching on the degree of client participation in treatment.

The five studies that explicitly matched clients who preferred a language other than English with a therapist who spoke the preferred language showed statistically significantly fewer benefits from a match based on race or ethnicity ($d = .08$) compared with the results of 18 studies with unknown procedures in which bilingual therapy or therapy in the preferred language may or may not have been provided to clients who spoke English as a second language ($d = .31$, $p < .05$). When therapy was provided in English to English speakers, the effect of racial or ethnic matching was $d = .18$, a value between those of the other two groups. These findings suggested that the effect of racial or ethnic matching was influenced by language matching for clients who preferred a language other than English. Specifically, the benefit of matching for clients who preferred to speak a language other than English was apparently more attributable to the match based on language than to the match based on race or ethnicity. When a therapist neither spoke the clients' preferred language nor shared the clients' race or ethnicity, the effect of racial or ethnic matching was almost four times as large as when language matching was provided.

Overall, the effect of racial or ethnic matching on client participation in treatment was moderated by language match, ethnic versus racial matching, percentage of White/European American therapists in the study, treatment completion versus treatment attendance, and year of publication. These several apparent moderating variables may have interacted with one another. We therefore sought to ascertain the degree to which these several variables affected effect sizes in the presence of one another by conducting random effects weighted regression models. Because the eight effect sizes specific to White/European Americans had previously been shown to be unrelated to client participation (Table 6.2), we excluded those data in the regression models to avoid confounding race with language matching and ethnic versus racial matching. Thus, the dependent variable for this analysis was the averaged effect size across only clients of color.

In the first model, which used all 53 studies, 38.9% of the variance in effect sizes was explained ($p < .0001$) by the combination of ethnic versus racial matching, treatment completion versus treatment attendance, language matching, and year of publication. At the univariate level, the two variables of explicit non-English language matching and year of publication reached statistical significance (standardized betas = $-.27$ and $-.37$, respectively, $p < .05$). In a second model, which considered the 27 studies that reported the racial composition of the therapists, the percentage of White/European American therapists in the study was entered along with the same four variables entered in the first model. This second model explained 46.4% of the variance in effect sizes ($p = .02$), again with only explicit non-English language matching (standardized beta = $-.45$, $p = .02$) and year of publication (standardized beta = $-.48$, $p = .01$) reaching statistical significance. Thus, although the combination of variables explained a substantial amount of effect size variance, apparent trends over time and explicit language matching among clients who preferred a language other than English were the variables that most explained study findings.

Likelihood of Publication Bias Adversely Influencing the Results

Meta-analytic results can be adversely affected by publication bias, given that unpublished studies are less likely to be located. In this meta-analysis, 32 published studies yielded stronger average effect sizes than 21 unpublished studies ($d = .27$ and $.14$, respectively, $p = .03$). Nevertheless, the inclusion of so many unpublished studies mitigated the possibility of publication bias. The overall data were fairly balanced on either side of the mean (see Figure 6.1), Egger's regression test (an estimate of asymmetry of effect sizes) did not reach statistical significance ($p > .05$), and one statistical method (Duval & Tweedie, 2000) did not identify any "missing" studies. These three analyses suggested that publication bias did not influence the overall findings.

DISCUSSION AND INTERPRETATION OF THE FINDINGS

Data from 53 research studies indicated that clients participated in mental health treatment at slightly higher rates and prematurely discontinued treatment less often when they had a therapist of their same race or ethnicity. However, the results differed across client race, with Asian American clients benefitting substantially when they had a therapist of their own race ($d = .46$), particularly a therapist of their own ethnicity (e.g., Japanese American client with a Japanese American therapist). In contrast, the treatment participation of White/European American clients differed to a small degree ($d = .09$) when they were matched or unmatched with the therapist.

On average, client age, education level, socioeconomic status, and gender did not affect findings across studies: Ethnic or racial matching yielded similar data irrespective of those attributes. Research findings have, however, changed substantially over time. The year in which a study was published was strongly related to the observed effect size ($d = -.48$), such that the impact of ethnic or racial matching on client participation levels has decreased markedly in recent years. Matching a client with a therapist of her or his same race would have been an important treatment consideration in the 1970s, but more recently that consideration would be one of several relevant to increasing client participation and decreasing premature termination.

Considerations for Future Research

The results of any meta-analysis are qualified by the quality, methodology, and research design of the studies included in the analysis (Cooper, Hedges, & Valentine, 2009). In this meta-analysis the majority of studies (87%) did not randomly select participants; thus, the available data lacked evidence of external validity. More problematic was that only 11% of the studies involved random assignment of clients to matched versus unmatched conditions. This flaw greatly restricts our confidence in the internal validity of the studies. Multiple plausible confounds could have adversely affected the research findings, including the fact that clients with a therapist of their same race or ethnicity may have preferred that arrangement. Such methodological confounds are so problematic that we see no value in conducting further research on this topic that does not involve randomization to matched versus unmatched conditions.

Prior research had indicated that potential clients tend to prefer a therapist of their own race or ethnicity but that this match improves therapeutic outcomes only to a small degree (Cabral & Smith, 2011). According to the data analyzed in this meta-analysis, that apparent discrepancy between strong client preferences and weak outcome effects cannot be primarily attributed to differential participant attrition across matched versus unmatched conditions. Client attrition is problematic and requires attention, but it is not strongly affected by therapist race or ethnicity except for Asian American clients.

The specific factors that influence Asian American clients' participation in treatment deserve additional research attention (e.g., S. Sue, Cheng, Saad, & Chu, 2012). Among other explanations, the differences across client race likely reflect underlying differences in worldviews. Psychotherapy originated in Europe and North America and was therefore initially designed for White/European American clients (Pedersen, 2000). Asian Americans who engage in mental health treatments appear to benefit when Asian American therapists understand and account for their cultural experiences and worldviews that are pertinent to mental health and symptom change. Research to confirm this assertion that acculturation to Western methods of treatment accounts for the observed differences across race would be helpful, particularly because research has not yet examined groups such as Native American Indians and Alaska Natives.

Researchers can also attend more to issues of language. Because of numerous logistical difficulties, people with limited English proficiency can be excluded from research studies (Acevedo, Reyes, Annett, & López, 2003). In our analysis, only five studies (9%) explicitly matched clients who preferred a language other than English with a therapist who spoke that language. Data analyses suggested that the effects of racial or ethnic matching were primarily accounted for by language matching for clients who spoke English as a second language. The field would benefit from further investigation of language issues and from taking seriously the benefits of conducting treatment in the clients' preferred language if other than English.

Researchers must keep in mind that although the variables of race and ethnicity are important, they are broad descriptions that tell us little about how a client and therapist may actually interact in therapy. Variables that may increase understanding of client–therapist interactions include the therapist's multicultural competence and worldview congruence with the client. Those more specific variables have not received nearly as much attention in the research literature, yet likely influence client participation in therapy more than therapist race or ethnicity. Clients and therapists who share the same race or ethnicity do not necessarily share similar worldviews (Ibaraki & Hall, 2014). Although matching may be important for some clients, not all will benefit from this practice (S. Sue, 1988). As S. Sue and Zane (1987) suggested several decades ago, researchers should shift their focus from distal to proximal variables.

Recommendations for Practitioners

Hypothetically, matching clients with therapists of their same race or ethnicity should foster feelings of being understood, improve the therapeutic relationship, and increase a client's level of participation in treatment. Clients of color, particularly African American clients, tend to prefer this arrangement (Cabral & Smith, 2011). Therapists working with clients from races or ethnicities other than their own may therefore have some concern about how the client will engage in treatment. Most clients seeking therapy are more interested in factors other than therapist race, notably decreasing emotional pain and working through difficulties. Although perceived similarities with the therapist can provide a feeling of immediate connection, genuine respect must eventually be earned by the therapist, irrespective of race.

In particular, therapists of color can be confident that racial differences typically do not affect White/European American clients' participation in treatment. On average White/European American clients' choice to remain in treatment is essentially unaffected by whether the therapist shares their racial or ethnic background.

Moreover, matching clients of color with therapists of their same race or ethnicity is often unfeasible for a variety of reasons, including the fact that there are fewer available therapists of color (American Psychological Association, 2005). Even if it were possible to consistently match clients and therapists according to race or ethnicity, doing so might have unintended negative consequences (Alladin, 2002). For example, well-intentioned therapists may inadvertently fail to acknowledge other meaningful differences (e.g., level of acculturation) or dismiss the fact that within-group differences can be larger than between-group differences. Such oversights could curtail the effectiveness of psychotherapy and inadvertently contribute to the client being misunderstood.

Nevertheless, the data from this meta-analysis do suggest that something systematic needs to be done to better retain Asian American clients who have a therapist from another background. When Chinese American therapists are available to work with Chinese American clients, for example, such an arrangement would likely increase client participation. However, other practices could also increase client retention, such as incorporating culturally sensitive adaptations to therapy and providing therapists with ongoing multicultural training. Therapists working with Asian American clients especially have to proactively explore and implement practices to improve engagement and retention.

Practitioners may increase client participation and retention by providing therapy in clients' preferred language when other than English. Clients for whom English is a second language can find this a barrier to receiving high quality services (Acevedo et al., 2003). American Psychological Association guidelines (2003) suggest that mental health professionals interact in the language requested by the client or provide a professional language interpreter.

CONCLUSION

When clients of color are matched with a therapist of their same race or ethnicity, they tend to remain in treatment somewhat longer and drop out less frequently than when they have a therapist from a different racial or ethnic background. The benefits were particularly notable for Asian American clients. However, the research findings were more robust in past decades than at present, and findings vary substantially across studies. Many factors other than therapist race or ethnicity affect client levels of participation in mental health treatment.

At present, the research literature is of insufficient quality to justify more solid conclusions. Nevertheless, given the declining influence of racial or ethnic matching on client participation rates, we do not believe that continuing this line of inquiry will yield as much benefit to treatment participation among clients of color as would other strategies. These may include working to increase the number of bilingual therapists and therapists of color and enhancing the multicultural competence of therapists from all racial and ethnic backgrounds. In effect, few clients who discontinue therapy would identify the therapist's race or ethnicity as the deciding factor. More likely, they would speak of misunderstandings, insufficient emotional support, diverging views, incompatible opinions about what should be done, and so forth. Those are the key issues for therapists and researchers to address. It is time to identify precisely the reasons why clients prematurely discontinue therapy—and implement solutions.

7

CULTURALLY ADAPTED MENTAL HEALTH SERVICES: AN UPDATED META-ANALYSIS OF CLIENT OUTCOMES

When clients from diverse backgrounds seek professional mental health services, several concerns may arise: Will this therapist respect my beliefs and values? Will this therapist promote mainstream (White/European American) worldviews and solutions? Can I truly be myself in therapy? Clients may not verbalize these specific concerns, but these are among many that may adversely affect client outcomes in traditional therapy (S. Sue & Zane, 1987; S. Sue et al., 2006). Thus, clinicians should ask this critical question: To what extent does the therapy I provide align with the cultural beliefs, values, and goals of this client?

Although mental health treatments have proliferated in recent decades, most treatments are based on theories that reflect European and European

Alberto Soto and Derek Griner, both of Brigham Young University, contributed to the writing of this chapter.

A complete list of references for the studies included in this chapter's meta-analysis is posted online. Readers can consult it at http://pubs.apa.org/books/supp/smith

http://dx.doi.org/10.1037/14733-007

American ideals and values (e.g., psychodynamic, client-centered, cognitive–behavioral). As such, these traditional mental health treatments have frequently ignored or minimized contextual variables such as culture, gender, race and ethnicity, socioeconomic status, and religious and spiritual values (G. C. N. Hall, 2001; Ibaraki & Hall, 2014; Ponterotto, Casas, Suzuki, & Alexander, 2010). Rather than assume that any particular treatment will meet the needs of every client, therapists must consider these contextual and environmental variables to effectively align the treatment with the needs and experiences of the client (Cardemil, 2010b; Norcross & Wampold, 2011).

Cultural adaptations should be made to traditional treatments to better meet the needs of a diverse clientele (Castro, Barrera, & Holleran Steiker, 2010; Gone & Trimble, 2012; T. B. Smith, 2010). For instance, because Western values such as assertive individuation may contradict psychological well-being as conceptualized by clients from collectivistic cultures, therapists working with these populations may find that explicitly addressing the clients' social cohesion may prove more effective than the individualistic focus of many mental health treatments. Thus, a therapist working with Hispanic/Latino(a) American clients could consider family involvement in treatment (Falicov, 2009; Hurwich-Reiss, Rindlaub, Wadsworth, & Markman, 2014). Alternatively, a therapist who generally practices a strictly behavioral orientation to treatment might benefit from considering the cultural beliefs of a client who may think that ancestral spirits cause depression, even if most of the interventions remain behavioral in nature. A therapist who has discerned that an Alaska Native client favors traditional worldviews could incorporate cultural imagery and metaphors. Culturally competent treatments involve adaptations to methods of delivery, content, and conceptualizations, such that the client becomes more likely to engage in and successfully complete the treatment provided (S. Sue, Zane, Nagayama Hall, & Berger, 2009; Zane & Ku, 2014).

Psychologists have an ethical obligation to provide the most effective service available to their clients (Trimble, Scharrón-del-Río, & Hill, 2012; Vasquez, 2012). Much of the therapy literature focuses attention on evidence-based practices (EBPs; Kazdin, 2008), but EBPs, like most standardized treatment approaches, do not account for the needs of culturally diverse clients (La Roche & Christopher, 2008). Treatments provided should be based on evidence, but therapists must remember that no single EBP will work with every client. They must attend to cultural factors that influence therapy (Cardemil, 2010a; T. B. Smith, 2010; S. Sue, 2003; Trimble et al., 2012) and realize that cultural adaptations to EBPs are justified (Castro et al., 2010). Therapists who assume that an EBP is equally effective across all cultures take a universalistic approach to treatment, giving deference to the particular EBP over the realities of a particular client. These therapists may inappropriately apply the EBP by setting goals and embracing values that coincide with their own culture but not the client's culture (Comas-Díaz, 2006; Falicov, 2009). The field of multicultural psychology should help to replace culturally insensitive treatments (even those that may be evidence based) with culturally appropriate services.

Although cultural adaptations to mental health treatments are beneficial, they must be done systematically, using empirical data to support implementation (Barrera, Castro, Strycker, & Toobert, 2013; Domenech Rodríguez & Bernal, 2012; Huey, Tilley, Jones, & Smith, 2014). Multicultural psychology cannot assume that particular culturally adapted treatments are superior to traditional treatments without evidence and without simultaneous reliance on empirical data to refine the cultural adaptations made (G. Bernal, Jiménez-Chafey, & Domenech Rodríguez, 2009; Cardemil, 2010b; Castro et al., 2010; Huey et al., 2014). Cultural adaptations should be subject to the same intense scrutiny necessary for any high-risk activity involving individuals' well-being. Research on the effectiveness of cultural adaptations will help mental health professionals understand how best to apply the abstract principles of multicultural psychology to real world practices, with the goal of improving the outcomes of diverse clients over outcomes of treatment as usual.

REVIEW OF THE LITERATURE

Relevant Conceptual Issues

Although psychotherapy is relatively modern, mental health treatments are ancient. Cultures across the world have long practiced healing rituals or provided worldviews to enhance coping with psychological distress and mental illness (Calabrese, 2008; McCubbin & Marsella, 2009). Significant improvements in mental health treatments over the past century should not be misinterpreted to mean that all other conceptualizations and practices relevant to mental health are invalid or archaic. Psychologists have no monopoly on effective mental health treatments.

Furthermore, although many individuals in North America have come to see psychotherapy as a socially acceptable method for treating mental health concerns, individuals from other cultural origins may not feel the same way. Many individuals from diverse cultural backgrounds consider Western forms of psychotherapeutic interventions to be strange, invalidating, and intrusive (C. C. I. Hall, 1997; Jackson, Schmutzer, Wenzel, & Tyler, 2006). Although psychotherapy is effective (Campbell, Norcross, Vasquez, & Kaslow, 2013; Lambert, 2007), racial and ethnic minorities may encounter barriers such as difficulties discussing the negative consequences of racism with White therapists (D. W. Sue, 2015) and may therefore have outcomes less positive than expected (S. Sue, 1998). Some scholars have therefore advocated that psychologists in North America attend to indigenous conceptualizations and practices, with methods specific to local contexts increasingly being developed (U. Kim, Yang, & Hwang, 2006; Ramos & Alegría, 2014). In situations where indigenous approaches to psychology are insufficiently understood or are impractical to inform mental health treatments, mental health practitioners can use existing EBPs, adapting them to align with clients' cultural values and worldviews (Barrera et al., 2013).

Several decades ago, Stanley Sue (1977) specifically recommended that therapists culturally adapt treatment at the client–therapist level as well as at a system level. His original suggestions have become a catalyst for subsequent culturally sensitive treatments. These suggestions included (a) conducting therapy in the client's preferred language, (b) matching clients and therapists according to race or ethnicity, (c) developing mental health clinics that cater to specific racial or ethnic groups, and (d) providing alternative methods for mental health services delivery (G. Bernal & Flores-Ortiz, 1982; Flaskerud, 1986; Miranda et al., 2005; S. Sue, 1977). The first suggestion, language matching, was an obvious improvement over the common English-only services, but simply translating content into a client's preferred language would not correct underlying cultural differences in conceptualizations of mental health or methods for enhancing well-being. The second recommendation, racial matching, has proven effective in delimited circumstances (Cabral & Smith, 2011; see also Chapter 6, this volume), such as those involving African Americans and immigrant populations. The third recommendation has not been widely heeded, because few contemporary clinics provide specialized services for a given racial or ethnic group. Over time, the fourth recommendation, providing alternative methods and cultural modifications to existing methods, has received more emphasis than the other three (e.g., S. W. Chen & Davenport, 2005; T. B. Smith, 2010; S. Sue et al., 2009).

Cultural adaptations can be made according to the concept of *dynamic sizing* (S. Sue, 1998), accounting for commonalities in culturally diverse groups while also respecting and attending to individual differences (La Roche & Lustig, 2010). For example, a Native American Indian client who embraces indigenous spirituality may benefit from a spiritual healing ritual integrated into therapy (Calabrese, 2008; Trimble, King, Morse, & Thomas, 2014). However, a Chinese American client who was raised and educated in the United States may prefer standard cognitive behavioral therapy (CBT) techniques to a version of CBT adapted to account for traditional Chinese worldviews and values (S. W. Chen & Davenport, 2005). Thus, therapists should be mindful to align treatment with individual clients' cultural worldviews (La Roche & Lustig, 2013), rather than assume that standard (nonadapted) treatment is sufficient (Cardemil, 2010a) or implement cultural adaptations without verifying whether they actually match the client's worldviews, including acculturation level (S. Sue, 2010). Therapists should tailor the treatment to the individual client (Norcross & Wampold, 2011), not assume generalization without evidence for generalization (Cardemil, 2010b; S. Sue, 1999).

Given the essential culturally specific expertise needed for such adaptations to treatment, clinicians may feel overwhelmed, particularly when considering the many possible ways that treatment could be modified to better align with cultural factors. To help specify the types of cultural adaptations that should be most effective in mental health treatments, scholars have developed conceptual frameworks to help guide clinicians.

An ecological validity model (G. Bernal, Bonilla, & Bellido, 1995) addressed eight specific cultural domains that clinicians should consider when working with culturally diverse clients:

- *language adaptions*—extending beyond interpretation and translation to include terminology and methods for communicating that are appropriate to the client's particular background (e.g., for Mexican Americans, the phrase *échale ganas* rather than "hang in there");
- *persons*—the attention that should be directed to the client–therapist relationship, particularly cultural similarities and differences (Asnaani & Hofmann, 2012);
- *metaphors*—the symbols, folklore, and concepts shared by a cultural group of individuals (Parra Cardona et al., 2012);
- *content*—culture-specific beliefs and practices (e.g., religious and spiritual beliefs, cultural history and traditions) that can be infused in therapeutic interventions (McCabe, Yeh, Lau, & Argote, 2012);
- *concepts*—ways in which presenting concerns are conceptualized in a culturally congruent manner (e.g., accepting somatic conceptualizations of depression vs. depression conceptualized only in terms of emotional distress; exploring religious or spiritual concepts to explain suffering and healing; S. W. Chen & Davenport, 2005);
- *goals* for treatment, which should align with the cultural worldview of the client (e.g., collectivism vs. individualism; see Diaz-Martinez, Interian, & Waters, 2010);
- *methods* of treatment, which should be adapted for the individual needs of the client, congruent with his or her worldview (e.g., family-centered therapy vs. individual therapy); and
- *context*—the broader issues (e.g., acculturative stress, racial microaggressions, immigration, poverty) that culturally diverse

clients may commonly face (Hinton, Rivera, Hofmann, Barlow, & Otto, 2012; La Roche, D'Angelo, Gualdron, & Leavell, 2006).

Therapists should attend to multiple dimensions such as these when culturally adapting mental health treatments. Additional considerations and frameworks for practice also provide guidance but cannot be detailed in this chapter (Barrera & Castro, 2006; Hwang, 2006, 2009; Lau, 2006; Leong, 2011; Whitbeck, 2006).

Although research-based models provide a framework for addressing cultural factors that may be ignored by traditional forms of therapy (Domenech Rodríguez & Bernal, 2012; Huey et al., 2014), clinicians should be receptive to client feedback about what has and has not worked for them (Lambert, 2010). Researchers and clinicians may find that appropriate adaptations can be assessed through focus groups with individuals from the relevant community. A therapist might also consult community leaders, religious and spiritual leaders, scholars, and client family members for insight into the appropriateness of proposed adaptations for a specific cultural group, rather than attempting to address several culturally diverse groups with the same intervention (T. B. Smith, Rodríguez, & Bernal, 2011). The balance of appropriate etic versus emic adaptations is difficult, but it can be attained by thoughtful and purposeful consultation with clients and examination of the relevant literature, which includes several books on the topic of cultural adaptations (G. Bernal & Rodríguez, 2012; La Roche, 2012; C. J. Yeh, Parham, Gallardo, & Trimble, 2011).

Narrative Review of the Research Literature

Several years after guidelines for cultural adaptations of treatments were publicized, culturally congruent services remained rare (S. Sue et al., 2006). Nevertheless, the topic has received increasing professional interest (G. Bernal et al., 2009; Cardemil, 2010b; Huey et al., 2014; Ramos & Alegría, 2014). Meta-analyses have shown that cultural adaptations of treatments are, in fact, effective (Benish, Quintana, & Wampold, 2011; Chowdhary et al., 2014; T. B. Smith et al., 2011; van Loon, van Schaik, Dekker, & Beekman, 2013). The first of these reviews (Griner & Smith, 2006) found that the average effect sizes for quasi-experimental and experimental designs were $d = .42$ and $d = .40$, respectively. A subsequent update to that meta-analysis (T. B. Smith et al., 2011) found that when the results were adjusted for apparent publication bias, the average effect size was $d = .27$. A review of culturally adapted treatments for youth reported an average effect size of $d = .22$ when the control group received treatment as usual (Huey & Polo, 2008). Another meta-analysis (Benish et al., 2011) reported an average effect size of $d = .32$ when comparing culturally adapted treatments with bona-fide treatments. A recent review, limited to nine studies of outpatient treatment for depression and anxiety (van Loon et al., 2013), found substantially greater effectiveness ($d = 1.06$). A review of 20 studies specific to the treatment of depression also found a large average effect size ($d = .72$; Chowdhary et al., 2014). Another recent review has summarized much of that work (Huey et al., 2014).

Overall, these meta-analyses and reviews have documented benefits of culturally adapted treatments when working with culturally diverse clients. Researchers and clinicians are, however, continually finding new and innovative ways to attend to cultural factors in therapy. The increasing number of research studies of culturally adapted treatments means that the literature must be continuously evaluated so practitioners can benefit from the latest findings and trends. Thus, we sought to update our previous meta-analysis of culturally adapted interventions by searching out additional data. After presenting the details of the meta-analysis, a summary of the findings is presented in a subsequent section.

QUANTITATIVE SYNTHESIS OF RESEARCH DATA

Our updated meta-analysis included studies identified in previous meta-analyses (Benish et al., 2011; T. B. Smith et al., 2011) that were conducted in the United States or Canada; evaluated clients' experiences in mental health services that were adapted on the basis of culture, race, or ethnicity; and involved a control group using a quasi-experimental or experimental research design. We included any type of control group, and we recorded the nature of the control group because we were planning to compare those studies involving equivalent mental health services not culturally adapted (e.g., treatment as usual) with no treatment (e.g., clients on a waiting list receiving no services). We excluded studies with more than 10% White/European American clients or control group members because the cultural adaptations were presumed to enhance the experiences of people of color, such that the treatments would have different meaning for White/European American clients.

Statistical estimates within studies were converted to Cohen's d using meta-analytic software. Positive values for effect sizes indicated improved client outcomes (decreased symptoms, higher treatment completion rates) over the control group, whereas negative values indicated worse client outcomes compared with the control group. General methods of the meta-analysis are reported in the Appendix of this book.

Description of the Existing Research Literature

We located 108 studies that evaluated a culturally adapted mental health treatment. However, we analyzed data from only 79 studies because 17 involved a single group of participants tracked over time (evaluating pre- to posttest changes without a control group), eight involved a substantial number (>10%) of White/European American participants, two involved correlational designs, one reported client treatment participation but no client outcome information, and one involved extended follow-up data to a previously published study already included in the review. As shown in Table 7.1, the 79 studies were conducted primarily during the past 2 decades, with most of the studies located being published. Subjects tended to be either children and adolescents or middle-aged adults, reflecting a trend in the literature for treatments to be either prevention-oriented (treating "at-risk" groups) or clinically oriented (examining groups in community mental health clinics). Asian Americans and Hispanic/Latino(a) Americans were the two groups most commonly evaluated in studies. By contrast, African Americans and Native American Indians were evaluated in only 14% and 7% of the studies, respectively.

Overall, the manuscripts contained data from 12,014 individual clients, but the median number of clients was 60, a small number of participants given that about half were in control group conditions. The types of cultural adaptations varied substantially across studies. Some studies clearly followed existing guidelines available in the professional literature (e.g., G. Bernal et al., 1995), but others had produced thin descriptions and/or had delimited adaptations to a few aspects of culture:

- 76% included explicit mention of cultural content and values in treatment,
- 70% provided treatment in the client's preferred language when other than English,
- 60% matched clients with therapists of similar ethnic and racial backgrounds,
- 53% addressed clients' contextual issues (e.g., experiences of racism, employment),
- 48% used metaphors from client cultures,
- 47% modified the methods of delivering therapy on the basis of cultural considerations,
- 46% indicated that they had developed the cultural adaptations through consultation with individuals from the culture,
- 43% adhered to the client's conceptualization of the presenting problem,

TABLE 7.1
Characteristics of 79 Studies of Culturally Adapted Treatments

Characteristic	M	No. of studies (k)	%
Year of report	2000		
Before 1980		0	0
1980–1989		8	10
1990–1999		26	33
2000–2012		45	57
Publication status			
Published		63	80
Unpublished dissertations		16	20
Research design			
Quasi-experimental		19	24
Experimental		60	76
Sample type			
Community members		9	11
At-risk clients		41	52
Clinical clients		29	37
Sample size	152		
<50		31	39
50–99		30	38
100–199		9	11
200–399		4	5
400–999		2	3
>1,000		3	4
Age of participants[a]	25.5		
Children (<13 years)		22	28
Adolescents (13–18 years)		20	25
Young adults (19–29 years)		4	5
Middle-aged adults (30–55 years)		29	37
Senior adults (>56 years)		4	5
Gender of participants (% female)	58.4		
Race of participants[b] (%)			
African American	14		
Asian American	44		
Hispanic/Latino(a) American	35		
Native American Indian	7		
Other	<1		

Note. Not all variables sum to the total number of studies because of missing data.
[a]Average age category of participants within studies, not all participants necessarily listed. [b]The racial composition of participants across all studies, calculated by multiplying the number of participants within studies by the percentage of participants from each racial group and dividing that product by the total number of participants.

- 42% based their cultural adaptations on published research or theoretical models,
- 21% reported that mental health staff had received training in the cultural adaptations,
- 18% modified the wording of outcome instrumentation to be culturally appropriate, and
- 11% explicitly solicited culturally congruent outcome goals from the client.

On average, studies reported 3.9 out of the eight components of G. Bernal's model (G. Bernal et al., 1995). Only 14 studies (18%) involved more than five of the eight components. Thus, on the whole, the studies made attempts to culturally adapt treatment without adhering closely to best practices.

The typical study involved an experimental design in which clients were randomly assigned to either a culturally adapted mental health treatment or "treatment as usual." In those studies, the effect size represents an estimate of the effectiveness of culturally adapted treatments. For the 24% of studies using quasi-experimental designs (nonrandom group composition) and the 47% of studies using no-treatment controls (clients on a waiting list), the magnitude of the effect size estimates would be influenced by factors other than the culturally adapted nature of the intervention; these studies thus warranted separate analyses. We also considered it essential to distinguish the results from studies using mental health treatments with clinical populations from results of studies involving prevention-oriented interventions for at-risk populations, because the nature of the services provided would necessarily differ, and client outcomes and rate of change would also likely differ.

Overall Findings by Research Design, Control Group Type, and Treatment Type

Across all 79 studies examining a culturally adapted mental health treatment, the random effects weighted effect size was $d = 0.47$ ($SE = .043$, 95% CI = [0.39, 0.57], $p < .0001$). The heterogeneity of the findings was high ($I^2 = 72.0$, 95% CI = [65, 78]; $Q_{(78)} = 278.9$, $p < .0001$), meaning that the results tended to be very inconsistent across studies (see Figure 7.1). In the 60 studies in which participants were randomly assigned to treatment conditions (true experimental designs), average results were statistically significantly more effective than in the 19 studies using nonrandom assignment of clients to treatment conditions (quasi-experimental designs; $d = 0.55$ vs. $d = 0.28$, $p = .004$). This finding was unexpected because experimental designs that remove some plausible confounds (e.g., impact of self-selection on treatment effectiveness) typically result in more conservative effect sizes than designs in which confounds

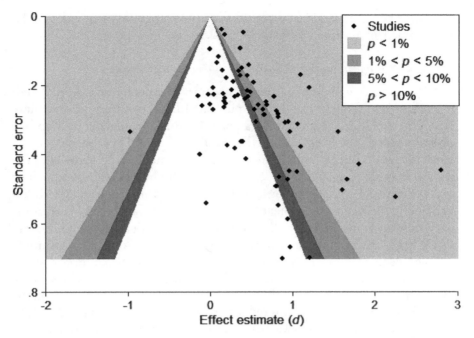

Figure 7.1. Contour-enhanced funnel plot of effect sizes (Cohen's *d*) by standard error for 79 studies of culturally adapted treatments. This graph shows the distribution of effect sizes as a function of the number of participants in the study (operationalized as standard error). The studies at the top of the graph are those with many participants (and small standard error values), studies that yielded results in the range of $d = 0.0–0.5$. The fewer the participants, the less consistent the results. Moreover, in the middle and bottom of the graph are few studies with nonsignificant results (note the absence of dots in the white area relative to the top of the graph and to the right of the graph). This distribution strongly suggests publication bias in the available literature; the overall average effect estimate should therefore be adjusted closer to zero ($d = .31$) to account for apparently "missing" nonsignificant findings.

are uncontrolled. Also contrary to expectations, no meaningful difference was evident between the findings of the 37 studies comparing outcomes of treatment groups to those of no-treatment control groups (i.e., clients on a waiting list) and the findings of the 42 studies comparing outcomes in the experimental group with outcomes of clients receiving a bona fide treatment (treatment as usual; $d = 0.49$ vs. $d = 0.46$, $p > .10$).

Comparison of treatments for clinical populations versus prevention-oriented programs for at-risk populations yielded similar results ($d = 0.47$ vs. $d = 0.52$, $p > .10$). When we restricted analyses of those two types of studies to experimental designs with comparison groups receiving a comparable (but nonadapted) intervention, 12 treatments for clinical populations yielded an effect size of $d = 0.56$, and 15 prevention-oriented programs for at-risk populations yielded an average effect size of $d = 0.59$.

Likelihood of Publication Bias Adversely Influencing the Results

When a researcher obtains results contrary to expectation (i.e., null findings), those results are less likely to be published and therefore more difficult to locate in a literature search and meta-analysis. This so-called publication bias can shift meta-analytic data toward the hypothesis favored by scholars, because nonsignificant results were unrepresented. In this meta-analytic review, publication bias apparently did influence the overall findings we reported. The data in Figure 7.1 were asymmetric, with a notable dearth of studies with few participants that did not achieve statistically significant results, indicating that studies with negative or null results had not been located in our literature search. Egger's regression test (an estimate of effect size asymmetry) was statistically significant ($p < .0001$), indicative of publication bias. In addition, one statistical method (Duval & Tweedie, 2000) identified 22 "missing" studies in the distribution. When those hypothetically missing data were accounted for, the resulting omnibus effect size was reduced to $d = 0.31$ (95% CI = [0.22, 0.40]). Evidence of publication bias was also found in the restricted sample of studies using an experimental design with a comparable treatment for the control group (i.e., culturally adapted treatment vs. "treatment as usual"). Thus, the results presented in the previous section represent liberal estimates, and the influence of publication bias will need to be accounted for when interpreting the results and in subsequent analyses.

Study and Participant Characteristics Influencing the Results

Study and participant characteristics had been found to moderate the results of a previous meta-analysis (T. B. Smith et al., 2011). Specifically, the effectiveness of culturally adapted mental health treatments had been found to be greater among (a) adult client populations older than 35 to 40 years, (b) racially homogeneous samples of clients (with homogeneity being one indicator of specificity of cultural adaptions), (c) Asian American clients, and (d) studies involving multiple cultural adaptations (with more cultural adaptations producing more effective treatments). We sought to ascertain whether these variables would remain predictors of treatment effectiveness when the influence of publication bias and experimental versus quasi-experimental research design were considered. A meta-regression including these six variables explained 33.1% of the variance in effect sizes ($p < .0001$), with the results depicted in Table 7.2. All variables contributed at least 1% of variance to the model, as indicated by beta weights above .10, but two variables—the percentage of Asian American participants and the racial homogeneity of

TABLE 7.2
Random Effects Regression Weights for Study
Characteristics Associated With Effect Sizes

Variable	R^2	β	p
	33.1***		
Estimate of publication bias[a]		.25	.006
Sum of cultural adaptations[b]		.25	.005
Random assignment to treatment type		.27	.005
Average client age		.26	.006
Percentage of Asian American clients		.14	.16
Client racial homogeneity within studies[c]		.11	.23

Note. [a]Inverse of the number of participants in the study (Peters, Sutton, Jones, Abrams, & Rushton, 2006). [b]Sum of the eight indicators of the ecological model (G. Bernal, Bonilla, & Bellido, 1995). [c]Contrast of studies in which all participants were of the same race with studies in which participants' race varied, *** $p < .001$.

the client participants—failed to reach statistical significance in the presence of the other variables ($k = 79$). The other four variables contributed equivalently to the model, each explaining between 6% and 7% of the variance in effect sizes. Culturally adapted mental health treatments continued to appear to be most effective for adult populations over age 40, likely interacting with acculturation level. And treatments involving multiple cultural adaptations were more effective than those with only a few types of cultural adaptations: The more closely a treatment aligned with recommended practices (e.g., G. Bernal et al., 1995), the more effective the treatment.

A separate meta-regression was conducted to examine whether any particular cultural adaptation was more predictive of positive client outcomes than any other. Indicators of the eight components of the ecological validity model (G. Bernal et al., 1995) explained 16.3% of the variance in effect sizes ($p = .02$). The two types of cultural adaptations that remained statistically significant in the presence of the others were (a) explicitly basing treatment on the client's goals, informed by cultural values (standardized beta = 0.25, $p = .03$) and (b) providing treatment in the clients' preferred language (standardized beta = 0.21, $p = .04$). Both of these adaptations had proven effective in a previous meta-analysis (Griner & Smith, 2006).

DISCUSSION AND INTERPRETATION OF THE FINDINGS

Compared with treatment as usual, culturally adapted treatments result in better outcomes for clients of color. Nevertheless, the underlying findings are highly variable (Figure 7.1), such that some culturally adapted treatments are clearly preferable to others. In fact, some culturally adapted treatments are about as effective as or worse than nonadapted treatment as usual (see also Huey et al., 2014). The distinguishing features of studies with findings of effective versus ineffective cultural adaptations were random assignment of clients to treatment conditions, treatment of adult clients above age 40 (likely conflated with level of acculturation), and more comprehensive cultural adaptations. Treatments were particularly effective when based on clients' goals, informed by cultural contexts, and provided in clients' preferred language. However, we observed a troubling trend for publication bias. Studies with null findings are apparently remaining unpublished. After accounting for publication bias, the magnitude of the overall results for studies using true experimental designs to compare culturally adapted treatments to bona fide treatments was $d = .31$.

Considerations for Future Research

Researchers must continually evaluate psychotherapeutic interventions to ensure that clients are receiving the best services available. Because several meta-analytic reviews have confirmed that cultural adaptations do result in better client outcomes than bona fide treatments, researchers can ask additional questions: What makes culturally adapted treatments more effective than traditional practices? Why are some culturally adapted treatments very effective but others not much better than control group conditions (see Figure 7.1)? In such examinations, scholars can explicitly evaluate the postulates of relevant conceptual models (Barrera & Castro, 2006; G. Bernal et al., 1995; Hwang, 2006, 2009; Lau, 2006; Leong, 2011; Whitbeck, 2006). We know that cultural adaptations work, but we now need more specific information about the underlying mechanisms and processes (T. B. Smith, 2010).

We need greater attention to cultural adaptations to treatments involving Native American Indian clients, who are currently underrepresented in research studies. Additional studies involving African American clients would also be useful. The field already has enough studies with relatively small numbers of participants, given that the median value was only 60 clients across 79 studies. With the variability in research findings among studies using relatively few participants (note range of effect sizes across bottom two thirds of Figure 7.1), large multi-site research projects would be more useful. We encourage scholars in the field to collaborate on large-scale projects rather than work on separate small ones.

We also invite scholars as well as journal reviewers and editors to consider the issue of publication bias. Studies with statistically significant findings appear to be published more frequently than studies with nonsignificant results. Authors may be reluctant to submit manuscripts with findings that contradict the data evaluated in previous meta-analyses, and editors may be reluctant to publish them. This reluctance creates a problem: Not all cultural adaptations work (note the many points in the center area of nonsignificant results in Figure 7.1), and we do not benefit from science when failures remain hidden.

Suggestions for Practitioners

In our review of the literature, we located several models and conceptual frameworks that can be used by clinicians to culturally adapt mental health treatments (Barrera & Castro, 2006; G. Bernal et al., 1995; Hwang, 2006, 2009; Lau, 2006; Leong, 2011; Whitbeck, 2006). Clinicians should follow these models (Castro et al., 2010), but we found few instances of clinical practice that were explicitly based on them. On average, the treatments in the 79 studies we examined used 3.9 out of eight aspects of G. Bernal's model (G. Bernal et al., 1995), with only 14% using more than five. Clinical practices reported in the literature are beneficial but fall short of the ideal. There are, no doubt, practical reasons why few clinicians consider the conceptual frameworks available in the literature and why only about half of the recommended dimensions of adaptation are implemented. Identification of those reasons can facilitate removal of barriers and eventual implementation of best practices. The more cultural adaptations a therapist makes to a treatment, the more effective that treatment is likely to be with clients of color. We urge practitioners to implement professional recommendations for culturally adapting mental health treatments.

Among the practices clinicians use to culturally adapt treatment, aligning treatment goals with the cultural worldviews and values of each client currently seems to be the most effective. This strategy yielded the strongest client outcomes across the few studies that implemented it. Therapists should give particular heed to working toward client-generated goals that incorporate cultural contexts. This process will help the clinician gain insight into the cultural worldview of the client and will also promote an egalitarian relationship, empowering the client.

The meta-analytic data also support providing treatment in the client's preferred language, consistent with existing professional guidelines:

> Psychologists interact in the language requested by the client and, if this is not feasible, make an appropriate referral. . . . If this is not possible, psychologists offer the client a translator with cultural knowledge and an appropriate professional background. When no translator is available, then a trained paraprofessional from the client's culture is used as a translator/culture broker. (American Psychological Association, 1993, p. 47)

We hope that practitioners will make services available to clients who prefer a language other than English by using language interpreters or by actively using referral networks to find professionals with the necessary language skills.

CONCLUSION

Culturally diverse clients benefit from efforts to align mental health treatments with their cultural values and worldviews. However, culturally adapted treatments vary in their effectiveness; some are very effective, whereas others are only slightly better, or even less effective, than nonadapted treatment as usual (Huey et al., 2014). Effective treatments tend to involve comprehensive cultural adaptations, as clinicians align their work with the cultural values and worldviews of the clients.

8

ACCULTURATION LEVEL AND PERCEPTIONS OF MENTAL HEALTH SERVICES AMONG PEOPLE OF COLOR: A META-ANALYSIS

> A number of behavioral and social scientists take the position that: Social change is accompanied by the intensification of social and cultural sources of psychological conflict, by new stresses and new adaptation require-ments in new milieus, and by the loss of the stabilizing effect of old cul-tural patterns.
>
> —Ari Kiev (1972, p. 9)

As psychiatrist Ari Kiev has pointed out, social and cultural change intensifies the psychological conflicts typically brought on by the need to adapt to new and unfamiliar circumstances. Vast societal and organizational changes in the Western world over the past 400 years have produced corre-sponding changes in both indigenous and immigrant populations. For indige-nous aboriginal populations, those changes were invariably imposed through colonization, legislation, war, and disease. In contrast, immigrants sought change. Indeed, many individuals from a wide variety of nations immigrated to the Western Hemisphere to find new lifestyles and opportunities. Change of any type has clear ramifications for psychology.

Changes require coping strategies. Sudden social changes are likely to be especially disruptive for individuals. A sudden change in cultural tradi-tions produces *acculturative stress* (Berry, 1980), increasing the likelihood

A complete list of references for the studies included in this chapter's meta-analysis is posted online. Readers can consult it at http://pubs.apa.org/books/supp/smith

http://dx.doi.org/10.1037/14733-008
Foundations of Multicultural Psychology: Research to Inform Effective Practice, by T. B. Smith and J. E. Trimble

of destructive coping mechanisms such as substance abuse at the individual level and massive disruption of cultural values and norms at the group level.

Among the most obvious and most frequently reported acculturation consequences are societal disintegration and personal crisis (Berry & Kim, 1986). As long-held cultural worldviews and norms disappear, individuals may report feeling "lost" amidst the change. At the group level, previous patterns of authority, civility, and welfare are absorbed. At the individual level, hostility, uncertainty, and depression may occur; some immigrants may even backtrack as they struggle with the challenges of acculturation. All together these changes comprise the negative side of acculturation, which can adversely affect family relationships, peer relationships, occupation, and physical health (Haasen, Demiralay, & Reimer, 2008; Mui & Kang, 2006; Steffen, Smith, Larson, & Butler, 2006; Vinokurov, Trickett, & Birman, 2002). Acculturation processes affect both interpersonal and intrapersonal functioning.

The challenges for the mental health profession lie in sensitively understanding the complexities of acculturation and social change, especially among people of color who encounter racism and sometimes stark cultural differences. This learning process for the clinician involves understanding both the stress of acculturation and the stress individuals may feel from their view of mental health and mental health treatment. Conceptualizations of mental health differ across cultures, and non-Western cultures have practices and beliefs about effective cures that differ from psychotherapy. Thus, understanding the degree to which the acculturation of clients of color affects their perceptions of and experiences in mental health services in North America is essential for practitioners working with those clients (e.g., Leong, Kim, & Gupta, 2011).

NARRATIVE REVIEW OF THE LITERATURE

The principal goal of mental health services is to improve client functioning and well-being. Achieving this goal is contingent on several factors related to the client's ethnic and racial background. One essential factor concerns the client's ability to adapt to sociocultural change, including the extent to which they (a) are capable of coping with the demands associated with the acculturative process and (b) understand and utilize Western methods of mental health treatment. Some basic background information contributes bases for understanding this point.

Immigrant populations are increasing. In the United States' last decade some 700,000 immigrants became naturalized citizens. According to news columnist John Cookson (2012),

In the 1990s, the annual average was 500,000, and in the 1980s it was 200,000 . . . yet as a share of the total population, this is a change from 0.1% of the population becoming naturalized citizens each year in the 1980s to 0.2% now. (p. 1)

In the past few years most of the naturalized citizens have been immigrants from Mexico, followed in prevalence by those from the Philippines, India, and China; over half of them live in California, Florida, and New York (Cookson, 2012). Data are inconsistent on mental health clinic visits by the immigrant populations, but there is a general expectation that some of the new immigrants will seek out mental health services: "A 2003 survey supported by the National Institutes of Health found that a sixth of new legal immigrants . . . became depressed during the [acculturation] process" (Cookson, 2012, p. 1). Such diverse clientele will require culturally appropriate services from mental health professionals.

As immigrant populations have increased, so has interest in acculturation as a psychosocial cultural construct; 93% of publications in PsycINFO on "acculturation and mental health" occurred since 1990. Acculturation has emerged as a leading variable in mental health research (Birman, 2011; Birman & Simon, 2014; Heath, Neimeyer, & Pedersen, 1988). The acculturation process, particularly its association with perceptions of and experiences in mental health services, should be a major concern for mental health practitioners who provide services for immigrant populations and others experiencing rapid sociocultural change.

Relevant Theory

Acculturation had been defined as "culture change that is initiated by the conjunction of two or more autonomous cultural systems, [including] the selective adaptation of value systems [and] the processes of integration and differentiation" (Social Science Research Council, 1954, p. 974). The most significant concepts in this 1954 definition were represented by the words *change* and *adaptation*. Subsequent research and exploration of the two processes generated different views of the acculturation construct. When considering such views, acculturation should be differentiated from *enculturation*, which is "the process by which a person learns the requirements of the culture by which he or she is surrounded, and acquires values and behaviors that are appropriate or necessary in that culture" (Grusec & Hastings, 2007, p. 547).

To these early formulations (which are concerned mainly with cultural phenomena) has been added a psychological component focusing on changes that individuals undergo during the acculturation of their group, referred to as *psychological acculturation* by Graves (1967). This construct refers to the dynamic process of transformation for a particular individual coming into contact with a new culture. With the variety of personal, community, and societal factors that shape individual immigrants' cultural experiences, psychological acculturation refers to more than the mere passage of time in a new country or generational status (Birman & Simon, 2014; Schwartz, Pantin, Sullivan, Prado, & Szapocznik, 2006).

The more traditional definition implies that a cultural group moves from a native or tradition-oriented state through a transitional stage and progresses eventually to an "elite acculturated" stage (Spindler & Spindler, 1967). According to this notion, cultural changes proceed away from one's own cultural lifeway in a linear manner to culminate in the full and complete internalization of another culture's lifeway. Contemporary social researchers have difficulty with the traditional view, claiming that acculturation is neither a linear process nor an achievable end, especially if the process occurs during the initial contact and change period.

Increasing evidence suggests that acculturation is a multifaceted phenomenon. Moderating variables, individual preferences, and the desire for ethnic affiliation must be factored into the process (B. S. K. Kim & Abreu, 2001; M. J. Miller, 2007; Tsai, Ying, & Lee, 2000; Zea, Asner-Self, Birman, & Buki, 2003). Thus, contemporary researchers have adopted bidirectional and multidimensional perspectives. Bidirectional perspectives view acculturation as a process in which elements of both one's own and the donor culture are retained and internalized (e.g., LaFromboise, Coleman, & Gerton, 1993; Mendoza, 1984).

Instead of attempting to isolate an individual on an index that approaches full assimilation, one must consider the possibility that many available options depend on the situation. Mendoza (1984) suggested that an acculturating individual may reject religious practices, assimilate dress customs, and integrate food preferences and selective holiday celebrations; one's acculturative status, therefore, is best understood from a composite of indices rather than from an aggregated summative index. Trimble (1988) advocated a similar view, emphasizing the intricate recursive relationship among person variables, situational characteristics, and acculturative patterns; his model emphasized the potency of contextual and situational variables in determining behavioral, perceptual, and cognitive appraisals. The context in which acculturation occurs contributes to the process (B. S. K. Kim & Abreu, 2001; B. S. K. Kim, Atkinson, & Umemoto, 2001; R. M. Lee, Yoon, & Liu-Tom, 2006). Along with indicating that acculturation involves seven dimensions (behavioral, affective, cognition, personality, identity, attitudes, and stress), Berry (1980, 1997; Berry & Sam, 1996) has pointed out that contextual factors such as politics and economics can significantly influence adaptation (S. Sue & Okazaki, 2009; Tran & Birman, 2010). Cabassa (2003) noted that the acculturative process depends on one's preimmigration history, the initiating means and reasons for immigration, and the postimmigration context.

From these definitions, characteristics of the process can be identified. First, contact or interaction between cultures must be continuous and first hand, excluding short-term accidental contact and single cultural practices diffused over long distances. Second, change occurs in the cultural or psychological phenomena among the people in contact. Thus, a distinction is apparent between acculturation as a process and as a state: In the process, dynamic activity occurs during and after contact, and the result is relatively stable, though ongoing change may continue.

Mental health workers must recognize that, like group-level phenomena, individual acculturation does not cohere as a neat predictable package. Groups and individuals vary in their response to and participation in acculturative influences; some domains of culture and behavior may be altered without changes in other domains. For example, attitudes toward the value of technology may change without parallel changes in associated beliefs and behaviors. Thus, the process of acculturation is uneven, not uniform in its cultural and psychological effects.

Much of the acculturation literature tends to emphasize negative and unhealthy adjustment outcomes. A few researchers, however, point out that groups that acculturate can adapt successfully to new environments. Individuals in pluralistic societies develop attitudes about the society as a whole as well as ways of relating to individuals and groups (Berry, Trimble, & Olmedo, 1986). Similarly, attitudes of those in the acculturation process largely determine orientations and perceptions of one's own group and relationships with other groups.

The most cited acculturation theory is the work of Canadian cross-cultural psychologist John Berry. According to Berry (1994, 1995, 1997), individuals can hold acculturation attitudes toward any of the following dimensions: assimilation, integration, separation, and marginalization. A review of the definitions of *adjustment, adaptation, acculturation, assimilation,* and *effectiveness,* especially as they relate to intercultural effectiveness, revealed several skills and traits that contribute to successful or effective adaptation, including ability to communicate, ability to establish and maintain relationships, orientation toward knowledge, capability in linguistics, disposition toward flexibility, realistic view of the target culture, and willingness to develop cultural empathy (Hannigan, 1990). Literature review findings also suggest that factors such as dependent anxiety, perfectionism, ethnocentrism, rigidity, narrow-mindedness, and self-centered role behaviors can contribute to negative adjustments. Mendenhall and Oddou (1985) also pointed out that expatriate acculturation is a multidimensional process that includes dimensions of self-orientation, other-orientation, perception, and cultural toughness. Such factors as relationship development, communicative openness, and stress reduction activities can promote effective adaptation. Groups and individuals can anticipate the effects of the acculturative process if culture contact is imminent.

In a related acculturation theory, Olmedo (1979) proposed that acculturation research use a "full-measurement model," which provides a way to investigate relationships among multidimensional sets of quantitatively defined variables. The model utilizes a set of acculturation scales or factors like those of a cognitive or personality test. This framework allows researchers to determine (a) the interdependence structure of acculturation variables, (b) the interdependence structure of cognitive or personality test variables, and (c) the structure of relationships between the two sets of variables. Thus, research may explore fully the possible relationships among variables, such as perceptions of and experiences in psychotherapy.

Acculturation theories have their critics and skeptics. Some contend that the construct is inadequately defined, the measures are sometimes limited to specific populations, and the scales may be measuring experiences that are confounded by multiple life situations (Birman & Simon, 2014; Hunt, Schneider, & Comer, 2004; Rudmin, 2003, 2009; Rudmin & Ahmadzadeh, 2001; Schwartz, Unger, Zamboanga, & Szapocznik, 2010). Considering the prevalence of debates and contentiousness of some critics in the field, Escobar and Vega (2000) suggested,

> Until such time as we have clarification of these important matters, we recommend suspending judgments about the necessity of including acculturation measures in peer reviewed research, or presupposing the meaning and value of acculturation measures in the absence of an explicit theoretical rationale for their inclusion. (p. 739)

Hence, it is time for a synthesis of research findings on the degree to which clients' level of acculturation is associated with their perceptions of and experiences in mental health services.

Summary of Previous Research Findings

Although most contemporary researchers emphasize that acculturative processes are multifaceted, bidirectional, and situational, inspection of a number of acculturation measures reveals unidimensional linear evaluations: Most measures yield a single score that identifies one's position on a nativist–traditionalist–assimilationist dimension. Moreover, some measures contain as few as three items, whereas a few others contain as many as 43, a discrepancy that can raise serious validity questions (Rudmin, 2003, 2009).

Acculturation scale content typically includes one theme or a combination of three themes: natality, behavioral predisposition, and subjective preferences. All three themes can contain items often found in measures of ethnic identification. Some researchers have identified an ethnic identity factor embedded in their acculturation scales, and researchers continue to use items in acculturation scales that also are found in ethnic identity scales (Trimble, 2005, 2007). Such issues are but a few of the emerging concerns about measuring acculturation.

In studying and assessing the acculturative process, cross-cultural psychologists prefer to emphasize an individual's experiences. As a consequence, the bulk of the studies flowing from this orientation measure psychological acculturation and attempt to isolate an individual's cultural orientation on a bipolar linear continuum. For example, Triandis, Kashima, Shimada, and Villareal (1986) used a participatory measure of acculturation to assess the existence of cultural differences in a sample of Hispanic and non-Hispanic navy recruits. They created a single acculturation score by summing four items: length of residence in the United States, media acculturation (e.g., preference for television, radio, and movies), number of non-Hispanic coworkers, and number of non-Hispanic friends and romantic partners.

Padilla (1980) proposed an acculturation framework that embraces elements of the contact-participation dimension and one's perceived loyalty to one's own culture. This framework includes 11 dimensions (e.g., language preferences, name preference for children) to measure loyalty and 15 dimensions to identify cultural awareness. Padilla (1980) concluded that "cultural awareness is the more general component," and "ethnic loyalty is the more tenuous" (p. 65). This model formed the basis of a multifactorial acculturation model developed by Richman, Gaviria, Flaherty, Biz, and Wintrob (1987) containing five dimensions: language, customs, ethnic identity, sociability, and discrimination. Many other multidimensional frameworks and measures have subsequently appeared (e.g., Cuéllar, Arnold, & Maldonado, 1995; Suinn, Khoo, & Ahuna, 1995; Zea et al., 2003).

A number of factors can influence the degree to which immigrants adapt and adjust to the new host cultural environment (Birman & Simon, 2014). One of the interesting questions arising from the literature is the degree to which one's own heritage and the host culture's general heritage contribute to psychological adaptation and adjustment. The research results are mixed, depending to some extent on the ethnic background of the immigrant. The degree to which immigrants identify with their cultural and ethnic background can partially influence adaptation, especially among Hispanic Americans (Rivera, 2007; Rodríguez, Mira, Paez, & Myers, 2007; Torres, 2010). In a few studies researchers found that for some Asian Americans adjustment was not difficult because they believed they were more assimilated than others (Hwang & Myers, 2007; Oh, Koeske, & Sales, 2002; C. J. Yeh, 2003).

Recently Eunju Yoon et al. (2013) published a meta-analysis of the relationship among acculturation, enculturation, and mental health. Examining data from 325 studies, the researchers found that acculturation was positively associated with mental health outcomes such as self-esteem, life satisfaction, depression, distress, anxiety, and so forth. In addition, they found that the use of language and certain behaviors related positively to mental health, as did the extent to which individuals identified with their cultural background. The authors concluded that the most favorable acculturation strategy was to strive for integration.

One of the major findings from a review of the literature suggested that most researchers rely heavily on correlating acculturation scales. This is a problem. Specific analyses must be conducted to investigate different dimensions of acculturation and account for possible curvilinear relationships (Birman & Simon, 2014; Rudmin, 2003). Authors should explicitly report and emphasize subscale as well as total score findings. Optimally, authors will identify classes of participants (e.g., cluster analysis) and report additional differences accordingly. Moreover, measurement should evaluate different components of the acculturative process rather than drawing limited conclusions from one or two factors. The different components seem likely to relate differently to mental health treatment, with cultural knowledge and attitudes mattering less than cultural values and cognitive styles. Finally, most acculturation research consists of surveys. Comparison designs that evaluate differences across contexts are minimal. Yet we know that acculturation contexts matter.

To summarize, change is an inevitable human and environmental condition, and acculturation is one form of sociocultural change that has clear implications for mental health, including perceptions of and experiences in mental health services. Originally identified and conceptualized by anthropologists, acculturation is recognized as central to the research agendas of psychologists, psychiatrists, sociologists, social workers, and educators. Most researchers in psychology have attempted to attribute the results of sociocultural change to the acculturative process, blaming negative adaptation and adjustment on acculturation as if it has a direct effect on mental health outcomes. Such attributions, however well meaning, have confounded the research process and muddled the field of inquiry. Yet there is no doubt that when two or more cultural groups come into direct contact, conflicting expectations regarding what constitutes "normal" mental health and its treatment are inevitable. How immigrants and people of color perceive and experience mental health services in North America continues to be an important and significant research question. The objectives of this meta-analytic review were to estimate the degree to which clients' level of acculturation has been associated with individuals' perceptions of and experiences with mental health services and to estimate the degree to which study and participant characteristics have moderated those findings.

META-ANALYSIS OF THE RESEARCH DATA

We reviewed U.S. and Canadian studies that included a quantitative measure of individuals' level of acculturation that was statistically associated with at least one quantitative measure of an aspect of mental health services (utilization, retention, treatment attitudes, clinical outcomes). We included studies measuring perceptions of mental health services (e.g., likelihood to seek mental health services, perceived usefulness of mental health services, evaluations of the helpfulness of mental health therapists), but we coded studies of individuals' perceptions separately from studies of actual clients. We transformed statistics in manuscripts into the common metric of Pearson's r, with positive values indicating that greater acculturation was associated with more favorable experiences in or perceptions about mental health services. The Appendix of this book contains additional information about methods of the meta-analysis.

Description of Existing Research Literature

Our literature search yielded 107 studies reporting data on 23,173 individuals' perceptions of or experiences with mental health services as a function of their level of acculturation while residing in the United States or Canada. As shown in Table 8.1, the topic has been consistently investigated over the past 2 decades, but few studies have involved actual mental health clients ($k = 15$). The modal study involved cross-sectional, correlational data obtained by convenience from nonclinical samples of young adults. Children, adolescents, and senior adults were rarely evaluated. Relatively few studies involved methodologically rigorous designs (i.e., randomly selected individuals who have experienced therapy in contrast to matched controls who have not). Researchers have typically administered a survey of people's perceptions of mental health services along with a measure of acculturation. Thus, the overall results of this meta-analysis primarily represent nonclient attitudes and perceptions about mental health services.

Notably, only three of the 107 studies involved multiple racial groups; in contrast to most of the other topics covered in this volume, data collection for acculturation tended to be limited to participants of a single racial group, primarily to individuals with Asian or Hispanic/Latino(a) ancestry. Few studies addressed African Americans, Native American Indians, Polynesian Americans, or other groups; specifically, the construct of acculturation has

TABLE 8.1
Characteristics of 107 Studies of the Association Between Acculturation and Perceptions of and/or Experiences With Mental Health Services

Characteristic	M	No. of studies (k)	%
Year of report			
Before 1980		6	6
1980–1989		8	7
1990–1999		46	43
2000–2007		47	44
Publication status			
Published		73	68
Unpublished		34	32
Sampling procedure			
Convenience		96	90
Representative (random selection)		11	10
Research design			
Cross-sectional		67	63
Longitudinal		2	2
Comparison groups		18	17
Other (e.g., analogue, archival)		20	18
Sample population			
General community members		87	81
At-risk group members		5	5
Clinical populations (in treatment)		15	14
Sample size	171		
<50		9	8
50–99		28	26
100–199		37	35
200–399		22	21
400–999		7	6
>1,000		4	4
Participant ages[a]	27.7		
Children (<13 years)		2	2
Adolescents (13–18 years)		3	3
Young adults (19–29 years)		53	52
Middle-aged adults (30–55 years)		43	42
Senior adults (>56 years)		1	1
Participant gender of (% female)	59.1		
Participant race[b] (%)			
African American	2		
Asian American	65		
Hispanic/Latino(a) American	28		
Native American Indian/Alaska Native	1		
Other	3		

Note. Not all variables sum to the total number of studies because of missing data.
[a]Average age category of participants within studies; not all participants within the study would necessarily be in the category listed. [b]The racial composition of participants across all studies was calculated by multiplying the number of participants within studies by the percentage of participants from each racial group and dividing that product by the total number of participants.

been most often applied by researchers to two racial groups with a recent history of large-scale immigration to the United States and Canada. In contemporary research, the construct of acculturation has not been widely applied to racial groups indigenous to North America or historically enslaved. This issue will be covered later in more detail. Overall, research data described in the remainder of this chapter should be qualified as applying primarily to Asian and Hispanic/Latino(a) Americans.

Overall Research Findings

Research findings included a high degree of variability. Across the 107 research studies identified, the observed correlations between individuals' level of acculturation and their perceptions of or experiences with mental health services ranged from −0.45 to 0.88; research studies reported anywhere from a strong inverse relationship to a very strong positive relationship. In essence, the results were "all over the map" (see Figure 8.1).

On average, across all types of measures of perceptions of or experiences with mental health services, the random effects weighted correlation with

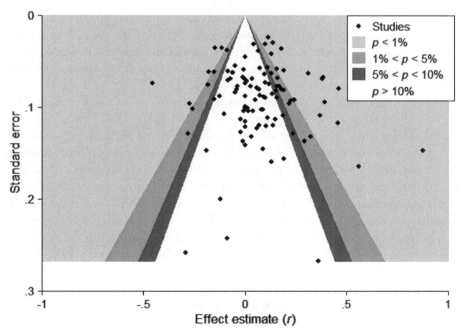

Figure 8.1. Contour-enhanced funnel plot of effect sizes (Pearson *r*) by standard error. Effect sizes ranged from *strongly negative* to *strongly positive*, with no consistent pattern. Although the overall average approximated zero, the results were too variable to be interpreted in the aggregate.

acculturation was .08 ($SE = .017$, 95% CI = [.05, .11], $p < .0001$). The heterogeneity of the findings ($I^2 = 82.1$, 95% CI = [79, 85], $Q_{(106)} = 592.7$, $p < .0001$) rendered problematic the exclusive reliance on a numerical average. Clearly, multiple factors influenced the association of acculturation with perceptions of and experiences in therapy. Acculturation is sometimes related to more favorable attitudes about mental health services and other times (although less frequently) to less favorable attitudes. Extreme values on both sides occur but are washed out in the averages. Interpreting the meaning of the data therefore benefitted from additional analytic steps.

Factors Influencing the Results

Study Characteristics

Studies evaluated different aspects of individuals' perceptions of or experiences in therapy, requiring that results be analyzed across the type of dependent variable used. The three broad types of variables were client utilization/retention in therapy, individuals' perceptions of therapy or the therapist, and client symptom reduction as a function of therapy. Specifically, 24 studies measured client utilization/retention, 86 measured individuals' perceptions of therapy or therapists, and eight measured client outcomes.[1] We conducted a multivariate meta-analysis of these data, using an estimate of $r = .60$ for the correlation of effect sizes within studies (to account for statistical interdependence). The random effects weighted effect sizes were low for client utilization/retention, $r = .09$ ($SE = .025$, 95% CI = [.04, .13]); for individuals' perceptions of therapy or therapists, $r = .09$ ($SE = .023$, 95% CI = [.04, .13]); and for client outcomes, $r = -.01$ ($SE = .062$, 95% CI = [-.13, .11]). These three types of data did not differ from one another ($p > .10$).

To evaluate whether our initial three categories of dependent variables were too broad, we grouped the data into five specific categories. However, no differences were found across the more specific categories of evaluation/outcome used across studies ($Q = 6.2$, $p = .19$; see Table 8.2). Studies of mental health service utilization or retention yielded similarly small results to studies of individuals' perceptions/expectations about mental health services. On average, acculturation was shown to be only minimally related to both actual involvement in therapy and perceptions about therapy—an important finding in our analyses, given its implications (see also Chapter 5, this volume).

When perceptions about therapy were broken down by the name of the instrument used, the results remained in the same minimal range

---

[1]Of the 107 total studies, two measured both client outcomes and client retention/utilization, two measured both client outcomes and client perceptions, and six measured both client perceptions and client retention/utilization.

TABLE 8.2
Weighted Mean Correlations Across Levels of Several
Moderator Variables in Studies of Perceptions of or Experiences
With Mental Health Services as a Function of Acculturation

Variable	Q_b	p	k	r_+	95% CI
Data source	2.3	.13			
Published			34	.04	[−.01, .10]
Unpublished			73	.10	[.06, .14]
Sampling procedure	0.1	.84			
Convenience			96	.08	[.04, .12]
Representative (random selection)			11	.07	[−.03, .17]
Research design	3.1	.37			
Cross-sectional			67	.09	[.05, .13]
Comparison groups			17	.06	[−.02, .15]
Analogue			13	.00	[−.10, .10]
Others			10	.11	[−.01, .22]
Sample population	0.1	.98			
General community members			87	.08	[.04, .12]
At-risk groups or clinical populations			20	.08	[.00, .16]
Participant gender[a]	1.5	.23			
Female			17	.17	[.07, .27]
Male			9	.07	[−.08, .20]
Participant race[b]	8.4	.04			
African American			4	.08	[−.12, .28]
Asian American			59	.12	[.07, .16]
Hispanic/Latino(a) American			35	.01	[−.05, .07]
Native American Indian/Alaska Native			2	.02	[−.25, .28]
Acculturation level	8.7	.03			
Low			16	.17	[.09, .25]
Moderate			47	.08	[.03, .13]
High			11	−.02	[−.12, .08]
Insufficient information			33	.07	[.01, .13]
Acculturation type	14.4	.003			
Proxy variable (i.e., language use, time)			10	.02	[−.08, .12]
Ethnic-specific acculturation measure			74	.06	[.02, .10]
General acculturation measure			12	.25	[.15, .34]
Miscellaneous (more than one above)			11	.12	[.02, .22]
Evaluation type[c]	6.2	.19			
Utilization of mental health services			18	.10	[.01, .18]
Retention in mental health services			6	.07	[−.07, .21]
Attitudes/expectations about services			81	.09	[.05, .13]
Client perceptions of therapists			9	−.04	[−.16, .08]
Client outcomes in therapy			8	−.02	[−.16, .12]
Measure[c]	8.8	.07			
ATSPPHS			46	.09	[.03, .14]
CERS			10	−.10	[−.23, .04]
CCCI			5	−.04	[−.22, .15]
CRF			4	.13	[−.07, .33]
Help-seeking			33	.10	[.03, .16]

Note. CI = confidence interval; k = number of studies; Q_b = Q-value for variance between groups; r_+ = random effects weighted correlation; ATSPPHS = Attitude Toward Seeking Professional Psychological Help Scale (E. H. Fischer & Farina, 1995); CERS = Counselor Effectiveness Rating Scale (L. K. Jones, 1974); CCCI = Cross-Cultural Counseling Inventory (LaFromboise, Coleman, & Hernandez, 1991); CRF = Counselor Rating Form (Atkinson & Wampold, 1982). [a]This analysis involved only studies with exclusively male or female participants. [b]This analysis involved studies with participants of a single racial group. [c]This analysis involved all effect sizes within studies that contained distinct outcome measures, such that studies could contribute more than one effect size to the analysis but only one effect size per category.

($Q = 8.8$, $p = .07$; see Table 8.2). Studies using the Counselor Effectiveness Rating Scale (L. K. Jones, 1974) tended to have negative effect sizes in contrast to the positive effect sizes of the Attitude Toward Seeking Professional Psychological Help Scale (E. H. Fischer & Farina, 1995) and general measures of help seeking for mental health. These findings may not be reliable, given the small number of studies using several of the instruments.

Differences were found across the way in which researchers operationalized acculturation ($Q = 14.4$, $p = .003$; see Table 8.2). Studies using general measures of acculturation to Western society (which included a variety of indicators) yielded much higher correlations than all other types of acculturation indicators.

The overall results obtained across all 107 studies were found to be consistent over time; the correlation between the year of study and its effect size was a trivial $r = -0.03$. As shown in Table 8.2, the results did not differ across the type of research design used or across the type of participant sampling used.

Participant Characteristics

Studies included a wide variety of participants, so we sought to determine whether systematic differences in findings could be attributable to participant characteristics: gender, age, age cohort, race, level of acculturation, aspect of acculturation reported, and clinical status.

The overall findings were not affected by participant gender. The correlation between studies' effect sizes and their percentage of female participants was very small ($r = 0.05$, $p > .10$), and there were trivial differences between studies using exclusively male or female participants (see Table 8.2). However, the average age of participants did moderate the results ($r = 0.25$, $p = .004$); studies with older participants tended to have higher effect sizes. Acculturation was more salient to middle-aged and senior adults' perceptions of or experiences with mental health services than to those of younger populations. This finding proved to be independent of age cohort: In a simultaneous random effects weighted regression, the association of effect size with average age remained moderate ($\beta = 0.22$), but estimated average year of participant birth (year of study minus average age of participants) did not at $\beta = -0.03$.

Minor differences were found across participants' race. Studies investigating Asian Americans had a somewhat higher average effect size (although still small) compared with studies investigating other racial groups ($Q = 8.4$, $p = .04$; see Table 8.2).

Participant level of acculturation moderated the overall results ($Q = 8.7$, $p = .03$; see Table 8.2). Studies with participants experiencing relatively low levels of acculturation (i.e., recent immigrants) had an average effect size more than double that of studies using more acculturated participants. Thus, lower acculturation levels affect perceptions of and experiences in therapy more than higher levels.

Overall results of the studies did not differ as a function of the clinical status of participants (Table 8.2). The average results across individuals receiving treatment and those receiving no treatment were virtually identical.

We next sought to determine which of the statistically significant participant characteristic variables remained statistically significant in the presence of the others. We conducted a random effects weighted metaregression to predict effect size with those variables found to be statistically significant in the univariate analyses. The model reached statistical significance ($R^2 = .14$, $Q = 19.6$, $p = .0006$).

The only variable that remained statistically significant in the model was participant level of acculturation ($b = -.20$, $p = .03$). To facilitate interpretation of the data, variables entered into both models were centered on their means. The B value for the variable labeled *constant* (see Table 8.3) represents the average effect size one would expect to find if all variables included in the model had the expected mean value. This value corresponds with the overall effect size reported earlier ($r = .08$). Interpretation of the B weights (Table 8.3, Column 1) reveals the extent to which each study characteristic would be expected to influence the observed overall effect size when controlling for the presence of the other variables. Thus, when researchers use samples of participants with low levels of acculturation, the expected effect size would be $r = .159$ ($.079 + .08$), and when they use samples of participants with high levels of acculturation, the expected effect size would be $r = -.001$ ($.079 - .08$). When people of color have acculturated to Western society, their level of acculturation is irrelevant to their perceptions of and experiences in therapy. However, when people of color have not acculturated to Western society, their level of acculturation is modestly associated with their average perceptions of or experiences in therapy.

TABLE 8.3
Random Effects Regression Weights for Study
Characteristics Associated With Effect Sizes

Variable	B	SE	p	β
$R^2 = .14$ ($k = 102$)				
Constant	.079	.018	.0006	
Participants' average age	.003	.002	.10	.15
Asian American participants[a]	.042	.057	.46	.10
Hispanic/Latino(a) American participants[a]	−.066	.061	.28	−.15
Participants' level of acculturation[b]	−.080	.037	.03	−.20

Note. SE = standard error. [a]Samples of participants exclusively from this racial group contrasted with samples of participants from all other racial groups. [b]Higher levels of acculturation have higher values.

Possible Influence of Publication Bias

Most studies (73 or 68%) in this meta-analysis were doctoral dissertations. It seemed improbable that the remaining 34 published manuscripts could have substantively affected the overall results in either direction. The average effect size obtained across published versus unpublished dissertations did not differ (Table 8.2).

As shown in Figure 8.1, effect sizes were widely distributed around the average value of $r = .08$. There were no obviously "missing" corners in the distribution that would suggest studies excluded unintentionally from analyses. One statistical method (Duval & Tweedie, 2000) did not identify any "missing" studies, and Egger's regression test was nonsignificant. Therefore, we concluded that publication bias was not a threat to the results of this meta-analysis.

DISCUSSION AND INTERPRETATION OF THE FINDINGS

What Do the Overall Results Suggest?

In terms of broad research findings, participant level of acculturation is inconsistently associated with perceptions of and experiences with mental health services. The observed correlations ranged from −0.45 to 0.88, suggesting a completely unreliable relationship. However, this meta-analysis identified several explanations for the observed inconsistencies.

The primary explanation for the overall variability is participant acculturation level. Low acculturation is more strongly associated with attitudes about and experiences with mental health services than moderate and high levels of acculturation. Because only 16 of the 107 research studies evaluated only participants with low levels of acculturation, those data were averaged out, such that the overall association with acculturation appeared to be minimal. However, acculturation is somewhat relevant to mental health services when it is low ($r = .17$), not half so much when it is moderate ($r = .08$), and not relevant at all when it is high ($r = −.02$).

Even among populations with low levels of acculturation, the average effect size of $r = .17$ is not exceptionally strong. Mental health services provided for clients of color may or may not be inconsistent with their traditionally held views about psychological disorders and their melioration. Averaged results reveal little about the underlying nature of the mental health treatments and the participants' experiences with them. Nevertheless, the findings of this meta-analysis suggested that acculturation level is more relevant to client utilization/retention and client perceptions of therapists than it is to client treatment outcome. More to the point, clients with low acculturation levels who engage in a mental health treatment and remain in that treatment tend to improve about the same as clients with higher levels (see also Chapter 5, this volume).

Other explanations for the variability in the overall research findings include three factors related to level of acculturation. First, the observed effect sizes varied across participant age. Studies with older participants tended to have higher effect sizes. However, this effect did not remain once the researchers accounted for the level of acculturation; older populations are less likely to be highly acculturated than younger groups. Second, the findings suggested a trend for acculturation to be more relevant to perceptions and experiences with mental health services by Asian Americans than by Hispanic/Latino(a) Americans. This finding could be attributable to differences in Western and Eastern worldviews, which have distinct cultural explanations for and stigma about mental illness, disclosure of personal problems, and so forth (Leong et al., 2011). Third, the way in which acculturation was measured influenced the data, with studies using general acculturation measures yielding higher correlations than all other acculturation indicators. This particular finding is both easy and difficult to explain. On one hand, a psychometrically robust instrument directly measuring the intended construct of acculturation should be more predictive than proxy variables such as time of residence in the United States, English language proficiency, and so forth. Indirect measures of acculturation typically function less effectively than direct measures. On the other hand, it is difficult to explain why general measures of acculturation would be more predictive of mental health attitudes than measures of acculturation that were designed for a specific ethnic group. This finding may be due to systematic differences in measurement or to a plausible curvilinear association that remained unaccounted for in correlational studies.

Considerations for Future Research

The findings of the meta-analysis present several challenges for research. Overall, the quality of research has to improve. The fact that two thirds of the studies on this topic are unpublished dissertations reflects the widespread use of surveys and correlational analyses that frankly yield limited information. At the very least, researchers using cross-sectional designs should have attended more to curvilinear relationships, rather than limiting themselves almost exclusively to linear associations. We now have conclusive evidence that research findings vary as a function of participant acculturation level, so future research must account for this relationship. And the focus of inquiry should shift to individuals with low levels of acculturation.

Optimally, researchers interested in mental health issues would have examined clinical populations, yet only 14% did. The field of multicultural psychology does not need any more surveys about attitudes in the general population that involve a few hundred participants and therefore lack external validity. The field does need many more studies of actual client experiences. Those studies can include qualitative investigations and case studies to illustrate the multiple ways in which acculturation level relates to mental health services. We also recommend that future research examine causal pathways: for example, evaluating individuals entering a medical clinic or social agency and then contrasting the individuals who do and do not follow through with a subsequent referral for mental health treatment. Until researchers systematically investigate causal pathways and collect data in clinical settings, we will lack useful information about acculturation and mental health services.

Most research studies included people of Asian and Hispanic/Latino(a) descent because those populations are often influenced by relocation and immigration experiences. Native American Indians were the least represented ethnic population in the sample, yet many tribal members continue to experience assimilation and adaptation difficulties and struggles. The struggles continue because many want to retain and maintain their historical lifestyles yet have to struggle with laws and conditions imposed by federal and state government regulations, ongoing historical oppression and discrimination, and the imposing lifestyles of the dominant culture. The same can be said about Polynesian Americans and Arab Americans. There is a pressing need for research with those populations.

Researchers should also consider increasing the number of research participants. About 60% of the study samples involved fewer than 200 participants, but the research findings were more consistent in studies with more than 300 participants. Using larger samples will also allow researchers to better examine factors that account for inconsistent findings: for example, differences that have been found across age; type of measure used and possible item bias or culturally uneven item translations; length of time in the host country; and variable personal, social, and economic experiences with relocation and contact with mainstream society.

Most critical, however, scholars have to ask more specific research questions and use methods and measures that will yield specific answers. The field will not benefit from additional scattered studies (Figure 8.1) that involve broad questions using generic measures. More specificity is needed with outcome variables and with ways measures of acculturation are operationalized, analyzed, and interpreted. If a research question concerns experiences in mental health treatment, then measuring generic acculturation status is totally insufficient; researchers must specifically focus on individuals' acculturation to Western worldviews about mental health and mental health treatments.

That someone is acculturated to the U.S. education system (adolescents) or workplace (adults) cannot be assumed to indicate that the individual perceives mental health and well-being in ways congruent (or incongruent) with mainstream mental health service providers. Researchers should measure precisely what needs to be known. And what mental health professionals need to know is the specific cultural attitudes about mental health, mental health treatments, and circumstances affecting well-being.

Suggestions for Practitioners

A therapist cannot assume that a client with low levels of acculturation will understand or appreciate the mental health treatment being offered. A mental health provider must seek to understand the cultural contexts and unique cultural characteristics of each client, extending his or her efforts beyond what is typical. Salzman (2001) recommended,

> [Therapists must] respect culture as a necessary psychological defense and design interventions accordingly; promote interventions emphasizing meaning construction at the community level and support the collective (community) and individual construction of meaning that sustains adaptive action; support and assist individuals and communities in the identification of standards and values within the cultural worldview they identify with that promote adaptive action in current realities; and support and assist communities in cultural recovery. (pp. 189–190)

The findings of this meta-analysis suggest that therapists and clinics should attend to client utilization/retention. If a clinic is presently not serving clients with low levels of acculturation, focusing on this population might present a significant opportunity; outreach and recruitment efforts will increase clientele for the clinic and meet a critical need for those individuals.

This meta-analysis also suggests that acculturation is a multifaceted phenomenon. Viewing acculturation as a univariate construct may result in an inconsistent prediction of how a client will respond in treatment. A clinician may find it optimal to discuss directly with clients their experiences and expectations about mental health treatments, rather than assuming anything. Clients unfamiliar with North American mental health treatments and psychotherapy may (a) hold excessively high expectations (e.g., of an instant cure), which could result in unmet expectations and dissatisfaction or (b) mistrust the methods, either failing to engage or misrepresenting their level of engagement to the therapist. Acculturation that has a minimal impact on a client's perceptions about treatment may still be highly relevant to the presenting symptoms, patterns of coping, and contextual life circumstances (Yoon et al., 2013).

CONCLUSION

Low acculturation, often found among immigrants and older adults, is relevant to perceptions of and experiences in mental health services. Among potential clients who are moderately to highly acculturated, the association varies too much to predict attitudes about mental health services. Future research using higher quality methods and more specific research questions and measures will be necessary before other conclusions can be reached.

Much work remains for scientists to understand the processes of acculturation, its relationship to social and sociocultural change, and the experiences of multicultural populations with mental health services. Our findings raise a few pointed questions for consideration. Which change-related constructs best describe acculturation processes relevant to mental health treatment utilization and outcomes (e.g., psychological acculturation, acculturative stress, sociocultural change, cultural borrowing/fusion)? Which cultural beliefs are most relevant to mental health and mental health services? Precisely when and how do North American mental health treatments align and not align with cultural worldviews of clients of color? Considering the contents of this chapter and others in this volume, relying on simplistic descriptions and measurements of acculturation and social change constructs would be insufficient and shortsighted. The challenges are significant, but so are the opportunities for improvement.

III

SYNTHESIS OF RESEARCH ON THE EXPERIENCES AND WELL-BEING OF PEOPLE OF COLOR

9

THE ASSOCIATION OF RECEIVED RACISM WITH THE WELL-BEING OF PEOPLE OF COLOR: A META-ANALYTIC REVIEW

A chapter on racism in the *Handbook of Multicultural Psychology* begins as follows:

> This chapter should not be here. In a more perfect world, a handbook celebrating the influence of and importance of multiculturalism within psychology would be complete without a specific analysis of prejudice and racism. The world's imperfection, however, makes this chapter an unfortunate necessity that can inform and improve us. (Czopp, Mark, & Walzer, 2014, p. 361)

Although the nature of racism has changed over time (Yoo & Pituc, 2013), it is engrained in many spheres of activity (D. W. Sue, 2005, 2013, 2015). Thus, this chapter, like that of Czopp et al. (2014), is critical because

Dr. Hokule'a Conklin of Brigham Young University contributed to the writing of this chapter.

A complete list of references for the studies included in this chapter's meta-analysis is posted online. Readers can consult it at http://pubs.apa.org/books/supp/smith

http://dx.doi.org/10.1037/14733-009

we need to more thoroughly understand the influence of racism and prejudice on mental health and well-being.

Racism and prejudice have always included both ideological and institutional dimensions (Neville, Spanierman, & Lewis, 2012) affecting multiple aspects of life, including employment, education, health care, and housing (National Research Council, 2004; U.S. Department of Health and Human Services, Office of the Surgeon General, 2001). Considerable evidence has revealed that multiple inequities attributable to racism have negative health consequences for people of color (Paradies, 2006). Racism clearly affects individuals' mental health and emotional well-being (Carter, 2007) and thus should be a concern for mental health professionals.

Scholars have increasingly investigated the psychological consequences of racism. The resulting data counter the false supposition that racism no longer poses a significant mental health risk for people of color (Constantine & Sue, 2006). Such data should embolden mental health professionals to oppose racism in all of its various forms (D. W. Sue, 2005, 2013).

This chapter summarizes research specific to the association between experiences of racism and psychological well-being among people of color in the United States and Canada. Mental health professionals who attend to the adverse effects of racism can bolster the well-being of the individuals, groups, and communities they serve.

REVIEW OF THE LITERATURE

Relevant Theory

Racism and its psychological consequences can be conceptualized in many ways. Several decades ago many theories focused on psychological processes. For instance, social comparison theory (Festinger, 1954) emphasized how self-evaluations are generated by contrasts with others. Individuals and groups whose race is judged negatively by others can internalize those negative evaluations (i.e., internalized racism). Although the basic components of Festinger's (1954) theory remain intact, significant contributions and advancements have extended to such variables as self-enhancement, self-evaluation maintenance, and closure avoidance, as well as various aspects of self and other attributions (Garcia, Tor, & Gonzalez, 2006; Suls, Martin, & Wheeler, 2002; Tesser & Campbell, 1982).

Other theories, such as relative deprivation theory (Walker & Smith, 2001), have addressed how self-evaluations differ as a function of inequitable distribution of power and resources. Intraindividual processes, such as resiliency factors, have also been addressed by the transactional model of stress and coping (Lazarus & Folkman, 1984), which posited that abilities to cope with stressors, such as racism, mediate an individual's appraisal of the racism and corresponding distress and responses to it. Nevertheless, scholars have noted that models emphasizing psychological interpretations of racism fail to account for other factors: "Research and theory on stress and coping . . . has fallen short of comprehensively capturing experiences and characteristics that emerge from person–environment transactions involving race and culture" (Harrell, 2000, p. 44).

In the past, psychological theories that emphasized the internalization of social experiences were clearly distinguished from sociological theories that emphasized systems and structures (i.e., inequitable access to resources). Contemporary conceptualizations attend to both and are termed the *psychosocial*, or "the interface between socially structured arrangements and intra-individual processes" (Schnittker & McLeod, 2005, p. 77). For example, a biopsychosocial model (R. Clark, Anderson, Clark, & Williams, 1999) explained differences in health outcomes by allowing for differences in individuals' perceptions, coping responses, environments, and level of exposure to racism.

Prominent among contemporary models, critical race theory (Delgado & Stefancic, 2012) posits that all structures that contribute to racial stratification place racial minority individuals at greater risk of various mental health problems (Brown, 2003). Five tenets of this theory are (a) racial stratification is ubiquitous, (b) racism is complex and difficult to remedy, (c) race is a social invention, (d) a phenomenological understanding of oppression is appropriate, and (e) critical race theorists should try to bring about social justice. The emphasis of this theory on dynamics of power and privilege has made it widely influential in multicultural psychology. Building on that foundation, Neville et al.'s (2012) expanded psychosocial model of racism illustrated how social structures and ideologies intersect and maintain racism over time.

Contemporary models thus emphasize a variety of mechanisms through which racism affects mental health, with some factors receiving substantial research attention. Steele's (2010) landmark work on stereotype threat has attracted the interest of the general public. Overall, the mental health professions are better positioned than ever to expand research investigations into how racism affects psychological well-being and to identify the degree to which other variables mediate and moderate that relationship (Harrell, 2000; Howe, Heim, & O'Connor, 2014).

Narrative Review of Previous Research

The increased attention to issues of racism in the recent research literature has been notable. One estimate indicated that from 1960 to 1970 only 115 studies of experiences of racism by racial or ethnic minority group members were published, whereas at least 4,669 studies on the topic appeared between 2000 and 2010 (Yoo & Pituc, 2013).

The growing corpus of research has already settled on one conclusion: The association of racism with well-being is complex. "Discrimination is, by its very nature, a subjective experience. By implication, reports of discrimination are subjective and depend on a complex process involving the perception, recall, and reporting of past life experiences" (Schnittker & McLeod, 2005, p. 90). Such complexity creates challenges for measurement and methodology. For obvious ethical reasons, the scientific study of racism should not involve experimental manipulation of racist encounters (A. R. Fischer & Shaw, 1999). The majority of research published in this area has been correlational and cross-sectional. These kinds of studies cannot isolate the effects of racism and do not easily distinguish among alternative explanations for decreased well-being.

Reliance on correlational research involving perception data has raised some questions about bidirectionality of effects. "Although many have argued that experiencing racial discrimination has deleterious consequences for mental health, it is also plausible that individuals experiencing lower levels of mental health are more inclined to interpret ambiguous events as being racially motivated" (Sellers & Shelton, 2003, p. 1081).

Individuals who are harmed by racism can acquire a protective sensitivity (Comas-Díaz & Jacobsen, 2001), which can be better understood in terms of race-based traumatic stress injury (Carter, 2007). Mental health professionals do not blame an individual who was raped for developing a protective sensitivity; similarly they should not speak of racism in ways that shift blame to people who are disadvantaged by it.

Although expressions of racism in North America are considerably less overt than in earlier decades, racism remains pervasive and problematic (D. W. Sue, 2015; Zárate, Quezada, Schenberger, & Lupo, 2014). Racial hierarchies and racial microaggressions (D. W. Sue et al., 2007) can result in anger, exhaustion, withdrawal, anxiety, and diminished self-esteem, among other adverse mental health symptoms, collectively described as racial battle fatigue (W. A. Smith, Allen, & Danley, 2007). It seems obvious that discrimination of any kind would have consequences that are primarily harmful, even though some consequences, such as increased resilience and willingness to combat injustice on behalf of others, could also accrue (D. W. Sue, 2005). At least four published literature reviews concluded that perceptions of racism are associated with decreased physical and psychological well-being (Carter, 2007; Paradies, 2006; D. R. Williams & Mohammed, 2009; D. R. Williams, Neighbors, & Jackson, 2003).

Four prior meta-analyses of the literature also found fairly consistent results. Across 23 studies specific to Asians and Asian Americans, the correlation between racial discrimination and mental health variables was $r = .23$

(D. L. Lee & Ahn, 2011). A separate meta-analysis of 66 studies of Black American adults reported an average correlation of $r = .20$ between perceived racism and mental health variables (Pieterse, Todd, Neville, & Carter, 2012). In a broader meta-analysis (Pascoe & Smart Richman, 2009), the average effect size was $r = .16$ across 105 studies after accounting for publication bias. In the fourth and most comprehensive meta-analysis (Schmitt, Branscombe, Postmes, & Garcia, 2014), racism correlated $-.21$ with well-being across 211 studies using correlational designs. The fourth meta-analysis also evaluated 11 experimental studies of racism, in which the average difference in well-being attributable to the conditions of racism was $d = .11$, a very modest value relative to the correlational data.

Across the four meta-analyses, different variables were found to moderate the overall association between psychological well-being and perceptions of racism. In the meta-analysis that examined several possible moderating variables (Pieterse et al., 2012), only the type of well-being measured moderated the results. In another (Pascoe & Smart Richman, 2009) the type of measurement of well-being did not moderate the results. The third (D. L. Lee & Ahn, 2011), which identified significant associations with resources and coping among Asian and Asian American populations, found some differences between studies involving participants from several ethnic backgrounds and studies involving only individuals with ancestry from China, India, or Vietnam. In the most comprehensive meta-analysis (Schmitt et al., 2014), the results from disadvantaged populations were of greater magnitude than those of relatively advantaged populations. Effect sizes obtained from African Americans were lower than those of other racial groups. No differences were observed across participant age, but measures of self-esteem yielded effect sizes that were about half the magnitude ($r = -.13$) of those involving measures of psychological distress ($r = -.25$). Pervasive experiences of discrimination proved more problematic than single events, as would be expected. Notably, the authors also found evidence for causality, through the results of longitudinal studies and studies in which the discrimination was manipulated.

Presently, we have not confirmed whether the association between racism and well-being truly differs across several study characteristics—such as the sampling procedures used, the research design implemented, the method for measuring racism, or the time period in which the study was conducted—with results possibly changing over several decades. We also cannot discern whether the results differ as a function of participant gender, clinical status, level of acculturation, or socioeconomic status.

To address these important considerations, we present the results of a meta-analysis that we had conducted prior to the publication of the four already described. Our meta-analysis involved moderation analyses not reported in the other four, but we analyzed only 81 studies. This lower number of studies was due in part to our use of different screening procedures: (a) restricting inclusion to populations in the United States and Canada; (b) excluding measures of perceived racism that included the construct of distress (which would artificially inflate the magnitude of the association between perceived racism and psychological well-being); and (c) including only studies with measures of individuals' personal experiences, excluding generic measures of people's perceptions of racism in society. We recently learned about a fifth meta-analysis, not yet published, being conducted by Robert Carter (mentioned in Carter & Pieterse, 2013). We regret our delay in publishing our analyses because of personal circumstances and the amount of time required to compile all chapters in this book, but we are pleased that data synthesis is occurring with increased frequency in multicultural psychology; the field will benefit from increased attention to data. After presenting the data, we summarize the findings in a subsequent section.

QUANTITATIVE SYNTHESIS OF RESEARCH DATA

In this section we describe our meta-analysis of the literature evaluating the association between racism and well-being among people of color living in the United States or Canada. We evaluated studies with a quantitative measure of individuals' experiences with or perceptions of racism (using the terms *racism* or *racial/ethnic prejudice*, *discrimination*, or *oppression*) that was statistically associated with at least one quantitative measure of a component of personal well-being (i.e., mental health, self-esteem). However, to avoid conceptual overlap we excluded studies using measures of racism that had embedded the construct of emotional distress in its items or scaling (e.g., evaluations of how stressful the individuals felt as a result of the racism they encountered). This procedure was essential to distinguish the occurrence of racist events from emotional reactions related to well-being. Statistical estimates in manuscripts were all converted to Pearson's r using meta-analytic software, with negative values indicating that more encounters with racism were associated with lower levels of well-being and positive values indicating that more encounters with racism were associated with higher levels of well-being. The general methods of this meta-analysis are reported in the Appendix to this book.

Description of the Existing Research Literature

We analyzed 81 studies reporting data on a total of 44,158 individuals' psychological well-being associated with their self-reported experiences with or perceptions of racism. Only three studies involved actual mental health clients (see Table 9.1). All age groups except adults over age 55 were represented.

TABLE 9.1
Characteristics of 81 Studies of the Association Between Received Racism and Well-Being

Characteristic	M	No. of studies (k)	%
Year of report	2003		
Before 1980		0	0
1980–1989		1	1
1990–1999		13	16
2000–2010		67	83
Publication status			
Published		69	85
Unpublished		12	15
Research design			
Cross-sectional survey		66	82
Longitudinal survey		13	16
Archival		1	1
Comparison groups		1	1
Sample type			
Community members		51	62
University students		24	29
Clinical clients		3	4
Mixed sample (more than one of the above)		4	5
Sample size	545		
<50		1	1
50–99		8	10
100–199		30	37
200–399		25	31
400–999		7	9
>1,000		10	12
Participant age[a]	25.9		
Children (<13 years)		4	5
Adolescents (13–18 years)		21	27
Young adults (19–29 years)		26	34
Middle-aged adults (30–55 years)		26	34
Senior adults (>56 years)		0	0
Participant gender (% female)	61.5		
Participant race[b] (%)			
African American	49		
Asian American	17		
Hispanic/Latino(a) American	25		
Native American	2		
Other/combined groups	7		

Note. Not all variables sum to the total number of studies because of missing data.
[a]Average age category of participants in studies is given, though not all participants in the study would necessarily be in the category listed. [b]The racial composition of participants across all studies was calculated by multiplying the number of participants within studies by the percentage of participants from each racial group and dividing that product by the total number of participants.

Half of the research studies were specific to African Americans, but no studies were specific to Polynesian Americans, American Indians, or Alaskan Natives.

The typical study involved cross-sectional correlational data obtained from convenience samples of participants who completed a questionnaire containing measures of experiences with or perceptions of racism received and one or more measures of psychological well-being. Thus, the overall results provided an estimate of the correlation expected from a survey about racism and psychological well-being administered to people of color.

Overall Research Findings

Across all types of measures of psychological well-being, the random effects weighted correlation with all types of measures of racism was −.183 ($SE = .003$, 95% CI = [−.21, −.16], $p < .0001$). The heterogeneity of the findings was very large ($I^2 = 84.1$, 95% CI = [81, 87], $Q_{(80)} = 503.4$, $p < .001$). Across the 81 studies, the observed correlations between indicators of individuals' well-being and their perceptions of racism ranged from −0.46 to 0.09, with about two thirds being between −.30 and −.10. On average, reports of racism were modestly associated with well-being, but the data were so inconsistent as to caution against reliance on the overall average. We examined several factors that could possibly explain the variability of the findings.

Factors Influencing the Results

Possible Influence of Publication Bias

As shown in Figure 9.1, effect sizes were scattered in a circular pattern around the average value of $r = −.18$, whereas typically such data take the shape of an elongated pyramid. This scattered distribution could possibly have indicated "missing" studies due to publication bias. Egger's regression test (a method to evaluate data symmetry) did not indicate publication bias, but one statistical method for estimating publication bias (Duval & Tweedie, 2000) identified 12 "missing" studies from the distribution. When those 12 studies were accounted for ("filled"), the newly computed effect size of $r = −.16$ remained statistically significant ($p < .01$, 95% CI = [−.18, −.13]) and similar to the previously reported overall average. Therefore, we concluded that even though about a dozen studies had likely been missing from the meta-analysis, correction for their absence changed the results to a very small degree, such that publication bias was only a minor threat to interpretation of the results.

Study Characteristics

Meta-analyses can detect differences in effect size across research study characteristics. We considered the influence of year of study publication,

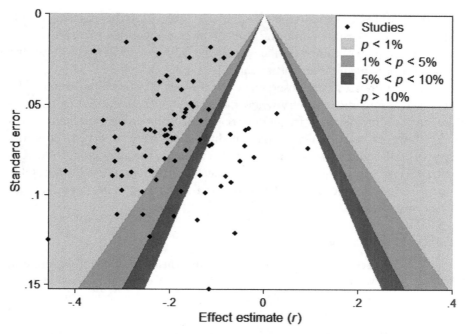

Figure 9.1. Contour-enhanced funnel plot of effect sizes (Pearson's *r*) by standard error for 81 studies of the association of perceived racism with well-being. The results were very inconsistent, irrespective of sample size. Moreover, there were fewer than expected studies with nonsignificant results (fewer dots in the white area adjacent to the left shaded portion of the graph) because the data should typically fall in the form of a pyramid, not the scatter depicted here. This distribution suggested that some studies may have been missing from the meta-analysis, with the overall average effect estimate adjusted to *r* = −.16.

research design, statistical controls, type of measure of racism, and type of well-being measured.

The results obtained across all 81 studies were found to be relatively stable over time (the correlation between the year of a study and its effect size was *r* = −.13, *p* = .13). Nevertheless, the majority of studies have occurred in the very recent past, and substantive social changes typically require more time for effects to be observed.

The results differed (*p* = .01) across the type of participant sampling, with eight large-scale surveys of participants randomly selected from the population having lower averaged results (*r* = −.11) than 67 studies using convenience sampling (*r* = −.19) and six studies involving random selection from a local setting or sampling with greater than 60% nonparticipation (*r* = −.23).

Correlation values obtained from 66 cross-sectional studies averaged *r* = −.18, which was essentially the same as the averaged value of *r* = −.19

obtained from 13 longitudinal studies. Moreover, the 12 studies that statistically controlled for possible confounds (age, education, gender, race, and socio-economic status) obtained similar averaged results ($r = -.17$) to the 69 studies that did not control for any other variable ($r = -.19$).

No differences were observed across the way racism was measured: The averaged results did not vary when racism was operationalized in terms of perceptions, incidence or frequency recall, or combined measurement methods. However, statistically significant differences were observed across the type of well-being that was measured. On average, the association of racism with adverse mental health symptoms (e.g., depression, anxiety) was notably stronger than with measures of positive well-being (e.g., self-esteem, life satisfaction; $r = -.22$ vs. $-.12$, $p = .01$).

Participant Characteristics

Characteristics of research participants varied widely across research studies, and we analyzed the possible influence of participants' average age, estimated birth year (for possible cohort effects), gender composition (% female), type of population (community members, students, clinical samples), estimated level of acculturation, estimated socioeconomic status, and race.

The results did not differ across race ($p > .10$). The findings of 32 studies specific to African Americans were similar ($r = -.18$) to the findings of 16 studies specific to Asian Americans ($r = -.20$) and to the findings of 16 studies specific to Hispanic/Latino(a) Americans ($r = -.16$); the percentages of participants from each racial group were unrelated to the study's results. Furthermore, no significant differences were found across participant age, estimated birth year, gender, education level, acculturation level, or socioeconomic status. Only three studies investigated clinical populations, which averaged $r = -.25$, and the averaged results from community members and university students averaged $r = -.175$.

DISCUSSION AND INTERPRETATION OF THE FINDINGS

Overall Findings

Abundant data has confirmed that experiences of racism are negatively associated with individuals' self-reported well-being (D. L. Lee & Ahn, 2011; Pascoe & Smart Richman, 2009; Pieterse et al., 2012; Schmitt et al., 2014). Our overall results were slightly less robust than those reported in the larger meta-analysis by Schmitt and colleagues (2014), and after adjusting for possible publication bias ($r = -.16$) our results were identical to those of Pascoe and Smart Richman (2009), who also adjusted for publication bias. To interpret, a correlation value of that magnitude is equivalent to the association between socioeconomic status and well-being (Pinquart & Sörensen, 2000) and also to the overall association between personality variables and well-being (DeNeve & Cooper, 1998). The association is not nearly as large as that between physical health and well-being ($r = .32$; Okun, Stock, Haring, & Witter, 1984), but it remains consequential. Nevertheless, the research findings are highly variable, so we cannot accurately predict how any particular group, let alone any single individual, will interpret and respond to racism.

Secondary Analyses

The primary contributions of this particular meta-analysis involve the investigation of potential moderating variables either unexamined in previous meta-analyses or inconsistently identified across meta-analyses. One of our notable findings involved an analysis of how well-being was measured in studies. Although Pascoe and Smart Richman (2009) did not find statistically significant differences across the form of well-being measurement used in studies, our results were essentially identical to those of the meta-analysis of Schmitt et al. (2014) and Pieterse et al. (2012), who both found that the association between perceived racism and positive aspects of well-being (e.g., self-esteem, quality of life) was much lower than the association when measurement involved negative well-being indicators (e.g., distress). We believe that these data are sufficiently robust to support the assumption that negative aspects of well-being are indeed more strongly associated with perceptions of racism than are positive aspects. We conjecture that this relationship exists because racism is a distressing series of events that overlap experientially with states of distress more than with overall life satisfaction or well-being.

Our meta-analysis confirmed no differences across participant race, gender, age, and socioeconomic status; the association between racism and well-being is independent of these variables. However, results differed between large-scale surveys with strong external validity and surveys with high rates of participant attrition. This finding suggests that the results of surveys with high participant attrition are suspect, due to possible selection bias: Individuals acutely affected by racism may be more likely to participate in the research than individuals with less distress ascribed to racism. Thus, even though the size of the correlation between perceived racism and well-being has remained fairly consistent across four meta-analyses, that association is inflated by the inclusion of studies with high rates of participant attrition.

Considerations for Future Research

Our findings suggest that research quality does matter. When the vast majority of research is correlational, a design highly susceptible to bias, efforts to reduce bias become even more essential. Specifically, if the people participating are more invested in the topic of racism (i.e., have had more negative experiences with racism) than nonparticipants, why should we trust the results? We also found that relatively few studies statistically controlled for possible confounds. Although those few studies with statistical controls yielded similar results to those using unadjusted data, in the future researchers should account for obvious sources of bias, and journal editors are encouraged to reject manuscripts with sources in which bias remains uncontrolled, particularly high rates of nonparticipation.

Measurement precision typically enhances the consistency of results. Unfortunately, the measures of racism in studies we examined were inconsistent in how participants were instructed (or not instructed) about the meaning of racism and what time period was evaluated (lifetime incidence vs. recent time periods). We cannot help but wonder whether the large heterogeneity of the findings was attributable to measurement issues such as cultural measurement equivalence and item bias (Trimble & Vaughn, 2013). We found that cross-sectional studies yielded essentially the same results as longitudinal studies ($r = -.18$ and $-.19$, respectively), indicating that the relationship between racism and well-being did not vary due to being measured concurrently or at a later time, perhaps because most measures were already retrospective, measuring encounters with racism distanced in time. We understand the convenience of using retrospective methods; however, the field now has more than enough studies examining racism in the undetermined past, a measure easily confounded by present mood and other factors affecting recall accuracy. Optimally, research should seek out participants who have recently experienced racism, provided representative samples can be obtained.

We were surprised to find few studies of mental health clients. Clinical research could be helpful in finding explanations for the differences in results concerning positive versus negative well-being. People vulnerable to mental illness may also be more likely to be targets of individual acts of racism. Or people may cope with racism less effectively because of their existing level of distress. In addition, some clients may present racist and discriminatory experience as their main concern yet feel as though the therapist does not truly understand the deeply damaging psychological effects they experience.

Psychological distress is correlated more strongly with racist events than general life satisfaction. Future research should explicitly confirm that this difference between positive and negative well-being is not solely attributable to preexisting levels of distress (Allen, Lewis, & Johnson-Jennings, 2015), although we sincerely doubt that preexisting levels of distress completely account for the severity of the racism perceived.

We found that almost half (49%) of the literature was specific to African Americans, yet the data suggest minimal differences across race, with the average effect size being smaller among African Americans relative to Asian Americans (Schmitt et al., 2014). Race-specific research can be valuable for many reasons, but such research could better consider the experiences of other groups, particularly Arab Americans, Polynesian Americans, Native American Indians, and Alaskan Natives. We also see little value in further comparisons among groups, as some researchers have a tendency to view the groups as more homogeneous than they are and thus gloss over deep cultural variations within groups (Trimble & Bhadra, 2013).

We encourage researchers to examine potential mediating variables, guided by the work of D. L. Lee and Ahn (2011). These authors found evidence that coping strategies, social support, cultural identity, and personal strengths influence the association between perceptions of racism and well-being. Investigating perceptions of racism in isolation, without concurrent consideration of mediating variables, does not seem particularly effective in moving the field forward.

Suggestions for Practitioners

If perceptions of racism are associated with well-being to about the same extent as personality or socioeconomic variables, therapists should consider clients' experiences of racism in the same ways they would account for personality and socioeconomic status. They cannot afford to ignore such experiences. Although individual clients vary widely in their experiences of racism and their reactions to it, similar variability characterizes personality attributes (DeNeve & Cooper, 1998), which are already seriously considered by many mental health professionals.

Given the differences of association between negative and positive measures of well-being, therapists should particularly attune to and interpret incidents of racism among populations in greatest distress. We assume but cannot yet confirm (given the correlational nature of the data) that high levels of distress make racism particularly problematic, both in terms of psychological impact and in terms of reactive coping. We also assume that the therapist can better assist clients by framing discussions of racism in terms of resilience and resistance, neither implicitly blaming individuals for their reactions nor implicitly assuming client passivity in the face of inequitable and dehumanizing situations.

Therapists should not have to worry about whether a client describes racism in terms of frequency or severity; no differences were found in the data across measures of perceptions of severity, incidence or frequency, or a combination. Thus, therapists can consider any method of client self-report; the associated negative consequences for well-being would be similar.

Finally, therapists should not assume that an individual of any particular background is more or less vulnerable to racism. It affects all groups. Its impact is equivalently adverse and equally unpredictable.

CONCLUSION

The findings of the present meta-analysis confirm and extend the results of other recent meta-analytic reviews: Racism is associated with diminished psychological well-being across racial and ethnic groups. In the lives of people of color, racism is as consequential to well-being as socioeconomic conditions (Pinquart & Sörensen, 2000). Mental health professionals should attend to clients' experiences interacting across social groups.

The data we reviewed reminded us of an anecdote shared by a colleague who studies issues of racism. Media coverage of that person's research generated a substantial amount of general public response. One correspondent, who had apparently experienced racism for decades, congratulated the researcher but also commented that it seemed bizarre that the scientific community would only now be validating what was so obvious—painfully obvious. Mental health professionals and researchers can catch up with the pace of reality.

We conclude with a recommendation for the profession that exceeds the bounds of the data we reviewed. We believe that mental health practices and research must be inspired by an objective even more consequential than validating past and current trauma and injury. Our primary objective must become to prevent racism (D. W. Sue, 2005, 2013; Zárate et al., 2014). No one would be satisfied with medical explanations of HIV or cancer that merely described individual suffering and its correlates. Mental health professionals attend to suffering, but that focus may have detracted from the work essential to prevention. Mental health professionals are well positioned to take a leading role in scientific efforts to understand racism in order to prevent it.

10

ETHNIC IDENTITY AND WELL-BEING OF PEOPLE OF COLOR: AN UPDATED META-ANALYSIS

For there are nearly as many ways in which such identities, fleeting or
enduring, sweeping or intimate, cosmopolitan or closed-in, amiable or
bloody-minded, are put together as there are materials with which to put
them together and reasons for doing so. . . . [A]nswers people sometimes
give to the question, whether self-asked or asked by others, as to who
(or, perhaps, more exactly, what) they are, simply do not form an orderly
structure.

—Clifford Geertz (2000, p. 225)

Culturally sensitive and multiculturally competent mental health professionals often ask about a client's ethnic and racial identity. Responses to
such queries can strengthen the therapist's understanding of the worldviews
relevant to the client's presenting concerns, make explicit the client's expectations for the treatment process, and enhance the client's comfort with
the therapist, among other factors. Yet, as cultural anthropologist Clifford
Geertz (2000) suggested, discussions and evaluations of ethnic identity are
complicated because human beings have multiple intertwined identities
that interact and affect one another in ways that are not fully understood.
Unfortunately, answers to the question of ethnic identity "simply do not form
an orderly structure" (Geertz, 2000, p. 225).

Most of the research on ethnic and racial identity has been limited
to the abstraction of race and ethnicity at a social and psychological level

A complete list of references for the studies included in this chapter's meta-analysis is posted online.
Readers can consult it at http://pubs.apa.org/books/supp/smith

http://dx.doi.org/10.1037/14733-010
Foundations of Multicultural Psychology: Research to Inform Effective Practice, by T. B. Smith and J. E. Trimble

of analysis (Amiot, de la Sablonnière, Terry, & Smith, 2007; Gong, 2007; Negy, Shreve, Jensen, & Uddin, 2003; Yip, Douglass, & Sellers, 2014). Other dimensions of an individual's identity, such as multiple identities, situational and contextual influences, and role expectations and enactments, are given less attention in the psychological literature. The widespread interest in the topic of ethnic identity suggests that we must stop and take stock of the field's progress and its future directions.

The growth in the field, with its attendant methodological and procedural problems and theoretical debates, points to the need for inquiry into the conceptualization and measurement of these seemingly elusive constructs. Accordingly, this chapter provides an overview of the construct of ethnic identity, particularly its relationship to psychological well-being, along with a brief discussion of ethnic identity measures. An updated meta-analysis summarizes research findings on the association between measures of ethnic identity and personal well-being. Although there is considerable literature on racial identity, those articles were not included in our analysis because of the differences between many racial identity and ethnic identity scales, including the ways the former are typically operationalized and measured.

NARRATIVE REVIEW OF THE LITERATURE

Origins of Ethnic Identity Constructs

Typically the term *identity* expresses the notion of sameness, likeness, and oneness. More precisely, identity means "the sameness of a person or thing at all times in all circumstances; the condition or fact that a person or thing is itself and not something else" (Simpson & Weiner, 1989, p. 620). Moynihan (1993) argued that identity is "a process located in the core of the individual and yet, also, in . . . his communal culture" (p. 64). It is a powerful conceptualization that strongly influences one's personality, sense of belonging and sameness, and quality of life.

To extend their understanding of identity, most social and psychological theorists must contend with the concept of self. And to approach an understanding of self-concept, one is obliged to provide plausible, if not substantial, explanations for the following domains: physical traits and characteristics, personal experiences past and present, social affiliations and integration, and personal values and behaviors, along with messages received from other people about those several issues (Cirese, 1985). Explanations for these domains consume volumes.

Although the bulk of the social and behavioral studies circumscribed by the ethnic variables concentrate on ethnic minority populations, generally the literature on ethnicity is actually far more inclusive. Social science interest in ethnicity, especially as a potential explanatory variable, began in the late 1940s (Cross, 1991; P. A. Katz & Taylor, 1988). Interest was fueled by at least two fundamental concerns: (a) the contentious notion of America as a melting pot of different nationalities, ethnic groups, and religious affiliations; and (b) the continuous concerns about pluralism and integration. The era "witnessed an outbreak of what might be called 'ethnic fever'" in which "the nation's racial and ethnic minorities sought to rediscover their waning ethnicity and to reaffirm their ties to the cultural past" (Steinberg, 1981, p. 3).

Although *ethnicity* and *race* are often used interchangeably, scholars have offered various distinct definitions for both constructs. The term *race* has multiple meanings and therefore is difficult to define. For example, "Ethnicity is often used as a euphemism for race," maintained Janet Helms (1994), "as well as for other sociocultural affiliations (such as religious and linguistic groups)." She continued, "Thus it might better be defined as social identity based on the culture of one's ancestors' national or tribal group as modified by the demands of the CULTURE in which one's group currently resides" (p. 293). To add to the complexity of the construct, Helms (1994) also suggested that "race has three types of definitions: (1) quasi-biological, (2) sociopolitical-historical, and (3) cultural. Each type may have relevance for how race becomes one of an individual's collective identities" (p. 297).

Helms (2007) firmly maintained that "racial identity theories do not suppose that racial groups in the United States are biologically distinct but rather suppose that they have endured different conditions of domination or oppression" (p. 181). Thus, for Helms, racial identity refers to the "psychological mechanisms that people develop to function effectively in a society where some people enjoy social and political advantage because of their ancestors' (presumed) physical appearances, but others suffer disadvantage and lower status for the same reasons" (Trimble, Helms, & Root, 2002, pp. 249–250; see Helms, 1994). As an alternative to *race*, Helms (1994) recommended using the term *sociorace* to acknowledge "the fact that typically the only criteria used to assign people to racial groups in this country are socially defined and arbitrary" (p. 147).

Research on ethnicity appears to dominate the social science literature; however as long as racism exists, the term *race* must continue to be used to draw attention to the racist experiences of millions of people who are constantly subjected to it. To merely classify these experiences with the terms *prejudice* or *discrimination* obfuscates the painful sting of racism; hence, to directly and forcefully confront racism, *race* must be kept at the forefront of our vocabulary when discussing intergroup and interpersonal relations (J. M. Jones, 2003).

Phinney (1990) noted "widely discrepant definitions and measures of ethnic identity, which makes generalizations and comparisons across studies difficult and ambiguous" (p. 500). Phinney (2003) developed the most widely used definition of the construct: "Ethnic identity is a dynamic, multidimensional construct that refers to one's identity, or sense of self as a member of an ethnic group" (p. 63). From her perspective, one claims an identity within the context of a subgroup; this subgroup claims a common ancestry and shares at least a similar culture, religion, language, kinship, or place of origin (Phinney & Ong, 2007). Phinney (2003) added, "Ethnic identity is not a fixed categorization, but rather is a fluid and dynamic understanding of self and ethnic background. Ethnic identity is constructed and modified as individuals become aware of their ethnicity, within the large (sociocultural) setting" (p. 63). At another level the term *identity* is almost synonymous with the term *ethnicity*, prompting some sociologists, such as Herbert Gans (2003), to suggest that *identity* is no longer a useful term.

Brief Overview of Relevant Theory

Social and psychological interest in ethnic and racial identity has resulted in a copious increase in journal articles and books on the subject. A few skeptics doubt that ethnicity is a benign topic; some refer to it as the "new ethnicity" because it is viewed as divisive, inegalitarian, and racist (Morgan, 1981). On occasion, the mention of ethnicity and identity, especially in academic circles, sparks discussion claiming that without segregation, ethnicity would not survive. Discussion can and often does turn to assertions that Americans tend to exaggerate the existence and beneficence of ethnicity (Yinger, 1986), with such phrases as "imagined ethnicity" and "pseudo-ethnicity" referring to those who foist some ethnic factor to justify an action. Similarly, concerning research on ethnic factors, Gordon (1978) asserted that "students of ethnicity run the risk of finding ethnic practices where they are not, of ascribing an ethnic social and cultural order where they do not in fact influence the person" (p. 151). Consequently, critics argue over some fanciful line to separate ethnic from nonethnic influences. The argument poses some questions: When can behavior, personality, values, attitudes, and so forth, be attributed to ethnic and racial factors? If an ethnic or racial attribution is not discernible, what sociocultural and psychological influence can account for the phenomenon?

Several anthropologists, historians, psychologists, and sociologists have written extensively on ethnic and racial identity (see reviews by M. E. Bernal & Knight, 1993; Carter, 1996; Cross, 1991; H. W. Harris, Blue, & Griffith, 1995; Helms, 1990, 1994; Sellers & Shelton, 2003; T. B. Smith & Silva, 2011; Steinberg, 1981; R. H. Thompson, 1989; Trimble, 2005; Trimble et al., 2002; van den Berghe, 1981; Yip et al., 2014). Theoretical positions vary, including some lodged in individual experiences and some formed from a sociobiological perspective. Barth's (1969) position represents the former: the native's worldview defines relationships, boundaries, lifestyles, and thought-ways. The sociobiological perspective, most fervently represented by Pierre van den Berghe (1981), is that "ethnic and racial sentiments are extensions of kinship sentiments" (p. 18) and that "descent . . . is the central feature of ethnicity" (p. 27). To support his argument, van den Berghe asserted that "there exists a general predisposition, in our species as in many others, to react favorably toward other organisms to the extent that those organisms are biologically related to the actor" (p. 19).

A review of the various treatises written about ethnicity leads one to an inevitable conclusion of its complexity (Helms, 2007; Phinney & Ong, 2007; Ponterotto & Park-Taylor, 2007; Trimble, 2007; Trimble & Dickson, 2005; Yip et al., 2014). In its broadest form, ethnicity refers to "any differentiation based on nationality, race, religion, or language" (Greeley, 1974, p. 187). Typically, ethnic identity is an affiliative construct by which an individual is viewed by self and others as belonging to a particular group. An individual can choose to associate with a group, especially if other choices are available (i.e., having mixed ethnic or racial heritage). Affiliation can be influenced by racial, natal, symbolic, and cultural factors (Cheung, 1993). Racial factors include physi-ognomic and physical characteristics; natal factors refer to "homeland" (or ancestral) origins of individuals, their parents, and kin; and symbolic factors include those that typify or exemplify an ethnic group (e.g., holidays, foods, clothing, artifacts). Symbolic ethnic identity usually implies that individuals choose their identity; however, to some extent, the cultural elements of the ethnic or racial group have a modest influence on their behavior (Kivisto & Nefzger, 1993). Cultural factors, which involve the specific lifeways and thoughtways of an ethnic group, are probably the most difficult to assess and measure (see Cheung, 1993, for more details). In conceptualizing ethnic iden-tity, the totality of racial, natal, symbolic, and cultural factors must be consid-ered to achieve a full and complete understanding of the construct. In the next section a few notable ethnic and racial identity scales are summarized to illus-trate the range of approaches researchers may use to measure the constructs.

Measurement of Ethnic Identity

In 1990 Jean Phinney summarized the existing ethnic identity literature for adolescents and adults, emphasizing primarily measurement and concep-tualization. She noted that "there is no widely agreed on definition of ethnic identity" and "the definitions that were given reflected quite different under-standings or emphasis regarding what is meant by ethnic identity" (p. 500). Undoubtedly, social and behavioral scientists believe they have a general sense for the ethnic construct; some indeed are rather firm about their posi-tions (van den Berghe, 1981; Weinreich, 1986; Weinreich & Saunderson,

2003). Identity as a psychological construct is also the subject of considerable debate; however, the addition of *ethnic* has cast the debate and subsequent hodgepodge of opinion into another domain. In fact, about a quarter of the studies reviewed by Phinney were not built on a theoretical framework.

Several conceptual approaches to ethnic identity emphasize an individual level of analysis linking notions of identity formation and development to self-concept. Much of the work in this area relies on Henri Tajfel's (1982) theory of social identity, which maintains that social identity strongly influences self-perception and thus should be the central locus of evaluation. When ethnicity forms the nexus of an in-group, self-identity will be influenced accordingly. One's distinctive ethnic characteristics, however, can be restrictive, as one may reject "externally based evaluations of the in-group" and therefore "may establish [one's] own standards and repudiate those of the dominant out-group" (M. E. Bernal, Saenz, & Knight, 1991, p. 135). Other responses are possible; individuals might withdraw or choose to dissociate with the referent, thereby adding psychological complications for themselves. Tajfel's social identity theory has generated considerable influence on ethnic identity research. Some prefer to carry out the work under the ethnic self-identification rubric (see Helms, 1994, 2007; Phinney, 1990, 1992; Phinney & Ong, 2007; Ponterotto & Park-Taylor, 2007; Trimble, 2007; Umaña-Taylor, 2004; Umaña-Taylor & Shin, 2007).

Approaches to measuring ethnic and racial identity range from use of a single item (Richman, Gaviria, Flaherty, Birz, & Wintrob, 1987) to scales containing several dimensions (Carter, 1996; Helms, 1990, 1994; Phinney, 1992; Umaña-Taylor, 2004; Weinreich, 1986; Weinreich & Saunderson, 2003). Whatever measurement approach or technique is being developed or used, one must factor in four domains of inquiry:

- natality, one's ancestral genealogy, including parents, siblings, and grandparents;
- subjective identification, a declaration of one's own ethnic or racial identity. Stephan and Stephan (2000) argued that "the goal of assessment of race/ethnicity is accuracy from the perspective of the respondent, and that the accuracy of such a social construct can only be obtained by individual self-designation" (p. 549);
- behavioral expressions of identity, as the respondent indicates preferences for activities germane to his or her ethnic affiliation, such as foods, music, books, and so forth; and
- situational or contextual influences, with the respondent indicating the situations that call for deliberate expression of the ethnic affiliation, such as traditional ceremonies, interaction with family and peers, neighborhood gatherings, and so forth

(Ponterotto & Park-Taylor, 2007; Trimble, 2000; Trimble et al., 2002; Umaña-Taylor, 2004; Umaña-Taylor & Shin, 2007; Yip et al., 2014).

At minimum, scales and measures should attempt to capture the essence of each domain to provide a full and complete profile or silhouette of an individual's identity. Helms (1994) added to this suggestion by pointing out that measures should be tridimensional and include items to tap individual characteristics, own-group affiliation, and out-group relations.

Simple nominal ethnic and racial procedures for declaring affiliation and membership have limited usefulness. Although categories are commonly used, Waters (1990) pointed out that

> one cannot tell what this identity means to be an individual, how and why people choose a particular ethnic identity from a range of possible choices; how often and in what ways that ethnic identity is used in everyday life; and how ethnic identity is intergenerationally transferred within families. (p. 11)

Building a scale on the social identity theory of Tajfel (1982) and the developmental stages advocated by Erik Erikson, Phinney (1992) created the Multigroup Ethnic Identity Measure (MEIM), which asks respondents to indicate their ethnic affiliation twice in the 15-item scale. This widely used scale has undergone revision and been reduced to six items that evaluate two components: identity exploration and identity commitment (Phinney & Ong, 2007).

Until recently, most of the published ethnic and racial identity measures have asked the respondent to state one ethnic affiliation. However, because many respondents have more than one ethnic identity, Oetting and Beauvais (1991) developed a full scale of over 50 items allowing an individual to "independently express identification or lack of identification" (p. 663) with several cultural groups. They claimed that "in large-scale surveys of adults, only two basic items may be needed to assess identification with any one culture reasonably well: (1) Do you live in the ____ way of life? and (2) Are you a success in the ____ way of life?" (p. 664). The researcher would fill in the blank space with an ethnic group such as Puerto Rican; the researcher can further specify the ethnic label by referring to a geographic locale or some other designation such as a neighborhood, reservation, village, or island grouping. Other items can be added to assess such things as family identification and tradition, cultural event participation, language preferences, and parental identification to expand the presumed effectiveness of the scale.

In the 1980s Weinreich put forth his theory and measurement technique, explicating Identity Structure Analysis (ISA), a complex, highly sophisticated approach to assessing individuals' ethnic identity as well as their identities with other facets of their lives. If an individual identifies to some degree with more than one ethnic or racial group, this multiple identity can be captured with the ISA approach (Weinreich, 1986; Weinreich & Saunderson, 2003). ISA is grounded in psychodynamic developmental theory, personal construct psychology, appraisal theory, social constructionism, cognitive–affective consistency theories, and symbolic interactionist theoretical perspectives. According to Weinreich and Saunderson (2003), "ISA conceptualizes one's appraisal of social situations as involving one's interpretation of their significance to self's identity from moment to moment. Appraisal provides and records experiences of situations and events" (p. 20). ISA can be custom designed to measure identity in an idiographic or nomothetic framework through use of bipolar constructs; thus, the approach can be tailored for an individual as well as for groups. Indices can be constructed to measure such constructs as self-image (past, current, and ideal), well-being, values, role models, reference groups, empathetic identification, and conflicting identification, in addition to evaluation of others and a few other related domains of identity.

The scales summarized in this section and those described in the literature are not without criticism. Indeed, researchers and scholars have subjected many of the measures and their corresponding theories to extensive scrutiny through cross-validation procedures, empirical testing, and theoretical speculation. For example, Root (2000) maintained that "the current models do not account for a range of ways in which people construct their core identities and determine the importance of race in them" (p. 214). Moreover, Root noted that "researchers have found no reliable method of extrapolating the core or breadth of one's identity from one context of identity or from a response to one question" (p. 212).

Association of Ethnic Identity With Well-Being

A close correspondence has been noted between an individual's sense of ethnic identity and subjective well-being (George, 2010). Both constructs involve personal assessment of the extent to which one identifies with an ethnic or racial group. Yip and her colleagues (2014) pointed out that "the contributions of both perspectives result in a common focus on the positive implications of a coherent sense of racial/ethnic identity for general well-being" (p. 180).

Subjective well-being can be defined as individuals' assessment of their cognitive satisfaction and emotional reactions to their lives. Some scholars claim that subjective well-being involves global assessment of all aspects of a person's life. However, important differences are found in the nature of well-being across multicultural groups. Thus, one might ask whether cognitive–affective evaluations represent a universal basis for defining well-being across multicultural groups. To assess well-being subjectively, rather than through a group normative standard, encompasses assumptions aligned with a cultural frame valuing personal independence, often labeled as *individualism*.

The status of well-being research is somewhat culturally situated within only one system of values and beliefs. For example, Ryff and Keyes (1995) proposed the following dimensions: self-acceptance, personal growth, life purpose, environmental mastery, autonomy, and positive interpersonal relations. Diener and Diener (1995) pointed out that subjective well-being can be defined as "a person's evaluative reactions to his or her life—either in terms of life satisfaction (cognitive evaluations) or affect (ongoing emotional reactions)" (p. 653). They identified three hallmarks of the well-being construct: (a) It resides within the experience of the individual, (b) it includes positive measures, and (c) it involves global assessment of all aspects of a person's life. Seligman (2011) proposed PERMA as a means to understand happiness and well-being: positive emotion, engagement, relationship, meaning, and accomplishments.

All of these approaches are framed within an individuocentric perspective and thus ignore the richness of "living life well" that exists in countless ethnocultural populations. On this point, cross-cultural psychologist Michael Bond (2013) asked, "What factors lead an individual on this planet to assess himself or herself as satisfied with life?" He contended that "four aspects of an individual's 'life as lived' will contribute to life satisfaction in any national culture: sound health, satisfaction with one's finances, a sense of autonomy, and happiness" (p. 158).

Limited consideration has been given to the contribution of ethnic and racial group identification in determining well-being outcomes. Some studies have found ethnic identity to be associated with a number of positive outcomes (e.g., Phinney, Horenczyk, Liebkind, & Vedder, 2001). Among a sample of 161 African American adults, Yap, Settles, and Pratt-Hyatt (2011) found that relationship centrality and private life satisfaction were mediated by perceptions of belonging. They also found that gender moderated the strength of each of these mediating effects: Belongingness mediated the relationships for women but not for men. In two somewhat related studies Mandara, Gaylord-Harden, Richards, and Ragsdale (2009) and Binning, Unzueta, Huo, and Molina (2009) found that ethnic identity may be as important as self-esteem to the mental health of African American adolescents and that those who identified with multiple groups tended to report either equal or higher psychological well-being and social engagement.

Recent research has now reached a critical mass sufficient to provide an empirical test of the relationships between the two constructs. Several decades ago Phinney (1990) found a reasonable distribution of studies show-ing a definitive relationship between ethnic identity and psychological well-being. A meta-analysis used data from 184 studies to systematically explore the relationship between ethnic identity and well-being among North American people of color (T. B. Smith & Silva, 2011), with the results indi-cating a modest but statistically significant average effect size of $r = .17$ for this relationship. However, the range of association expressed in effect sizes was highly variable, and secondary analysis revealed a number of pertinent com-plexities to these data. The effect sizes were strongest for measures of positive aspects of well-being, which included happiness, life satisfaction, quality of life, self-esteem, and self-mastery. Effect sizes were weakest for mental health symptoms such as depression and anxiety. Ethnic identity appears to function more efficaciously among people of color by enhancing positive components of well-being than by buffering against psychopathology.

In a study of over 600 high school students born in the United States, researchers found among African Americans, White/European Americans, and Hispanic/Latino(a) Americans a positive association between self-esteem and ethnic identity (Phinney, Cantu, & Kurtz, 1997). Similar pat-terns have been observed among Korean American college students: clarity, pride, and engagement in individuals' ethnic identity was positively related to self-esteem and negatively related to depressive symptoms (R. M. Lee, 2005). However, when these associations were examined over time, no evidence was found for any longitudinal associations between ethnic identity and self-esteem (Umaña-Taylor, Vargas-Chanes, Garcia, & Gonzales-Backen, 2008).

In a seminal paper examining cultural perspectives of well-being, Wong (2011) identified "four pillars" of the good life as meaning, virtue, resilience, and well-being. Regarding these points, Wong maintained, "Given that there are cultural differences, subjective well-being still provides a useful index on how we are doing and how well we live at the individual and national level" (p. 15). Similarly, Diener and Tov (2009) reported that life satisfaction and positive affects exist in different forms in many countries, concluding,

> The World Poll shows that differences in society can make an enor-mous difference in levels of subjective well-being. The differences in well-being between societies are as large as the differences between very happy and depressed individuals. The role of institutions and societies should not be underplayed in our attempts to understand and improve the world. (p. 218)

Allen, Rivkin, and López (2014) agreed, adding,

> A significant body of evidence strongly suggests dimensions of well-being are not the same across cultures, and even what seems to outwardly

appear a common element can instead involve different acts, scripts, and meanings across multicultural groups. However, despite their central relevance in addressing the situation, elaboration of indigenous theories of well-being are generally early in development, largely incomplete, and often raise many more questions than they answer. In developing this knowledge base, psychology would do well to remain ever vigilant of the ecological fallacy, whereby knowledge based on the perspective of an aggregate is assumed to apply to an individual. (p. 308)

By way of summary, social and behavioral scientists vary in how they conceptualize and measure the constructs of ethnic and racial identity, which at their core involve multiple issues of sameness and differentiation. Thus, the measurement of ethnicity and ethnic identity is no small task, especially given the debate surrounding its theoretical foundations and its usefulness. Researchers must consider the "various cultural and structural dimensions of ethnicity" (Cheung, 1989, p. 72) and "distinguish between general aspects of ethnic identity that apply across groups and specific aspects that distinguish groups" (Phinney, 1990, p. 508). To accomplish this we must move away from viewing ethnic groups as homogeneous entities; in fact, there may be more heterogeneity within certain ethnic and racial groups than among the dominant groups in North American society (Cheung, 1993; Trimble, 1990; Trimble & Dickson, 2005).

This chapter focuses on psychological well-being and its correspondence with ethnic identity. Most of the literature on the subject emphasizes an *individuocentric* orientation, with the locus of analysis in an individual's assessment of his or her sense of well-being, satisfaction with life, and levels and depths of ethnic identity. More research is necessary to fully understand the contributions of different lifeways and thoughtways to "living life well."

This chapter began with an observation by Clifford Geertz (2000), and the review of literature closes at this point with another of his astute observations:

As the world becomes more thoroughly interconnected, economically and politically, as people move about in unforeseen, only partially controllable, and increasingly massive, ways, and new lines are drawn and old ones erased . . . the catalogue of available identifications expands, contracts, changes shape, ramifies, involutes, and develops. (p 225)

Accordingly, the only principled way we can meet the challenge posed by the enlarging catalogue is to engage in a thorough inquiry. The following section reports an updated meta-analysis of the literature, with a summary of the findings presented in the section after that.

QUANTITATIVE SYNTHESIS OF RESEARCH ON THE ASSOCIATION BETWEEN ETHNIC IDENTITY AND PERSONAL WELL-BEING

This section consists of a meta-analysis that includes 31 studies beyond those analyzed by T. B. Smith and Silva (2011). Moreover, additional information regarding the racial heterogeneity of samples and the magnitude of ethnic identity are included in this review. We sought to determine the degree to which additional data modified the findings of the 2010 publication and to ascertain whether additional variables affected the findings across studies. The methods of this meta-analysis are reported in the Appendix of this book.

Description of the Existing Research Literature

We located a total of 215 studies that reported data on 50,717 individuals' psychological well-being as a function of their self-reported level of ethnic identity. As shown in Table 10.1, the number of studies investigating the topic has increased substantively over the past 2 decades, but few studies have involved actual mental health clients. All age groups except adults over age 55 were adequately represented in the literature. Asian Americans were overrepresented relative to their percentage of the U.S. population. Native American Indians were underrepresented, with 16 studies including Native American Indians and only eight being specific to that population. Only one study evaluated Polynesian Americans, Native Hawaiians.

The typical study involved cross-sectional (correlational) data obtained from convenience samples of participants who completed a questionnaire containing measures of ethnic identity (most often the MEIM) and one or more measures of psychological well-being, typically self-esteem. Thus, the overall results provide an estimate of the correlation expected when administering a survey about ethnic identity and well-being to people of color.

Overall Research Findings

Across all types of measures of well-being, the random effects weighted correlation with ethnic identity was .182 (SE = .009, 95% CI = [.16, .20], $p < .0001$). The heterogeneity of the findings was moderately high (I^2 = 72, 95% CI = [67, 75], $Q_{(214)}$ = 753, $p < .001$). Across the 215 research studies, the observed correlations between individuals' level of ethnic identity and their perceptions of well-being ranged from −0.18 to 0.60. However, most of the effect sizes (80%) fell between 0.0 and 0.35. A positive ethnic identity was associated with slightly poorer well-being in 10% of the studies, but was strongly

TABLE 10.1
Characteristics of 215 Studies of the Association
Between Ethnic Identity and Well-Being

Characteristic	M	No. of studies (k)	%
Year of report	2001		
Before 1980		0	0
1980–1989		3	1
1990–1999		68	32
2000–2008		121	67
Publication status			
Published		93	43
Unpublished		122	57
Sampling procedure			
Convenience		200	93
Representative (random selection)		15	7
Research design			
Cross-sectional		203	94
Longitudinal		12	6
Population			
General community members		62	29
Students		136	63
At-risk group members		14	7
Clinical populations (in treatment)		3	1
Sample size	236		
<50		7	3
50–99		55	26
100–199		79	37
200–399		50	23
400–999		18	8
>1,000		6	3
Participant age[a]	23.0		
Children (<13 years)		16	7
Adolescents (13–18 years)		72	34
Young adults (19–29 years)		76	35
Middle-aged adults (30–55 years)		33	15
Senior adults (>55 years)		6	3
Not reported		12	6
Participant gender (% female)	61.8		
Participant race[b] (%)			
African American	36		
Asian American	34		
Hispanic/Latino(a) American	25		
Native American Indian	2		
Pacific Islander American	1		
Other	2		

Note. Not all variables sum to the total number of studies because of missing data.
[a]Average age category of participants within studies (not all participants necessarily in the category listed).
[b]The racial composition of participants across all studies, calculated by multiplying the number of participants within studies by the percentage of participants from each racial group and dividing that product by the total number of participants.

associated with high levels of well-being in about 10% of the studies. On average, the strength of individuals' ethnic identity was found to be modestly associated with their well-being.

Factors Influencing the Results

Study Characteristics

Meta-analyses can sometimes detect differences in effect size across different types of research studies. We considered the possible influence of the year in which the study was published, the research design, the type of measure of ethnic identity, and the type of measure of well-being.

The results obtained across all 215 studies were stable over time. The correlation between the year of study publication and its effect size was $r = -.02$ (see Table 10.2). However, the majority of studies were conducted in the recent past, and substantive social changes typically require more time to observe any effects. As shown in Table 10.3, the results did not differ across the type of participant sampling, and although cross-sectional studies did have higher effect sizes ($r = .19$) than longitudinal studies ($r = .12$), this difference was not statistically significant.

No differences were apparent across the type of measure of ethnic identity. Although the clear majority of research reviewed here (70%) involved

TABLE 10.2
Random Effects Weighted Correlations of Effect Sizes With Study
and Sample Characteristics

Variable	r	k
Study characteristics		
Year of publication	−.02	215
Total number of participants	−.06	215
Participants' characteristics		
Age	−.17*	186
Average birth year[a]	.13	186
Gender of client[b]	−.13	211
Education level	−.01	119
Socioeconomic status	.05	117
% African Americans	−.14	96
% Hispanic/Latino(a) Americans	−.14	72
% Asian Americans	−.29**	92
% Native American Indians	−.53*	16
Average strength of ethnic identity[c]	.25**	136

Note. *$p < .05$. **$p < .01$.
[a]Year of study minus average age of clients at time of study (to estimate cohort effects). [b]Percentage of female participants within studies. [c]Averaged item-level score on the Multiethnic Ethnic Identity Measure (Phinney, 1992).

TABLE 10.3
Weighted Mean Correlations Across Levels of Several Moderator Variables in Studies of the Association of Ethnic Identity With Well-Being

Variable	Q_b	p	k	r_+	95% CI
Data source	2.0	.15			
Published			93	.20	[.17, .22]
Unpublished			122	.17	[.15, .19]
Sampling procedure	0.1	.78			
Convenience			200	.18	[.16, .20]
Representative (random selection)			15	.17	[.11, .23]
Research design	3.2	.08			
Cross-sectional			203	.19	[.17, .21]
Longitudinal			12	.12	[.05, .19]
Population	6.5	.04			
General community members			62	.15	[.11, .18]
Students			136	.20	[.18, .22]
At-risk groups or clinical populations			17	.18	[.12, .24]
Socioeconomic Status	0.5	.78			
Lower class			29	.16	[.11, .21]
Lower middle class			27	.18	[.13, .24]
Middle class and above			61	.18	[.14, .22]
Gender[a]	6.1	.02			
Female			39	.13	[.08, .18]
Male			12	.25	[.17, .33]
Participant race[b]	4.2	.24			
African American			58	.19	[.16, .23]
Asian American			61	.16	[.11, .18]
Hispanic/Latino(a) American			34	.16	[.12, .21]
Native American Indian			8	.15	[.07, .26]
Racial composition	8.9	.003			
Heterogeneous			49	.23	[.19, .26]
Homogeneous			165	.17	[.15, .19]
Acculturation level	9.1	.03			
Low (immigrants)			6	.05	[−.05, .16]
Moderate			28	.15	[.10, .19]
High			40	.19	[.15, .21]
Insufficient information reported			141	.19	[.17, .21]
Ethnic identity measure	1.3	.52			
MEIM			150	.19	[.17, .21]
Other, research supported			35	.17	[.12, .21]
Other, homemade			26	.17	[.12, .22]
Well-being types	32.6	>.0001			
Mental health symptoms[c]			23	.09	[.04, .13]
Self-esteem			69	.23	[.21, .26]
General well-being/coping			18	.22	[.16, .27]
Multiple indicators			105	.16	[.14, .19]
Well-being sub-types[d]	75.3	>.0001			
General mental health symptoms[c]			16	.11	[.04, .18]
Anxiety[c]			24	.08	[.02, .13]
Stress/distress[c]			10	.05	[−.03, .13]

(continues)

TABLE 10.3
Weighted Mean Correlations Across Levels of Several Moderator Variables
in Studies of the Association of Ethnic Identity With Well-Being *(Continued)*

Variable	Q_b	p	k	r_+	95% CI
Depression/hopelessness[c]			58	.14	[.11, .17]
Other mental health symptoms[c]			18	.03	[−.03, .10]
Global well-being			37	.20	[.15, .24]
Self-esteem			136	.23	[.21, .25]
Self-mastery/self-control			22	.20	[.14, .25]
Coping skills			18	.16	[.10, .22]
Social support			31	.16	[.11, .20]
Problematic behavior[c]			13	.12	[.05, .19]
Multiple indicators (>1 above)			10	.11	[.02, .20]

Note. CI = confidence interval; k = number of studies; Q_b = Q-value for variance between groups; r_+ = random effects weighted correlation; MEIM = Multigroup Ethnic Identity Measure (Phinney, 1992).
[a]Analysis involving only studies with exclusively male or female participants. [b]Analysis involving data from studies with participants of a single racial group. [c]Inverse scaling, such that positive correlations denote less pathology. [d]Analysis involving all effect sizes within studies that contained distinct outcome measures, such that studies could contribute more than one effect size to the analysis but only one effect size per category.

the MEIM, the results obtained with other measures were of equivalent magnitude. Thus, the averaged results did not appear to depend on how ethnic identity was operationalized.

However, large differences were observed across the type of well-being measured (see Table 10.3). On average, the association of ethnic identity with measures of mental health symptoms was notably lower than with measures of self-esteem or general well-being. When the data were disaggregated by the type of measurement used, the same trend was apparent.

Nevertheless, the disaggregated results yielded interesting qualifications. Measures of symptoms of depression yielded a higher association ($r = .13$) with ethnic identity than all other measures of mental health symptoms. Measures of distress yielded a low correlation ($r = .05$), perhaps reflecting the temporary nature of distress relative to the more pervasive nature of other mental health indicators. Measures of problematic behavior (i.e., the Child Behavioral Checklist, typically administered in educational settings) yielded an average correlation of similar size to general mental health symptoms. Measures of self-esteem resulted in the highest overall correlations with ethnic identity. The direction of all these correlations were standardized for purposes of comparison, such that positive values indicated that ethnic identity was associated with positive states of well-being (i.e., fewer problematic behaviors or mental health symptoms).

Participant Characteristics

Characteristics of research participants varied widely across research studies, prompting investigation of the degree to which those differences might account for differences in the findings across studies. We analyzed the possible influence of participants' average age, estimated birth year (to investigate possible cohort effects), gender composition (% female), racial composition, population type (community members, students, at-risk groups, clinical samples), and ethnic identity level.

The average age of participants moderated the overall results ($r = -0.17$, $p = .02$); studies with younger participants (i.e., adolescents and young adults) tended to have larger effect sizes than studies of middle-aged and senior adults. Thus, ethnic identity appeared more relevant to the well-being of younger populations. This association was found irrespective of age cohort; when the estimated birth year of participants and the age of participants were regressed simultaneously, the magnitude of the association for age increased to $b = -0.26$, whereas the estimated year of participants' birth remained low ($b = -0.10$). This finding suggested that ethnic identity might be more pertinent to individual development than to changing social trends over time.

The differences among samples of community members, students, and at-risk or clinical populations (Table 10.3) were partially explained by differences in age. Compared with the other two types of studies, those with students had higher effect sizes, not unexpected because they consisted of younger participants. When age and population type were simultaneously regressed on effect size, age remained the same as it had been for the overall sample ($b = -0.17$), and the variables representing population type were lower ($b = 0.06$ for students as contrasted with community samples, and $b = 0.03$ for at-risk and clinical populations contrasted with community samples). Thus, there were no significant differences across population type after accounting for age.

Differences in the overall findings were evident across participant gender composition. The correlation between studies' effect sizes and their percentage of female participants was $r = -0.13$ ($p = .05$), and significant differences were found between studies using exclusively male versus female participants ($p = .02$, see Table 10.3). Taken together, these findings suggest that ethnic identity may be somewhat more salient to the well-being of males than females.

There were no differences across studies using participants from distinct racial groups (Table 10.3). This finding seems to indicate that ethnic identity equivalently predicts well-being among participant cultures. However, the racial heterogeneity of the research sample did moderate the results. Studies with populations representing one race reported lower effect sizes ($r = .17$) than those with racially mixed samples ($r = .23$), which could imply that ethnic identity is more relevant to well-being in mixed racial settings. This finding was confirmed by the consistent negative direction of the correlations of effect sizes with the percentages of participants from each racial group. This trend was particularly notable among samples including Asian American and Native American Indian participants; studies with relatively higher percentages of those populations (more homogeneous samples) tended to have smaller effect sizes than studies with low percentages of participants from these populations (Table 10.2).

The strength of participants' ethnic identity also moderated the results. Table 10.2 shows a correlation between the average item-level score on the MEIM (total score divided by the number of items) and the effect size obtained from that study, $r = .25$ ($p < .01$). Studies with participants reporting relatively higher levels of ethnic identity tended to demonstrate a stronger association between ethnic identity and well-being than studies with participants reporting lower levels of ethnic identity. This finding likely indicates that ethnic identity is relevant to an individual's well-being if he or she considers it somewhat important, but relevance increases when ethnic identify is strongly affirmed. One's level of ethnic identity influences perceptions.

Having found that several participant characteristics moderated the overall results, we next sought to ascertain which of the statistically significant variables remained statistically significant in the presence of the others. We therefore conducted a meta-regression using the variables that had been found to be statistically significant in the univariate analyses. Random effects weighted meta-regression is an analogue to multiple regression analysis for effect sizes. We evaluated two models because data regarding participants' average level of ethnic identity (average item-level scores measured by the MEIM) were unavailable in many reports. The first model excluded the level of ethnic identity in order to maximize the number of studies included in the analysis. This model better represents the literature (200 studies included), so it should be the one interpreted unless considering the variable representing level of ethnic identity, which only appears in the second model. Both models (see Table 10.4) reached statistical significance ($R^2 = .19$, $Q = 48.7$, $p < .0001$ and $R^2 = .24$, $Q = 38.5$, $p < .0001$).

To facilitate interpretation of the data, variables entered into both models were centered on their means. The B value for the variable labeled "constant" (Table 10.4) represents the average effect size one would expect to find if all variables included in the model had the expected mean value. These values correspond with the overall effect size reported earlier ($r = .18$). Interpretation of the B weights (Table 10.4, first column) reveals the extent to which each study characteristic would be expected to influence the observed overall effect size when controlling for the presence of the other variables. Thus, for Model 1, researchers using measures of mental health symptoms could expect an effect size of $r = .108$ ($.182 - .074$), and those using measures of self-esteem or global well-being would have expected effect sizes of $r = .238$ ($.182 + .056$) and $r = .236$ ($.182 + .054$), respectively. Overall, the variables that remained significant in the model were the type of well-being measured, along with participant gender (with stronger effect sizes among studies with

TABLE 10.4
Random Effects Regression Weights for Study Characteristics Associated With Effect Sizes

Variable	B	SE	p	β
Model 1 (k = 200) R² = .19				
Constant	.182	.009	<.0001	
Participants' average age	−.001	.001	.12	−.10
Percentage female participants	−.001	.001	.01	−.16
Immigrant status[a]	−.094	.051	.04	−.13
Homogeneous racial composition[b]	−.031	.022	.16	−.09
Measures of well-being[c]				
Mental health symptoms	−.074	.028	.009	−.18
Self-esteem	.056	.021	.008	.18
Global well-being	.054	.033	.10	.11
Model 2 (k = 128) R² = .24				
Constant	.181	.010	<.0001	
Participants' average age	−.001	.001	.30	−.09
Percentage female participants	−.001	.001	.12	−.13
Immigrant status[a]	−.066	.072	.36	−.07
Homogeneity of racial composition[b]	−.035	.025	.17	−.12
Well-being measures[c]				
Mental health symptoms	−.041	.035	.24	−.10
Self-esteem	.054	.025	.03	.18
Global well-being	.072	.034	.03	.19
Ethnic identity level[d]	.150	.038	.0001	.33

Note. Separate models were conducted because only 128 reports included information about item-level Multi-group Ethnic Identity Measure (MEIM; Phinney, 1992) scores. Model 1 better represents the literature and should be the one used, except when interpreting the effects of ethnic identity level, which was included in Model 2. [a]Low acculturation (immigrants) contrasted with studies not reporting information on participant acculturation level. [b]Samples of participants of all the same race contrasted with samples of participants from multiple racial groups. [c]Contrasted with multidimensional measures of well-being. [d]Average item-level score on the MEIM.

greater percentages of male participants), and immigrant status (predicting lower associations between ethnic identity and well-being). In the presence of the other variables, participant age and sample racial homogeneity no longer reached statistical significance. In Model 2, the level of ethnic identity (mean item score on the MEIM) remained a strong moderator of effect size ($b = .33$) in the presence of the other variables. The more strongly people of color endorse ethnic identity, the more relevant it is to their well-being.

Possible Influence of Publication Bias

A majority of studies (122; 57% of the total) in this meta-analysis were unpublished dissertations. The average effect size obtained across published versus unpublished studies did not differ (see Table 10.3), so we had no reason to suspect that unaccounted (unpublished) studies would adversely affect the findings.

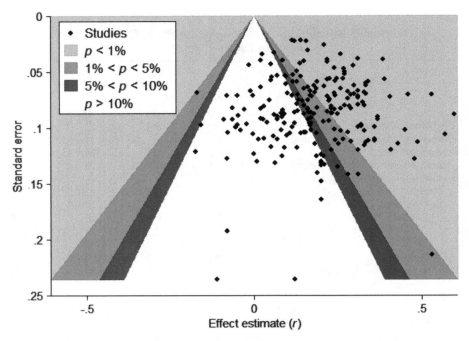

Figure 10.1. Contour-enhanced funnel plot of effect sizes (Pearson *r*) by standard error. The results across studies are highly variable, ranging from *somewhat negative* to *very strongly positive*. Thus, an overall average masks the true heterogeneity of the data; the association between ethnic identity and well-being is imprecise but predominantly positive.

As shown in Figure 10.1, effect sizes were relatively evenly distributed around the average value of *r* = .18. There were no "missing" corners in the distribution that would suggest studies excluded unintentionally from analyses. One statistical method to estimate publication bias (Duval & Tweedie, 2000) did not identify any "missing" studies, and Egger's regression test was nonsignificant. Therefore, we concluded that publication bias was not a threat to the results of this meta-analysis.

DISCUSSION AND INTERPRETATION OF THE FINDINGS

The psychosocial literature on ethnic identity and well-being is substantial. This topic has attracted considerable inquiry, especially in the past 2 decades. Results from the studies, however, have been mixed—they have been neither persuasive nor robust. On average, ethnic identity explains about 3.3% of the variance in measures of well-being among people of color.

The correlations between the self-reported measures of ethnic identity and well-being ranged from –.18 to .60, with most between 0.0 and 0.35. The findings open up an assortment of questions concerning the unexplained variance.

The wide variability in the research findings confirms the obvious: Many factors influence both ethnic identity and well-being. Present research practices have not accounted for that complexity. For instance, few researchers evaluate variables such as social status that can influence both self-esteem and ethnic identity. If an ethnic group has been through a history of prejudice and discrimination, group members could experience a devalued sense of self (Tajfel, 1982), but if the group has been evaluated positively, commitment is likely to be strong, contentment high, and involvement in ethnic practices significant (Phinney, 1991).

In short, decades of scholarship have produced a large body of research that tells little beyond what could have been guessed intuitively. A positive relationship exists between self-esteem and ethnic identity, but even that basic conclusion could be attributed to the wording of measurement items, which emphasize the certainty and importance of one's ethnic declaration and affiliation—for example, "I feel a strong attachment toward my own ethnic group." People who feel strongly affiliated to others would probably also report higher levels of well-being than individuals who feel unaffiliated or uncertain about where their allegiance can be placed.

Considerations for Future Research

The sample of studies represented almost all age groups except those over the age of 55. Asian Americans were the most represented ethnic group, and Native American Indians, Alaska Natives, and Polynesian Americans were the least represented in the literature. Some researchers disaggregated groups into subgroups such as Chinese, Japanese, Korean, and Southeast Asians. However, most often researchers tended to lump their participants into one overarching inclusive ethnic label, a practice contributing to *ethnic gloss*: the appearance of ethnic and cultural homogeneity that may be inaccurate (Trimble & Bhadra, 2013).

The tendency for researchers and scholars to gloss over depth of cultural lifeways and thoughtways raises serious methodological questions. Ethnic gloss through imprecise categorization of participants provides little or no information on the richness and cultural variation within ethnocultural groups and may ignore the existence of numerous subgroups characterized by unique cultural traditions. This sorting method minimizes the deep cultural influences that guide a group member's thought, feelings, and behavior. Broad ethnic categorizations can generate biased and flawed scientific research as well as promote stereotypes. In addition, use of an ethnic gloss does not enhance external validity, the potential to generalize findings within and across subgroups.

An associated finding is that current research practices have inadequately accounted for multiethnic individuals, who may affirm multiple sources of identity, seek ways to pass as members of one group but not the other, and/or denigrate the value of one group relative to another. Individuals whose heritage includes multiple ethnic groups may choose to identify with a particular group regardless of how others may view them, although parental influences and gender alignment with parents, racism, emotional security, and several other factors are influential in the complex processes of identification (Root, 1994). The data we analyzed did not account for those dynamics, which require more specific evaluations.

This meta-analysis extended information available on the association between ethnic identity and psychological well-being by confirming that the absolute level of ethnic identity does influence that association to a marked degree. This finding confirms theoretical expectations: Individuals with high levels of ethnic identity tend to view their ethnic identity as salient to well-being; individuals with low levels of ethnic identity tend to see it as less connected to well-being. Hence individuals' level of ethnic identity should be more clearly evaluated and understood, including the reasons why ethnic identity is or is not particularly strong, thus refocusing methods of inquiry to account for individual variation.

Although research with clinical populations occurs rarely, in the general population ethnic identity appears to be more relevant to self-esteem than to mental health symptoms. According to Tajfel's (1982) theory of social identity, one's social identity strongly influences self-perception, and in the general population self-perception is more accurately represented by self-esteem than by psychopathology. Nevertheless, this finding could also suggest that the commonly held assumption that ethnic identity buffers against distress may be problematic. Analyses of the relationship of ethnic identity with self-esteem and distress could benefit from more explicit consideration of detailed theoretical frameworks such as that provided by Tajfel, rather than the all-too-common practice of correlating sets of variables without a solid heuristic model and then testing that model. For instance, this meta-analysis identified differences in the degree to which ethnic identity is associated with well-being when the participants are examined in ethnically homogeneous versus heterogeneous settings. This finding is consistent with Tajfel's social identity theory, which indicates that identity is more salient in mixed settings than homogeneous ones; identity must be evaluated relative to the available social contrasts. Although research in the social psychology literature has taken care to evaluate situational factors and to explicitly test theories, multicultural psychology research has typically involved broad research questions without systematic inquiry into the specifics of an association.

We have to be explicit about some questionable practices in the multicultural psychology literature that we reviewed. We found that 93% of the studies used convenience samples. If the field intends to produce generalizable research findings, it has to randomly select research participants to establish external validity. We also found that 94% of the studies involved cross-sectional surveys. How can the field prove, let alone understand, causality when relationships are not evaluated across time?

The relationship between ethnic identity and well-being was found to be minimal among participants with low levels of acculturation to North American society (i.e., recent immigrants and refugees), but only six studies evaluated those populations. Thus, we cannot discern with confidence whether individuals with low acculturation levels, who tend to have ethnically homogeneous social networks (Phinney et al., 2001), may take their ethnic identity for granted in terms of their well-being, despite high absolute levels of in-group identification (Phinney, 2006). Social identity theory (Tajfel, 1982) posits that a group would have to experience contrast (opposition/oppression) for ethnic identity to be activated as a coping strategy, but recent immigrants who reside in ethnic enclaves, or who alternatively seek to minimize their differences by trying to fit in with mainstream society, may not initially activate ethnic identity as a coping strategy. Nevertheless, theories of acculturation (Berry, 2003) emphasize that multiple processes influence the affirmation of one's own ethnicity and its relevance to well-being, such that an accurate interpretation of our finding would require a more detailed understanding of the participants' contexts than is possible in a meta-analysis. Future research is needed to clarify the relationship between ethnic identity and well-being as a function of acculturation.

Another challenge facing those who are advancing inquiry into ethnic and racial identity is that the number of ethnic and racial groups in North America is increasing not declining, and the populace does not appear to be assimilating at the rate many demographers and sociologists have predicted. All over the world geopolitical boundaries are changing because of political turmoil, colonialism, and globalization; thus, individuals are changing their ethnic allegiances and identities as they move to a new environment or as rearranged boundaries move them into a new environment (Arnett, 2002). Indigenous groups are asserting sovereign rights and demanding recognition and access to their ancestral lands. Voices that were once suppressed are demanding to be recognized. Consequently, ethnic groups worldwide are becoming more independent and visible; this diversity presents new challenges for the field of ethnic and racial identity, particularly to its relationship to well-being.

Suggestions for Practitioners

More now than ever, multicultural awareness is being integrated into classroom curricula and public discourse. And people are becoming interested in tracing their genealogy and learning about their ancestral heritage. For example, Black History Month is one of several popular opportunities for acknowledging and celebrating diversity and ethnic differences. Many individuals are coming to believe that they must declare an ethnic background so that they may join in the celebration. In their work with clients, therapists can attune to motives such as self-affirmation and sense of belonging that may be relevant to this exploration of and affiliation with ethnic heritage.

Unfortunately, many clients may be negatively concerned about their expression of identity; some presenting problems may emanate from feelings of guilt over assimilation or from a longing to better understand their ethnic heritage that was wrested away from them when they were adopted or moved to an area where their ethnic group was misunderstood or victimized. In such instances, the therapist should explicitly help clients to develop skills to cope with those circumstances, as well as assist them in valuing their ethnic origins and expressing them without fear of ostracism and rejection.

The data finding that ethnic identity tends to be more pertinent to the well-being of younger individuals than older groups aligns with theories that emphasize the importance of identity development among adolescents and young adults. Clinicians working with those populations can particularly attune to client experiences relevant to ethnic identity.

Clinicians must keep in mind the complexity of clients' identity development and expression, including ethnic identity. Our review of the literature did not resolve uncertainties about the causal relationship between ethnic identity and well-being. The relationship might be that individuals who already have a strong self-esteem are more likely to embrace their ethnic identity, rather than the other way around. Practitioners should not presume ethnic identity to be linear or in any way simplistic—even though that position has been common in the literature. Rather, they should look more deeply into clients' troubling conditions for the possible contributions of ethnic identity to wellness and resilience.

CONCLUSION

Our meta-analysis included 215 published studies involving over 50,000 participants from several ethnic groups. The overall results provide an estimate of the expected correlation when a survey concerning ethnic identity and well-being is administered to people of color ($r = .18$), a value falling not quite midway between mild and moderate according to J. Cohen's (1988) guidelines for interpreting effect size. However, that average value masks variability. A positive ethnic identity was associated with somewhat lower well-being in 10% of the studies, but was strongly associated with high levels of well-being in about 10% of the studies.

Several decades of research on the topic of ethnic identity generated the scatter depicted in Figure 10.1. Investigating global research issues such as the overall association between ethnic identity and well-being is not particularly helpful because of multifaceted underlying constructs. We therefore need to ask more specific research questions. What are the causal pathways? Under what circumstances does ethnic identity prove most protective against distress? For the construct of ethnic identity to become deserving of the widespread attention it has received, research efforts must yield information more useful than the data depicted in Figure 10.1.

IV

FOUNDATIONS
FOR THE FUTURE

11

PHILOSOPHICAL CONSIDERATIONS FOR THE FOUNDATION OF MULTICULTURAL PSYCHOLOGY

> If we are to achieve a richer culture, rich in contrasting values, we must recognize the whole gamut of human potentialities, and so weave a less arbitrary social fabric, one in which each diverse human gift will find a fitting place.
>
> —Margaret Mead (1963, p. 218)

People's experiences require interpretation. Research data require interpretation. In a book otherwise about experience and data, this chapter addresses the topic of interpretation. This shift from evidence to ideas requires explanation, which we offer in the form of an anecdote.

At a recent professional conference, a participant asked a prominent panel member why he had dropped his successful career in neuropsychology to teach philosophy—of all things! The question was asked with a tone of unmistakable incredulity. Although not directly raising the issue of sanity, the question seemed based on an underlying disbelief that a rational individual could possibly make such a decision. Why philosophy?

The question "Why philosophy?" articulated what many individuals in the audience had thought privately. Is the "big money" not in neuropsychology? After all, the panelist was quite famous in neuropsychology. Why study ideas rather than save lives? Is philosophy not the antithesis of neuroscience? Hundreds of challenges could have been offered, but the point of this anecdote

http://dx.doi.org/10.1037/14733-011

Foundations of Multicultural Psychology: Research to Inform Effective Practice, by T. B. Smith and J. E. Trimble

is that each challenge would have required the panelist to justify his position—in contrast to alternatives. Each alternative would align with a particular worldview—a philosophy. Philosophy is omnipresent, acknowledged or not.

The premise of this book, that data should inform clinical practice, is based on multiple assumptions. So are mental health treatments. So are cultural worldviews. Multicultural counseling and psychology seeks to understand and question these assumptions.

WHY ASK QUESTIONS?

When asked sincerely and thoughtfully, questions seek to bridge gaps between worldviews. Questions seek interpretation. They seek clarity in terms that we already understand. Thus, questions expose the assumptions and values of the questioner. What we already know or assume influences what we believe we need to find out. And when we believe we know already, we do not ask. Or, we ask in a way that limits or precludes actually bridging worldviews.

In the introductory anecdote, the incredulous participant did not ask why the famous panelist had started out in neuropsychology in the first place—assuming intrinsic value in the study of neuropsychology. The audience had many assumptions about such things as the optimal means for advancing knowledge (empiricism vs. rationalism), the usefulness of neuroscience over philosophy (pragmatism or perhaps utilitarianism), or the individual's own personal interests (psychological egoism). Questions reveal underlying assumptions and values. The process of identifying assumptions and evaluating ideals relative to alternatives is the work of philosophy. Seen in this light, psychology itself is an attempt to apply philosophy to understand and improve human experience (Robinson, 1995).

HOW DOES PHILOSOPHY RELATE TO MULTICULTURAL PSYCHOLOGY?

Why include a chapter on philosophical considerations in a book about multicultural research? We purposefully use the term *philosophy* rather than the terms *conceptualization* or *framework* to emphasize the readers' obligation to engage the material through questioning and critical thinking. We seek to prompt thoughtful analysis (Machado & Silva, 2007). And we do so by questioning assumptions in contemporary multicultural psychology. No doubt some individuals who have read previous chapters in this book bypassed this chapter after a single glance at a title including the word *philosophical*. To them, we can offer no explanation. To the hurried readers who dared to skim this far into the introductory section, we offer no promises. To the one who continues, we offer more questions. The point of this chapter is that multicultural psychologists should ask questions like the incredulous conference participant. When questions are asked, assumptions and values can be identified. When questions are asked, dialogue occurs. And dialogue explicitly informed by values and assumptions is the essence of multicultural psychology.

WHY DO ASSUMPTIONS MATTER?

Assumptions embedded within ideas have substantive power, especially if they remain unchallenged. They influence decisions and actions without the benefit of thoughtful evaluation. Adverse consequences of assumptions can be obvious: Presidential decisions to support the invasion of Cuba in 1962 or of Iraq in 2003 gave more weight to presuppositions than to contraindications. Such examples are easily apparent. But equally apparent are pathologies in which individuals assume fallacies about their own worth on the basis of evaluations of others (e.g., not "good enough") and minimize evidence contradicting their assumptions. Assumptions influence thoughts and behaviors until identified and contrasted with alternatives.

Psychotherapy can challenge faulty assumptions, but reflecting and identifying assumptions are not the exclusive responsibility of clients. Clinicians, students, and instructors assuming certain tenets about multicultural psychology can also benefit from self-evaluation. The data presented in the preceding chapters of this book indicate that several of the assumptions in multicultural psychology research have been proven unreliable. Or perhaps some of the assumptions are correct but the data were unreliable. Which assumptions or which data sets are accurate? To what degree? Under which circumstances? Questioning prevailing assumptions in multicultural psychology may generate new explanations better aligned with the research data—and may also yield data characterized by greater reliability.

Multicultural psychology does not benefit from maintaining unreliable assumptions. Multicultural psychology benefits when we strive to align our assumptions with the needs and experiences of historically disadvantaged populations.

IS IT TIME TO ASK HARD (PHILOSOPHICAL) QUESTIONS IN MULTICULTURAL PSYCHOLOGY?

Examining one's own limitations can be painful. Would it not be better for a book promoting multicultural psychology to remain positive, rather than ask questions that might be uncomfortable? We desire to improve multicultural psychology, but we understand that questioning traditional practices may provoke varied reactions. We intend no offense. But even the most cherished ideas in multicultural psychology fail to explain the vast complexity of reality, so a re-vision and revision of our profession's ideas is inevitable, no matter how presently influential they may be.

In the spirit of working collaboratively, we offer a historical analogy. Like the scientific and philosophical traditions it broke from in the late 1800s, early work in psychology relied exclusively on intellectuals from Europe and North America to the exclusion of alternative worldviews. Assumptions about race and ethnicity influenced the early practice of psychology in a myriad of ways, many harmful (D. W. Sue & Sue, 2013). Women and people of color who received indoctrination as psychologists initially experienced little freedom to question those assumptions without incurring marginalization (Guthrie, 2004), but over several decades harder and harder questions about race and racism kept coming. For instance, psychologists recognizing inaccurate assumptions opposed racial segregation (K. B. Clark & Clark, 1939) and other forms of prejudgment based on stereotypes (Allport, 1954). Multicultural psychology exists today on the basis of scholarship that uncovered and corrected assumptions.

We honor the women and men who questioned prevailing paradigms in psychology and those of the subsequent generation who built multicultural psychology on their work (i.e., elders recognized at the National Multicultural Conference and Summit). After many decades of struggle, multicultural psychology is here to stay (D. W. Sue, Bingham, Porché-Burke, & Vasquez, 1999). However, much work remains to be done, with the rising generation of graduate students needing better preparation to effectively negotiate the complex social realities of our time. In their interest and in the interest of the communities they will serve, will we now collectively improve multicultural psychology by asking harder and harder (philosophical) questions that challenge our previous assumptions?

SOME QUESTIONS TO CONSIDER (WITH HOPES FOR MANY MORE TO COME)

In our collective efforts to enhance multicultural psychology, open dialogue should not only accelerate its improvement but also model the process it seeks to promote: learning from differences. The field has matured in recent decades, but the complexity of multiculturalism will ensure that the discipline will continue to expand over the next century and beyond. Thousands of questions remain unanswered. Although we provide tentative responses to the three "example questions" we ask in this section, we recognize that it is the process of asking questions that has greatest worth. Questions can prompt additional queries and responses in an iterative cycle.

What "Is" Multicultural Psychology?

Numerous definitions and descriptions of multicultural psychology are available. Their consistent theme is that psychology must embrace the whole gamut of human potentialities, as the esteemed cultural anthropologist Margaret Mead (1963) suggested.

Most descriptions of multicultural psychology are aspirational: They describe what ought to be. In his seminal book *Multiculturalism as a Fourth Force*, Paul Pedersen (1999) pointed out, "Multiculturalism refers to a new perspective in mainstream psychology characterized as a fourth force complementing the three other theoretical orientations in psychology, i.e., psychodynamic theory, existentialistic theory, and cognitive–behavioral theory, addressing the needs of culturally diverse populations" (p. 113). He added, "Multiculturalism recognizes the complexity of culture" (p. 113). In addition, Pedersen quoted eminent cross-cultural psychologist John Berry (1991): "Multiculturalism is meant to create a socio-political context within which individuals can develop healthy identities and mutually positive intergroup attitudes" (p. 24).

We share these aspirations. We also recognize that we have not yet arrived at a point where undergraduate students are as familiar with multicultural psychology (the "fourth force") as they are with behavioral, psychodynamic, and humanistic psychology. And multicultural psychological research rarely accounts for "the complexity of culture." We are still largely discussing antibias strategies rather than creating sociocultural contexts conducive to "mutually positive intergroup attitudes." In short, an obvious gap exists between multicultural psychology as practiced and as frequently defined. It is time to bridge that gap, starting with an evaluation of reality. Taking inventory of what multicultural psychology "is" in the real world can help determine where we are relative to what it "ought" to be, with the aim of achieving the envisioned "ought."

When we, the authors, have spoken with psychologists who are unaware of our affiliation with multicultural psychology, we have sensed three general approaches to the topic, with a fourth, atypical approach. Polite, surface acknowledgement is by far the most common response. Yes, multiculturalism is important, but when the conversation starts to go further, no substantive methods, theories, or even rationale are mentioned. A second approach involves strong and apparently genuine affirmation of multiculturalism, with general principles understood but disconnected from their application; people "talk the talk" but do not know how to "walk the walk." A third approach is silence, a disengagement rooted in apathy or skepticism. We are thankful we encounter the latter approach with decreasing frequency. The rarest of all, thus not yet one of the three "general" approaches, is to successfully practice multicultural psychology.

We occasionally meet people who engage in genuine collaboration with local communities. They understand complex personal, situational, political, and historical influences. They have stretched their methodological, theoretical, and analytic skills to the point that they have acquired new perspective and skills. So the envisioned aspirations are possible to attain. We see it. We would like to see it more. For that to happen, future scholarship has to address what multicultural psychology means to the people who are attempting to apply it ("What 'is' multicultural psychology?"). Understanding what people perceive multicultural psychology to be will be essential to lifting their vision of what it can become.

How Will We More Equitably Serve Historically Oppressed Populations?

Government initiatives to fund mental health care for economically disadvantaged populations can help improve access to services, but reliance on such programs will be insufficient to meet the vast need. Presently we see few graduate students interested in serving impoverished communities; as students they increasingly incur debt that precludes their entertaining such a notion. Understandably, graduates often seek the highest paying positions available. Professional psychology graduate programs can help by seeking investments and endowments to help offset tuition costs. Even more beneficial, graduate programs can emphasize a service-oriented mentality, providing practicum and/or externship experiences in high need areas. Internship sites serving disadvantaged populations could be promoted (Casas, Park, & Cho, 2010).

Individual practitioners can also take personal responsibility for better meeting the needs of impoverished individuals needing care. Most psychologists in private practice have a few spare hours in their caseload. Reduced rates (sliding scales) and networking in local communities can increase client service utilization. Rather than merely challenging others to serve impoverished groups, we can take action ourselves. To paraphrase a better statement, we need not ask what our community can do for us, but what we can do for our community.

What Aims Should Multicultural Psychology Work to Achieve?

Multicultural psychology has broad ambitions: no less than to eradicate prejudice and discrimination and to promote the well-being of historically oppressed populations. Nevertheless, it may be useful to specify aims that can contribute to meeting those long-term objectives. For instance, what essential aspects of applied mental health services might bring about the greatest improvements in traditional practices? Within the delimited sphere of mental health services (including prevention and wellness initiatives), four specific aims seem most desirable: (a) reduction of mental health disparities, (b) access to services by those in need, (c) retention of those receiving services, and (d) improved outcomes to the satisfaction of those receiving services.

Other praiseworthy initiatives, such as promoting multicultural competence among therapists, should not divert the primary focus from these four aims. In fact, the ultimate purpose of therapist multicultural competence is to address the four aims, although most contemporary research into this competence relates only indirectly to them. The same could be said of applied psychological research concerning perceived racism, acculturation, ethnic identity, and so forth. Although the relationship of ethnic identity to well-being is interesting, the application of that knowledge to enhance the efficacy of therapy or prevention initiatives with at-risk youth is of more use. Multicultural psychology cannot continue to influence the broader profession (Pedersen, 1999; D. W. Sue et al., 1999) by drifting into interesting topics at the expense of the essential ones.

Many authors affirm social justice as an objective for mental health service providers (Toporek, 2006). Social justice is a far nobler objective than the four comparatively mundane aims proposed here. However, these four aims could be considered the focal point of social justice work within psychology, serving as concrete benchmarks for progress in mental health settings toward the broader aim of social justice, a paradigm worthy of our efforts and therefore of our questions.

QUESTIONING A PARADIGM: RECONCEPTUALIZING SOCIAL JUSTICE

Early in this chapter we emphasized that assumptions pervasively influence both collectives and individuals. We then asked three "example questions" about multicultural psychology. We now focus on the topic of social justice to explore possible assumptions at the paradigmatic level and to suggest a possible alternative conceptualization. As with the example questions discussed earlier, the content of this inquiry matters much less than the process. Any paradigm influential in multicultural psychology could and should be similarly questioned.

How Central Is Social Justice to Multicultural Psychology?

Few concepts can rival the influence of social justice on contemporary multicultural psychology. Commonly defined as the application of the concept of justice to a societal level, *social justice* is more specifically set out by Rawls (1999):

> Each person possesses an inviolability founded on justice that even the welfare of society as a whole cannot override. For this reason justice denies that the loss of freedom for some is made right by a greater good shared by others. (pp. 3–4)

Social justice, because it aims to promote equity by eradicating discrimination and poverty, has profoundly shaped multicultural psychology (Arredondo & Perez, 2003; Leong, Comas-Díaz, Hall, McLoyd, & Trimble, 2014; Toporek, Gerstein, Fouad, Roysircar, & Israel, 2006). Social justice perspectives have moved multicultural psychology forward in many essential ways, including (a) equity in power structures, (b) orientation toward action, and (c) empowerment of community.

Why question a paradigm with benefits so obvious and so widely recognized? Although the concept of social justice is repeated often in multicultural psychology literature, most authors merely mention it in passing, at times seeming to use it as a type of code word to show familiarity with contemporary parlance, with little relevance actually shown in the research. Genuine adherence to the concept of social justice does occur (D'Andrea & Daniels, 2010), but infrequently (Baluch, Pieterse, & Bolden, 2004). Are there assumptions in present articulations of social justice that might constrain its influence or preclude its widespread application?

What Assumptions Might Be Embedded in the Concept of Social Justice?

The concept of social justice has been invoked by a variety of scholars advocating for change in psychology (e.g., Arredondo & Perez, 2003; Vera & Speight, 2003) and higher education generally (Worthington, Hart, & Khairallah, 2010), so any generic examination of the concept will fail to represent all perspectives. Although a systematic examination of all possible assumptions within a social justice paradigm would fill an entire volume, we restrict our list to three strengths that frequently receive attention in applied psychology.

- Primacy of power. Attending to power (i.e., resources, social influence) is the optimal focus of scholarship, with an aim to promote equality through social change.
- Role of advocacy. Mental health professionals should advocate for oppressed people.
- Emphasis on empowerment. Power plus advocacy lead to empowerment—giving voice to the voiceless; bottom-up processes are key.

To continue the conceptual analysis, we could examine relevant philosophical positions sharing similar assumptions. However, few authors in psychology mention underlying philosophy. Moreover, social justice is multifaceted (Toporek et al., 2006). Nevertheless, the three assumptions seem related to the following philosophical concepts: (a) dialectical materialism and critical pedagogy, (b) praxis and political activism, and (c) liberation psychology. Although these positions are rarely cited in manuscripts, their links with social justice have been well articulated (Ivey & Collins, 2003; Ivey & Zalaquett, 2009; Vera & Speight, 2003).

Which of These Assumptions Might Conflict With Pragmatic Realities in (North American) Multicultural Psychology?

In our review we found that much of the multicultural psychology literature did not align with the three assumptions just listed. For example, far from giving credence to "the primacy of power," researchers hardly ever measure or even operationalize issues of power (i.e., resources, social influence), even those clearly relevant to their investigation. They pay even less attention to advocacy for social change. Few publications are driven by "bottom up" community involvement. Undermining the field's intended emphasis on social justice, the variables commonly measured in contemporary multicultural psychology research (e.g., assessment validity, ethnic and racial identity, acculturation) are ancillary to issues of power, advocacy, and empowerment.

Although this neglect may be excused in research (because detachment from reality is sometimes attributed to inhabitants of ivory towers), we find the same trends in literature describing clinical practice, with allusions to issues of power, advocacy, and empowerment but few specifics (Vera & Speight, 2003). Recently, a prominent multicultural psychology leader lamented that her work with disadvantaged communities was not valued by her peers and that she knew of few psychologists who shared her passion or role as advocate, despite prevailing rhetoric. Rarely do we hear of true community empowerment in the literature. Fields such as development studies, social work, and social anthropology have developed traditions conducive to participatory action research (designed to promote community empowerment by meeting people's needs and answering their questions); however, we find hardly any of that work in multicultural psychology. Despite years of appeals in the literature, the promotion of social justice seems incongruent with present practices.

The most obvious reason for such incongruence is reluctance of adherents to practice the principles (Baluch et al., 2004; Speight & Vera, 2004).

But why is social justice not more commonly practiced when the entire field seems to be based on it? The following reasons may apply:

- Issues of power, empowerment, and so forth, may be too abstract or complex for psychologists to address in therapy or research; these concepts may need to be grounded in lived experience (Gergen, 1995) and operationalized (Cooren, 2006).
- North American psychologists have been raised in a capitalist society that obfuscates power dynamics, even those that are obvious to others. People are rarely paid to be social justice advocates, so they rarely engage in the work.
- Practitioners may perceive liberation psychology as a theory, rather than as a worldview for engagement with reality.
- People who select a career in the mental health professions may prefer working with individuals and small groups, rather than dealing with macro-level issues.
- Methods of social change beyond advocacy and political activism may be overlooked by individuals who narrowly interpret liberation psychology. Not all contexts or personalities are compatible with advocacy or activism; multiple methods can be effective in raising awareness or facilitating desirable change.

In addition to these practical reasons why the concept of social justice has been characterized more by verbal posturing than the intended actions, we suggest that part of that problem stems from the underlying philosophy. Materialism, a philosophy informing liberation psychology, praxis, and critical pedagogy, was a response to oppression, with roots in European intellectual paradigms. The underlying assumptions are reactionary and thus delimited, not necessarily aligning with cultures of other origins. That is, philosophical materialism adds a layer of interpretation that can preclude acceptance of other worldviews, an objective of multicultural psychology. Philosophical materialism is a popular worldview among intellectuals, but many indigenous cultures abide by different conceptualizations. Academics and advocates commonly interpret experiences of indigenous populations through the lens of materialism, although they criticize comparable interpretation through the lens of capitalism, individualism, and so forth. Such interpretation must be distinguished from acceptance of an indigenous cultural worldview as worthy on its own merits.

Although Marx, Fanon, Freire, Martín-Baró, and others advocating philosophical materialism both criticized power dynamics and emphasized relations across all of humanity (humanization), many proponents of social justice do little more than condemn those who abuse power. Motivated by indignation, justified anger, they become "like the oppressors, mimicking their patterns of domination and dehumanization" (Gaztambide, 2009,

p. 216). Freire (1973) termed this reactionary stance *naïve transitivity*. His urging to transcend reactivity aligns with even novice students' perceptions about animated social justice advocates pounding the pulpit at professional conferences: They seem to be selling a version of psychology insufficiently self-reflective to earn admiration. A genuinely multicultural psychology would not fix attention on symbols of status (money, influence) at the expense of omitting other important contexts (social/intimate, holistic/spiritual).

So long as social justice is obtained, a pragmatist would embrace any means to achieve that end. But if the end is not being achieved (which is certainly the case), the pragmatist would explore reasons why and replace those most likely negating efficacy. For instance, if philosophical materialism is an uncertain fit with many indigenous cultures of Africa, Asia, Australia, North and South America, and the Pacific Islands, other motivations for promoting justice may be more desirable for multicultural psychology.

Section Summary: Values and Assumptions

Values and assumptions pervade multicultural psychology—as they do every discipline. Although we cannot escape values and assumptions, we can seek to identify them and improve on them if possible.

In this section we have explored the concept of social justice, demonstrating its relevance to multicultural psychology, listing three assumptions embedded within it, identifying some philosophical underpinnings, and finally listing possible limitations of those assumptions in the practice of multicultural psychology. Any idea or theory prominent in multicultural psychology can be similarly evaluated. However, the purpose of such deconstruction must be reconstruction: to retain what is useful and improve on the rest. To that effort we now turn.

How Can Social Justice Be Reconceptualized Through a Relational Paradigm?

Karl Marx articulated philosophical materialism in response to his era, the industrial revolution of the latter 1800s. Abuses of power were universal. Protections for citizens were minimal, and protections for disenfranchised groups were either nonexistent or ignored. Certainly oppression of the powerless had always existed—and will always exist—but through materialism the masses gained the allegiance of scholars, who articulated their plight and proposed means for their empowerment.

Equal opportunity remains an aim to be sought. However, social and global dynamics have changed with the times. International cultural exchange now occurs at unprecedented levels. Electronic networks provide enhanced connection with global as well as local diversity, with opportunities for more equity in access to knowledge. Our collective interests now depend on multiculturalism and internationalism, requiring that we move beyond a self-preservation mentality. Just as Marx provided a powerful response to the needs of his time, contemporary multicultural psychology would benefit from a philosophy (not merely a set of loosely connected arguments about power and privilege) that directly responds to an increasingly Internet-based society with its need for unity amid diversity. Although the laudable work of Martín-Baró, Aron, and Corne (1994) on liberation psychology provides philosophical underpinning for social justice, our thesis is that a broader relational paradigm can provide a more useful philosophical foundation that is compatible with that work but not dependent on materialism.

Humans are innately social beings. A relational paradigm asserts that social interactions are central, not tangential, to psychology (Gergen, 1995; Jordan, 2010; Slife & Wiggins, 2009). Individuals' interactions with others form the structure, process, and content of their lives. Primary relationships (childhood and current) influence other relationships, which vary in importance across time and across contexts. Each person has a unique pattern of relationships that is constantly changing, but clear similarities can be found across individuals and even across cultures because some similar contexts are shared, most notably physiologic but also environmental, linguistic, historic, and so forth (D. Cohen, 2001). New relationships and repaired relationships alter individuals' perceptions, emotions, cognitions, and behaviors, which all influence other relationships in interactive processes.

Aspects of a relational paradigm can be found across history. The philosophy of Confucius emphasized social roles. Aristotle conceived humans as primarily political, by which he meant interactive (Robinson, 1995), necessary parts of the whole—the *polis* (community or city). Our ultimate interests are those of the community.

The relational paradigm is a contemporary movement that links with the tenets of feminism (J. B. Miller, 1986), interpersonal psychotherapy (Weissman, Markowitz, & Klerman, 2000), object relations (Clarke, Hahn, & Hoggett, 2008), symbolic interactionism (Charon, 2001), social constructionism (Gergen, 2009), liberation psychology (Martín-Baró et al., 1994), and philosophies advanced by Levinas (1969, 1998) and Bakhtin (1981) among others. The term *relational paradigm* denotes a broad worldview, a meta-theory. A variety of synonymous terms have been used in the literature: *relational meta-theory* (Lerner & Overton, 2008), *relationism* (Overton & Ennis, 2006b), *relational ontology* (Slife, 2004), *relationality* (Slife & Wiggins, 2009), *relational perspective* (T. B. Smith & Draper, 2004; Weissman et al., 2000), and *relational methodological research approaches* (Trimble & Mohatt, 2006). Although specific assertions and assumptions differ (e.g., Oliver, 2001), the core principles align to emphasize reciprocal effects embedded in interpersonal and intergroup interactions. To understand people, we must understand their relationships. The following seven general principles help to clarify how individuals are best understood, not solely as individuals but also as interactive agents in the context of multiple relationships past, present, and potential.

Connectedness (Mutual Edification)

An innate yearning for attachment with others characterizes human life (Cassidy & Shaver, 2008). Social engagement provides information exchange and learning (Bandura, 1977), but at deeper levels it can be emotionally fulfilling and mutually edifying. Interpersonal intimacy provides meaning and purpose in life. In fact, an insufficient social network affects longevity as much as light smoking and much more than alcoholism, obesity, and hypertension (Holt-Lunstad, Smith, & Layton, 2010). The absence of genuine intimacy coincides with psychological disturbance and poor health (S. Cohen, 2004; Holt-Lunstad, Smith, et al., 2015). The principle of mutual edification provides a philosophical and psychological basis for the aim of multicultural psychology to eradicate oppression and segregation: People who are socially distanced experience negative outcomes; people who are socially integrated experience enhanced well-being.

Holism

A relational paradigm emphasizes contextualization (Overton & Ennis, 2006a). We cannot see the parts without seeing the whole, and we cannot understand the whole without considering the parts. To understand psychological processes, we have to learn about both specific events and their contexts. Multicultural psychology, with its emphasis on contextualization, has provided a holistic perspective previously absent from individualistic conceptualizations of human experience.

Interactive Volition

Individuals possess an innate will and volition called *agency* (Adams & Markus, 2001; Magyar-Moe & López, 2008; R. N. Williams, 1992), but that volition interacts with the environment (Robichaud, 2006). External forces, such as sociopolitical oppression, clearly influence and restrict an individual's choices. Nevertheless, we retain the power to work to modify external environments (e.g., combat oppression). We are not free from external influences, including our own relationship history and culture, but we are free to change our perspective, repair damaged relationships, form new relationships, strengthen our own abilities, and work to modify the environment.

Becoming

Relational development is ongoing. Personal identity and capacity evolve as relationships evolve. Whereas most of psychology fixes its focus on the present, a relational paradigm emphasizes ongoing processes and potentials: the ontology of becoming (Overton & Ennis, 2006b).

Self-in-Relation

In a relational paradigm, the self is seen not as a fixed entity, isolated and independent, but as a highly complex and fluid pattern, a *self-in-relation* (Adams & Markus, 2001; Kaplan, 1986). People understand themselves through their interactions with others, who serve as points of comparison and contrast across circumstances and across time (Overton & Ennis, 2006a). For instance, ethnic identity develops not only through emulation of desired models but also by contrast with other ethnic groups, particularly oppressive ones (Tajfel, 2010).

Responsibility to Others (Moral Sensibility)

Whenever people interact, they influence one another, even if implicitly. Thus, people remain responsible to one another for their influence (Gergen, 2009; Levinas, 1969). Given this responsibility, a relational paradigm advocates an *other-engagement* (meaningfully interacting in ways mutually beneficial) and a *we-consciousness* (explicit attentiveness to the relationship; Levinas, 1998). Other-engagement and we-consciousness diminish self-interest (Stapel & Koomen, 2001), which helps keep interpersonal and intergroup interactions benign rather than oppressive. Thus, therapists maintain not only focus on the client but also vigilance for effects on the client of their own actions and assumptions (Richardson, Fowers, & Guignon, 1999). Sensibility and responsibility to the client constitute the essence of multicultural counseling competence.

Rights

Interpersonal relationships occur across disparate contexts, including different nations and legal systems. However, crossing a geopolitical boundary should not change the core human. Thus, the notion of human rights is necessarily grounded in relationships, not in myriad contexts. People bear rights with them wherever they go, irrespective of organizational policy or national law.

From this perspective a *right* denotes a deserved protection. Rights "follow the person" (irrespective of national and organizational boundaries) because people remain vulnerable to others wherever the location. Human vulnerabilities necessitate protection, so rights link to vulnerabilities (Harré & Robinson, 1995). Social institutions that protect human rights (i.e., government, professional organizations such as the American Psychological Association) hold accountable anyone prepared to compromise others' well-being or take advantage of their vulnerabilities. Multiculturalism has helped to promote recognition of human vulnerability and to promote accompanying protections.

How Might a Relational Paradigm Benefit Multicultural Psychology?

An abstract metatheory, like the relational paradigm, is useful to practitioners and researchers to the extent that it facilitates interpretation of lived experience and research data. A relational paradigm has clear implications for social justice and community empowerment, as alluded to in the preceding section. For example, the Miami Youth Development Project applies a relational approach to promoting social justice by relying on contextual resources and the relationships of youth to their parents, peers, teachers, and mentors (Lerner & Overton, 2008).

Most scholars who advise about the conduct of mental health treatments and research with populations other than their own devote attention to the principles and codes of professional ethical standards and norms; that is, they are concerned about what is right and wrong, good or bad, harmless or harmful, intrusive or nonintrusive, and an assortment of other moral and humanistic considerations. Scholars have expanded on normative professional standards to include often unstated ethical principles and guidelines that focus on the importance of establishing firm collaborative relationships with community leaders, especially in conducting research with ethnocultural groups (Fisher et al., 2002; G. V. Mohatt, 1989).

> It is time to place the collaboration concept in the center of inquiry and work out its importance for community research and intervention. Although some would see it as merely a tool or strategy to getting the "real" work of behavioral science done, our strong preference is to view the research relationship in community research and intervention as a critical part of the "real" work itself. (Trickett & Espino, 2004, p. 62)

A relational paradigm also has clear implications for psychotherapy (Gelso, 2011; Slife, 2004; Slife & Wiggins, 2009; T. B. Smith & Draper, 2004; Wachtel, 2008). This chapter cannot include the many ways a relational paradigm can improve clinical practices, but the basic tenets are obvious: building interpersonal trust with the client, exploring clients' relationship patterns to gain insights into positive and negative coping, strengthening clients' social skills and intimacy with others, involving others in the clients' efforts to improve, attending to countertransference, modeling desirable interpersonal interactions in the here and now, and so forth. "Research studies demonstrate that it is the relationship between the client and the psychotherapist, more than any other factor, which determines the effectiveness of psychotherapy" (Clarkson, 2003, p. 4).

The specific implications of a relational paradigm for multicultural psychology are too many to list, but we briefly highlight the relevance of a relational paradigm to the construct of ethnic identity as one example that may suggest possibilities for other topics. Research and theory focused on identity development have received much attention in the literature, but this scholarship typically involves assumptions associated with individualism: Identity is often assumed to be a trait, something an individual "possesses" (e.g., noting that Ms. Kim has a strong Korean American identity). In contrast, a relational paradigm would emphasize the dynamic shared nature of identity (e.g., examining Ms. Kim's relationships with her grandparents, workmates, etc., and attending to how those interactions invoke and suppress her perceptions and actions relevant to cultural values as a Korean American). From this perspective, scholarship on identity development should attend to social influences, primarily family socialization (e.g., L. L. Liu & Lau, 2013; Trimble, 2005). Identity undergoes challenges and redefinitions as social encounters broaden outside the home, but then stabilizes as social interactions become predictable and controllable.

> For example, a person's complex identity as bisexual Catholic female accountant with a learning disability is dependent on her interactions with other women, bisexuals, Catholics, accountants, and individuals with learning disabilities, who provide essential modeling and sources of comparison, and people who share none of those attributes, who serve as sources of contrast. If the woman has had positive key interactions with others about her gender, she will likely strongly affirm her identity as a woman. But if she has had negative interactions with others about her learning disability and has failed to meet a positive role model with a learning disability, she may likely minimize or avoid openly acknowledging that aspect of her experience. Identity parallels social interactions. Models of racial identity, gender identity, spiritual identity, etc. may therefore benefit from incorporating interpersonal-level variables such as socialization and predictability of interactions. (T. B. Smith & Draper, 2004, pp. 319–320)

Although identity development theories often mention social dynamics, relevant research has remained steeped in individualism, measuring the individual without regard to social context.

Similarly, many other variables in multicultural psychology (e.g., the effects of racism on well-being) have clear social foundations that have typically been ignored because of assumptions embedded in individualism. A relational paradigm attempts to balance prevailing notions with alternative explanations hopefully representative of lived experience.

We have many reasons to believe that a relational paradigm aligns well with multicultural psychology (Comstock et al., 2008; Fay, 1996). Conceptualizations and assumptions based on a relational paradigm may offer several advantages over existing conceptualizations and assumptions based on alternative paradigms, detailed in the following paragraphs.

Congruence With Psychological Perspectives

A relational paradigm fits well within social and applied psychology, thus corresponding to psychotherapy better than philosophical paradigms originally conceived by scholars in economics, comparative literature, sociology, or political science. For example, a psychotherapist can work with the relational concept of collective/group well-being (Peterson, Park, & Sweeney, 2008) while also attending to socioeconomic power (for an alternative conceptualization see Gergen, 1995).

Congruence With Well-Being

Having sufficient resources to sustain life with reasonable predictability is essential to well-being (Diener & Oishi, 2000; Howell & Howell, 2008). Once individuals have sufficient material resources, the basis for human well-being is interpersonal relationships (e.g., Dwyer, 2000; Magyar-Moe & López, 2008; Peterson et al., 2008). This research finding, consistent across world cultures (e.g., Haller & Hadler, 2006), has necessarily focused inquiry on social factors associated with well-being. Personal and collective happiness is largely a function of the quality of interpersonal relationships (Myers, 2008, 2012). A multicultural psychology incorporating principles of connectedness, holism, becoming, and so forth, could improve current efforts to promote well-being (N. V. Mohatt, Fok, Burket, Henry, & Allen, 2011). A multicultural psychology informed by these relational principles can easily integrate with positive psychology, a possibility open for exploration (Pedrotti, Edwards, & López, 2009). A relational paradigm aligns with the psychology of well-being.

Congruence With a Primary Cause of Trauma and Mental Illness

A relational paradigm is not restricted to a positive psychology focus on well-being, although that is its strength (Magyar-Moe & López, 2008). When negative or unpredictable, relationships yield harmful psychological consequences, sometimes terribly destructive ones. Psychological damage results from violations of intimacy and dignity: incest, rape, verbal abuse, spousal infidelity, and similar interpersonal desecration unfortunately common among individuals seeking mental health services. Mental illness that is not directly explainable by neurochemistry has social underpinnings. The psychology of abuse, trauma, and pathology fit within a relational paradigm.

Congruence With Means to Promote Social Change

Multicultural psychologists explicitly promote change in their profession and in society (Ivey & Zalaquett, 2009; Totikidis & Prilleltensky, 2006). Change must involve the social world, particularly relationships, if it is to be sustained. Confrontation and political advocacy can transform institutional policies, but ultimately, individuals need to adopt a different worldview for change to persist. For instance, people may continue to tell racist jokes in private despite an antiracism policy, but they typically stop telling racist jokes once peers frown rather than smile. Real changes occur when social networks reinforce stated organizational values. Multicultural psychology seeks not merely policy change but genuine social inclusion, with efforts that address many social levels being the most effective.

Congruence With Cultural Values

A relational paradigm seems aligned with the values of many cultures worldwide. Indigenous African worldviews, Native American Indian worldviews, Central and South American worldviews, Asian worldviews, and Pacific Islander worldviews tend to emphasize family relationships over individualism.

A relational paradigm challenges and stretches individualistic cultures, but it does not necessarily conflict with them. Even in the most extreme individualistic cultures, genuine interpersonal intimacy has remained a cohesive force (i.e., families); thus, these cultures already attend to relational issues to some degree. A relational paradigm provides a bridge between individualistic and collectivistic cultures. It also provides explicit affirmation of cultural values not adequately represented in mainstream psychology.

Congruence With the Notion of Intersectionality

Race and culture interact with gender and sexual orientation, which interact with family structures and geographic region, among many other variables. Multiculturalism increasingly attends to these intersections (McNeill, 2009; T. B. Smith & Draper, 2004). A relational paradigm offers a framework from which to conceptualize and operationalize the complex intersections of human diversity, which ultimately have social meanings, functions, and consequences. We are not merely groups and not merely individuals; investigation of intersections necessitates holistic reasoning.

Clarification Summary of Benefits of a Relational Paradigm for Social Justice Work

Earlier we listed three strengths of the concept of social justice for multicultural psychology: its emphasis on power, action, and empowerment. These strengths do not require a paradigm associated with philosophical materialism. Holding people accountable for abuses of power does not necessitate critical pedagogy, but it does require the moral principle of accountability. Accountability pervades the relational paradigm. Its emphasis on interdependence checks self-interest, the primary reason for abuses of power. Moreover, the whole notion of power remains grounded in lived experiences arising from intergroup and interpersonal exchange (Gergen, 1995). Thus, the conceptualization of power is made explicitly relevant to applied psychology when power is viewed through a relational lens.

Similarly, the need to take action against oppression does not necessarily require political activism, but it does require the principle of social responsibility. Responsibility to others is keenly felt through a we-consciousness. Action orientation characterizes the principle of other-engagement. Interaction necessarily entails action.

Likewise, empowerment of oppressed peoples can occur not only through raising liberation consciousness but also through integrating social networks. A relational paradigm affirms individual, family, and group rights and their associated protections by emphasizing that separate but equal is not equal. It is insufficient for groups to assert their own rights. Protest may receive attention, but it does not necessarily promote engagement among parties. Equality is not equality without social network integration.[1] A relational paradigm promotes interactions as equals (e.g., Oliver, 2001). When justice is disallowed, steps are taken to reengage dialogue, such as affirmations of equality, appeals to moral sensibilities, appeals to influential third parties, and explanations for refusals to submit to injustice. A relational paradigm seeks genuine integration and equity that includes but extends beyond the economic and political.

Within a relational paradigm, a primary motive is mutual engagement as equals and rejection of the roles of oppressor or oppressed. This approach seeks to change the contexts that led to the power imbalance in the first place and to replace the disempowering notions that oppressed groups too often internalize when reacting from defensive postures. Rather than promote social justice in terms of "us versus them," mutual edification provides motivation for continued engagement across divides. Thus, a relational paradigm sustains action against oppression because the motivation transcends self-interest.

A relational paradigm and philosophical materialism both attend to issues of power, access, status, coercion, and so forth (see Table 11.1). One cannot accurately conceptualize individuals, families, or groups without those concepts, but to those important concepts a relational paradigm adds sources of affiliation, ideals, and so forth, such as abilities, gender, geographic region, race, religion,

---

[1]Social integration does not necessarily entail assimilation or acculturation. Engagement across difference is one component of well-being.

TABLE 11.1
Comparison of Two Philosophical Positions for Fostering
Social Justice Through Multicultural Psychology

	Philosophical materialism	Relational paradigm
Primary aspiration	Equality	Mutual enrichment
Primary emphasis	Access to power	Holistic well-being
Conceptualizations of power	Critical pedagogy, dialectical materialism	Accountability, interdependence, moral principles
Action orientation	Advocacy, praxis, transformation of systems	Social responsibility, protection of human rights
Empowerment	Liberation psychology, grassroots political activism	Social network integration, skill development
Level of primary focus	Macro level systems (and other levels as appropriate)	Intergroup, interpersonal
Motivations	Emancipation, fighting against oppression to obtain justice	Engagement as equals, dismantling oppressed/ oppressor roles

Note. Common features include the following: emphasis on local community empowerment, action-oriented promotion of equality and self-determination, explicit opposition to all forms of oppression, and attention to human conditions and contexts, including issues of power, opportunity, status, coercion, and so forth.

and sexual orientation, that are only indirectly addressed by philosophical materialism. Material considerations are crucial, even paramount, in desperate situations, and they overlap with social considerations. Thus, a relational paradigm maintains the focus on poverty, inequity, oppression, and so forth (the strength of materialism), while contextualizing those issues in lived experience.

For these reasons, we propose that for applied psychology a relational paradigm is preferable to alternative social justice conceptualizations. Specifically, we believe that social justice (an aim of multicultural psychology) can be better measured, evaluated, and promoted within a relational paradigm relative to prevailing conceptualizations based on philosophical materialism. Whether or not future scholarship takes up this issue, we have attempted to emphasize the point that ideational foundations do matter. Assumptions influence outcomes.

What Assumptions and Limitations Must Be Expected for a Relational Paradigm?

Every approach has assumptions and limitations. Just as the strengths of materialism led us to uncover its possible weaknesses, the strengths of a relational paradigm also point to its weaknesses. The following limitations characterize a relational paradigm.

Psychological Explanations Can Obfuscate the Value of Other Perspectives

Human behavior can be explained at numerous levels, from the micro (neurochemical) to the macro (environmental). A relational paradigm clearly emphasizes interpersonal and intergroup exchanges at the expense of other levels of explanation. Relational theorists have tended to ignore biologically oriented research findings, such as those of neuropsychology. Macro issues such as warfare and access to health care are relevant to but clearly distanced from purely social causes. And with few exceptions, relational scholarship shies away from the traditionally influential cornerstones of psychology, such as comparative psychology and radical behaviorism, as well as technically oriented dimensions, such as computer simulations of human cognition. Excessive reliance on the interpersonal level of explanation, even if congruent with the worldviews of mental health professionals, artificially constrains attention when other mechanisms (e.g., ambient pollution or neurochemistry) may be more pertinent.

Complexity Restricts the Isolation of Variables

Although a relational paradigm accounts for the contextuality of human experience, the resulting complexity diminishes the likelihood of isolating explanatory variables. Even when a specific characteristic is isolated, the conditions affecting that characteristic are potentially infinite. Contextuality cannot coexist with simplicity; causality becomes difficult to explain.[2]

Reliance on correlation more than causal models has been one of the primary weaknesses of psychological research. Nevertheless, we are just now reaching a point where statistics may enable sufficient complexity in our data collection and analyses to move beyond correlation. Social network analyses have increased in their complexity and utility over time (e.g., Borgatti, Mehra, Brass, & Labianca, 2009; Kirke, 2007), but additional simplification of the tools for conducting social network statistics is necessary before graduate curricula in psychology will routinely cover those statistics. Nevertheless, given the explosion of Internet-based inquiry and statistical modeling of social networks, we see their widespread use as an eventuality: Analytics possible through supercomputers will examine trillions of paths of social influence such that the network shape and directional flow become apparent and open to inquiry. Until such statistical tools become widely available, however, research conducted within a relational paradigm must rely on traditional methods for attempting to provide causal explanations (Kuhn, 1996).

---

[2]Nevertheless, true experimental designs can be used within a relational paradigm. Social psychologists use a remarkable variety of research methods that could be adopted in multicultural psychology.

Including Notions of Morality Would Require Discourse Beyond Current Parameters

If human interactions are fundamentally moral, as a relational paradigm affirms, morality must be addressed by psychology. Except for the publication of self-regulating codes of ethics, the profession of psychology has largely sidestepped morality. In fact, psychology was originally developed in partial reaction against the notion of morality and the institutions, religious and aristocratic, that overtly enforced their own versions of morality. Thus, psychologists may have difficulties accepting the emphasis of the relational paradigm on moral issues. Nevertheless, psychologists constantly confront questions of meaning, not merely questions of description.

Some scholars have argued for decades that psychology's discomfort with moral conceptualizations has not served its interests. Specifically, they have emphasized that all scientific inquiry remains influenced by human values; thus, openly acknowledging those values is in the profession's best interest. Theory and research should be contextualized (Slife & Williams, 1995). And psychology will benefit from greater self-awareness and accompanying transparency. Multicultural psychology advocates for greater self-awareness and transparency as well.

A paramount fear is that entertaining professional discourse about morality would paralyze the field. Would progress not degenerate into the morass of debate and counter-accusation? With little prior experience engaging moral issues, this could happen. Researchers have been systematically taught to hide personal values in professional writing. To overcome discomfort in debating the value, meaning, and purpose of their work, psychology researchers would have to first recognize that questions of value, meaning, and purpose are in fact the most important questions. Discussions of whether variable X correlates with or even causes variable Y becomes appropriate in psychotherapy only after we understand the ramifications of messing with X and Y for a particular client. Justification for research should be based on arguments about value, meaning, and purpose, with those justifications subject to challenges and refutation. We have to invoke the "so what?" question much more often with our own work and with the work that appears in multicultural psychology journals.

Section Summary: Values and Assumptions

Social justice is a value—a value based on assumptions about human dignity and fairness. Work that promotes principles of justice and fairness is a moral endeavor. Multicultural psychology embodies that work; thus, it is a moral as well as a professional and empirical movement.

Multicultural psychology seeks to promote the well-being of historically oppressed people. The more clearly multicultural psychology can articulate its objectives and its proposed means to achieve them, the more support it is likely to draw. Contemporary struggles for equity, such as the denunciation of racial microaggressions (D. W. Sue et al., 2007), require this articulation in the face of opposition or, more prevalent, apathy. Ultimately, psychologists will embrace and infuse multiculturalism in psychotherapy (and in their personal lives) to the extent that it becomes recognized as the right thing to do. Moral sensibility is embedded in social relations.

In this section we have attempted to delineate how a relational paradigm may provide grounding for social justice work in multicultural psychology. Assumptions and values of the relational paradigm include the aim of mutual edification, the necessity of holistic thinking, the existence of human volition and agency, the developmental perspective of becoming, the understanding of identity as a self-in-relation, the inescapability of responsibility for others, and the existence of human rights—moral obligations to protect human vulnerabilities.

The objective of multicultural psychology is not to achieve mere tolerance, the "recognition" of differences (see Oliver, 2001). Rather, multicultural psychology has sought to promote human well-being through self-affirmation and, although not articulated as such, other-affirmation. If multicultural psychology seeks these broad aims, its work extends beyond even social justice. It may rightly advocate for any salutary principle, such as reconciliation, personal sacrifice for the well-being of others, and deepened interchange across apparent and genuine ideational differences. Applied psychologists are already in the business of promoting values (e.g., Magyar-Moe & López, 2008); multicultural psychologists can promote values that benefit disenfranchised populations.

A relational conceptualization of multicultural psychology espouses values that promote mutual enrichment. Whereas the concept of self-affirmation may presently be popular, a relational conceptualization includes the paired concept of other-affirmation. Individuals do not exist in a social vacuum. Affirmation of self yields reciprocity through affirmation of others. In other words, when people engage in other-affirmation (e.g., schoolteachers who empower students in an otherwise harsh environment), we call them praiseworthy (affirming the person who affirms others), but praise for oneself without genuine engagement with others we call narcissism. So it is with multicultural psychology: Our work is insufficient if we merely affirm multicultural voices, each one calling out its own music. Expression is far preferable to voicelessness, but cacophony attracts few listeners. No, self-affirmation of culture, race, gender, or any other partitioned aspect of human identity is an aim too delimited for multicultural psychology, even if justice were technically achieved because no one restricted expression.

Continuing the metaphor of vocal music, a relational conceptualization offers multicultural psychology the equivalent of a music school. Voices can tune to surroundings. The quality of individuals' and groups' expressions can improve. In a music school the ear can be taught to hear others' tone and timbre and to recognize the themes and motifs already native to their inflections. Schools of music enable compositions, orchestrations, and production of quality performances that generate an audience. Unity amid diversity can be attained through multicultural psychology, a school for relationships learned through experience.

A relational conceptualization of multicultural psychology seeks justice toward the aim of mutual enrichment. Voices must not merely be heard but understood, appreciated, and joined.

BRINGING IT ALL TOGETHER

Psychology consists of ideas about human experience. Those ideas stem from underlying philosophies and their associated assumptions. For most of its history, psychology has presumed the experiences, worldviews, and philosophies of cultures with origins in Western Europe, to the detriment of others (D. W. Sue, 2015). Multicultural psychology has sought to represent people previously excluded from mainstream dialogue, and it has brought attention to significant ideas, such as those covered in previous chapters of this volume (e.g., multicultural competence). Those ideas can be refined not only through improvements in empirical methods (e.g., assessment, participant selection, theory testing) but also through appraisal of their underlying values and assumptions (Machado & Silva, 2007; Slife & Williams, 1995). Just as the assumptions of psychology have benefitted from scrutiny with a multicultural perspective (D. W. Sue, 2015; D. W. Sue & Sue, 2013), the assumptions of multicultural psychology should benefit from evaluation.

Questioning assumptions, a few readers have likely wondered whether this chapter about philosophy was necessary in a book otherwise about data. We ask these readers to consider our intended messages. We hope that many readers who have previously been skeptical about the relevance of a broad concept such as *justice* to psychology have become aware that real-world psychological implications and applications are generated by such principles as "injustice anywhere is a threat to justice everywhere" (quoted from Martin Luther King Jr.'s "Letter from Birmingham Jail"). Such ideas motivated millions during the civil rights movement. Such ideas also motivate our work as mental health professionals: If a relational paradigm enables me to recognize my interconnectedness, I will be more likely to act when I see injustice, but if I fixate on the inequities, I may be more likely to react from a stance akin to naive transitivity. Is this contrast merely a nuance, too subtle to be consequential? Ask about a person's motives, and you will be in a better position to understand resulting actions and reactions. That sounds like the work of a psychologist.

Too few mental health professionals have addressed the philosophical foundations of multicultural psychology, with the notable exceptions focused on research methods and guiding principles (Cauce, 2011; David, Okazaki, & Giroux, 2014; Gone, 2011; Ponterotto, 2010). Questions posed in this chapter openly challenge commonplace apathy about conceptual analysis. Table 11.2 contains some steps to consider. Of all people, multicultural psychologists should be keenly aware of our own assumptions and values.

TABLE 11.2
Example Components of Conceptual Analysis

Conceptual analysis component	Rationale
Define constructs precisely.	Specification is essential to all subsequent steps of conceptual analysis. Problems arise from imprecision.
Identify the level(s) of analysis to be undertaken (macro to micro, abstract to concrete).	Most constructs are pertinent or valid at only one level of explanation, but multiple levels of explanation are typically necessary in psychology. Constructs should not be generalized beyond their realistic limits.
Identify essential parts of the construct.	Breaking down constructs can help distinguish truly essential features, circumstances, and so forth, including parts that must be included for the concept to remain viable.
Identify how the parts relate to one another and to the whole.	Dynamics must be observed and considered, particularly relationships between parts that are not explained by the proposed theory or construct.
Identify strengths and limitations.	Construct application requires understanding of when and how it works most and least effectively. Strengths and limitations can be paired: A strength can be a limitation; a limitation can be a strength.
Identify a concrete case that demonstrates the construct, and contrast it with contradictory or hypothetical cases.	Practice requires understanding of when, where, and how concepts fit and do not fit in the real world, including exceptions that remain unexplained.
Identify alternative explanations.	Understanding of similar constructs should be used to inform analysis. This includes existing relevant theories and other disciplines that have addressed similar issues, possibly using other terms.
Identify metaphysics, epistemology, ontology, and so forth.	Every construct has foundational assumptions: for example, the nature of reality, ways we can know about the world, and so forth.
Consider real-world consequences.	Constructs have many possible ramifications: people who will benefit or be harmed, possible misinterpretations and misuses, consequences of ignoring it, and so forth.

No field can solve astoundingly complex social situations through a single lens. Many voices contribute to effective solutions. Scholarly synthesis and contrast, rather than reverential adherence to a few popular ideas, promotes the aims of multicultural psychology. We are reminded of the words of a Mexican Nobel laureate in literature:

> What sets worlds in motion is the interplay of differences, their attractions and repulsions. Life is plurality, death is uniformity. By suppressing differences and peculiarities, by eliminating different civilizations and cultures, progress weakens life and favors death. The ideal of a single civilization for everyone, implicit in the cult of progress and technique, impoverishes and mutilates us. Every view of the world that becomes extinct, every culture that disappears, diminishes a possibility of life. (Paz, 1985, p. 117)

Across human history, few societies have been multicultural. What can we learn from those societies that have been? Across human history, no age has been so globally networked as the present. How will we of the present age connect while retaining cultural plurality? Across human history, no age has had greater intellectual and material resources. How will we foster mutual enrichment? Questions expand the vista of multicultural psychology.

12

FIRMING UP THE FOUNDATION FOR AN EVIDENCE-BASED MULTICULTURAL PSYCHOLOGY

Psychotherapy and related mental health services are based on decades of research (Norcross, 2011). Mental health professionals understand the benefits of research in improving treatment practices and fostering individuals' well-being. Indeed, evidence-based practices have become the standard for the profession (American Psychological Association [APA] 2005 Presidential Task Force on Evidence-Based Practice, 2006).

Multicultural psychology should also be based on research evidence (G. Bernal & Domenech Rodríguez, 2012; Cauce, 2011; Leong, Comas-Díaz, Nagayama Hall, McLoyd, & Trimble, 2014; G. C. N. Hall & Yee, 2014). A primary purpose of this book was to evaluate the degree to which multicultural psychology is being built on a solid research foundation. This book covered only select topics within multicultural psychology that were specific to race and ethnicity, but in general, the conclusions were positive. Although there are still pressing needs for greater empirical evidence stemming from a lack of

http://dx.doi.org/10.1037/14733-012
Foundations of Multicultural Psychology: Research to Inform Effective Practice, by T. B. Smith and J. E. Trimble
Copyright © 2016 by the American Psychological Association. All rights reserved.

attention to multiculturalism in some segments of the mental health professions, remarkable gains have been made in recent decades. And those gains deserve acknowledgement. Multiculturalism is no longer a peripheral issue in many professional circles, and increased influence in both research and practice is the current trajectory. Looking to the future, the continued influence of multicultural psychology on psychotherapy and other mental health treatments seems certain (Pedersen, 1999).

Notwithstanding the noble ambitions and rapidly increasing influence of multicultural psychology, it seems wise to not extend the reach of advocacy too far beyond the available research evidence (Huey, Tilley, Jones, & Smith, 2014). Many details of multicultural issues relevant to mental health and well-being remain presumed or unknown. We have much to learn.

RECOMMENDATIONS FOR STRENGTHENING THE RESEARCH FOUNDATION OF MULTICULTURAL PSYCHOLOGY

To solidify the research foundation of multicultural psychology, four areas for improvement can be considered: (a) maintaining focus on the essential dependent variables; (b) attending to meta-analytic data to prioritize independent variables; (c) increasing specificity and improving research methods; and (d) developing, testing, and refining theories. These recommendations deserve serious attention (see also Awad & Cokley, 2010; B. M. Byrne et al., 2009; Huey et al., 2014; M. J. Miller & Sheu, 2008; Ponterotto, 2010; Worthington, Soth-McNett, & Moreno, 2007). They will help solidify knowledge foundational for the construction of a truly multicultural psychology.

Focus on the Essential Dependent Variables in Mental Health Service Provision

Empirical data can and should inform multicultural psychology (Cauce, 2011), but as pointed out in the previous chapter (Chapter 11), data are generated and interpreted on the basis of assumptions about what is important and what is not (see also Slife, 2009). And because values and assumptions differ, research agendas vary. Even a casual perusal of the multicultural psychology literature quickly confirms wide variability in the topics covered. Although diversity of thought can improve the profession, scattered research agendas can be problematic if they inadequately address the most consequential dependent variables. For mental health professionals, those would be variables within the scope of their influence that would have the greatest impact on the clients they serve. In the previous chapter we proposed four: (a) reduction of mental health disparities, (b) access to services by those in need, (c) retention of those receiving services, and (d) improved outcomes to the satisfaction of those receiving services.

Does the field adequately address those four aims? To evaluate the amount of research covering the four aims, we conducted a content analysis of the applied psychology literature relevant to race, ethnicity, or culture covering a 6-year period. We sought to evaluate scholarship explicitly addressing psychotherapy and related mental health services, so we limited our search to the PsycINFO database using a string of keywords specific to mental health treatments crossed with variants of the terms *race*, *ethnicity*, and *culture*. Our searches yielded 3,484 hits, of which 805 turned out to be irrelevant on further examination; 895 tangentially mentioned race, ethnicity, or culture in the abstract but the manuscript was primarily relevant to another topic; and 239 were book reviews. Using established procedures for content analysis (Krippendorff, 2012), coders assigned the remaining 1,545 manuscripts to 33 content categories, with manuscripts having content that overlapped categories (i.e., both social justice and ethical issues) being coded in a separate column from manuscripts having content pertinent to a single category. This procedure enabled calculation of percentages representative of multiple categories. In the end, however, the percentages observed for the single-category studies were virtually the same as those of the multiple-category studies, so we report only the former for the sake of parsimony. Two coders independently reviewed every manuscript, with the data averaged between coders reported in Table 12.1 for 22 of the 33 content-area categories because the remaining 11 categories had only a few manuscripts each.

Table 12.1 provides a snapshot of the content for publications mentioning race, ethnicity, or culture that were specific to mental health treatments.

TABLE 12.1
Topics Relevant to Race, Ethnicity, or Culture in the Literature Specific
to Mental Health Treatment

More common topics	%	Less common topics	%
Diagnosis rates by race/ethnicity	13	Perceived racial/ethnic discrimination	3
Therapist multicultural competence	12	Ethnic identity	3
Cultural adaptations to treatment	10	Ethical issues relevant to race/ethnicity	2
Client expectations about treatment	9		
Therapist multicultural education/training	8	Multicultural supervision	2
		Racial identity	2
Client treatment outcomes by race/ethnicity	8	Client–therapist racial/ethnic match	1
		Individualism/collectivism	1
Client utilization of treatment	7	Social justice	1
Assessment/measurement issues	4	Client participation in treatment	1
Attitudes toward mental illness	4	Client spirituality	1
Therapist prejudice/bias	4	Color-blind racial attitudes	1
Acculturation	4		

Topics central to mental health treatment were represented more often than topics peripheral to mental health treatment. The topic most often addressed was diagnostic rates by race or ethnicity, which is directly relevant to the first of the four proposed aims of the field. Therapist multicultural competence and cultural adaptations to treatment were the second and third most commonly addressed topics, which are both relevant to the other three aims. When considering the whole, about three fourths of the literature could be construed to align with one or more of the four proposed aims presented earlier in this chapter. Some scatter characterizes the multicultural psychology literature, but at present, two recommendations for improvement of research focus may suffice.

First, greater attention can be given to client outcomes. Only 8% of manuscripts addressed client outcomes in treatment, a percentage that seems low given (a) the importance of documenting client improvement in treatment and (b) the fact that many of the manuscripts retrieved did not contain data, meaning that fewer than 8% of manuscripts actually evaluated client outcomes. We urge greater attention in the multicultural psychology literature to clients' outcomes in treatment (see also Lau, Chang, & Okazaki, 2010).

Second, researchers may have to more frequently evaluate the degree of client participation in treatment (i.e., completion and drop-out rates). The fact that only 1% of manuscripts addressed client participation in treatment seems problematic. The third of the four proposed aims appears to be neglected. Nevertheless, there may justifiable reasons why client participation in mental health treatments has not been examined more frequently. Specifically, the data in Chapter 5 of this book suggested that racial discrepancies in client participation rates may be less severe than previously imagined.

Overall, aligning multicultural psychology research with the experiences of individuals in need of mental health services will greatly improve the utility of present scholarship. Whereas 1,545 manuscripts that addressed race, ethnicity, or culture and that were specific to mental health treatments were identified in the PsycINFO database over a 6-year period, over 40,000 manuscripts that addressed race, ethnicity, or culture during that same time frame did not mention mental health treatment (no mention of the root terms *psychotherapy*, *treatment*, *therapy*, *intervention*, *program*, *service*, *clinic*, *counseling*, *patient*, or *client*). It would appear that although issues of race, ethnicity, and culture are being widely attended to, proportionately little research in psychology addresses dependent variables essential to mental health services.

Synthesize Research Findings and Prioritize Efforts Using Those Data

Prioritizing research foci involves both conceptual and empirical considerations. Systematic literature reviews and meta-analyses prove useful in making those decisions. Whereas thousands of systematic literature reviews and meta-analyses have been conducted in the general psychology literature (Cooper & Koenka, 2012), relatively few have been conducted in multicultural psychology.

As one step toward informing the field of priorities for investigation, the meta-analyses reported in this book can be considered together, with the data portrayed in a single display. Figure 12.1 depicts the effect sizes found within the several meta-analyses, all converted to the metric of Cohen's d. When depicted in this manner, several points can be made after sounding a caution.[1] At one level of interpretation, Figure 12.1 provides the numbers of manuscripts (k) with data on each topic. A comparison of the number of manuscripts with data makes it clear that studies of therapist multicultural competence were underrepresented in the literature relative to other topics; a field cannot establish its credibility on solely 16 studies. Conversely, other topics may have received relatively excessive research attention. Specifically, a substantial investment has been made to investigate strength of ethnic identity, yet ethnic identity accounts for an average of 3.3% of the variance in the well-being of people of color—and the direction of causality has not been established (see Chapter 10). The overall mental health literature on ethnic identity consists of several thousands of research studies, which represent millions of hours of effort expended (hours of work by authors × number of authors × number of studies, plus hours spent by participants). In the future it may be more advantageous to invest research efforts in variables with demonstrated causality that account for substantial variance in well-being, such as socioeconomic conditions (e.g., McKee-Ryan, Song, Wanberg, & Kinicki, 2005), coping strategies (e.g., Ano & Vasconcelles, 2005), relationship and family qualities (e.g., Proulx, Helms, & Buehler, 2007), and variables associated with positive psychology (Sin & Lyubomirsky, 2009). Professionals

---

[1]The data in the several meta-analyses cannot be compared against one another without an accurate understanding of the context of each meta-analysis. The topics are entirely distinct in content, measurement, and methodology, just as apples are distinct from oranges, even though both can be digested. Given the severity of concerns about data misinterpretation, we hesitated to generate Figure 12.1. Nevertheless, we trust the reader to become informed by reviewing each meta-analysis and thus avoiding uninformed comparisons. As one of several errors that can be made when considering Figure 12.1, a reader observing the very large effect size found when client experiences in therapy are associated with client ratings of their therapist's multicultural competence (the third row in Figure 12.1) could falsely conclude that that topic is the most important or (even worse) the most effective. Those conclusions would be erroneous because the information presented in Chapter 3 made it clear that that large effect size is highly problematic for several reasons, particularly when contrasted with the small effect size obtained when therapists' rate their own multicultural competence. In this instance, the benefit of the graph is the clear contrast between the two types of measurement, not the pretentiously large effect size observed when using one problematic measure. Another source of error in interpreting Figure 12.1 would be a failure to account for the size of the corresponding literature. The numbers of studies (k) for the data from Chapter 3 (the second and third rows) are much fewer than the numbers of studies in the other meta-analyses; only seven studies evaluated therapists' perceptions and only 11 studies evaluated clients' perceptions.

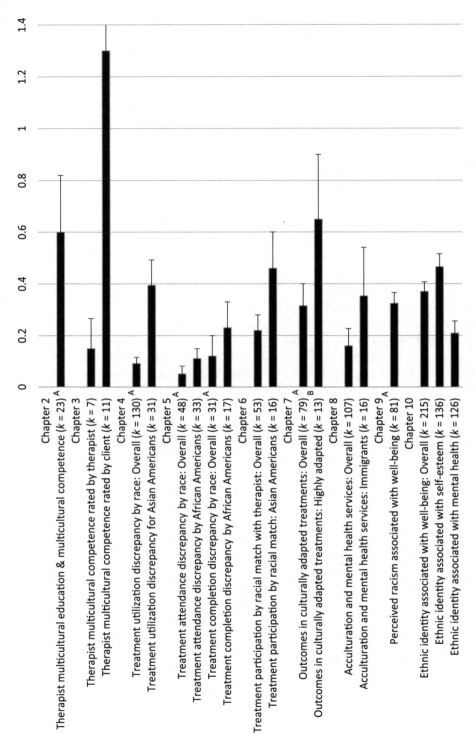

Figure 12.1. Effect sizes (Cohen's *d*) and 95% confidence intervals for meta-analyses reported in chapters of this book. A = adjusted for publication bias; B = studies with at least six of eight recommended cultural adaptations; *k* = number of studies.

intent on enhancing the well-being of people of color will benefit from attending to variables such as these to a greater degree than variables that have proven less consequential.

Acculturation to North American society has also been widely examined, with over 1,500 relevant studies appearing in PsycINFO. Yet the review in Chapter 8 found fewer than two dozen studies investigating immigrants' experiences in mental health treatments. The data indicate the obvious: The construct of acculturation is most salient for immigrant populations. Professionals can therefore align with the data and either analyze differences within samples (including curvilinear associations) or discontinue the common practice of administering generic measures of acculturation when level of acculturation is unlikely to account for variance in the dependent measure administered to individuals with moderate or high levels of acculturation.

Culturally adapted mental health treatments are increasingly recognized as evidence-based alternatives to traditional treatments (Cardemil, 2010a; Huey et al., 2014). According to the meta-analysis in Chapter 7, clients appear to benefit most when the adaptations are systematic (following established guidelines) and multifaceted. That is, the more a treatment aligns with the cultural worldviews and experiences of a client, the more effective the treatment is likely to be.

In general, clients engage in and attend or complete mental health treatments at similar rates across race (Chapters 4 and 5). The clear exceptions are that Asian Americans are much less likely than other groups to enter professional treatment and are much more likely to remain in treatment when the therapist is of the same race or ethnicity, and African Americans are much less likely than other groups to remain in treatment. Attention to the explanations for those discrepancies can facilitate the implementation of needed steps to remove them.

In short, the field of multicultural psychology will benefit from attending closely to systematic literature reviews and meta-analyses. At present, the lack of clinical studies (research with actual mental health clients) appears to be the greatest gap in the overall corpus of scholarship (see also Lau et al., 2010; Worthington et al., 2007). Future meta-analytic reviews will continue to redirect efforts in the ongoing process of improvement based on data.

Specify Constructs and Improve Research Methods

Multicultural psychology seeks to inform mental health professionals of the essential variability in human conditions and experiences. Nevertheless, that intention is undercut by the high degree of variability that characterizes research findings in multicultural psychology, as evidenced by the scatterplots (and large I^2 values) accompanying each meta-analysis in this book. Effect sizes vary in any field. In our analyses, they varied so much that the random effects weighted averages reported in some chapters could be criticized as informative fiction. Yes, the averaged effect sizes represent the best overall estimate, but a single research study might yield anything, from moderately positive to moderately negative results. Under these circumstances, trust in the findings of any single quantitative study, particularly those with few participants, becomes restricted to a degree approaching disregard.

Wide variations in circumstances and participant characteristics already introduce multiple explanations for the variability of research findings in multicultural psychology, but when both known sources of variation and threats to internal validity are unaccounted for in studies, when research procedures are inadequately described, and when there are no standard approaches to evaluating a given phenomenon, ascertaining the "true effect size" is highly improbable (J. Miller & Schwarz, 2011). For our estimates to become more reliable, our measurements and our methods must improve.

Greater specificity is one solution. Multicultural psychology is complex, but its literature is characterized by frequent use of categorical assumptions. Categories of race, ethnicity, gender, sexual orientation, religion, and so forth, are assumed to suffice as independent variables, yet we have known for decades about extreme variability within groups (e.g., Phinney, 1996) and overlap across groups (e.g., biracial identification; Young, Sanchez, & Wilton, 2013). As one negative consequence among many, graduate classes in multicultural psychology often provide categorical group-level descriptions implicitly portrayed as sufficient. Categories and categorical thinking can be useful heuristics for the completely uninformed, but at what cost do we perpetuate group stereotypes among individuals being trained as experts in human behavior?

Scholars affirm that professionals should attend to proximal variables, such as the meanings and consequences of ethnicity, not merely categorical ethnicity (e.g., S. Sue, 1988). Categorical operationalization of race, ethnicity, and culture is too imprecise to yield more than general trends. As important as the constructs of race, ethnicity, and culture are, an entire field cannot help but crawl forward while relying so heavily on generic, distal variables. It is time to break apart categorical approaches and precisely describe aspects of experience, such as the multiple components of racial socialization or cultural values of holism, useful to improving mental health and quality of life. Researchers should specify their questions, measurements, and analyses, rather than continue to rely on the easily generated but largely ineffective check box.

Another solution is to use methods that explicitly account for variability and control for potential confounds. Presently, much of the multicultural psychology literature consists of surveys and correlational studies, with a relative absence of research designs that account for sources of error and differences across contexts. Multicultural psychology is important. It is so important that the research deserves to be done well (e.g., Awad & Cokley, 2010; B. M. Byrne et al., 2009; Lau et al., 2010; Ponterotto, 2010). With that consideration in mind, university research advisors, journal editorial board members, and anyone now informed by the scatterplots in this book can commit to elevate expectations for research quality in multicultural psychology.

Improving the quality of quantitative research need not entail inordinate amounts of effort. Six steps should have a consequential impact: (a) precisely define constructs, optimally broken down into subcomponents; (b) evaluate proximal variables rather than distal or proxy variables; (c) investigate sources of within-group and between-group variability; (d) control for likely confounds, randomly select participants, and randomly assign participants to conditions when ethical or feasible; (e) use very conservative estimates of effect size when conducting a power analysis to estimate the number of participants needed in a study; and (f) have theory guide research questions and test theory in the research. Other recommendations specific to qualitative research can also be followed (e.g., Ponterotto, 2010), but steps such as these six will enhance the utility of quantitative research efforts. Believing the sixth recommendation, to attend to theory, to be particularly important, we elaborate on that recommendation.

Develop, Test, and Refine Theory

In conducting our meta-analytic reviews of multicultural psychology research (Chapters 2 to 10), we observed that few manuscripts involved research questions explicitly based on relevant theories, and even fewer attempted to evaluate theories. Those that did were predominantly the notable leaders in the field and their graduate students. Although the work of those leaders is truly admirable and has attracted followers, the work of the followers does not elaborate much on what has already been proposed. Collectively, we seem reluctant to critically engage theory and push one another to reconsider and refine. Metaphorically, it seems that we are more interested in riding comfortably along on the bandwagon than in terrain exploration.

As pointed out in the previous chapter (Chapter 11), we are often reluctant to engage in the terrain exploration of theory development chiefly because we are unaccustomed to doing so, not because we are unsuited to the work. And the benefits of theory development are substantial. At a time when laboratory experimentation was the norm, a revolutionary young physicist, Albert Einstein, engaged in thought experiments (Ono, 1982). Revolutions in science begin with novel conceptualizations (Kuhn, 2012). At a time when most multicultural psychology research involves self-report surveys, we need both more laboratory experimentation and more thought experiments. Trailblazing enables progress.

At this point it may be helpful to consider a concrete example of the need for explanatory theories in multicultural psychology. A conceptual challenge to both categorical notions of race, ethnicity, and culture and to the attempts at specificity intended to correct for the problems of that categorization, as discussed in the previous section, comes from *intersectionality* (e.g., McNeill, 2009). Intersectionality involves a holistic perspective inclusive of the multiplicity of identities and experiences that cannot easily be categorized or specified without committing misrepresentation. An individual is simultaneously racial, ethnic, and cultural along with having multiple other attributes (age, gender, etc.). Although we applaud emerging scholarship that accounts for intersectionality (e.g., Miville & Ferguson, 2014), much work remains to be done. How will such complexity be operationalized in research and in professional training? How will intersectionality be put into practice? We anticipate the development of relevant theories.

Given the overall need for theory development, where should scholars in multicultural psychology begin? Which of the many topics and challenges in the field should be targeted in the future? In considering how to narrow recommendations, it seemed appropriate to solicit input from renowned scholars in the field. They have been engaged in the work for decades, and their broad vision can inform speculation about pressing future needs. We therefore requested the opinions of several leaders in multicultural psychology about what the profession should consider for the future, given demographic projections and likely social conditions. We received the following responses, which we have edited for brevity.

- "I would gravitate to the challenges related to the three P's: power, privilege, and person. We need to attend to social and economic disparities."
- "We need to address the role of religion in people's lives. Underfunding of traditionally ethnic religious institutions is limiting access to important support systems. This leads to loss of traditions, creates schisms between generations, and presents in counseling as loss of direction, diminished hope, and struggle to find meaning in life."
- "A challenge to all of the helping professions is the recruitment and training of clinicians who are members of diverse groups (broadly and inclusively defined). The overall field runs the risk of failing to keep pace with demographics trends. Collectively, we are training a different population of therapists (e.g., upper-middle class) than the clients we serve."
- "Problems often arise in supervision and consultation. I'm also reminded that issues of oppression extend to political issues, such as voter suppression."

- "All counseling is likely to be multicultural in some sense and to some degree, given the multiple identities and affiliations that each of us has. So counselors must think about and address culture and its implications from a dynamic perspective. To date, our approach to culture has been much too static."
- "A topic that comes to mind is internalization of hatred, manifested as complacency."
- "My prediction is that we're going to need to do more macro systemic advocacy around political and economic issues, as there simply won't be enough social services for most people in need."
- "Your question reminded of a client I saw last week. She was hungry. She could not obtain food stamps for two to three more days. How do I manage that in counseling? She said, 'You look like you do OK. Can you tell me, how do I rise out of poverty?' That is very humbling. What is our role in that scenario?"
- "Sexual and gender minorities (individuals who identify as lesbian, gay, bisexual, or transgender) will be more open with their families of origin about LGBT status than they might have been in prior generations. This creates new opportunities for family closeness, but it also creates more of a need for extended family members to work out their acceptance of each other."
- "Endangered languages are becoming even more endangered. People who speak an endangered language will feel torn between their duties or desires to cultivate their cultural inheritance and their desires to operate in a dominant culture."
- "White people continue to occupy policy, judicial, and power broker positions. As psychologists and counselors, what role do we play in addressing those inequities?"
- "We need to address gender issues related to gender identity and to violence among intimate partners."
- "Younger people did not experience the racism of the past, so they may feel it is irrelevant to their lives. Older Whites may fear becoming a minority group with diminished power."
- "Three recommendations: (1) indigenous peoples and their growing awareness of settler decolonization issues, (2) lingering assimilation efforts and racial microaggressions, and (3) sensitivity to unique historical issues of diverse groups."

Distilling the experts' informal comments, we make two observations. First, several of the experts recommended that the field focus on issues of power, particularly socioeconomic status and poverty, although other recommended topics could also be conceptualized in terms of power inequities. In

Chapter 11, we described a philosophical framework from which this kind of work may gain more traction than attempts based on philosophical materialism have thus far generated in the mental health professions. Irrespective of the paradigms or methods used, the primary point that several experts in the field are making is that we must no longer act as if power inequities do not affect mental health. They do, and we must attend to them.

Second, beyond the topics of power and poverty, there was no consensus on priorities for the future. Many challenges plead for solutions. Encompassing all of human diversity, multicultural psychology is so broad that organization and prioritization proves daunting. Sorting and sifting through myriad important topics will require our best efforts, so we repeat our recommendations to focus squarely on the four dependent variables most essential to the work of mental health professionals (listed above) and to consider research data when selecting among the many independent variables that call for our attention. And we emphasize the central role that strong theories can play in explaining the relationships among variables, providing essential guidance for targeting underlying causes, rather than surface-level descriptions.

Admittedly, the complexity of multicultural psychology resists the artificial imposition of theoretical concepts. No theory can account for all exceptions, so it seems unlikely for a single approach to unify all aspects of the field's complexity (Cauce, 2011). Nevertheless, it is abundantly clear that the field needs theories that go beyond description to explanation. We need strong theories that move beyond *what* questions to answer *how* and eventually *why* questions. This line of scholarship can focus on (a) micro-theories, those delimited by circumstances or attributes; and (b) middle-range theories, those that explain events common to multiple settings but do not claim universality (Merton, 1968). Thus far, theory development has been limited to a few topics in multicultural psychology, yet it will be obvious to those familiar with the multicultural psychology literature how very much those theories have contributed to the field. Existing theories have to be tested and subsequently refined, but even further upstream, efforts at theory development have not even come close to keeping pace with the torrent of need. If the complexity of human diversity is to be described in terms that promote well-being and decrease psychopathology, that work has a place in multicultural psychology.

CONCLUSION

Multicultural psychology has great potential. Metaphorically, multicultural psychology can be compared to a construction project, not a single edifice but a vast complex of buildings. In a word, it is a community, a community in which all are welcomed, none excluded. It has the potential to

EXHIBIT 12.1
Data-Based Implications for Mental Health Practitioners

Therapists benefit from obtaining experience and education on multicultural competence (see Chapter 2, this volume).

Therapists working with clients of color should remain attuned to client perceptions, which predict client experiences in therapy much better than the therapist's self-perceptions of multicultural competence (Chapter 3).

People of color underutilize mental health services, but the racial discrepancies are lower than commonly assumed, except for Asian Americans. Clinicians can take steps to increase the relevance, availability, and appeal of their services for people of color, particularly Asian Americans (Chapter 4).

People of color have a small risk of prematurely terminating mental health services. African Americans are at greatest risk, but even that risk is lower than commonly assumed (Chapter 5). Clients with a therapist of their own race or ethnicity are somewhat less likely to prematurely terminate mental health services, particularly Asian Americans (Chapter 6). Clinicians can address factors that could decrease the risk of premature termination.

The more a treatment aligns with the cultural experiences of a client, the better the clients' outcome (Chapter 7).

Clinicians should attend to the perceptions of and experiences with mental health services for populations with low levels of acculturation (e.g., first generation immigrants; Chapter 8).

Experiences of racism are negatively associated with the well-being of people of color, such that clinicians should empower clients' reporting racist encounters (Chapter 9).

Strength of ethnic identity is positively associated with well-being, such that clinicians should attend to the interactions of that identity with psychological functioning (Chapter 10).

Research results vary widely (all chapters). Averaged data (Figure 12.1) provides general direction, but clinicians should understand the worldviews and experiences of individual clients and not impose their own preconceptions, even when those come from data. In particular, practitioners have to learn directly from clients from groups inadequately represented in the literature: Native American Indians, Alaska Natives, Polynesian Americans, and Arab Americans.

be a force for unity amidst diversity. It has the potential to improve mental health practices (see Exhibit 12.1) and to unite North American practices with those found elsewhere. It is a large community indeed.

The community of mental health professionals relies on evidence-based practices (APA 2005 Presidential Task Force on Evidence-Based Practice, 2006). To what degree is multicultural psychology supported by research (G. C. N. Hall & Yee, 2014)? On the basis of research data, cultural adaptations to mental health services result in greater client improvement than traditional mental health services ("treatment as usual"); in fact, the more aligned with clients' culture, the more effective the treatment. On the basis of research data, psychologists should account for level of acculturation among immigrant populations in mental health services and should address experiences of racism and level of ethnic identity among people of color generally.

On the basis of research data, mental health professionals should understand that Asian Americans do not enter mental health services to the same extent as other groups nor remain in treatment as long as other groups if the therapist is not of their same racial or ethnic background; findings indicate that steps beyond current practices must be taken to meet the mental health needs of Asian Americans (e.g., S. Sue, Cheng, Saad, & Chu, 2012). On the basis of similar research data, mental health professionals should understand that because African American clients discontinue treatment at rates higher than those of other groups, steps beyond current practices must be taken to effectively engage and retain individual clients (e.g., Snowden, 2012). On the basis of research data, therapists benefit when receiving education designed to enhance multicultural competence. And on the basis of research data, mental health professionals should understand that their own perceptions of multicultural competence may not align with the experiences of their clients of color but that clients of color do perceive therapist multicultural competence to be very strongly associated with their own experiences in treatment.

In summary, with thousands of manuscripts now providing both quantitative and qualitative data, the research basis for multicultural psychology appears to be in place. With the foundation cleared and soon to be solidified, construction is underway. Construction workers are needed.

APPENDIX: GENERAL METHODS OF THE META-ANALYSES (CHAPTERS 2–10)

Chapters 2 to 10 in this book report the results of meta-analyses. Those meta-analyses involved similar methods, so a detailed description of the meta-analytic methods in each chapter proved redundant.

This Appendix provides information specified in professional guidelines for publishing meta-analyses (APA Publications and Communications Board Working Group on Journal Article Reporting Standards, 2008; Moher, Liberati, Tetzlaff, Altman, & the PRISMA Group, 2009). Procedures used in the meta-analyses reported in this book were adapted to those professional guidelines; several meta-analyses had already commenced prior to the publication of the professional guidelines. A supplemental file available online (http://pubs.apa.org/books/supp/smith) provides a detailed comparison of the methods used in the meta-analyses reported in this book compared with the Meta-Analysis Reporting Standards (APA Publications and Communications Board Working Group on Journal Article Reporting Standards, 2008) and Preferred Reporting Items for Systematic Reviews and Meta-Analyses (Moher et al., 2009).

GENERAL ELIGIBILITY CRITERIA

We restricted our meta-analytic reviews to data collected in the United States or Canada because cultural values and mental health practices may systematically differ in other nations. When the research question was specific to people of color, data from White/European Americans and Canadians were excluded from the analyses (Chapters 5–8), but biracial and multiracial individuals were included. We analyzed manuscripts written in English because our research team lacked sufficient coders fluent in other languages. All quantitative research designs except case studies and single-N studies were eligible for inclusion.

Given the relative dearth of previous systematic reviews in the field of multicultural psychology, our intention[1] was to review broad constructs, rather than restrict analyses to a particular conceptualization or measurement of a given construct. This approach appeared justified because we found

---

[1]We affirm that our decisions and analyses were not influenced by external parties and that we are solely responsible for the contents of the book. Brigham Young University funded the research assistants.

inconsistent terminology in the literature: Different authors used slightly different terms when intending similar meaning. For instance, authors referred to the degree of client participation in mental health services (Chapter 5) using a variety of terms (e.g., *usage, attendance, completion*), such that had we restricted our review to certain synonyms, we would have inaccurately excluded manuscripts with pertinent data. We preferred to err on the side of conceptual similarity rather than on the side of precision, given that the field has yet to conclude which operationalization of complex constructs would be preferable among the many available.

In our reviews, we defined *mental health services* as any treatment, outpatient or inpatient, explicitly intended to improve emotional or psychological well-being, whether provided by a psychologist, psychiatrist, psychiatric nurse, clinical social worker, or mental health counselor. When a manuscript contained information about mental health treatments provided by both general practitioner physicians and mental health specialists, we extracted only the information pertaining to mental health specialists. We excluded studies that were limited to substance abuse treatments because of the complicating issues of mandated versus voluntary treatment, multiple types of substances with different impacts, dynamics of substance abuse dependence, and relapse rates that differ from treatments for mental health concerns. When a manuscript contained information about both mental health services and substance abuse treatment, we coded only the data pertaining to services provided by mental health professionals. Otherwise, we did not restrict manuscripts on any particular mental health problem or treatment modality. Prevention-oriented interventions with at-risk populations or community members were included but coded separately from treatments with clinical populations.

Our several meta-analyses took substantial time to complete, with staggered cutoff dates for data inclusion, as follows: Chapter 2 (multicultural education for therapists) by October 2008; Chapter 3 (therapist multicultural competence) by June 2012; Chapter 4 (mental health service utilization) by April 2008; Chapter 5 (participation in mental health services) by April 2008; Chapter 6 (ethnic matching) by March 2013; Chapter 7 (culturally adapted treatments) by July 2012; Chapter 8 (acculturation and mental health services) by July, 2008; Chapter 9 (racism and well-being) by June 2010; and Chapter 10 (ethnic identity and well-being) by August 2009. Because findings may have changed over time, we coded and analyzed the year of publication.

INFORMATION SOURCES AND SEARCH STRATEGIES

To locate relevant published and unpublished studies, at least three and up to eight members of the research team conducted extensive searches of the following electronic databases: PsycINFO, PsycArticles, Science Citation

Index, Social Sciences Abstracts, Social Sciences Citation Index, and Digital Dissertations. In these electronic searches, lists of synonymous words and phrases were cross-referenced with one another. For instance, in the meta-analysis of acculturation and mental health services (Chapter 8), the word root *acculturat* was crossed with a list of word roots and phrases relevant to mental health services: *client, counsel, treatment, clinic, therapy, psychotherapy, session, intake, screening,* "mental health treatment," "psychological service," and "mental health service" using the Boolean OR to include all terms. Full search strings for all chapters are available from the first author. After identifying studies that met coding criteria, a team member examined the references cited within those manuscripts to locate additional articles that fit the inclusion criteria but were not initially located in the electronic databases. Attempts were also made to contact authors who had published three or more articles on the topic of the meta-analysis to request information regarding other (unpublished) studies to include in the review. In three instances, solicitations for unpublished manuscripts were posted on professional listservs. Reference lists of all studies included within each chapter are published online (http://pubs.apa.org/books/supp/smith).

DATA COLLECTION PROCESSES

A research team consisting of a university faculty member, at least one graduate student, and at least three undergraduate students coded manuscripts after receiving extensive training on relevant procedures. Team members worked in pairs to enhance the accuracy of coding decisions and data entry. Each article was coded by two separate pairs of coders. In addition to effect size data, coders extracted information about possible moderating variables, including participant characteristics (e.g., age, gender, race) and study characteristics (e.g., study setting, study design, sample size). The interrater agreement of initial coding decisions was evaluated for categorical variables using Cohen's kappa and for continuous variables using intraclass correlation coefficients (ICC) generated in one-way random effects models for single measures. Across all meta-analyses, the average coefficients obtained for coding pairs were acceptably high, as follows: Chapter 2 (multicultural education for therapists) kappa = 0.77, ICC = 0.89; Chapter 3 (therapist multicultural competence) kappa = 0.72, ICC = 0.94; Chapter 4 (mental health service utilization) kappa = 0.74, ICC = 0.95; Chapter 5 (participation in mental health services) kappa = 0.83, ICC = 0.82; Chapter 6 (ethnic matching) kappa = 0.78, ICC = 0.96; Chapter 7 (cultural adaptations to treatment) kappa = 0.75, ICC = 0.97; Chapter 8 (acculturation and mental health services) kappa = 0.86, ICC = 0.98; Chapter 9 (racism and well-being) kappa = 0.83, ICC = .95;

and Chapter 10 (ethnic identity and well-being) kappa = 0.85, ICC = 0.89. Discrepancies between pairs were resolved by a third round of review by at least one member from both original pairs. The first author adjudicated unresolved disagreements.

DATA ANALYSES

We used meta-analytic software to transform statistical estimates derived from a variety of metrics (e.g., t, F, and p values) to one of three types of effect sizes: (a) Cohen's d for meta-analyses involving differences between groups or conditions (Chapters 2, 5–7), (b) Pearson's r for meta-analyses evaluating associations between variables, with the data analyzed after Fisher's z transformation (Chapters 3, 8–10), and (c) odds ratios for the meta-analysis involving a binary comparison of mental health service utilization, with the data analyzed after natural log transformation (Chapter 4).

When a study contained multiple effect sizes, the values were averaged (weighted by the standard error or number of participants included in each analysis) to compute an aggregate effect size for that particular study, such that each study contributed only one data point to the calculation of the omnibus effect size. Because the variables measured in studies (a) had been imprecisely defined across research studies, (b) were influenced by many factors beyond those measured within studies, and thus (c) were expected to yield effect size estimates that differed across individual participants and across individual studies, inverse variance weighted random effects models were used in analyzing the data using the 2006 version of macros for SPSS developed by Lipsey and Wilson (2001). Random effects models allowed for generalization beyond the studies included in the analyses.

For the analyses conducted in several of the chapters, we expected the results to differ by participant race, so in those instances we conducted multivariate meta-analyses (Becker, 2000) using all effect sizes in studies by racial or ethnic group, with those analyses accounting for within-study correlations among effect sizes. The multivariate analyses were specific to data from African Americans, Asian Americans, and Hispanic/Latino(a) Americans, but data specific to Native Americans or Alaska Natives were insufficient across studies so were combined with the data from unspecified and "other" racial categories. Because participant race remained unspecified in manuscripts when authors used the catchall term "ethnic minorities" when describing clients with ancestry primarily outside Europe, the "unspecified/other" racial category analyzed in the multivariate analyses represented a generic contrast of limited interpretability.

REFERENCES

Abreu, J. M., Gim Chung, R. H., & Atkinson, D. R. (2000). Multicultural counseling training: Past, present, and future directions. *The Counseling Psychologist, 28,* 641–656. http://dx.doi.org/10.1177/0011000000285003

Acevedo, M. C., Reyes, C. J., Annett, R. D., & López, E. M. (2003). Assessing language competence: Guidelines for assisting persons with limited English proficiency in research and clinical settings. *Journal of Multicultural Counseling and Development, 31,* 192–204. http://dx.doi.org/10.1002/j.2161-1912.2003.tb00543.x

Adams, G., & Markus, H. R. (2001). Culture as patterns: An alternative approach to the problem of reification. *Culture & Psychology, 7,* 283–296. http://dx.doi.org/10.1177/1354067X0173002

Ægisdóttir, S., & Gerstein, L. H. (2010). International counseling competencies: A new frontier in multicultural training. In J. G. Ponterotto, J. M. Casas, L. A. Suzuki, & C. Alexander (Eds.), *Handbook of multicultural counseling* (3rd ed., pp. 175–188). Thousand Oaks, CA: Sage.

Ajzen, I., & Fishbein, M. (1977). Attitude–behavior relations: A theoretical analysis and review of empirical research. *Psychological Bulletin, 84,* 888–918. http://dx.doi.org/10.1037/0033-2909.84.5.888

Alegría, M., Canino, G., Ríos, R., Vera, M., Calderón, J., Rusch, D., & Ortega, A. N. (2002). Inequalities in use of specialty mental health services among Latinos, African Americans, and non-Latino Whites. *Psychiatric Services, 53,* 1547–1555. http://dx.doi.org/10.1176/appi.ps.53.12.1547

Alegría, M., Chatterji, P., Wells, K., Cao, Z., Chen, C. N., Takeuchi, D., . . . Meng, X. L. (2008). Disparity in depression treatment among racial and ethnic minority populations in the United States. *Psychiatric Services, 59,* 1264–1272. http://dx.doi.org/10.1176/ps.2008.59.11.1264

Alegría, M., Polo, A., Gao, S., Santana, L., Rothstein, D., Jimenez, A., . . . Normand, S. L. (2008). Evaluation of a patient activation and empowerment intervention in mental health care. *Medical Care, 46,* 247–256. http://dx.doi.org/10.1097/MLR.0b013e318158af52

Alladin, W. J. (2002). Ethnic matching in counselling. In S. Palmer (Ed.), *Multicultural counselling: A reader* (pp. 175–180). London, England: Sage.

Allen, J., Lewis, J., & Johnson-Jennings, M. (2015). Well-being and health. In P. Pedersen, J. Draguns, W. Lonner, J. E. Trimble, & M. Sharron-del Rio (Eds.), *Counseling across cultures* (7th ed., pp. 435–455). Thousand Oaks, CA: Sage.

Allen, J., Rivkin, I. D., & López, E. D. S. (2014). Health and well-being. In F. T. L. Leong, L. Comas-Díaz, G. C. Nagayama Hall, V. C. McLoyd, & J. E. Trimble (Eds.), *APA handbook of multicultural psychology: Vol. 1. Theory and research* (pp. 299–311). Washington, DC: American Psychological Association.

Allport, G. W. (1954). *The nature of prejudice*. Oxford, England: Addison-Wesley.

Alvidrez, J. (1999). Ethnic variations in mental health attitudes and service use among low-income African American, Latina, and European American young women. *Community Mental Health Journal, 35*, 515–530. http://dx.doi.org/10.1023/A:1018759201290

Alvidrez, J., Snowden, L. R., & Patel, S. G. (2010). The relationship between stigma and other treatment concerns and subsequent treatment engagement among Black mental health clients. *Issues in Mental Health Nursing, 31*, 257–264. http://dx.doi.org/10.3109/01612840903342266

American Psychological Association. (1986). *Accreditation handbook*. Washington, DC: Author.

American Psychological Association. (1993). Guidelines for providers of psychological services to ethnic, linguistic, and culturally diverse populations. *American Psychologist, 48*, 45–48. http://dx.doi.org/10.1037/0003-066X.48.1.45

American Psychological Association. (1994). *Guidelines and principles for accreditation of programs in professional psychology*. Washington, DC: Author.

American Psychological Association. (2003). Guidelines on multicultural education, training, research, practice, and organizational change for psychologists. *American Psychologist, 58*, 377–402.

American Psychological Association. (2005). *APA presidential task force on enhancing diversity: Final report*. Washington, DC: Author.

American Psychological Association. (2009). *Report of the APA task force on the implementation of the multicultural guidelines*. Washington, DC: Author.

American Psychological Association. (2014). *Proposed standards of accreditation in health service psychology*. Retrieved from http://www.apa.org/ed/accreditation/

Amiot, C. E., de la Sablonnière, R., Terry, D. J., & Smith, J. R. (2007). Integration of social identities in the self: Toward a cognitive–developmental model. *Personality and Social Psychology Review, 11*, 364–388. http://dx.doi.org/10.1177/1088868307304091

Ancis, J. R. (2003). Teaching multicultural competencies using the Internet and other technologies. In D. B. Pope-Davis, H. L. K. Coleman, & R. L. Toporek (Eds.), *Handbook of multicultural competencies in counseling & psychology* (pp. 575–588). Thousand Oaks, CA: Sage. http://dx.doi.org/10.4135/9781452231693.n36

Ancis, J. R., & Ali, S. R. (2005). Multicultural counseling training approaches: Implications for pedagogy. In C. Z. Enns & A. L. Sinacore (Eds.), *Teaching and social justice: Integrating multicultural and feminist theories in the classroom* (pp. 85–97). Washington, DC: American Psychological Association. http://dx.doi.org/10.1037/10929-005

Andersen, R., & Newman, J. F. (1973). Societal and individual determinants of medical care utilization in the United States. *The Milbank Memorial Fund Quarterly. Health and Society, 51*, 95–124. http://dx.doi.org/10.2307/3349613

Angold, A., Erkanli, A., Farmer, E. M. Z., Fairbank, J. A., Burns, B. J., Keeler, G., & Costello, E. J. (2002). Psychiatric disorder, impairment, and service use in rural African American and White youth. *Archives of General Psychiatry, 59*, 893–901. http://dx.doi.org/10.1001/archpsyc.59.10.893

Ano, G. G., & Vasconcelles, E. B. (2005). Religious coping and psychological adjustment to stress: A meta-analysis. *Journal of Clinical Psychology, 61*, 461–480. http://dx.doi.org/10.1002/jclp.20049

APA 2005 Presidential Task Force on Evidence-Based Practice. (2006). Evidence-based practice in psychology. *American Psychologist, 61*, 271–285. http://dx.doi. org/10.1037/0003-066X.61.4.271

APA Publications and Communications Board Working Group on Journal Article Reporting Standards. (2008). Reporting standards for research in psychology: Why do we need them? What might they be? *American Psychologist, 63*, 839–851. http://dx.doi.org/10.1037/0003-066X.63.9.839

Arnett, J. J. (2002). The psychology of globalization. *American Psychologist, 57*, 774–783. http://dx.doi.org/10.1037//0003-066X.57.10.774

Arredondo, P., & Perez, P. (2003). Expanding multicultural competence through social justice leadership. *The Counseling Psychologist, 31*, 282–289. http://dx.doi.org/ 10.1177/0011000003031003003

Arredondo, P., Rosen, D. C., Rice, T., Perez, P., & Tovar-Gamero, Z. G. (2005). Multicultural counseling: A 10-year content analysis of the *Journal of Counseling & Development. Journal of Counseling & Development, 83*, 155–161. http://dx.doi. org/10.1002/j.1556-6678.2005.tb00592.x

Arredondo, P., & Toporek, R. (2004). Multicultural counseling competencies = ethical practice. *Journal of Mental Health Counseling, 26*, 44.

Arredondo, P., Toporek, R., Brown, S. P., Jones, J., Locke, D. C., Sanchez, J., & Stadler, H. (1996). Operationalization of the multicultural counseling competencies. *Journal of Multicultural Counseling and Development, 24*, 42–78. http:// dx.doi.org/10.1002/j.2161-1912.1996.tb00288.x

Arredondo, P., & Tovar-Blank, Z. G. (2014). Multicultural competencies: A dynamic paradigm for the 21st century. In F. T. L. Leong, L. Comas-Díaz, G. C. Nagayama Hall, V. C. McLoyd, & J. E. Trimble (Eds.), *APA handbook of multicultural psychology: Vol. 2. Applications and training* (pp. 19–34). Washington, DC: American Psychological Association.

Asnaani, A., & Hofmann, S. G. (2012). Collaboration in multicultural therapy: Establishing a strong therapeutic alliance across cultural lines. *Journal of Clinical Psychology, 68*, 187–197. http://dx.doi.org/10.1002/jclp.21829

Atkinson, D. R., & Wampold, B. E. (1982). A comparison of the Counselor Rating Form and the Counselor Effectiveness Rating Scale. *Counselor Education and Supervision, 22*, 25–36. http://dx.doi.org/10.1002/j.1556-6978.1982.tb00927.x

Awad, G. H., & Cokley, K. O. (2010). Designing and interpreting quantitative research in multicultural counseling. In J. G. Ponterotto, J. M. Casas, L. Suzuki, & C. Alexander (Eds.), *Handbook of multicultural counseling* (pp. 385–396). Thousand Oaks, CA: Sage.

Baca, L., Ridley, C. R., Kelly, S. M., Sue, S., Takooshian, H., Grimes, T. R., & Taylor, L. (2007). Future directions for practitioners, trainers, and researchers: Interdisciplinary perspectives. In G. B. Esquivel, E. C. López, & S. G. Nahari (Eds.), *Handbook of multicultural school psychology: An interdisciplinary perspective* (pp. 659–694). Mahwah, NJ: Erlbaum.

Bakhtin, M. M. (1981). *Dialogic imagination: Four essays.* Austin: University of Texas Press.

Baluch, S. P., Pieterse, A. L., & Bolden, M. A. (2004). Counseling psychology and social justice: Houston . . . we have a problem. *The Counseling Psychologist, 32,* 89–98. http://dx.doi.org/10.1177/0011000003260065

Bandura, A. (1977). *Social learning theory.* Oxford, England: Prentice-Hall.

Barrera, M., Jr., & Castro, F. G. (2006). A heuristic framework for the cultural adaptation of interventions. *Clinical Psychology: Science and Practice, 13,* 311–316. http://dx.doi.org/10.1111/j.1468-2850.2006.00043.x

Barrera, M., Jr., Castro, F. G., Strycker, L. A., & Toobert, D. J. (2013). Cultural adaptations of behavioral health interventions: A progress report. *Journal of Consulting and Clinical Psychology, 81,* 196–205. http://dx.doi.org/10.1037/a0027085

Barrett, M. S., Chua, W.-J., Crits-Christoph, P., Gibbons, M. B., & Thompson, D. (2008). Early withdrawal from mental health treatment: Implications for psychotherapy practice. *Psychotherapy: Theory, Research, Practice, Training, 45,* 247–267. http://dx.doi.org/10.1037/0033-3204.45.2.247

Barth, F. (Ed.). (1969). *Ethnic groups and boundaries.* Boston, MA: Little, Brown.

Becker, B. J. (2000). Multivariate meta-analysis. In H. E. A. Tinsley & S. D. Brown (Eds.), *Handbook of applied multivariate statistics and mathematical modeling* (pp. 499–525). San Diego, CA: Academic Press. http://dx.doi.org/10.1016/B978-012691360-6/50018-5

Benish, S. G., Quintana, S., & Wampold, B. E. (2011). Culturally adapted psychotherapy and the legitimacy of myth: A direct-comparison meta-analysis. *Journal of Counseling Psychology, 58,* 279–289. http://dx.doi.org/10.1037/a0023626

Berkman, L. F., Glass, T., Brissette, I., & Seeman, T. E. (2000). From social integration to health: Durkheim in the new millennium. *Social Science & Medicine, 51,* 843–857. http://dx.doi.org/10.1016/S0277-9536(00)00065-4

Bernal, G., Bonilla, J., & Bellido, C. (1995). Ecological validity and cultural sensitivity for outcome research: Issues for the cultural adaptation and development of psychosocial treatments with Hispanics. *Journal of Abnormal Child Psychology, 23,* 67–82. http://dx.doi.org/10.1007/BF01447045

Bernal, G., & Domenech Rodríguez, M. M. (2012). *Cultural adaptations: Tools for evidence-based practice with diverse populations.* Washington, DC: American Psychological Association. http://dx.doi.org/10.1037/13752-000

Bernal, G., & Flores-Ortiz, Y. (1982). Latino families in therapy: Engagement and evaluation. *Journal of Marital and Family Therapy, 8,* 357–365. http://dx.doi.org/10.1111/j.1752-0606.1982.tb01458.x

Bernal, G., Jiménez-Chafey, M. I., & Domenech Rodríguez, M. M. (2009). Cultural adaptation of treatments: A resource for considering culture in evidence-based practice. *Professional Psychology: Research and Practice, 40,* 361–368. http://dx.doi.org/10.1037/a0016401

Bernal, M. E., & Castro, F. G. (1994). Are clinical psychologists prepared for service and research with ethnic minorities? Report of a decade of progress. *American Psychologist, 49,* 797–805. http://dx.doi.org/10.1037/0003-066X.49.9.797

Bernal, M. E., & Knight, G. P. (Eds.). (1993). *Ethnic identity: Formation and transmission among Hispanics and other minorities.* Albany: State University of New York Press.

Bernal, M. E., Saenz, D. S., & Knight, G. P. (1991). Ethnic identity and adaptation of Mexican American youths in school settings. *Hispanic Journal of Behavioral Sciences, 13,* 135–154. http://dx.doi.org/10.1177/07399863910132002

Berry, J. W. (1980). Social and cultural change. In H. C. Triandis & R. Brislin (Eds.), *Handbook of cross-cultural psychology: Vol. 5. Social* (pp. 211–279). Boston, MA: Allyn & Bacon.

Berry, J. W. (1991). Understanding and managing multiculturalism: Some possible implications of research in Canada. *Psychology and Developing Societies, 3,* 17–49. http://dx.doi.org/10.1177/097133369100300103

Berry, J. W. (1994). Acculturation and psychological adaptation: An overview. In A. Bouvy, F. J. R. Van de Vijver, P. Boski, & P. Schmitz (Eds.), *Journeys into cross-cultural psychology* (pp. 129–141). Berwyn, PA: Swets & Zeitlinger.

Berry, J. W. (1995). Psychology of acculturation. In N. R. Goldberger & J. B. Veroff (Eds.), *The culture and psychology reader* (pp. 457–488). New York: New York University Press.

Berry, J. W. (1997). Immigration, acculturation, and adaptation. *Applied Psychology, 46,* 5–34.

Berry, J. W. (2003). Conceptual approaches to acculturation. In K. M. Chun, P. Balls Organista, & G. Marín (Eds.), *Acculturation: Advances in theory, measurement, and applied research* (pp. 17–37). Washington, DC: American Psychological Association.

Berry, J. W., & Kim, U. (1986). Acculturation and mental health. In P. Dasen, J. W. Berry, & N. Sartorius (Eds.), *Applications of cross-cultural psychology to healthy human development* (pp. 207–236). Beverly Hills, CA: Sage.

Berry, J. W., Poortinga, Y. H., Segall, M. H., & Dasen, P. R. (1992). *Cross-cultural psychology: Research and applications.* New York, NY: Cambridge University Press.

Berry, J. W., & Sam, D. L. (1996). Acculturation and adaptation. In J. W. Berry, M. H. Segall, & C. Kagitcibasi (Eds.), *Handbook of cross-cultural psychology: Vol. 3. Social behavior and applications* (pp. 291–326). Boston, MA: Allyn & Bacon.

Berry, J. W., Trimble, J. E., & Olmedo, E. (1986). Assessment of acculturation. In W. J. Lonner & J. W. Berry (Eds.), *Field methods in cross-cultural research* (pp. 291–324). Newbury Park, CA: Sage.

Binning, K. R., Unzueta, M. M., Huo, Y. J., & Molina, L. E. (2009). The interpretation of multiracial status and its relation to social engagement and psychological well-being. *Journal of Social Issues, 65*, 35–49. http://dx.doi.org/10.1111/j.1540-4560.2008.01586.x

Birman, D. (2011). Migration and well-being: Beyond the macrosystem. *Psychosocial Intervention, 20*, 339–341. http://dx.doi.org/10.5093/in2011v20n3a11

Birman, D., & Simon, C. D. (2014). Acculturation research: Challenges, complexities, and possibilities. In F. T. L. Leong, L. Comas-Díaz, G. C. Nagayama Hall, V. C. McLoyd, & J. E. Trimble (Eds.), *APA handbook of multicultural psychology: Vol. 1. Theory and research* (pp. 207–230). Washington, DC: American Psychological Association.

Bojuwoye, O., & Sodi, T. (2010). Challenges and opportunities to integrating traditional healing into counselling and psychotherapy. *Counselling Psychology Quarterly, 23*, 283–296. http://dx.doi.org/10.1080/09515070.2010.505750

Bond, M. H. (2013). The pan-culturality of well-being: But does culture fit into the equation? *Asian Journal of Social Psychology, 16*, 158–162. http://dx.doi.org/10.1111/ajsp.12024

Bonham, V. L., Warshauer-Baker, E., & Collins, F. S. (2005). Race and ethnicity in the genome era: The complexity of the constructs. *American Psychologist, 60*, 9–15. http://dx.doi.org/10.1037/0003-066X.60.1.9

Borgatti, S. P., Mehra, A., Brass, D., & Labianca, G. (2009). Network analysis in the social sciences. *Science, 323*, 892–895. http://dx.doi.org/10.1126/science.1165821

Bosworth, H. B., Parsey, K. S., Butterfield, M. I., McIntyre, L. M., Oddone, E. Z., Stechuchak, K. M., & Bastian, L. A. (2000). Racial variation in wanting and obtaining mental health services among women veterans in a primary care clinic. *Journal of the National Medical Association, 92*, 231–236.

Broman, C. L. (1987). Race differences in professional help seeking. *American Journal of Community Psychology, 15*, 473–489.

Brown, T. N. (2003). Critical race theory speaks to the sociology of mental health: Mental health problems produced by racial stratification. *Journal of Health and Social Behavior, 44*, 292–301. http://dx.doi.org/10.2307/1519780

Bynum, W. F., & Porter, R. (Eds.). (2013). *Companion encyclopedia of the history of medicine*. New York, NY: Routledge.

Byrne, B. M., Oakland, T., Leong, F. T., van de Vijver, F. J., Hambleton, R. K., Cheung, F. M., & Bartram, D. (2009). A critical analysis of cross-cultural research and testing practices: Implications for improved education and training in psychology. *Training and Education in Professional Psychology, 3*, 94–105. http://dx.doi.org/10.1037/a0014516

Byrne, D. E. (1971). *The attraction paradigm*. New York, NY: Academic Press.

Cabassa, L. J. (2003). Measuring acculturation: Where we are and where we need to go. *Hispanic Journal of Behavioral Sciences, 25*, 127–146. http://dx.doi.org/10.1177/0739986303025002001

Cabral, R. R., & Smith, T. B. (2011). Racial/ethnic matching of clients and therapists in mental health services: A meta-analytic review of preferences, perceptions, and outcomes. *Journal of Counseling Psychology, 58*, 537–554. http://dx.doi.org/10.1037/a0025266

Cachelin, F. M., & Striegel-Moore, R. H. (2006). Help seeking and barriers to treatment in a community sample of Mexican American and European American women with eating disorders. *International Journal of Eating Disorders, 39*, 154–161.

Cachelin, F. M., Veisel, C., Barzegarnazari, E., & Striegel-Moore, R. H. (2000). Disordered eating, acculturation, and treatment-seeking in a community sample of Hispanic, Asian, Black, and White women. *Psychology of Women Quarterly, 24*, 244–253. http://dx.doi.org/10.1111/j.1471-6402.2000.tb00206.x

Calabrese, J. D. (2008). Clinical paradigm clashes: Ethnocentric and political barriers to Native American efforts at self-healing. *Ethos, 36*, 334–353. http://dx.doi.org/10.1111/j.1548-1352.2008.00018.x

Campbell, L. F., Norcross, J. C., Vasquez, M. J., & Kaslow, N. J. (2013). Recognition of psychotherapy effectiveness: The APA resolution. *Psychotherapy, 50*, 98–101. http://dx.doi.org/10.1037/a0031817

Cardemil, E. V. (2010a). The complexity of culture: Do we embrace the challenge or avoid it? *The Scientific Review of Mental Health Practice, 7*(2), 41–47.

Cardemil, E. V. (2010b). Cultural adaptations to empirically supported treatments: A research agenda. *The Scientific Review of Mental Health Practice, 7*(2), 8–21.

Carter, R. T. (1996). Exploring the complexity of racial identity attitude measures. In G. R. Sodowsky & J. C. Impara (Eds.), *Multicultural assessment in counseling and clinical psychology* (pp. 193–223). Lincoln, NE: Buros Institute of Mental Measurements.

Carter, R. T. (2003). Becoming racially and culturally competent: The racial–cultural counseling laboratory. *Journal of Multicultural Counseling and Development, 31*, 20–30. http://dx.doi.org/10.1002/j.2161-1912.2003.tb00527.x

Carter, R. T. (2007). Racism and psychological and emotional injury recognizing and assessing race-based traumatic stress. *The Counseling Psychologist, 35*, 13–105. http://dx.doi.org/10.1177/0011000006292033

Carter, R. T., & Pieterse, A. (2013, October). *A review and critique of the current status of race-related scholarship in counseling psychology.* Paper presented at the Diversity Challenge Conference, Chestnut Hill, MA.

Carter, R. T., & Qureshi, A. (1995). A typology of philosophical assumptions in multicultural counseling and training. In J. G. Ponterotto, J. M. Casas, & C. M. Alexander (Eds.), *Handbook of multicultural counseling* (pp. 239–262). Thousand Oaks, CA: Sage.

Cartwright, B. Y., Daniels, J., & Zhang, S. (2008). Assessing multicultural competence: Perceived versus demonstrated performance. *Journal of Counseling & Development, 86*, 318–322. http://dx.doi.org/10.1002/j.1556-6678.2008.tb00515.x

Casas, J. M., Park, Y. S., & Cho, B. (2010). The multicultural and international-ization counseling psychology movements: When all is said and done, it's all multicultural, isn't it? In J. G. Ponterotto, J. M. Casas, L. A. Suzuki, & C. M. Alexander (Eds.), *Handbook of multicultural counseling* (3rd ed., pp. 189–200). Thousand Oaks, CA: Sage.

Case, L., & Smith, T. B. (2000). Ethnic representation in a sample of the literature of applied psychology. *Journal of Consulting and Clinical Psychology, 68,* 1107–1110. http://dx.doi.org/10.1037/0022-006X.68.6.1107

Cassidy, J., & Shaver, P. R. (Eds.). (2008). *Handbook of attachment: Theory, research, and clinical applications* (2nd ed.). New York, NY: Guilford Press.

Castillo, L. G., Brossart, D. F., Reyes, C. J., Conoley, C. W., & Phoummarath, M. J. (2007). The influence of multicultural training on perceived multicultural coun-seling competencies and implicit racial prejudice. *Journal of Multicultural Counsel-ing and Development, 35,* 243–255. http://dx.doi.org/10.1002/j.2161-1912.2007.tb00064.x

Castro, F. G., Barrera, M., Jr., & Holleran Steiker, L. K. (2010). Issues and chal-lenges in the design of culturally adapted evidence-based interventions. *Annual Review of Clinical Psychology, 6,* 213–239. http://dx.doi.org/10.1146/annurev-clinpsy-033109-132032

Cates, J. T., Schaefle, S. E., Smaby, M. H., Maddux, C. D., & Le Beauf, I. (2007). Com-paring multicultural with general counseling knowledge and skill competency for students who completed counselor training. *Journal of Multicultural Coun-seling and Development, 35,* 26–39. http://dx.doi.org/10.1002/j.2161-1912.2007.tb00047.x

Cauce, A. M. (2011). Is multicultural psychology a-scientific? Diverse methods for diversity research. *Cultural Diversity and Ethnic Minority Psychology, 17,* 228–233. http://dx.doi.org/10.1037/a0023880

Chao, R. C., & Nath, S. R. (2011). The role of ethnic identity, gender roles, and multicultural training in college counselors' multicultural counseling compe-tence: A mediation model. *Journal of College Counseling, 14,* 50–64. http://dx.doi.org/10.1002/j.2161-1882.2011.tb00063.x

Chao, R. C., Wei, M., Good, G. E., & Flores, L. Y. (2011). Race/ethnicity, color-blind racial attitudes, and multicultural counseling competence: The moderating effects of multicultural counseling training. *Journal of Counseling Psychology, 58,* 72–82. http://dx.doi.org/10.1037/a0022091

Charon, J. M. (2001). *Symbolic interactionism: An introduction, an interpretation, an integration.* Upper Saddle River, NJ: Prentice Hall.

Chen, S., Sullivan, N. Y., Lu, Y. E., & Shibusawa, T. (2003). Asian Americans and mental health services: A study of utilization patterns in the 1990s. *Journal of Ethnic & Cultural Diversity in Social Work, 12,* 19–42. http://dx.doi.org/10.1300/J051v12n02_02

Chen, S. W., & Davenport, D. S. (2005). Cognitive–behavioral therapy with Chinese American clients: Cautions and modifications. *Psychotherapy: Theory, Research, Practice, Training, 42,* 101–110. http://dx.doi.org/10.1037/0033-3204.42.1.101

Cheung, Y. W. (1989). Making sense of ethnicity and drug use: A review and suggestions for future research. *Social Pharmacology, 3,* 55–82.

Cheung, Y. W. (1993). Approaches to ethnicity: Clearing roadblocks in the study of ethnicity and substance use. *International Journal of the Addictions, 28,* 1209–1226.

Chow, J. C., Jaffee, K., & Snowden, L. (2003). Racial/ethnic disparities in the use of mental health services in poverty areas. *American Journal of Public Health, 93,* 792–797. http://dx.doi.org/10.2105/AJPH.93.5.792

Chowdhary, N., Jotheeswaran, A. T., Nadkarni, A., Hollon, S. D., King, M., Jordans, M. J., . . . Patel, V. (2014). The methods and outcomes of cultural adaptations of psychological treatments for depressive disorders: A systematic review. *Psychological Medicine, 44,* 1131–1146. http://dx.doi.org/10.1017/S0033291713001785

Cirese, S. (1985). *Quest: A search for self.* New York, NY: HOH, Rurehard, & Winston.

Clark, K. B., & Clark, M. K. (1939). Segregation as a factor in the racial identification of Negro pre-school children. *Journal of Experimental Education, 8,* 161–163. http://dx.doi.org/10.1080/00220973.1939.11010160

Clark, R., Anderson, N. B., Clark, V. R., & Williams, D. R. (1999). Racism as a stressor for African Americans. A biopsychosocial model. *American Psychologist, 54,* 805–816. http://dx.doi.org/10.1037/0003-066X.54.10.805

Clarke, S., Hahn, H., & Hoggett, P. (Eds.). (2008). *Object relations and social relations: The implications of the relational turn in psychoanalysis.* London, England: Karnac Books.

Clarkson, P. (2003). *The therapeutic relationship.* London, England: Whurr.

Cohen, D. (2001). Cultural variation: Considerations and implications. *Psychological Bulletin, 127,* 451–471. http://dx.doi.org/10.1037/0033-2909.127.4.451

Cohen, J. (1988). *Statistical power analysis for the behavioral sciences.* New York, NY: Routledge.

Cohen, S. (2004). Social relationships and health. *American Psychologist, 59,* 676–684. http://dx.doi.org/10.1037/0003-066X.59.8.676

Coleman, H. L. K. (2004). Multicultural counseling competencies in a pluralistic society. *Journal of Mental Health Counseling, 26,* 56–66.

Coleman, H. L. K., Wampold, B. E., & Casali, S. L. (1995). Ethnic minorities' ratings of ethnically similar and European American counselors: A meta-analysis. *Journal of Counseling Psychology, 42,* 55–64. http://dx.doi.org/10.1037/0022-0167.42.1.55

Coleman, M. N. (2006). Critical incidents in multicultural training: An examination of student experiences. *Journal of Multicultural Counseling and Development, 34,* 168–182. http://dx.doi.org/10.1002/j.2161-1912.2006.tb00036.x

Comas-Díaz, L. (2006). Cultural variation in the therapeutic relationship. In C. Goodheart, A. Kazdin, & R. Sternberg (Eds.), *Evidence-based psychotherapy: Where practice and research meet* (pp. 81–105). Washington, DC: American Psychological Association. http://dx.doi.org/10.1037/11423-004

Comas-Díaz, L., & Jacobsen, F. M. (2001). Ethnocultural allodynia. *The Journal of Psychotherapy Practice and Research, 10,* 246–252.

Comstock, D. L., Hammer, T. R., Strentzsch, J., Cannon, K., Parsons, J., & Salazar, G., II. (2008). Relational-cultural theory: A framework for bridging relational, multicultural, and social justice competencies. *Journal of Counseling & Development, 86,* 279–287. http://dx.doi.org/10.1002/j.1556-6678.2008.tb00510.x

Conner, K. O., Koeske, G., & Brown, C. (2009). Racial differences in attitudes toward professional mental health treatment: The mediating effect of stigma. *Journal of Gerontological Social Work, 52,* 695–712. http://dx.doi.org/10.1080/01634370902914372

Connolly Gibbons, M. B., Rothbard, A., Farris, K. D., Wiltsey Stirman, S., Thompson, S. M., Scott, K., . . . Crits-Christoph, P. (2011). Changes in psychotherapy utilization among consumers of services for major depressive disorder in the community mental health system. *Administration and Policy in Mental Health and Mental Health Services Research, 38,* 495–503. http://dx.doi.org/10.1007/s10488-011-0336-1

Constantine, M. G. (2001). Multiculturally-focused counseling supervision: Its relationship to trainees' multicultural counseling self-efficacy. *The Clinical Supervisor, 20,* 87–98. http://dx.doi.org/10.1300/J001v20n01_07

Constantine, M. G. (2002). Predictors of satisfaction with counseling: Racial and ethnic minority clients' attitudes toward counseling and ratings of their counselors' general and multicultural counseling competence. *Journal of Counseling Psychology, 49,* 255–263. http://dx.doi.org/10.1037/0022-0167.49.2.255

Constantine, M. G. (2007). Racial microaggressions against African American clients in cross-racial counseling relationships. *Journal of Counseling Psychology, 54,* 1–16. http://dx.doi.org/10.1037/0022-0167.54.1.1

Constantine, M. G., & Ladany, N. (2000). Self-report multicultural counseling competence scales: Their relation to social desirability attitudes and multicultural case conceptualization ability. *Journal of Counseling Psychology, 47,* 155–164. http://dx.doi.org/10.1037/0022-0167.47.2.155

Constantine, M. G., & Ladany, N. (2001). New visions for defining and assessing multicultural counseling competence. In J. G. Ponterotto, J. M. Casas, L. A. Suzuki, & C. Alexander (Eds.), *Handbook of multicultural counseling* (2nd ed., pp. 482–498). Thousand Oaks, CA: Sage.

Constantine, M. G., & Sue, D. W. (2006). *Addressing racism: Facilitating cultural competence in mental health and educational settings.* Hoboken, NJ: Wiley.

Cook, B. L., Doksum, T., Chen, C. N., Carle, A., & Alegría, M. (2013). The role of provider supply and organization in reducing racial/ethnic disparities in mental health care in the U.S. *Social Science & Medicine, 84,* 102–109. http://dx.doi.org/10.1016/j.socscimed.2013.02.006

Cookson, J. (2012, June 7). How much do you know about U.S. immigrants? *CNN World*. Retrieved from http://globalpublicsquare.blogs.cnn.com/2012/06/07/immigration-nation-what-you-need-to-know/

Cooper, H., Hedges, L. V., & Valentine, J. C. (2009). *The handbook of research synthesis and meta-analysis*. New York, NY: Russell Sage Foundation.

Cooper, H., & Koenka, A. C. (2012). The overview of reviews: Unique challenges and opportunities when research syntheses are the principal elements of new integrative scholarship. *American Psychologist, 67,* 446–462. http://dx.doi.org/10.1037/a0027119

Cooren, F. (2006). The organizational world as a plenum of agencies. In E. J. Van Every (Ed.), *Communication as organizing: Empirical and theoretical explorations in the dynamic of text and conversation* (pp. 81–100). Mahwah, NJ: Erlbaum.

Corning, A. F., & Malofeeva, E. V. (2004). The application of survival analysis to the study of psychotherapy termination. *Journal of Counseling Psychology, 51,* 354–367. http://dx.doi.org/10.1037/0022-0167.51.3.354

Corrigan, P. (2004). How stigma interferes with mental health care. *American Psychologist, 59,* 614–625. http://dx.doi.org/10.1037/0003-066X.59.7.614

Crook-Lyon, R., O'Grady, K. A., Smith, T. B., Jensen, D. R., Golightly, T., & Potkar, K. A. (2012). Addressing religious and spiritual diversity in graduate training and multicultural education for professional psychologists. *Psychology of Religion and Spirituality, 4,* 169–181. http://dx.doi.org/10.1037/a0026403

Cross, W. (1991). *Shades of black: Diversity in African American identity*. Philadelphia, PA: Temple University Press.

Cuéllar, I., Arnold, B., & Maldonado, R. (1995). Acculturation Rating Scale for Mexican Americans–II: A revision of the original ARSMA scale. *Hispanic Journal of Behavioral Sciences, 17,* 275–304.

Czopp, A. M., Mark, A. Y., & Walzer, A. S. (2014). Prejudice and racism. In F. T. L. Leong, L. Comas-Díaz, G. C. Nagayama Hall, V. C. McLoyd, & J. E. Trimble (Eds.), *APA handbook of multicultural psychology: Vol. 1. Theory and research* (pp. 361–377). Washington, DC: American Psychological Association.

D'Andrea, M., & Daniels, J. (2010). Promoting multiculturalism, democracy, and social justice in organizational settings: A case study. In J. G. Ponterotto, J. M. Casas, L. A. Suzuki, & C. M. Alexander (Eds.), *Handbook of multicultural counseling* (3rd ed., pp. 591–602). Thousand Oaks, CA: Sage.

D'Andrea, M., Daniels, J., & Heck, R. (1991). Evaluating the impact of multicultural counseling training. *Journal of Counseling & Development, 70,* 143–150. http://dx.doi.org/10.1002/j.1556-6676.1991.tb01576.x

D'Andrea, M., & Heckman, E. (2008). A 40-year review of multicultural counseling outcome research: Outlining a future research agenda for the multicultural counseling movement. *Journal of Counseling & Development, 86,* 356–363. http://dx.doi.org/10.1002/j.1556-6678.2008.tb00520.x

David, E. J. R., Okazaki, S., & Giroux, D. (2014). A set of guiding principles to advance multicultural psychology and its major concepts. In F. T. L. Leong, L. Comas-Díaz, G. C. Nagayama Hall, V. C. McLoyd, & J. E. Trimble (Eds.), *APA handbook of multicultural psychology: Vol. 1. Theory and research* (pp. 85–104). Washington, DC: American Psychological Association.

Dawson, J. L. M. (1971). Theory and research in cross-cultural psychology. *Bulletin of the British Psychological Society, 24,* 291–306.

Delgado, R., & Stefancic, J. (2012). *Critical race theory.* New York: New York University Press.

DeNeve, K. M., & Cooper, H. (1998). The happy personality: A meta-analysis of 137 personality traits and subjective well-being. *Psychological Bulletin, 124,* 197–229. http://dx.doi.org/10.1037/0033-2909.124.2.197

de Smith, M. J., Goodchild, M. F., & Longley, P. A. (2007). *Geospatial analysis: A comprehensive guide to principles, techniques and software tools* (2nd ed.). Leicester, England: Troubador.

Diala, C., Muntaner, C., Walrath, C., Nickerson, K. J., LaVeist, T. A., & Leaf, P. J. (2000). Racial differences in attitudes toward professional mental health care and in the use of services. *American Journal of Orthopsychiatry, 70,* 455–464. http://dx.doi.org/10.1037/h0087736

Diaz-Martinez, A., Interian, A., & Waters, D. (2010). The integration of CBT, multicultural and feminist psychotherapies with Latinas. *Journal of Psychotherapy Integration, 20,* 312–326. http://dx.doi.org/10.1037/a0020819

Dickson, G. L., Argus-Calvo, B., & Tafoya, N. G. (2010). Multicultural counselor training experiences: Training effects and perceptions of training among a sample of predominately Hispanic students. *Counselor Education and Supervision, 49,* 247–265. http://dx.doi.org/10.1002/j.1556-6978.2010.tb00101.x

Dickson, G. L., & Jepsen, D. A. (2007). Multicultural training experiences as predictors of multicultural competencies: Students' perspectives. *Counselor Education and Supervision, 47,* 76–95. http://dx.doi.org/10.1002/j.1556-6978.2007.tb00040.x

Diener, E., & Diener, M. (1995). Cross-cultural correlates of life satisfaction and self-esteem. *Journal of Personality and Social Psychology, 68,* 653–663. http://dx.doi.org/10.1037/0022-3514.68.4.653

Diener, E., & Oishi, S. (2000). Money and happiness: Income and subjective well-being across nations. In E. M. Suh (Ed.), *Culture and subjective well-being* (pp. 185–218). Cambridge, MA: The MIT Press.

Diener, E., & Tov, W. (2009). Well-being on planet Earth. *Psychological Topics, 18,* 213–219.

Domenech Rodríguez, M. M., & Bernal, G. (2012). Frameworks, models, and guidelines for cultural adaptation. In G. Bernal & M. M. Domenech Rodríguez (Eds.), *Cultural adaptations: Tools for evidence-based practice with diverse populations* (pp. 23–44). Washington, DC: American Psychological Association. http://dx.doi.org/10.1037/13752-002

Dressler, W. W., Oths, K. S., & Gravlee, C. C. (2005). Race and ethnicity in public health research: Models to explain health disparities. *Annual Review of Anthropology, 34*, 231–252. http://dx.doi.org/10.1146/annurev.anthro.34.081804.120505

Drinane, J. M., Owen, J., Adelson, J. L., & Rodolfa, E. (2014). Multicultural competencies: What are we measuring? *Psychotherapy Research*, 1–10. http://dx.doi.org/10.1080/10503307.2014.983581

Dumas, J. E., Moreland, A. D., Gitter, A. H., Pearl, A. M., & Nordstrom, A. H. (2008). Engaging parents in preventive parenting groups: Do ethnic, socioeconomic, and belief match between parents and group leaders matter? *Health Education & Behavior, 35*, 619–633. http://dx.doi.org/10.1177/1090198106291374

Dunn, T. W., Smith, T. B., & Montoya, J. A. (2006). Multicultural competency instrumentation: A review and analysis of reliability generalization. *Journal of Counseling & Development, 84*, 471–482. http://dx.doi.org/10.1002/j.1556-6678.2006.tb00431.x

Duval, S., & Tweedie, R. (2000). Trim and fill: A simple funnel-plot-based method of testing and adjusting for publication bias in meta-analysis. *Biometrics, 56*, 455–463. http://dx.doi.org/10.1111/j.0006-341X.2000.00455.x

Dwyer, D. (2000). *Interpersonal relationships*. Florence, KY: Taylor & Frances/Routledge.

Escobar, J., & Vega, W. (2000). Mental health and immigration's AAAs: Where are we and where do we go from here? *Journal of Nervous and Mental Disorders, 188*, 736–740.

Evans, B., & Whitfield, J. (Eds.). (1988). *Black males in the United States: An annotated bibliography from 1967–1987*. Washington, DC: American Psychological Association.

Falicov, C. J. (2009). Commentary: On the wisdom and challenges of culturally attuned treatments for Latinos. *Family Process, 48*, 292–309. http://dx.doi.org/10.1111/j.1545-5300.2009.01282.x

Fay, B. (1996). *Contemporary philosophy of social science: A multicultural approach*. Malden, MA: Blackwell.

Festinger, L. (1954). A theory of social comparison processes. *Human Relations, 7*, 117–140. http://dx.doi.org/10.1177/001872675400700202

Fischer, A. R., & Shaw, C. M. (1999). African Americans' mental health and perceptions of racist discrimination: The moderating effects of racial socialization experiences and self-esteem. *Journal of Counseling Psychology, 46*, 395–407. http://dx.doi.org/10.1037/0022-0167.46.3.395

Fischer, E. H., & Farina, A. (1995). Attitudes toward seeking professional psychological help: A shortened form and considerations for research. *Journal of College Student Development, 36*, 368–373.

Fisher, C. B., Hoagwood, K., Boyce, C., Duster, T., Frank, D. A., Grisso, T., . . . Zayas, L. H. (2002). Research ethics for mental health science involving ethnic minority children and youths. *American Psychologist, 57*, 1024–1040. http://dx.doi.org/10.1037/0003-066X.57.12.1024

Flaskerud, J. H. (1986). The effects of culture-compatible intervention on the utilization of mental health services by minority clients. *Community Mental Health Journal, 22,* 127–141. http://dx.doi.org/10.1007/BF00754551

Flaskerud, J. H., & Liu, P. Y. (1990). Influence of therapist ethnicity and language on therapy outcomes of Southeast Asian clients. *International Journal of Social Psychiatry, 36,* 18–29. http://dx.doi.org/10.1177/002076409003600103

Flicker, S. M., Waldron, H. B., Turner, C. W., Brody, J. L., & Hops, H. (2008). Ethnic matching and treatment outcome with Hispanic and Anglo substance-abusing adolescents in family therapy. *Journal of Family Psychology, 22,* 439–447. http://dx.doi.org/10.1037/0893-3200.22.3.439

Fouad, N. A. (2006). Multicultural guidelines: Implementation in an urban counseling psychology program. *Professional Psychology: Research and Practice, 37,* 6–13. http://dx.doi.org/10.1037/0735-7028.37.1.6

Fouad, N. A., & Arredondo, P. (2007). *Becoming culturally oriented: Practical advice for psychologists and educators.* Washington, DC: American Psychological Association. http://dx.doi.org/10.1037/11483-000

Freire, P. (1973). *Education for critical consciousness.* New York, NY: Seabury.

Fuertes, J. N., Stracuzzi, T. I., Bennett, J., Scheinholtz, J., Mislowack, A., Hersh, M., & Cheng, D. (2006). Therapist multicultural competency: A study of therapy dyads. *Psychotherapy: Theory, Research, Practice, Training, 43,* 480–490. http://dx.doi.org/10.1037/0033-3204.43.4.480

Gans, H. (2003, March 7). Identity. *The Chronicle of Higher Education,* p. B4.

Garcia, S. M., Tor, A., & Gonzalez, R. (2006). Ranks and rivals: A theory of competition. *Personality and Social Psychology Bulletin, 32,* 970–982. http://dx.doi.org/10.1177/0146167206287640

Garland, A. F., Hough, R. L., Landsverk, J. A., McCabe, K., Yeh, M., Ganger, W., & Reynolds, B. J. (2000). Racial and ethnic variations in mental health care utilization among children in foster care. *Children's Services: Social Policy, Research, & Practice, 3,* 133–146. http://dx.doi.org/10.1207/S15326918CS0303_1

Garroutte, E. M., Kunovich, R. M., Jacobsen, C., & Goldberg, J. (2004). Patient satisfaction and ethnic identity among American Indian older adults. *Social Science & Medicine, 59,* 2233–2244. http://dx.doi.org/10.1016/j.socscimed.2004.03.032

Gaztambide, D. J. (2009). *Religion as a wellspring of healing and liberation: Toward a liberation psychology of religion* (Unpublished doctoral dissertation). Union Theological Seminary, New York, NY.

Gaztambide, D. J. (2012). Addressing cultural impasses with rupture resolution strategies: A proposal and recommendations. *Professional Psychology: Research and Practice, 43,* 183–189. http://dx.doi.org/10.1037/a0026911

Geertz, C. (2000). *Available light: Anthropological reflections on philosophical topics.* Princeton, NJ: Princeton University Press.

Gelso, C. J. (2011). *The real relationship in psychotherapy: The hidden foundation of change*. Washington, DC: American Psychological Association. http://dx.doi.org/10.1037/12349-000

George, L. K. (2010). Still happy after all these years: Research frontiers on subjective well-being in later life. *Journal of Gerontology: Social Sciences, 10*, 1–9. http://dx.doi.org/10.1093/geronb/gbq006

Gergen, K. J. (1995). Relational theory and the discourses of power. In K. J. Gergen (Ed.), *Management and organization: Relational alternatives to individualism* (pp. 29–50). Brookfield, VT: Avebury/Ashgate.

Gergen, K. J. (2009). *Relational being: Beyond self and community*. New York, NY: Oxford University Press.

Gladwell, M. (2006). *The tipping point: How little things can make a big difference*. New York, NY: Hachette Digital.

Glass, G. (1976). Primary, secondary, and meta-analysis of research. *Educational Researcher, 5*, 3–8. http://dx.doi.org/10.3102/0013189X005010003

Golding, J. M., & Wells, K. B. (1990). Social support and use of mental health services by Mexican Americans and non-Hispanic Whites. *Basic and Applied Social Psychology, 11*, 443–458. http://dx.doi.org/10.1207/s15324834basp1104_7

Gómez, L. E., & López, N. (2013). *Mapping race: Critical approaches to health disparities research*. New Brunswick, NJ: Rutgers University Press.

Gone, J. P. (2011). Is psychological science a-cultural? *Cultural Diversity and Ethnic Minority Psychology, 17*, 234–242. http://dx.doi.org/10.1037/a0023805

Gone, J. P., & Trimble, J. E. (2012). American Indian and Alaska Native mental health: Diverse perspectives on enduring disparities. *Annual Review of Clinical Psychology, 8*, 131–160. http://dx.doi.org/10.1146/annurev-clinpsy-032511-143127

Gong, L. (2007). Ethnic identity and identification with the majority group: Relations with national identity and self-esteem. *International Journal of Intercultural Relations, 31*, 503–523. http://dx.doi.org/10.1016/j.ijintrel.2007.03.002

Gordon, M. M. (1978). *Human nature, class, and ethnicity*. New York, NY: Oxford University Press.

Graves, T. D. (1967). Acculturation, access, and alcohol in a tri-ethnic community. *American Anthropologist, 69*, 306–321. http://dx.doi.org/10.1525/aa.1967.69.3-4.02a00030

Greeley, A. M. (1974). *Ethnicity in the United States*. New York, NY: Wiley.

Griner, D., & Smith, T. B. (2006). Culturally adapted mental health intervention: A meta-analytic review. *Psychotherapy: Theory, Research, Practice, Training, 43*, 531–548. http://dx.doi.org/10.1037/0033-3204.43.4.531

Grusec, J. E., & Hastings, P. D. (2007). *Handbook of socialization: Theory and research*. New York, NY: Guilford Press.

Guthrie, R. V. (1976). *Even the rat was White: A historical view of psychology*. New York, NY: Harper & Row.

Guthrie, R. V. (2004). *Even the rat was White: A historical view of psychology* (2nd ed.). Upper Saddle River, NJ: Pearson.

Haasen, C., Demiralay, C., & Reimer, J. (2008). Acculturation and mental distress among Russian and Iranian migrants in Germany. *European Psychiatry, 23*, 10–13. http://dx.doi.org/10.1016/S0924-9338(08)70056-7

Hall, C. C. I. (1997). Cultural malpractice. The growing obsolescence of psychology with the changing U.S. population. *American Psychologist, 52*, 642–651. http://dx.doi.org/10.1037/0003-066X.52.6.642

Hall, G. C. N. (2001). Psychotherapy research with ethnic minorities: Empirical, ethical, and conceptual issues. *Journal of Consulting and Clinical Psychology, 69*, 502–510. http://dx.doi.org/10.1037//0022-006X.69.3.502

Hall, G. C. N., & Yee, A. H. (2014). Evidence-based practice. In F. T. L. Leong, L. Comas-Díaz, G. C. Nagayama Hall, V. C. McLoyd, & J. E. Trimble (Eds.), *APA handbook of multicultural psychology: Vol. 2. Applications and training* (pp. 59–79). Washington, DC: American Psychological Association.

Haller, M., & Hadler, M. (2006). How social relations and structures can produce happiness and unhappiness: An international comparative analysis. *Social Indicators Research, 75*, 169–216. http://dx.doi.org/10.1007/s11205-004-6297-y

Hannigan, T. (1990). Traits, attitudes, and skills that are related to intercultural effectiveness and their implications for cross-cultural training: A review of the literature. *International Journal of Intercultural Relations, 14*, 89–111. http://dx.doi.org/10.1016/0147-1767(90)90049-3

Harré, R., & Robinson, D. N. (1995). On the primacy of duties. *Philosophy, 70*, 513. http://dx.doi.org/10.1017/S0031819100065773

Harrell, S. P. (2000). A multidimensional conceptualization of racism-related stress: Implications for the well-being of people of color. *American Journal of Orthopsychiatry, 70*, 42–57. http://dx.doi.org/10.1037/h0087722

Harris, H. W., Blue, H. C., & Griffith, E. H. (Eds.). (1995). *Racial and ethnic identity*. New York, NY: Routledge.

Harris, P. M. (1998). Attrition revisited. *American Journal of Evaluation, 19*, 293–305. http://dx.doi.org/10.1177/109821409801900303

Hayes, J. A., Owen, J., & Bieschke, K. J. (2015). Therapist differences in symptom change with racial/ethnic minority clients. *Psychotherapy*. Advance online publication. http://dx.doi.org/10.1037/a0037957

Heath, A. E., Neimeyer, G. J., & Pedersen, P. B. (1988). The future of cross-cultural counseling: A Delphi poll. *Journal of Counseling & Development, 67*, 27–30. http://dx.doi.org/10.1002/j.1556-6676.1988.tb02005.x

Helms, J. E. (1990). (Ed.) *Black and White racial identity: Theory, research, and practice*. Westport, CT: Greenwood Press.

Helms, J. E. (1994). The conceptualization of racial identity and other "racial" constructs. In E. J. Trickett, R. J. Watts, & D. Birman (Eds.), *Human diversity: Perspectives on people in context* (pp. 285–311). San Francisco, CA: Jossey-Bass.

Helms, J. E. (2007). Some better practices for measuring racial and ethnic identity constructs. *Journal of Counseling Psychology, 54,* 235–246. http://dx.doi.org/10.1037/0022-0167.54.3.235

Helms, J. E., Jernigan, M., & Mascher, J. (2005). The meaning of race in psychology and how to change it: A methodological perspective. *American Psychologist, 60,* 27–36. http://dx.doi.org/10.1037/0003-066X.60.1.27

Henderson, R. C., Williams, P., Gabbidon, J., Farrelly, S., Schauman, O., Hatch, S., . . . the MIRIAD study group. (2014). Mistrust of mental health services: Ethnicity, hospital admission and unfair treatment. *Epidemiology and Psychiatric Sciences,* 1–8. http://dx.doi.org/10.1017/S2045796014000158

Henrich, J., Heine, S. J., & Norenzayan, A. (2010). The weirdest people in the world? *Behavioral and Brain Sciences, 33,* 61–83. http://dx.doi.org/10.1017/S0140525X0999152X

Hinton, D. E., Rivera, E. I., Hofmann, S. G., Barlow, D. H., & Otto, M. W. (2012). Adapting CBT for traumatized refugees and ethnic minority patients: Examples from culturally adapted CBT (CA-CBT). *Transcultural Psychiatry, 49,* 340–365. http://dx.doi.org/10.1177/1363461512441595

Holt-Lunstad, J., Smith, T. B., Baker, M., Harris, T., & Stephenson, D. (2015). Loneliness and social isolation as risk factors for mortality: A meta-analytic review. *Perspectives on Psychological Science, 10,* 227–237. http://dx.doi.org/10.1177/1745691614568352

Holt-Lunstad, J., Smith, T. B., & Layton, J. B. (2010). Social relationships and mortality risk: A meta-analytic review. *PLoS Medicine, 7,* e1000316–e1000316. http://dx.doi.org/10.1371/journal.pmed.1000316

Howe, C., Heim, D., & O'Connor, R. (2014). Racism, identity and psychological well-being: A longitudinal perspective on politically embattled relations. *Ethnic and Racial Studies, 37,* 2457–2474. http://dx.doi.org/10.1080/01419870.2013.835057

Howell, R. T., & Howell, C. J. (2008). The relation of economic status to subjective well-being in developing countries: A meta-analysis. *Psychological Bulletin, 134,* 536–560. http://dx.doi.org/10.1037/0033-2909.134.4.536

Hoyt, W. T., Warbasse, R. E., & Chu, E. Y. (2006). Construct validation in counseling psychology research. *The Counseling Psychologist, 34,* 769–805. http://dx.doi.org/10.1177/0011000006287389

Huey, S. J., Jr., & Polo, A. J. (2008). Evidence-based psychosocial treatments for ethnic minority youth. *Journal of Clinical Child and Adolescent Psychology, 37,* 262–301. http://dx.doi.org/10.1080/15374410701820174

Huey, S. J., Jr., Tilley, J. L., Jones, E. O., & Smith, C. A. (2014). The contribution of cultural competence to evidence-based care for ethnically diverse populations. *Annual Review of Clinical Psychology, 10,* 305–338. http://dx.doi.org/10.1146/annurev-clinpsy-032813-153729

Hunt, L. M., Schneider, S., & Comer, B. (2004). Should "acculturation" be a variable in health research? A critical review of research on U.S. Hispanics. *Social Science & Medicine, 59,* 973–986. http://dx.doi.org/10.1016/j.socscimed.2003.12.009

Hurwich-Reiss, E., Rindlaub, L. A., Wadsworth, M. E., & Markman, H. J. (2014). Cultural adaptation of a family strengthening intervention for low-income Spanish-speaking families. *Journal of Latina/o Psychology, 2,* 21.

Hwang, W. C. (2006). The psychotherapy adaptation and modification framework: Application to Asian Americans. *American Psychologist, 61,* 702–715. http://dx.doi.org/10.1037/0003-066X.61.7.702

Hwang, W. C. (2009). The formative method for adapting psychotherapy (FMAP): A community-based developmental approach to culturally adapting therapy. *Professional Psychology: Research and Practice, 40,* 369–377. http://dx.doi.org/10.1037/a0016240

Hwang, W. C., & Myers, H. F. (2007). Major depression in Chinese Americans: The roles of stress, vulnerability, and acculturation. *Social Psychiatry and Psychiatric Epidemiology, 42,* 189–197. http://dx.doi.org/10.1007/s00127-006-0152-1

Ibaraki, A. Y., & Hall, G. C. N. (2014). The components of cultural match in psychotherapy. *Journal of Social and Clinical Psychology, 33,* 936–953. http://dx.doi.org/10.1521/jscp.2014.33.10.936

Imel, Z. E., Baldwin, S., Atkins, D. C., Owen, J., Baardseth, T., & Wampold, B. E. (2011). Racial/ethnic disparities in therapist effectiveness: A conceptualization and initial study of cultural competence. *Journal of Counseling Psychology, 58,* 290–298. http://dx.doi.org/10.1037/a0023284

Ivey, A. E., & Collins, N. M. (2003). Social justice: A long-term challenge for counseling psychology. *The Counseling Psychologist, 31,* 290–298. http://dx.doi.org/10.1177/0011000003031003004

Ivey, A. E., & Zalaquett, C. P. (2009). Psychotherapy as liberation: Multicultural counseling and psychotherapy (MCT) contributions to the promotion of psychological emancipation. In J. L. Chin (Ed.), *Diversity in mind and in action: Vol. 3. Social justice matters.* (pp. 181–199). Santa Barbara, CA: Praeger/ABC-CLIO.

Jackson, L. C., Schmutzer, P. A., Wenzel, A., & Tyler, J. D. (2006). Applicability of cognitive–behavior therapy with American Indian individuals. *Psychotherapy: Theory, Research, Practice, Training, 43,* 506–517. http://dx.doi.org/10.1037/0033-3204.43.4.506

Jahoda, G. (1979). A cross-cultural perspective on experimental social psychology. *Personality and Social Psychology Bulletin, 5,* 142–148. http://dx.doi.org/10.1177/014616727900500203

Jahoda, G. (1988). J'Accuse. In M. Bond (Ed.), *The cross-cultural challenge to social psychology* (pp. 86–95). Newbury Park, CA: Sage.

Jones, J. M. (2003). Constructing race and deconstructing racism: A cultural psychology approach. In G. Bernal, J. E. Trimble, A. K. Burlew, & F. T. Leong (Eds.), *Handbook of racial and ethnic minority psychology* (pp. 276–290). London, England: Sage. http://dx.doi.org/10.4135/9781412976008.n14

Jones, L. K. (1974). The Counselor Evaluation Rating Scale: A valid criterion of counselor effectiveness? *Counselor Education and Supervision, 14,* 112–116. http://dx.doi.org/10.1002/j.1556-6978.1974.tb00852.x

Jordan, J. V. (2010). *Relational–cultural therapy.* Washington, DC: American Psychological Association.

Kaplan, A. (1986). The "self-in-relation": Implications for depression in women. *Psychotherapy: Theory, Research, Practice, Training, 23,* 234–242. http://dx.doi.org/10.1037/h0085603

Kaslow, N. J., Rubin, N. J., Bebeau, M. J., Leigh, I. W., Lichtenberg, J. W., Nelson, P. D., . . . Smith, I. L. (2007). Guiding principles and recommendations for the assessment of competence. *Professional Psychology: Research and Practice, 38,* 441–451. http://dx.doi.org/10.1037/0735-7028.38.5.441

Katz, A. D., & Hoyt, W. T. (2014). The influence of multicultural counseling competence and anti-Black prejudice on therapists' outcome expectancies. *Journal of Counseling Psychology, 61,* 299–305. http://dx.doi.org/10.1037/a0036134

Katz, M. H., & Hauck, W. W. (1993). Proportional hazards (Cox) regression. *Journal of General Internal Medicine, 8,* 702–711. http://dx.doi.org/10.1007/BF02598295

Katz, P. A., & Taylor, D. A. (Eds.). (1988). *Eliminating racism: Profiles in controversy.* New York, NY: Plenum Press. http://dx.doi.org/10.1007/978-1-4899-0818-6

Kazdin, A. E. (1996). Dropping out of child psychotherapy: Issues for research and implications for practice. *Clinical Child Psychology and Psychiatry, 1,* 133–156. http://dx.doi.org/10.1177/1359104596011012

Kazdin, A. E. (2008). Evidence-based treatment and practice: New opportunities to bridge clinical research and practice, enhance the knowledge base, and improve patient care. *American Psychologist, 63,* 146–159. http://dx.doi.org/10.1037/0003-066X.63.3.146

Keita, G., & Petersen, A. (Eds.). (1996). *Blacks in the United States: Abstracts of the psychological and behavioral Literature, 1987–1995.* Washington, DC: American Psychological Association.

Kelly, T. A., & Strupp, H. H. (1992). Patient and therapist values in psychotherapy: Perceived changes, assimilation, similarity, and outcome. *Journal of Consulting and Clinical Psychology, 60,* 34–40. http://dx.doi.org/10.1037/0022-006X.60.1.34

Kiev, A. (1972). *Transcultural psychiatry.* New York, NY: Free Press.

Kim, B. S. K., & Abreu, J. M. (2001). Acculturation measurement: Theory, current instruments, and future directions. In J. Ponterotto, M. Casas, L. Suzuki, & C. Alexander (Eds.), *Handbook of multicultural counseling* (2nd ed.; pp. 394–424). Thousand Oaks, CA: Sage.

Kim, B. S. K., Atkinson, D. R., & Umemoto, D. (2001). Asian cultural values and the counseling process: Current knowledge and directions for future research. *The Counseling Psychologist, 29,* 570–603. http://dx.doi.org/10.1177/0011000001294006

Kim, U., Yang, K., & Hwang, K. (Eds.). (2006). *Indigenous and cultural psychology.* New York, NY: Springer. http://dx.doi.org/10.1007/0-387-28662-4

Kirke, D. M. (2007). Social network analysis and psychological research. *The Irish Journal of Psychology, 28*(1–2), 53–61. http://dx.doi.org/10.1080/03033910.2007.10446248

Kiselica, M. S. (1998). Preparing Anglos for the challenges and joys of multiculturalism. *The Counseling Psychologist, 26*, 5–21. http://dx.doi.org/10.1177/0011000098261001

Kivisto, P., & Nefzger, B. (1993). Symbolic ethnicity and American Jews: The relationship of ethnic identity to behavior and group affiliation. *The Social Science Journal, 30*, 1–12. http://dx.doi.org/10.1016/0362-3319(93)90002-D

Kleinman, A., Eisenberg, L., & Good, B. (1978). Culture, illness, and care: Clinical lessons from anthropologic and cross-cultural research. *Annals of Internal Medicine, 88*, 251–258. http://dx.doi.org/10.7326/0003-4819-88-2-251

Knox, S., Adrians, N., Everson, E., Hess, S., Hill, C., & Crook-Lyon, R. (2011). Clients' perspectives on therapy termination. *Psychotherapy Research, 21*, 154–167. http://dx.doi.org/10.1080/10503307.2010.534509

Knox, S., Burkard, A. W., Johnson, A. J., Suzuki, L. A., & Ponterotto, J. G. (2003). African American and European American therapists' experiences of addressing race in cross-racial psychotherapy dyads. *Journal of Counseling Psychology, 50*, 466–481. http://dx.doi.org/10.1037/0022-0167.50.4.466

Krippendorff, K. (2012). *Content analysis: An introduction to its methodology* (3rd ed.). Thousand Oaks, CA: Sage.

Kuhn, T. S. (1996). *The structure of scientific revolutions* (3rd ed.). Chicago, IL: University of Chicago Press. http://dx.doi.org/10.7208/chicago/9780226458106.001.0001

Kuhn, T. S. (2012). *The structure of scientific revolutions* (50th anniversary ed.). Chicago, IL: University of Chicago Press.

LaFromboise, T. D., Coleman, H. L. K., & Gerton, J. (1993). Psychological impact of biculturalism: Evidence and theory. *Psychological Bulletin, 114*, 395–412. http://dx.doi.org/10.1037/0033-2909.114.3.395

LaFromboise, T. D., Coleman, H. L. K., & Hernandez, A. (1991). Development and factor structure of the Cross-Cultural Counseling Inventory—Revised. *Professional Psychology: Research and Practice, 22*, 380–388. http://dx.doi.org/10.1037/0735-7028.22.5.380

Lambert, M. J. (2007). What we have learned from a decade of research aimed at improving psychotherapy outcome in routine care. *Psychotherapy Research, 17*, 1–14. http://dx.doi.org/10.1080/10503300601032506

Lambert, M. J. (2010). *Prevention of treatment failure: The use of measuring, monitoring, and feedback in clinical practice*. Washington, DC: American Psychological Association. http://dx.doi.org/10.1037/12141-000

Landis, D., & Brislin, R. W. (Eds.). (2013). *Handbook of intercultural training: Vol. 1. Issues in theory and design*. New York, NY: Elmsfeld.

Langer, N. (1999). Culturally competent professionals in therapeutic alliances enhance patient compliance. *Journal of Health Care for the Poor and Underserved, 10*, 19–26. http://dx.doi.org/10.1353/hpu.2010.0770

La Roche, M. J. (2012). *Cultural psychotherapy: Theory, methods, and practice*. Atlanta, GA: Sage.

La Roche, M. J., & Christopher, M. S. (2008). Culture and empirically supported treatments: On the road to a collision? *Culture & Psychology, 14*, 333–356. http://dx.doi.org/10.1177/1354067X08092637

La Roche, M. J., D'Angelo, E., Gualdron, L., & Leavell, J. (2006). Culturally sensitive guided imagery for allocentric Latinos: A pilot study. *Psychotherapy: Theory, Research, Practice, Training, 43*, 555–560. http://dx.doi.org/10.1037/0033-3204.43.4.555

La Roche, M. J., & Lustig, K. (2010). Cultural adaptations: Unpacking the meaning of culture. *The Scientific Review of Mental Health Practice, 7*(2), 26–30.

La Roche, M. J., & Lustig, K. (2013). Being mindful about the assessment of culture: A cultural analysis of culturally adapted acceptance-based behavior therapy approaches. *Cognitive and Behavioral Practice, 20*, 60–63. http://dx.doi.org/10.1016/j.cbpra.2012.04.002

Lassiter, P. S., Napolitano, L., Culbreth, J., & Ng, K. (2008). Developing multicultural competence using the structured peer group supervision model. *Counselor Education and Supervision, 47*, 164–178. http://dx.doi.org/10.1002/j.1556-6978.2008.tb00047.x

Lau, A. S. (2006). Making the case for selective and directed cultural adaptations of evidence-based treatments: Examples from parent training. *Clinical Psychology: Science and Practice, 13*, 295–310. http://dx.doi.org/10.1111/j.1468-2850.2006.00042.x

Lau, A. S., Chang, D. F., & Okazaki, S. (2010). Methodological challenges in treatment outcome research with ethnic minorities. *Cultural Diversity and Ethnic Minority Psychology, 16*, 573–580. http://dx.doi.org/10.1037/a0021371

Lazarus, R. S., & Folkman, S. (1984). *Stress, appraisal, and coping*. New York, NY: Springer-Verlag.

Lee, D. L., & Ahn, S. (2011). Racial discrimination and Asian mental health: A meta-analysis. *The Counseling Psychologist, 39*, 463–489. http://dx.doi.org/10.1177/0011000010381791

Lee, R. M. (2005). Resilience against discrimination: Ethnic identity and other-group orientation as protective factors for Korean Americans. *Journal of Counseling Psychology, 52*, 36–44. http://dx.doi.org/10.1037/0022-0167.52.1.36

Lee, R. M., Chalk, L., Conner, S. E., Kawasaki, N., Jannetti, A., LaRue, T., & Rodolfa, E. (1999). The status of multicultural counseling training at counseling internship sites. *Journal of Multicultural Counseling and Development, 27*, 58–74. http://dx.doi.org/10.1002/j.2161-1912.1999.tb00215.x

Lee, R. M., Yoon, E., & Liu-Tom, H. T. (2006). Structure and measurement of acculturation/enculturation for Asian Americans using the ARSMA-II. *Measurement and Evaluation in Counseling and Development, 39*, 42–55.

Leong, F. T. L. (2011). Cultural accommodation model of counseling. *Journal of Employment Counseling, 48*, 150–152. http://dx.doi.org/10.1002/j.2161-1920.2011.tb01099.x

Leong, F. T. L., Comas-Díaz, L., Nagayama Hall, G. C., McLoyd, V. C., & Trimble, J. E. (Eds.). (2014). *APA handbook of multicultural psychology* (Vols. 1–2). Washington, DC: American Psychological Association. http://dx.doi.org/10.1037/14189-000

Leong, F. T. L., Holliday, B. G., Trimble, J. E., Padilla, A. M., & McCubbin, L. D. (2012). Ethnic minority psychology. In I. B. Weiner (Ed.), *Handbook of psychology: Vol. 1. Ethnic minority psychology* (2nd ed., pp. 530–561). Hoboken, NJ: Wiley.

Leong, F. T. L., Kim, H. H., & Gupta, A. (2011). Attitudes toward professional counseling among Asian-American college students: Acculturation, conceptions of mental illness, and loss of face. *Asian American Journal of Psychology, 2,* 140–153. http://dx.doi.org/10.1037/a0024172

Leong, F. T. L., & Whitfield, J. R. (Eds.). (1992). *Asians in the United States: Abstracts of the psychological and behavioral literature, 1967–1991.* Washington, DC: American Psychological Association.

Lerner, R. M., & Overton, W. F. (2008). Exemplifying the integrations of the relational developmental system: Synthesizing theory, research, and application to promote positive development and social justice. *Journal of Adolescent Research, 23,* 245–255. http://dx.doi.org/10.1177/0743558408314385

Levinas, E. (1969). *Totality and infinity: An essay on exteriority.* Pittsburgh, PA: Duquesne University Press.

Levinas, E. (1998). *Entre nous: On thinking-of-the-other.* New York, NY: Columbia University Press.

Li, L. C., & Kim, B. S. (2004). Effects of counseling style and client adherence to Asian cultural values on counseling process with Asian American college students. *Journal of Counseling Psychology, 51,* 158–167. http://dx.doi.org/10.1037/0022-0167.51.2.158

Lipsey, M. W., & Wilson, D. B. (2001). *Practical meta-analysis.* Thousand Oaks, CA: Sage.

Liu, L. L., & Lau, A. S. (2013). Teaching about race/ethnicity and racism matters: An examination of how perceived ethnic racial socialization processes are associated with depression symptoms. *Cultural Diversity and Ethnic Minority Psychology, 19,* 383–394. http://dx.doi.org/10.1037/a0033447

Lo, C. C., Cheng, T. C., & Howell, R. J. (2014). Access to and utilization of health services as pathway to racial disparities in serious mental illness. *Community Mental Health Journal, 50,* 251–257. http://dx.doi.org/10.1007/s10597-013-9593-7

Lonner, W. J. (2000). On the growth and continuing importance of cross-cultural psychology. *Eye on Psi Chi, 4*(3), 22–26.

López, S. R., Barrio, C., Kopelowicz, A., & Vega, W. A. (2012). From documenting to eliminating disparities in mental health care for Latinos. *American Psychologist, 67,* 511–523. http://dx.doi.org/10.1037/a0029737

López, S. R., Grover, K. P., Holland, D., Johnson, M. J., Kain, C. D., Kanel, K., ... Rhyne, M. C. (1989). Development of culturally sensitive psychotherapists. *Professional Psychology: Research and Practice, 20,* 369–376. http://dx.doi.org/10.1037/0735-7028.20.6.369

Machado, A., & Silva, F. J. (2007). Toward a richer view of the scientific method. The role of conceptual analysis. *American Psychologist, 62,* 671–681. http://dx.doi.org/10.1037/0003-066X.62.7.671

Magyar-Moe, J., & López, S. J. (2008). Human agency, strengths-based development, and well-being. In W. B. Walsh (Ed.), *Biennial review of counseling psychology* (Vol. 1, pp. 157–175). New York, NY: Routledge/Taylor & Francis.

Mandara, J., Gaylord-Harden, N. K., Richards, M. H., & Ragsdale, B. L. (2009). The effects of changes in racial identity and self-esteem on changes in African American adolescents' mental health. *Child Development, 80,* 1660–1675. http://dx.doi.org/10.1111/j.1467-8624.2009.01360.x

Maramba, G. G., & Nagayama Hall, G. C. (2002). Meta-analyses of ethnic match as a predictor of dropout, utilization, and level of functioning. *Cultural Diversity and Ethnic Minority Psychology, 8,* 290–297. http://dx.doi.org/10.1037/1099-9809.8.3.290

Martín-Baró, I. M., Aron, A., & Corne, S. (1994). *Writings for a liberation psychology.* Cambridge, MA: Harvard University Press.

McCabe, K., Yeh, M., Lau, A., & Argote, C. B. (2012). Parent–child interaction therapy for Mexican Americans: Results of a pilot randomized clinical trial at follow-up. *Behavior Therapy, 43,* 606–618. http://dx.doi.org/10.1016/j.beth.2011.11.001

McCubbin, L. D., & Marsella, A. (2009). Native Hawaiians and psychology: The cultural and historical context of indigenous ways of knowing. *Cultural Diversity and Ethnic Minority Psychology, 15,* 374–387. http://dx.doi.org/10.1037/a0016774

McCutcheon, S. R., & Imel, Z. E. (2009). Valuing diversity implementing our best intentions. *The Counseling Psychologist, 37,* 760–771. http://dx.doi.org/10.1177/0011000009334094

McGuire, T. G., Alegría, M., Cook, B. L., Wells, K. B., & Zaslavsky, A. M. (2006). Implementing the Institute of Medicine definition of disparities: An application to mental health care. *Health Services Research, 41,* 1979–2005. http://dx.doi.org/10.1111/j.1475-6773.2006.00583.x

McGuire, T. G., & Miranda, J. (2008). New evidence regarding racial and ethnic disparities in mental health: Policy implications. *Health Affairs, 27,* 393–403. http://dx.doi.org/10.1377/hlthaff.27.2.393

McKee-Ryan, F., Song, Z., Wanberg, C. R., & Kinicki, A. J. (2005). Psychological and physical well-being during unemployment: A meta-analytic study. *Journal of Applied Psychology, 90,* 53–76.

McNeill, B. W. (Ed.). (2009). *Intersections of multiple identities: A casebook of evidence-based practices with diverse populations.* New York, NY: Routledge/Taylor & Francis.

McPherson, M., Smith-Lovin, L., & Cook, J. M. (2001). Birds of a feather: Homophily in social networks. *Annual Review of Sociology, 27,* 415–444. http://dx.doi.org/10.1146/annurev.soc.27.1.415

Mead, M. (1963). *Sex and temperament in three primitive societies.* New York, NY: Morrow.

Mendenhall, M., & Oddou, G. (1985). The dimensions of expatriate acculturation: A review. *The Academy of Management Review, 10,* 39–47.

Mendoza, R. (1984). Acculturation and sociocultural variability. In J. L. Martinez & R. Mendoza (Eds.), *Chicano Psychology* (2nd ed., pp. 61–75). Orlando, FL: Academic Press. http://dx.doi.org/10.1016/B978-0-12-475660-1.50011-5

Merton, R. K. (1968). *Social theory and social structure* (Rev ed.). New York, NY: Free Press.

Meyer, O. L., & Takeuchi, D. T. (2014). Help seeking and service utilization. In F. T. L. Leong, L. Comas-Díaz, G. C. Nagayama Hall, V. C. McLoyd, & J. E. Trimble (Eds.), *APA handbook of multicultural psychology: Vol. 2. Applications and training* (pp. 529–541). Washington, DC: American Psychological Association.

Miller, J., & Schwarz, W. (2011). Aggregate and individual replication probability within an explicit model of the research process. *Psychological Methods, 16*, 337–360. http://dx.doi.org/10.1037/a0023347

Miller, J. B. (1986). *Toward a new psychology of women* (2nd ed.). Boston, MA: Beacon Press.

Miller, M. J. (2007). A bilinear multidimensional measurement model of Asian American acculturation and enculturation: Implications for counseling interventions. *Journal of Counseling Psychology, 54*, 118–131. http://dx.doi.org/10.1037/0022-0167.54.2.118

Miller, M. J., & Sheu, H. (2008). Conceptual and measurement issues in multicultural psychology research. In S. D. Brown & R. W. Lent (Eds.), *Handbook of counseling psychology* (4th ed., pp. 103–120). New York, NY: Wiley.

Miller, N. B. (1982). Social work services to urban Indians. In J. W. Green (Ed.), *Cultural awareness in the human services* (pp. 157–183). Englewood Cliffs, NJ: Prentice Hall.

Miranda, J., Bernal, G., Lau, A., Kohn, L., Hwang, W. C., & LaFromboise, T. (2005). State of the science on psychosocial interventions for ethnic minorities. *Annual Review of Clinical Psychology, 1*, 113–142. http://dx.doi.org/10.1146/annurev.clinpsy.1.102803.143822

Miville, M. L., & Ferguson, A. D. (Eds.). (2014). *Handbook of race–ethnicity and gender in psychology*. New York, NY: Springer. http://dx.doi.org/10.1007/978-1-4614-8860-6

Mohatt, G. V. (1989). The community as informant or collaborator? *American Indian and Alaska Native Mental Health Research, 2*(3), 64–70. http://dx.doi.org/10.5820/aian.0203.1989.64

Mohatt, N. V., Fok, C. C. T., Burket, R., Henry, D., & Allen, J. (2011). Assessment of awareness of connectedness as a culturally-based protective factor for Alaska native youth. *Cultural Diversity and Ethnic Minority Psychology, 17*, 444–455. http://dx.doi.org/10.1037/a0025456

Moher, D., Liberati, A., Tetzlaff, J., Altman, D. G., & the PRISMA Group. (2009). Preferred reporting items for systematic reviews and meta-analyses: The PRISMA statement. *Annals of Internal Medicine, 151*, 264–269, W64. http://dx.doi.org/10.7326/0003-4819-151-4-200908180-00135

Mollen, D., Kelly, S. M., & Ridley, C. R. (2011). Therapeutic change: The raison d'être for counseling competence. *The Counseling Psychologist, 39*, 918–927. http://dx.doi.org/10.1177/0011000011405221

Morgan, H. W. (1981). *Drugs in America.* Syracuse, NY: Syracuse University Press.

Moynihan, D. P. (1993). Pandaemonium: Ethnicity in international politics. New York, NY: Oxford University Press.

Mui, A. C., & Kang, S. Y. (2006). Acculturation stress and depression among Asian immigrant elders. *Social Work, 51*, 243–255. http://dx.doi.org/10.1093/sw/51.3.243

Murdock, N. L., Edwards, C., & Murdock, T. B. (2010). Therapists' attributions for client premature termination: Are they self-serving? *Psychotherapy: Theory, Research, Practice, Training, 47*, 221–234. http://dx.doi.org/10.1037/a0019786

Myers, D. G. (2008). Will money buy happiness? In S. J. López (Ed.), *Positive psychology: Exploring the best in people: Vol. 4. Pursuing human flourishing* (pp. 37–56). Westport, CT: Praeger/Greenwood.

Myers, D. G. (2012). Human connections and the good life: Balancing individuality and community in public policy. In S. Joseph (Ed.), *Positive psychology in practice* (pp. 641–657). Hoboken, NJ: Wiley. http://dx.doi.org/10.1002/9780470939338.ch38

National Research Council. (2004). *Measuring racial discrimination.* Washington, DC: National Academies Press.

Negy, C., Shreve, T. L., Jensen, B. J., & Uddin, N. (2003). Ethnic identity, self-esteem, and ethnocentrism: A study of social identity versus multicultural theory of development. *Cultural Diversity and Ethnic Minority Psychology, 9*, 333–344. http://dx.doi.org/10.1037/1099-9809.9.4.333

Neighbors, H. W., Caldwell, C., Williams, D. R., Nesse, R., Taylor, R. J., Bullard, K. M., . . . Jackson, J. S. (2007). Race, ethnicity, and the use of services for mental disorders: Results from the National Survey of American Life. *Archives of General Psychiatry, 64*, 485–494. http://dx.doi.org/10.1001/archpsyc.64.4.485

Neville, H. A., Spanierman, L. B., & Lewis, J. A. (2012). The expanded psychosocial model of racism: A new model for understanding and disrupting racism and White privilege. In N. A. Fouad, J. A. Carter, & L. M. Subich (Eds.), *APA handbook of counseling psychology: Vol. 2. Practice, interventions, and applications* (pp. 333–360). Washington, DC: American Psychological Association. http://dx.doi.org/10.1037/13755-014

Newell, M. L., Nastasi, B. K., Hatzichristou, C., Jones, J. M., Schanding, G. T., & Yetter, G. (2010). Evidence on multicultural training in school psychology: Recommendations for future directions. *School Psychology Quarterly, 25*, 249–278. http://dx.doi.org/10.1037/a0021542

Norcross, J. C. (2011). *Psychotherapy relationships that work* (2nd ed.). New York, NY: Oxford University Press. http://dx.doi.org/10.1093/acprof:oso/9780199737208.001.0001

Norcross, J. C., & Lambert, M. J. (2011). Evidence-based therapy relationships. In J. C. Norcross (Ed.), *Psychotherapy relationships that work* (2nd ed., pp. 3–21). New York, NY: Oxford University Press.

Norcross, J. C., & Wampold, B. E. (2011). What works for whom: Tailoring psychotherapy to the person. *Journal of Clinical Psychology, 67,* 127–132. http://dx.doi.org/10.1002/jclp.20764

Ober, A. M., Granello, D. H., & Henfield, M. S. (2009). A synergistic model to enhance multicultural competence in supervision. *Counselor Education and Supervision, 48,* 204–221. http://dx.doi.org/10.1002/j.1556-6978.2009.tb00075.x

O'Donohue, W., & Benuto, L., (2010). The many problems with cultural sensitivity. *Scientific Review of Mental Health Practice, 7,* 34–37.

Oetting, E. R., & Beauvais, F. (1991). Orthogonal cultural identification theory: The cultural identification of minority adolescents. *International Journal of Addictions, 25,* 655–685.

Oh, Y., Koeske, G. F., & Sales, E. (2002). Acculturation, stress, and depressive symptoms among Korean immigrants in the United States. *The Journal of Social Psychology, 142,* 511–526. http://dx.doi.org/10.1080/00224540209603915

Okun, M. A., Stock, W. A., Haring, M. J., & Witter, R. A. (1984). Health and subjective well-being: A meta-analysis. *International Journal of Aging & Human Development, 19,* 111–132. http://dx.doi.org/10.2190/QGJN-0N81-5957-HAQD

Oliver, K. (2001). *Witnessing: Beyond recognition.* Minneapolis: University of Minnesota Press.

Olmedo, E. (1979). Acculturation: A psychometric perspective. *American Psychologist, 34,* 1061–1070. http://dx.doi.org/10.1037/0003-066X.34.11.1061

Olmedo, E., & Walker, V. (Eds.). (1990). *Hispanics in the United States: Abstracts of the psychological and behavioral literature, 1980–1989.* Washington, DC: American Psychological Association.

Ono, Y. A. (1982). How I created the theory of relativity. *Physics Today, 35,* 45–47. http://dx.doi.org/10.1063/1.2915203

Overton, W. F., & Ennis, M. D. (2006a). Cognitive–developmental and behavior-analytic theories: Evolving into complementarity. *Human Development, 49,* 143–172. http://dx.doi.org/10.1159/000091893

Overton, W. F., & Ennis, M. D. (2006b). Relationism, ontology, and other concerns. *Human Development, 49,* 180–183. http://dx.doi.org/10.1159/000091895

Owen, J. J., Imel, Z., Adelson, J., & Rodolfa, E. (2012). 'No-show': Therapist racial/ethnic disparities in client unilateral termination. *Journal of Counseling Psychology, 59,* 314–320. http://dx.doi.org/10.1037/a0027091

Owen, J. J., Leach, M. M., Wampold, B., & Rodolfa, E. (2011a). Client and therapist variability in clients' perceptions of their therapists' multicultural competencies. *Journal of Counseling Psychology, 58,* 1–9. http://dx.doi.org/10.1037/a0021496

Owen, J. J., Leach, M. M., Wampold, B., & Rodolfa, E. (2011b). Multicultural approaches in psychotherapy: A rejoinder. *Journal of Counseling Psychology, 58,* 22–26. http://dx.doi.org/10.1037/a0022222

Owen, J. J., Tao, K., Leach, M. M., & Rodolfa, E. (2011). Clients' perceptions of their psychotherapists' multicultural orientation. *Psychotherapy, 48,* 274–282. http://dx.doi.org/10.1037/a0022065

Padgett, D. K., Patrick, C., Burns, B. J., & Schlesinger, H. J. (1994). Women and outpatient mental health services: Use by Black, Hispanic, and White women in a national insured population. *Journal of Mental Health Administration, 21,* 347–360. http://dx.doi.org/10.1007/BF02521354

Padilla, A. (1980). The role of cultural awareness and ethnic loyalty in acculturation. In A. Padilla (Ed.), *Acculturation: Theory, models and some new findings* (pp. 47–84). Boulder, CO: Westview.

Paniagua, F. A., & Yamada, A. M. (Eds.). (2013). *Handbook of multicultural mental health: Assessment and treatment of diverse populations.* San Diego, CA: Academic Press.

Paradies, Y. (2006). A systematic review of empirical research on self-reported racism and health. *International Journal of Epidemiology, 35,* 888–901. http://dx.doi.org/10.1093/ije/dyl056

Parra Cardona, J. R., Domenech Rodríguez, M. M., Forgatch, M., Sullivan, C., Bybee, D., Holtrop, K., . . . Bernal, G. (2012). Culturally adapting an evidence-based parenting intervention for Latino immigrants: The need to integrate fidelity and cultural relevance. *Family Process, 51,* 56–72. http://dx.doi.org/10.1111/j.1545-5300.2012.01386.x

Pascoe, E. A., & Smart Richman, L. (2009). Perceived discrimination and health: A meta-analytic review. *Psychological Bulletin, 135,* 531–554. http://dx.doi.org/10.1037/a0016059

Paz, O. (1985). *The labyrinth of solitude and other writings.* New York, NY: Grove Press.

Pedersen, P. B. (1999). *Multiculturalism as a fourth force.* Philadelphia, PA: Brunner/Mazel.

Pedersen, P. B. (2000). *A handbook for developing multicultural awareness* (3rd ed.). Alexandria, VA: American Counseling Association.

Pedersen, P. B. (2004). *110 experiences for multicultural learning.* Washington, DC: American Psychological Association.

Pedersen, P. B. (2008). Ethics, competence, and professional issues in cross-cultural counseling. In P. B. Pedersen, J. G. Draguns, W. J. Lonner, & J. E. Trimble (Eds.), *Counseling across cultures* (6th ed., pp. 5–20). Thousand Oaks, CA: Sage. http://dx.doi.org/10.4135/9781483329314.n1

Pedersen, P. B., Draguns, J. G., & Lonner, W. J. (Eds.). (1976). *Counseling across cultures.* Honolulu: University of Hawaii Press.

Pedersen, P. B., Draguns, J. G., Lonner, W. J., & Trimble, J. E. (Eds.). (2008). *Counseling across cultures* (6th ed.). Thousand Oaks, CA: Sage. http://dx.doi.org/10.4135/9781483329314

Pedrotti, J. T., Edwards, L. M., & López, S. J. (2009). Positive psychology within a cultural context. In S. J. López & C. R. Snyder (Eds.), *Oxford handbook of positive psychology* (2nd ed., pp. 49–57). New York, NY: Oxford University Press.

Peters, J. L., Sutton, A. J., Jones, D. R., Abrams, K. R., & Rushton, L. (2006). Comparison of two methods to detect publication bias in meta-analysis. *JAMA, 295,* 676–680. http://dx.doi.org/10.1001/jama.295.6.676

Peterson, C., Park, N., & Sweeney, P. J. (2008). Group well-being: Morale from a positive psychology perspective. *Applied Psychology, 57,* 19–36. http://dx.doi.org/10.1111/j.1464-0597.2008.00352.x

Phinney, J. S. (1990). Ethnic identity in adolescents and adults: Review of research. *Psychological Bulletin, 108,* 499–514. http://dx.doi.org/10.1037/0033-2909.108.3.499

Phinney, J. S. (1991). Ethnic identity and self-esteem: A review and integration. *Hispanic Journal of Behavioral Sciences, 13,* 193–208. http://dx.doi.org/10.1177/07399863910132005

Phinney, J. S. (1992). The multigroup ethnic identity measure: A new scale for use with diverse groups. *Journal of Adolescent Research, 7,* 156–176. http://dx.doi.org/10.1177/074355489272003

Phinney, J. S. (1996). When we talk about American ethnic groups, what do we mean? *American Psychologist, 51,* 918–927. http://dx.doi.org/10.1037/0003-066X.51.9.918

Phinney, J. S. (2003). Ethnic identity and acculturation. In K. M. Chun, P. B. Organista, & G. Marín (Eds.), *Acculturation: Advances in theory, measurement, and applied research* (pp. 63–81). Washington, DC: American Psychological Association. http://dx.doi.org/10.1037/10472-006

Phinney, J. S. (2006). Ethnic identity exploration in emerging adulthood. In J. J. Arnett & J. L. Tanner (Eds.), *Emerging adults in America: Coming of age in the 21st century* (pp. 117–134). Washington, DC: American Psychological Association.

Phinney, J. S., Cantu, C. L., & Kurtz, D. A. (1997). Ethnic and American identity as predictors of self-esteem among African American, Latino, and White adolescents. *Journal of Youth and Adolescence, 26,* 165–185. http://dx.doi.org/10.1023/A:1024500514834

Phinney, J. S., Horenczyk, G., Liebkind, K., & Vedder, P. (2001). Ethnic identity, immigration, and well-being: An interactional perspective. *Journal of Social Issues, 57,* 493–510. http://dx.doi.org/10.1111/0022-4537.00225

Phinney, J. S., & Ong, A. (2007). Conceptualization and measurement of ethnic identity: Current status and future directions. *Journal of Counseling Psychology, 54,* 271–281. http://dx.doi.org/10.1037/0022-0167.54.3.271

Pieterse, A. L. (2009). Teaching antiracism in counselor training: Reflections on a course. *Journal of Multicultural Counseling and Development, 37,* 141–152. http://dx.doi.org/10.1002/j.2161-1912.2009.tb00098.x

Pieterse, A. L., Evans, S. A., Risner-Butner, A., Collins, N. M., & Mason, L. B. (2009). Multicultural competence and social justice training in counseling psychology and counselor education: A review and analysis of a sample of multicultural course syllabi. *The Counseling Psychologist, 37*, 93–115. http://dx.doi.org/10.1177/0011000008319986

Pieterse, A. L., Todd, N. R., Neville, H. A., & Carter, R. T. (2012). Perceived racism and mental health among Black American adults: A meta-analytic review. *Journal of Counseling Psychology, 59*, 1–9. http://dx.doi.org/10.1037/a0026208

Pinquart, M., & Sörensen, S. (2000). Influences of socioeconomic status, social network, and competence on subjective well-being in later life: A meta-analysis. *Psychology and Aging, 15*, 187–224. http://dx.doi.org/10.1037/0882-7974.15.2.187

Piselli, A., Halgin, R. P., & MacEwan, G. H. (2011). What went wrong? Therapists' reflections on their role in premature termination. *Psychotherapy Research, 21*, 400–415. http://dx.doi.org/10.1080/10503307.2011.573819

Ponterotto, J. G. (1997). Multicultural counseling training: A competency model and national survey. In D. B. Pope-Davis, & H. L. K. Coleman (Eds.), *Multicultural counseling competencies: Assessment, education and training, and supervision* (pp. 111–130). Thousand Oaks, CA: Sage. http://dx.doi.org/10.4135/9781452232072.n5

Ponterotto, J. G. (1998). Charting a course for research in multicultural counseling training. *The Counseling Psychologist, 26*, 43–68. http://dx.doi.org/10.1177/0011000098261004

Ponterotto, J. G. (2010). Qualitative research in multicultural psychology: Philosophical underpinnings, popular approaches, and ethical considerations. *Cultural Diversity and Ethnic Minority Psychology, 16*, 581–589. http://dx.doi.org/10.1037/a0012051

Ponterotto, J. G., & Austin, R. (2005). Emerging approaches to training psychologists to be culturally competent. In R. T. Carter (Ed.), *Handbook of racial–cultural psychology and counseling: Vol. 2. Training and practice* (pp. 19–35). Hoboken, NJ: Wiley.

Ponterotto, J. G., Casas, J. M., Suzuki, L. A., & Alexander, C. M. (Eds.). (2010). *Handbook of multicultural counseling* (3rd ed.). Thousand Oaks, CA: Sage.

Ponterotto, J. G., Fuertes, J. N., & Chen, E. C. (2000). Models of multicultural counseling. In R. W. Lent (Ed.), *Handbook of counseling psychology* (3rd ed., pp. 639–669). Hoboken, NJ: Wiley.

Ponterotto, J. G., & Park-Taylor, J. (2007). Racial and ethnic identity theory, measurement, and research in counseling psychology: Present status and future directions. *Journal of Counseling Psychology, 54*, 282–294. http://dx.doi.org/10.1037/0022-0167.54.3.282

Pope-Davis, D. B., Coleman, H. L. K., Liu, W. M., & Toporek, R. L. (2003). *Handbook of multicultural competencies in counseling and psychology*. Thousand Oaks, CA: Sage.

Pope-Davis, D. B., Liu, W. M., Toporek, R. L., & Brittan-Powell, C. S. (2001). What's missing from multicultural competency research: Review, introspection, and recommendations. *Cultural Diversity and Ethnic Minority Psychology, 7*, 121–138. http://dx.doi.org/10.1037/1099-9809.7.2.121

Presnell, A., Harris, G., & Scogin, F. (2012). Therapist and client race/ethnicity match: An examination of treatment outcome and process with rural older adults in the deep south. *Psychotherapy Research, 22*, 458–463. http://dx.doi.org/10.1080/10503307.2012.673022

Priester, P. E., Jones, J. E., Jackson-Bailey, C. M., Jana-Masri, A., Jordan, E., & Metz, A. J. (2008). An analysis of content and instructional strategies in multicultural counseling courses. *Journal of Multicultural Counseling and Development, 36*, 29–39. http://dx.doi.org/10.1002/j.2161-1912.2008.tb00067.x

Proulx, C. M., Helms, H. M., & Buehler, C. (2007). Marital quality and personal well-being: A meta-analysis. *Journal of Marriage and Family, 69*, 576–593. http://dx.doi.org/10.1111/j.1741-3737.2007.00393.x

Ramos, Z., & Alegría, M. (2014). Cultural adaptation and health literacy refinement of a brief depression intervention for Latinos in a low-resource setting. *Cultural Diversity and Ethnic Minority Psychology, 20*, 293–301. http://dx.doi.org/10.1037/a0035021

Rawls, J. (1999). *A theory of justice*. Cambridge, MA: Harvard University Press.

Reis, B. F., & Brown, L. G. (1999). Reducing psychotherapy dropouts: Maximizing perspective convergence in the psychotherapy dyad. *Psychotherapy: Theory, Research, Practice, Training, 36*, 123–136. http://dx.doi.org/10.1037/h0087822

Reynolds, A. L. (1997). Using the multicultural change intervention matrix (MCIM) as a multicultural counseling training model. In D. B. Pope-Davis & H. L. K. Coleman (Eds.), *Multicultural counseling competencies: Assessment, education and training, and supervision* (pp. 209–226). Thousand Oaks, CA: Sage. http://dx.doi.org/10.4135/9781452232072.n9

Reynolds, A. L. (2011). Understanding the perceptions and experiences of faculty who teach multicultural counseling courses: An exploratory study. *Training and Education in Professional Psychology, 5*, 167–174. http://dx.doi.org/10.1037/a0024613

Richards, G. (2012). *"Race," racism and psychology: Towards a reflexive history* (2nd ed.). New York, NY: Routledge/Taylor & Francis.

Richardson, F. C., Fowers, B. J., & Guignon, C. B. (1999). *Re-envisioning psychology: Moral dimensions of theory and practice*. San Francisco, CA: Jossey-Bass.

Richman, J. A., Gaviria, M., Flaherty, J. A., Birz, S., & Wintrob, R. M. (1987). The process of acculturation: Theoretical perspectives and an empirical investigation in Peru. *Social Science & Medicine, 25*, 839–847. http://dx.doi.org/10.1016/0277-9536(87)90042-6

Ridley, C. R., Espelage, D. L., & Rubinstein, K. J. (1997). Course development in multicultural counseling. In D. B. Pope-Davis & H. L. K. Coleman (Eds.), *Multicultural counseling competencies: Assessment, education and training, and supervision* (pp. 131–158). Thousand Oaks, CA: Sage. http://dx.doi.org/10.4135/9781452232072.n6

Ridley, C. R., Mendoza, D. W., & Kanitz, B. E. (1994). Multicultural training: Reexamination, operationalization, and integration. *The Counseling Psychologist, 22,* 227–289. http://dx.doi.org/10.1177/0011000094222001

Ridley, C. R., Mollen, D., & Kelly, S. M. (2011a). Beyond microskills: Toward a model of counseling competence. *The Counseling Psychologist, 39,* 825–864. http://dx.doi.org/10.1177/0011000010378440

Ridley, C. R., Mollen, D., & Kelly, S. M. (2011b). Counseling competence: Application and implications of a model. *The Counseling Psychologist, 39,* 865–886. http://dx.doi.org/10.1177/0011000010378443

Ridley, C. R., & Shaw-Ridley, M. (2011). Multicultural counseling competencies: An analysis of research on clients' perceptions: Comment on Owen, Leach, Wampold, and Rodolfa (2011). *Journal of Counseling Psychology, 58,* 16–21. http://dx.doi.org/10.1037/a0022221

Rivera, F. I. (2007). Contextualizing the experience of young Latino adults: Acculturation, social support, and depression. *Journal of Immigrant and Minority Health, 9,* 237–244. http://dx.doi.org/10.1007/s10903-006-9034-6

Robichaud, D. (2006). Steps toward a relational view of agency. In E. J. Van Every (Ed.), *Communication as organizing: Empirical and theoretical explorations in the dynamic of text and conversation* (pp. 101–114). Mahwah, NJ: Erlbaum.

Robinson, D. N. (1995). *An intellectual history of psychology* (3rd ed.). Madison: University of Wisconsin Press.

Rodríguez, N., Mira, C. B., Paez, N. D., & Myers, H. F. (2007). Exploring the complexities of familism and acculturation: Central constructs for people of Mexican origin. *American Journal of Community Psychology, 39,* 61–77. http://dx.doi.org/10.1007/s10464-007-9090-7

Rogers, M. R., & O'Bryon, E. C. (2014). Multicultural training models and curriculum. In F. T. L. Leong, L. Comas-Díaz, G. C. Nagayama Hall, V. C. McLoyd, & J. E. Trimble (Eds.), *APA handbook of multicultural psychology: Vol. 2. Applications and training* (pp. 659–679). Washington, DC: American Psychological Association.

Rogers-Sirin, L. (2008). Approaches to multicultural training for professionals: A guide for choosing an appropriate program. *Professional Psychology: Research and Practice, 39,* 313–319. http://dx.doi.org/10.1037/0735-7028.39.3.313

Rooney, S. C., Flores, L. Y., & Mercier, C. A. (1998). Making multicultural education effective for everyone. *The Counseling Psychologist, 26,* 22–32. http://dx.doi.org/10.1177/0011000098261002

Root, M. P. P. (1994, Summer). Reasons racially mixed persons identify as people of color. *Focus: Notes from the Psychological Study of Ethnic Minority Issues, 8,* 14–16.

Root, M. P. P. (2000). Rethinking racial identity development. In P. Spickard & W. J. Burroughs (Eds.), *We are a people: Narrative and multiplicity in constructing ethnic identity* (pp. 205–220). Philadelphia, PA: Temple University Press.

Rosenstock, I. M. (1966). Why people use health services. *The Milbank Memorial Fund Quarterly, 44,* 94–127. http://dx.doi.org/10.2307/3348967

Rosenthal, R. (1991). Meta-analysis: A review. *Psychosomatic Medicine, 53,* 247–271. http://dx.doi.org/10.1097/00006842-199105000-00001

Rudmin, F. W. (2003). Critical history of the acculturation psychology of assimilation, separation, integration, and marginalization. *Review of General Psychology, 7,* 3–37. http://dx.doi.org/10.1037/1089-2680.7.1.3

Rudmin, F. W. (2009). Constructs, measurements and models of acculturation and acculturative stress. *International Journal of Intercultural Relations, 33,* 106–123. http://dx.doi.org/10.1016/j.ijintrel.2008.12.001

Rudmin, F. W., & Ahmadzadeh, V. (2001). Psychometric critique of acculturation psychology: The case of Iranian migrants in Norway. *Scandinavian Journal of Psychology, 42,* 41–56. http://dx.doi.org/10.1111/1467-9450.00213

Ruglass, L. M., Hien, D. A., Hu, M. C., Campbell, A. N., Caldeira, N. A., Miele, G. M., & Chang, D. F. (2014). Racial/ethnic match and treatment outcomes for women with PTSD and substance use disorders receiving community-based treatment. *Community Mental Health Journal, 50,* 811–822. http://dx.doi.org/10.1007/s10597-014-9732-9

Ryff, C. D., & Keyes, C. L. M. (1995). The structure of psychological well-being revisited. *Journal of Personality and Social Psychology, 69,* 719–727. http://dx.doi.org/10.1037/0022-3514.69.4.719

Salzman, M. (2001). Cultural trauma and recovery: Perspectives from terror management theory. *Trauma, Violence, & Abuse, 2,* 172–191. http://dx.doi.org/10.1177/1524838001002002005

Sarason, S. B. (1974). *The psychological sense of community: Prospects for a community psychology.* Oxford, England: Jossey-Bass.

Schmitt, M. T., Branscombe, N. R., Postmes, T., & Garcia, A. (2014). The consequences of perceived discrimination for psychological well-being: A meta-analytic review. *Psychological Bulletin, 140,* 921–948. http://dx.doi.org/10.1037/a0035754

Schnittker, J., & McLeod, J. D. (2005). The social psychology of health disparities. *Annual Review of Sociology, 31,* 75–103. http://dx.doi.org/10.1146/annurev.soc.30.012703.110622

Schwartz, S. J., Pantin, H., Sullivan, S., Prado, G., & Szapocznik, J. (2006). Nativity and years in the receiving culture as markers of acculturation in ethnic enclaves. *Journal of Cross-Cultural Psychology, 37,* 345–353. http://dx.doi.org/10.1177/0022022106286928

Schwartz, S. J., Unger, J. B., Zamboanga, B. L., & Szapocznik, J. (2010). Rethinking the concept of acculturation: Implications for theory and research. *American Psychologist, 65,* 237–251. http://dx.doi.org/10.1037/a0019330

Seligman, M. E. P. (2011). *Flourish: A visionary new understanding of happiness and well-being.* New York, NY: Free Press.

Sellers, R. M., & Shelton, J. N. (2003). The role of racial identity in perceived racial discrimination. *Journal of Personality and Social Psychology, 84,* 1079–1092. http://dx.doi.org/10.1037/0022-3514.84.5.1079

Sevig, T., & Etzkorn, J. (2001). Transformative training: A year-long multicultural counseling seminar for graduate students. *Journal of Multicultural Counseling and Development, 29,* 57–72. http://dx.doi.org/10.1002/j.2161-1912.2001.tb00503.x

Sharf, J., Primavera, L. H., & Diener, M. J. (2010). Dropout and therapeutic alliance: A meta-analysis of adult individual psychotherapy. *Psychotherapy: Theory, Research, Practice, Training, 47,* 637–645. http://dx.doi.org/10.1037/a0021175

Sheu, H. B., & Lent, R. W. (2007). Development and initial validation of the Multicultural Counseling Self-Efficacy Scale–Racial Diversity Form. *Psychotherapy: Theory, Research, & Practice, 44,* 30–45. http://dx.doi.org/10.1037/0033-3204.44.1.30

Shin, S., Chow, C., Camacho-Gonsalves, T., Levy, R. J., Allen, I. E., & Leff, H. S. (2005). A meta-analytic review of racial–ethnic matching for African American and Caucasian American clients and clinicians. *Journal of Counseling Psychology, 52,* 45–56. http://dx.doi.org/10.1037/0022-0167.52.1.45

Simons, H. W., Berkowitz, N. N., & Moyer, R. J. (1970). Similarity, credibility, and attitude change: A review and a theory. *Psychological Bulletin, 73,* 1–16. http://dx.doi.org/10.1037/h0028429

Simpson, J. A., & Weiner, E. S. (1989). *The Oxford English dictionary* (2nd ed., Vol. 7). Oxford, England: Clarendon Press.

Sin, N. L., & Lyubomirsky, S. (2009). Enhancing well-being and alleviating depressive symptoms with positive psychology interventions: A practice-friendly meta-analysis. *Journal of Clinical Psychology, 65,* 467–487. http://dx.doi.org/10.1002/jclp.20593

Slife, B. D. (2004). Taking practice seriously: Toward a relational ontology. *Journal of Theoretical and Philosophical Psychology, 24,* 157–178. http://dx.doi.org/10.1037/h0091239

Slife, B. D. (2009). A primer of the values implicit in counseling research methods. *Counseling and Values, 53,* 8–21. http://dx.doi.org/10.1002/j.2161-007X.2009.tb00110.x

Slife, B. D., & Wiggins, B. J. (2009). Taking relationship seriously in psychotherapy: Radical relationality. *Journal of Contemporary Psychotherapy, 39,* 17–24. http://dx.doi.org/10.1007/s10879-008-9100-6

Slife, B. D., & Williams, R. (1995). *What's behind the research? Discovering hidden assumptions in the behavioral sciences.* Thousand Oaks, CA: Sage. http://dx.doi.org/10.4135/9781483327372

Smith, T. B. (2010). Culturally congruent practices in counseling and psychotherapy: A review of research. In J. G. Ponterotto, J. M. Casas, L. A. Suzuki, & C. M. Alexander (Eds.), *Handbook of multicultural counseling* (3rd ed., pp. 439–450). Thousand Oaks, CA: Sage.

Smith, T. B., Constantine, M. G., Dunn, T. W., Dinehart, J. M., & Montoya, J. A. (2006). Multicultural education in the mental health professions: A meta-analytic review. *Journal of Counseling Psychology, 53*, 132–145. http://dx.doi.org/10.1037/0022-0167.53.1.132

Smith, T. B., & Draper, M. (2004). Understanding individuals in their context: A relational perspective of multicultural counseling and psychotherapy. In T. B. Smith (Ed.), *Practicing multiculturalism: Affirming diversity in counseling and psychology* (pp. 313–323). Boston, MA: Allyn & Bacon.

Smith, T. B., Richards, P. S., Granley, M., & Obiakor, F. (2004). Practicing multiculturalism: An introduction. In T. B. Smith (Ed.), *Practicing multiculturalism: Affirming diversity in counseling and psychology* (pp. 3–16). Boston, MA: Allyn & Bacon.

Smith, T. B., Rodríguez, M. D., & Bernal, G. (2011). Culture. *Journal of Clinical Psychology, 67*, 166–175. http://dx.doi.org/10.1002/jclp.20757

Smith, T. B., & Silva, L. (2011). Ethnic identity and personal well-being of people of color: A meta-analysis. *Journal of Counseling Psychology, 58*, 42–60. http://dx.doi.org/10.1037/a0021528

Smith, W. A., Allen, W. R., & Danley, L. L. (2007). "Assume the position . . . you fit the description": Psychosocial experiences and racial battle fatigue among African American male college students. *American Behavioral Scientist, 51*, 551–578. http://dx.doi.org/10.1177/0002764207307742

Snowden, L. R. (2012). Health and mental health policies' role in better understanding and closing African American–White American disparities in treatment access and quality of care. *American Psychologist, 67*, 524–531. http://dx.doi.org/10.1037/a0030054

Snowden, L. R., Storey, C., & Clancy, T. (1989). Ethnicity and continuation in treatment at a Black community mental health center. *Journal of Community Psychology, 17*, 111–118. http://dx.doi.org/10.1002/1520-6629(198904)17:2<111::AID-JCOP2290170202>3.0.CO;2-2

Snowden, L. R., & Yamada, A. M. (2005). Cultural differences in access to care. *Annual Review of Clinical Psychology, 1*, 143–166. http://dx.doi.org/10.1146/annurev.clinpsy.1.102803.143846

Social Science Research Council. (1954). Acculturation: An exploratory formulation. *American Anthropologist, 56*, 973–1002.

Soheilian, S. S., Inman, A. G., Klinger, R. S., Isenberg, D. S., & Kulp, L. E. (2014). Multicultural supervision: Supervisees' reflections on culturally competent supervision. *Counselling Psychology Quarterly, 27*, 379–392. http://dx.doi.org/10.1080/09515070.2014.961408

Spanierman, L. B., Oh, E., Heppner, P. P., Neville, H. A., Mobley, M., Wright, C. V., . . . Navarro, R. (2011). The multicultural teaching competency scale: Development and initial validation. *Urban Education, 46*, 440–464. http://dx.doi.org/10.1177/0042085910377442

Spanierman, L. B., Poteat, V. P., Wang, Y., & Oh, E. (2008). Psychosocial costs of racism to White counselors: Predicting various dimensions of multicultural counseling competence. *Journal of Counseling Psychology, 55,* 75–88. http://dx.doi.org/10.1037/0022-0167.55.1.75

Speight, S. L., & Vera, E. M. (2004). A social justice agenda: Ready, or not? *The Counseling Psychologist, 32,* 109–118. http://dx.doi.org/10.1177/0011000003260005

Spindler, L., & Spindler, G. (1967). Male and female adaptations in culture change: Menominee. In R. Hunt (Ed.), *Personalities & cultures* (pp. 56–78). New York, NY: Natural History Press.

Stapel, D. A., & Koomen, W. (2001). I, we, and the effects of others on me: How self-construal level moderates social comparison effects. *Journal of Personality and Social Psychology, 80,* 766–781. http://dx.doi.org/10.1037/0022-3514.80.5.766

Statistics Canada. (2011). *2011 census profile.* Retrieved from http://www12.statcan.gc.ca

Steele, C. (2010). *Whistling Vivaldi: And other clues to how stereotypes affect us.* New York, NY: Norton.

Steffen, P. R., Smith, T. B., Larson, M., & Butler, L. (2006). Acculturation to Western society as a risk factor for high blood pressure: A meta-analytic review. *Psychosomatic Medicine, 68,* 386–397. http://dx.doi.org/10.1097/01.psy.0000221255.48190.32

Steinberg, S. (1981). *The ethnic myth: Race, ethnicity, and class in America.* New York, NY: Atheneum.

Stephan, C. W., & Stephan, W. G. (2000). The measurement of racial and ethnic identity. *International Journal of Intercultural Relations, 24,* 541–552. http://dx.doi.org/10.1016/S0147-1767(00)00016-X

Sue, D. W. (2005). Racism and the conspiracy of silence. *The Counseling Psychologist, 33,* 100–114. http://dx.doi.org/10.1177/0011000004270686

Sue, D. W. (2013). Race talk: The psychology of racial dialogues. *American Psychologist, 68,* 663–672. http://dx.doi.org/10.1037/a0033681

Sue, D. W. (2015). *Race talk and the conspiracy of silence: Understanding and facilitating difficult dialogues on race.* New York, NY: Wiley.

Sue, D. W., Arredondo, P., & McDavis, R. J. (1992a). Multicultural competencies/standards: A pressing need. *Journal of Counseling and Development, 70,* 477–486.

Sue, D. W., Arredondo, P., & McDavis, R. J. (1992b). Multicultural counseling competencies and standards: A call to the profession. *Journal of Multicultural Counseling and Development, 20,* 64–88. http://dx.doi.org/10.1002/j.2161-1912.1992.tb00563.x

Sue, D. W., Bernier, J. E., Durran, A., Feinberg, L., Pedersen, P., Smith, E. J., & Vasquez-Nuttall, E. (1982). Position paper: Cross-cultural counseling competencies. *The Counseling Psychologist, 10,* 45–52. http://dx.doi.org/10.1177/0011000082102008

Sue, D. W., Bingham, R. P., Porché-Burke, L., & Vasquez, M. (1999). The diversification of psychology: A multicultural revolution. *American Psychologist, 54,* 1061–1069. http://dx.doi.org/10.1037/0003-066X.54.12.1061

Sue, D. W., Capodilupo, C. M., Torino, G. C., Bucceri, J. M., Holder, A. M. B., Nadal, K. L., & Esquilin, M. (2007). Racial microaggressions in everyday life:

Implications for clinical practice. *American Psychologist, 62,* 271–286. http://dx.doi.org/10.1037/0003-066X.62.4.271

Sue, D. W., & Sue, D. (2013). *Counseling the culturally diverse: Theory and practice* (6th ed.). Hoboken, NJ: Wiley.

Sue, S. (1977). Community mental health services to minority groups. Some optimism, some pessimism. *American Psychologist, 32,* 616–624. http://dx.doi.org/10.1037/0003-066X.32.8.616

Sue, S. (1988). Psychotherapeutic services for ethnic minorities. Two decades of research findings. *American Psychologist, 43,* 301–308. http://dx.doi.org/10.1037/0003-066X.43.4.301

Sue, S. (1998). In search of cultural competence in psychotherapy and counseling. *American Psychologist, 53,* 440–448. http://dx.doi.org/10.1037/0003-066X.53.4.440

Sue, S. (1999). Science, ethnicity, and bias: Where have we gone wrong? *American Psychologist, 54,* 1070–1077. http://dx.doi.org/10.1037/0003-066X.54.12.1070

Sue, S. (2003). In defense of cultural competency in psychotherapy and treatment. *American Psychologist, 58,* 964–970. http://dx.doi.org/10.1037/0003-066X.58.11.964

Sue, S. (2010). Cultural adaptations in treatment. *The Scientific Review of Mental Health Practice, 7*(2), 31–32.

Sue, S., Cheng, J. K. Y., Saad, C. S., & Chu, J. P. (2012). Asian American mental health: A call to action. *American Psychologist, 67,* 532–544. http://dx.doi.org/10.1037/a0028900

Sue, S., Fujino, D. C., Hu, L., Takeuchi, D. T., & Zane, N. W. S. (1991). Community mental health services for ethnic minority groups: A test of the cultural responsiveness hypothesis. *Journal of Consulting and Clinical Psychology, 59,* 533–540. http://dx.doi.org/10.1037/0022-006X.59.4.533

Sue, S., & Okazaki, S. (2009). Asian-American educational achievements: A phenomenon in search of an explanation. *Asian American Journal of Psychology, 1,* 45–55. http://dx.doi.org/10.1037/1948-1985.S.1.45

Sue, S., & Zane, N. (1987). The role of culture and cultural techniques in psychotherapy. A critique and reformulation. *American Psychologist, 42,* 37–45. http://dx.doi.org/10.1037/0003-066X.42.1.37

Sue, S., Zane, N., Levant, R. F., Silverstein, L. B., Brown, L. S., Olkin, R., & Taliaferro, G. (2006). How well do both evidence-based practices and treatment as usual satisfactorily address the various dimensions of diversity? In J. C. Norcross, L. E. Beutler, & R. F. Levant (Eds.), *Therapy in the real world: Effective treatments for challenging problems* (pp. 329–374). Washington, DC: American Psychological Association.

Sue, S., Zane, N., Nagayama Hall, G. C., & Berger, L. K. (2009). The case for cultural competency in psychotherapeutic interventions. *Annual Review of Psychology, 60,* 525–548. http://dx.doi.org/10.1146/annurev.psych.60.110707.163651

Suinn, R. M., Khoo, G., & Ahuna, C. (1995). The Suinn-Lew Asian Self-Identity Acculturation Scale: Cross-cultural information. *Journal of Multicultural Counsel-*

ing and Development, 23, 139–148. http://dx.doi.org/10.1002/j.2161-1912.1995. tb00269.x

Suls, J., Martin, R., & Wheeler, L. (2002). Social comparison: Why, with whom, and with what effect? Current Directions in Psychological Science, 11, 159–163. http://dx.doi.org/10.1111/1467-8721.00191

Sussman, L. K., Robins, L. N., & Earls, F. (1987). Treatment-seeking for depression by Black and White Americans. Social Science & Medicine, 24, 187–196. http://dx.doi.org/10.1016/0277-9536(87)90046-3

Swartz, M. S., Wagner, H. R., Swanson, J. W., Burns, B. J., George, L. K., & Padgett, D. K. (1998). Administrative update: Utilization of services comparing use of public and private mental health services: The enduring barriers of race and age. Community Mental Health Journal, 34, 133–144.

Swift, J. K., & Callahan, J. L. (2011). Decreasing treatment dropout by addressing expectations for treatment length. Psychotherapy Research, 21, 193–200. http://dx.doi.org/10.1080/10503307.2010.541294

Swift, J. K., Callahan, J. L., & Levine, J. C. (2009). Using clinically significant change to identify premature termination. Psychotherapy: Theory, Research, Practice, Training, 46, 328–335. http://dx.doi.org/10.1037/a0017003

Swift, J. K., & Greenberg, R. P. (2012). Premature discontinuation in adult psychotherapy: A meta-analysis. Journal of Consulting and Clinical Psychology, 80, 547–559. http://dx.doi.org/10.1037/a0028226

Tajfel, H. (1982). Social identity and intergroup relations. Cambridge, England: Cambridge University Press.

Tajfel, H. (2010). Social identity and intergroup relations (Vol. 7). Cambridge, England: Cambridge University Press.

Talebi, H. (2006). An examination of differences in time to treatment, pretreatment symptomatology, and attrition rates in a sample of maltreated European American and Latino youth (Unpublished doctoral dissertation). University of California, Santa Barbara.

Tesser, A., & Campbell, J. (1982). Self-evaluation maintenance and the perception of friends and strangers. Journal of Personality, 50, 261–279. http://dx.doi.org/10.1111/j.1467-6494.1982.tb00750.x

Thomas, K. C., & Snowden, L. R. (2001). Minority response to health insurance coverage for mental health services. Journal of Mental Health Policy and Economics, 4, 35–41.

Thompson, C. E., & Neville, H. A. (1999). Racism, mental health, and mental health practice. The Counseling Psychologist, 27, 155–223. http://dx.doi.org/10.1177/0011000099272001

Thompson, R. H. (1989). Theories of ethnicity: A critical appraisal. New York, NY: Greenwood Press.

Tomlinson-Clarke, S., & Clarke, D. (2010). Culturally focused community-centered service learning: An international cultural immersion experience. Journal of Multicultural Counseling and Development, 38, 166–175. http://dx.doi.org/10.1002/j.2161-1912.2010.tb00124.x

Toporek, R. (Ed.). (2006). *Handbook for social justice in counseling psychology: Leadership, vision, and action*. Thousand Oaks, CA: Sage.

Toporek, R. L., Gerstein, L. H., Fouad, N. A., Roysircar, G., & Israel, T. (Eds.). (2006). *Handbook for social justice in counseling psychology: Leadership, vision, and action*. Thousand Oaks, CA: Sage.

Toporek, R. L., & Vaughn, S. R. (2010). Social justice in the training of professional psychologists: Moving forward. *Training and Education in Professional Psychology, 4*, 177–182. http://dx.doi.org/10.1037/a0019874

Torres, L. (2010). Predicting levels of Latino depression: Acculturation, acculturative stress, and coping. *Cultural Diversity and Ethnic Minority Psychology, 16*, 256–263. http://dx.doi.org/10.1037/a0017357

Totikidis, V., & Prilleltensky, I. (2006). Engaging community in a cycle of praxis: Multicultural perspectives on personal, relational, and collective wellness. *Community, Work & Family, 9*, 47–67. http://dx.doi.org/10.1080/13668800500420889

Tran, N., & Birman, D. (2010). Questioning the model minority: Studies of Asian American academic performance. *Asian American Journal of Psychology, 1*, 106–118. http://dx.doi.org/10.1037/a0019965

Triandis, H. C. (1976). *Variations in Black and White perceptions of the social environment*. Oxford, England: University of Illinois Press.

Triandis, H. C., Kashima, Y., Shimada, E., & Villareal, M. (1986). Acculturation indices as a means of confirming cultural differences. *International Journal of Psychology, 21*, 43–70. http://dx.doi.org/10.1080/00207598608247575

Trickett, E. J., & Espino, S. L. (2004). Collaboration and social inquiry: Multiple meanings of a construct and its role in creating useful and valid knowledge. *American Journal of Community Psychology, 34*, 1–69. http://dx.doi.org/10.1023/B:AJCP.0000040146.32749.7d

Trimble, J. E. (1988). Multilinearity of acculturation: Person–situation interactions. In D. Keats, D. Munro, & L. Mann (Eds.), *Heterogeneity in cross-cultural psychology* (pp. 173–186). Berwyn, PA: Swets & Zeitlinger.

Trimble, J. E. (1990). Ethnic specification, validation prospects, and the future of drug use research. *International Journal of the Addictions, 25*, 149–168.

Trimble, J. E. (1995). Ethnic minorities. In R. Coombs & D. Ziedonis (Eds.), *Handbook on drug abuse prevention: A comprehensive strategy to prevent the abuse of alcohol and other drugs* (pp. 379–410). Needham Heights, MA: Allyn & Bacon.

Trimble, J. E. (2000). Social psychological perspectives on changing self-identification among American Indians and Alaska Natives. In R. H. Dana (Ed.), *Handbook of cross-cultural and multicultural personality assessment* (pp. 197–222). Mahwah, NJ: Erlbaum.

Trimble, J. E. (2005). An inquiry into the measurement of racial and ethnic identity. In R. Carter (Ed.), *Handbook of racial–cultural psychology and counseling: Theory and research* (Vol. 1, pp. 320–359). New York, NY: Wiley.

Trimble, J. E. (2007). Prolegomena for the connotation of construct use in the measurement of ethnic and racial identity. *Journal of Counseling Psychology, 54*, 247–258. http://dx.doi.org/10.1037/0022-0167.54.3.247

Trimble, J. E., & Bagwell, W. (Eds.). (1995). *North American Indians and Alaska Natives: Abstracts of psychological and behavioral literature, 1967–1995*. Washington, DC: American Psychological Association.

Trimble, J. E., & Bhadra, M. (2013). Ethnic gloss. In K. Keith (Ed.), *Encyclopedia of cross-cultural psychology* (pp. 500–504). New York, NY: Wiley. http://dx.doi.org/10.1002/9781118339893.wbeccp204

Trimble, J. E., & Dickson, R. (2005). Ethnic identity. In C. B. Fisher & R. M. Lerner (Eds.), *Applied developmental science: An encyclopedia of research, policies, and programs*. Thousand Oaks: Sage. http://dx.doi.org/10.4135/9781412950565.n160

Trimble, J. E., Helms, J. E., & Root, M. P. (2002). Social and psychological perspectives on ethnic and racial identity. In G. Bernal, J. Trimble, K. Burlew, & F. Leong (Eds.), *Handbook of racial and ethnic minority psychology* (pp. 239–275). Thousand Oaks, CA: Sage.

Trimble, J. E., King, J., Morse, G. S., & Thomas, L. R. (2014). North American Indian and Alaska Native spirituality and psychotherapy. In P. S. Richards (Ed.), *Handbook of psychotherapy and religious diversity* (2nd ed.). Washington, DC: American Psychological Association.

Trimble, J. E., & Mohatt, G. V. (2006). Coda: The virtuous and responsible researcher in another culture. In J. E. Trimble & C. B. Fisher (Eds.), *Handbook of ethical and responsible research with ethnocultural populations and communities* (pp. 325–334). Thousand Oaks, CA: Sage.

Trimble, J. E., Scharrón-del-Río, M. R., & Hill, J. S. (2012). Ethical considerations in the application of cultural adaptation models with ethnocultural populations. In G. Bernal & M. M. D. Rodríguez (Eds.), *Cultural adaptations: Tools for evidence-based practice with diverse populations* (pp. 45–67). Washington, DC: American Psychological Association. http://dx.doi.org/10.1037/13752-003

Trimble, J. E., & Vaughn, L. (2013). Cultural measurement equivalence. In K. Keith (Ed.), *Encyclopedia of cross-cultural psychology* (pp. 313–319). New York, NY: Wiley.

Tsai, J., Ying, Y. W., & Lee, P. A. (2000). The meaning of "being Chinese" and "being American". *Journal of Cross-Cultural Psychology, 31*, 302–332. http://dx.doi.org/10.1177/0022022100031003002

Tummala-Narra, P. (2009). Teaching on diversity: The mutual influence of students and instructors. *Psychoanalytic Psychology, 26*, 322–334. http://dx.doi.org/10.1037/a0016444

Umaña-Taylor, A. J. (2004). Ethnic identity and self-esteem: Examining the role of social context. *Journal of Adolescence, 27*, 139–146. http://dx.doi.org/10.1016/j.adolescence.2003.11.006

Umaña-Taylor, A. J., & Shin, N. (2007). An examination of ethnic identity and self-esteem with diverse populations: Exploring validation by ethnicity and geography. *Cultural Diversity & Ethnic Minority Psychology, 13*, 178–186.

Umaña-Taylor, A. J., Vargas-Chanes, D., Garcia, C. D., & Gonzales-Backen, M. (2008). A longitudinal examination of Latino adolescents' ethnic identity, coping with discrimination, and self-esteem. *The Journal of Early Adolescence, 28*, 16–50. http://dx.doi.org/10.1177/0272431607308666

U.S. Census Bureau. (2010). *Overview of race and Hispanic origin, 2010*. Washington, DC: Government Printing Office.

U.S. Census Bureau. (2011). *Income, poverty, and health insurance coverage in the United States: 2010*. Retrieved from http://www.census.gov/prod/2011pubs/p60-239.pdf

U.S. Department of Health and Human Services, Office of the Surgeon General. (2001). *Mental health: Culture, race, and ethnicity—A supplement to mental health: A report of the Surgeon General*. Rockville, MD: Author.

Utsey, S. O., Grange, C., & Allyne, R. (2006). Guidelines for evaluating the racial and cultural environment of graduate training programs in professional psychology. In M. G. Constantine & D. W. Sue (Eds.), *Addressing racism: Facilitating cultural competence in mental health and educational settings* (pp. 213–232). Hoboken, NJ: Wiley.

Valentine, A., DeAngelo, D., Alegría, M., & Cook, B. L. (2014). Translating disparities research to policy: A qualitative study of state mental health policymakers' perceptions of mental health care disparities report cards. *Psychological Services, 11*, 377–387. http://dx.doi.org/10.1037/a0037978

van den Berghe, P. (1981). *The ethnic phenomenon*. New York, NY: Elsevier.

van Loon, A., van Schaik, A., Dekker, J., & Beekman, A. (2013). Bridging the gap for ethnic minority adult outpatients with depression and anxiety disorders by culturally adapted treatments. *Journal of Affective Disorders, 147*, 9–16. http://dx.doi.org/10.1016/j.jad.2012.12.014

Vasquez, M. J. T. (2012). Psychology and social justice: Why we do what we do. *American Psychologist, 67*, 337–346. http://dx.doi.org/10.1037/a0029232

Vera, E. M., & Speight, S. L. (2003). Multicultural competence, social justice, and counseling psychology: Expanding our roles. *The Counseling Psychologist, 31*, 253–272. http://dx.doi.org/10.1177/0011000003031003001

Vereen, L. G., Hill, N. R., & McNeal, D. T. (2008). Perceptions of multicultural counseling competency: Integration of the curricular and the practical. *Journal of Mental Health Counseling, 30*, 226–236.

Vinokurov, A., Trickett, E. J., & Birman, D. (2002). Acculturative hassles and immigrant adolescents: A life-domain assessment for Soviet Jewish refugees. *The Journal of Social Psychology, 142*, 425–445. http://dx.doi.org/10.1080/00224540209603910

Wachtel, P. L. (2008). *Relational theory and the practice of psychotherapy*. New York, NY: Guilford Press.

Walker, I., & Smith, H. J. (Eds.). (2001). *Relative deprivation: Specification, development, and integration*. West Nyack, NJ: Cambridge University Press. http://dx.doi.org/10.1017/CBO9780511527753

Waters, M. C. (1990). *Ethnic options: Choosing identities in America*. Berkeley: University of California Press.

Watkins, M. P., & Portney, L. G. (2009). *Foundations of clinical research: Applications to practice* (3rd ed.). New York, NY: Pearson/Prentice Hall.

Webb, C. A., DeRubeis, R. J., & Barber, J. P. (2010). Therapist adherence/competence and treatment outcome: A meta-analytic review. *Journal of Consulting and Clinical Psychology, 78*, 200–211. http://dx.doi.org/10.1037/a0018912

Weinrach, S. G., & Thomas, K. R. (2002). A critical analysis of the multicultural counseling competencies: Implications for the practice of mental health counseling. *Journal of Mental Health Counseling, 24*, 20–35.

Weinrach, S. G., & Thomas, K. R. (2004). The AMCD multicultural counseling competencies: A critically flawed initiative. *Journal of Mental Health Counseling, 26*, 81–93.

Weinreich, P. (1986). The operationalization of identity theory in racial and ethnic relations. In J. Rex & D. Mason (Eds.), *Theories of race and ethnic relations* (pp. 299–320). Cambridge, England: Cambridge University Press. http://dx.doi.org/10.1017/CBO9780511557828.016

Weinreich, P., & Saunderson, W. (Eds.). (2003). *Analyzing identity: Cross-cultural, societal, and clinical contexts*. New York, NY: Routledge.

Weissman, M. M., Markowitz, J. C., & Klerman, G. L. (2000). *Comprehensive guide to interpersonal psychotherapy*. New York, NY: Basic Books.

Wendt, D. C., Gone, J., & Nagata, D. (2014). Potentially harmful therapy and multicultural counseling: Bridging two disciplinary discourses. *The Counseling Psychologist*. http://dx.doi.org/10.1177/0011000014548280

Whaley, A. L. (2001). Cultural mistrust and mental health services for African Americans: A review and meta-analysis. *The Counseling Psychologist, 29*, 513–531. http://dx.doi.org/10.1177/0011000001294003

Whitbeck, L. B. (2006). Some guiding assumptions and a theoretical model for developing culturally specific preventions with Native American people. *Journal of Community Psychology, 34*, 183–192. http://dx.doi.org/10.1002/jcop.20094

Whiting, B. B. (1963). *Six cultures: Studies of child rearing*. Oxford, England: Wiley.

Wierzbicki, M., & Pekarik, G. (1993). A meta-analysis of psychotherapy dropout. *Professional Psychology: Research and Practice, 24*, 190–195. http://dx.doi.org/10.1037/0735-7028.24.2.190

Williams, D. R., & Mohammed, S. A. (2009). Discrimination and racial disparities in health: Evidence and needed research. *Journal of Behavioral Medicine, 32*, 20–47. http://dx.doi.org/10.1007/s10865-008-9185-0

Williams, D. R., Neighbors, H. W., & Jackson, J. S. (2003). Racial/ethnic discrimination and health: Findings from community studies. *American Journal of Public Health, 93*, 200–208. http://dx.doi.org/10.2105/AJPH.93.2.200

Williams, R. N. (1992). The human context of agency. *American Psychologist, 47*, 752–760. http://dx.doi.org/10.1037/0003-066X.47.6.752

Wong, P. T. P. (2011). Positive psychology 2.0: Towards a balanced interactive model of the good life. *Canadian Psychology/Psychologie Canadienne, 52,* 69–81. http://dx.doi.org/10.1037/a0022511

Worthington, R. L., & Dillon, F. R. (2011). Deconstructing multicultural counseling competencies research: Comment on Owen, Leach, Wampold, and Rodolfa (2011). *Journal of Counseling Psychology, 58,* 10–15. http://dx.doi.org/10.1037/a0022177

Worthington, R. L., Hart, J., & Khairallah, T. S. (2010). Counselors as diversity change agents in higher education. In J. G. Ponterotto, J. M. Casas, L. A. Suzuki, & C. M. Alexander (Eds.), *Handbook of multicultural counseling* (3rd ed., pp. 563–576). Thousand Oaks, CA: Sage.

Worthington, R. L., Soth-McNett, A. M., & Moreno, M. V. (2007). Multicultural counseling competencies research: A 20-year content analysis. *Journal of Counseling Psychology, 54,* 351–361. http://dx.doi.org/10.1037/0022-0167.54.4.351

Yap, S. C. Y., Settles, I. H., & Pratt-Hyatt, J. S. (2011). Mediators of the relationship between racial identity and life satisfaction in a community sample of African American women and men. *Cultural Diversity and Ethnic Minority Psychology, 17,* 89–97. http://dx.doi.org/10.1037/a0022535

Yeh, C. J. (2003). Age, acculturation, cultural adjustment, and mental health symptoms of Chinese, Korean, and Japanese immigrant youths. *Cultural Diversity & Ethnic Minority Psychology, 9,* 34–48. http://dx.doi.org/10.1037/1099-9809.9.1.34

Yeh, C. J., Parham, T. A., Gallardo, M. E., & Trimble, J. E. (2011). *Culturally adaptive counseling skills: Demonstrations of evidence-based practices.* Thousand Oaks, CA: Sage.

Yeh, M., McCabe, K., Hough, R. L., Lau, A., Fakhry, F., & Garland, A. (2005). Why bother with beliefs? Examining relationships between race/ethnicity, parental beliefs about causes of child problems, and mental health service use. *Journal of Consulting and Clinical Psychology, 73,* 800–807. http://dx.doi.org/10.1037/0022-006X.73.5.800

Yinger, J. M. (1986). Intersecting strands in the theorization of race and ethnic relations. In J. Rex & D. Mason (Eds.), *Theories of race and ethnic relations* (pp. 20–41). Cambridge, England: Cambridge University Press. http://dx.doi.org/10.1017/CBO9780511557828.003

Yip, T., Douglass, S., & Sellers, R. M. (2014). Ethnic and racial identity. In F. T. L. Leong, L. Comas-Díaz, G. C. Nagayama Hall, V. C. McLoyd, & J. E. Trimble (Eds.), *APA handbook of multicultural psychology: Vol. 1. Theory and research* (pp. 179–205). Washington, DC: American Psychological Association.

Yoo, H. C., & Pituc, S. T. (2013). Assessments of perceived racial stereotypes, discrimination, and racism. In K. F. Geisinger, B. A. Bracken, J. F. Carlson, J. C. Hansen, N. R. Kuncel, S. P. Reise, & M. C. Rodriguez (Eds.), *APA handbook of testing and assessment in psychology: Vol. 2. Testing and assessment in clinical and counseling psychology* (pp. 427–451). Washington, DC: American Psychological Association. http://dx.doi.org/10.1037/14048-025

Yoon, E., Chang, C.-T., Kim, S., Clawson, A., Cleary, S. E., Hansen, M., . . . Gomes, A. M. (2013). A meta-analysis of acculturation/enculturation and mental health. *Journal of Counseling Psychology, 60,* 15–30. http://dx.doi.org/10.1037/a0030652

Young, D. M., Sanchez, D. T., & Wilton, L. S. (2013). At the crossroads of race: Racial ambiguity and biracial identification influence psychological essentialist thinking. *Cultural Diversity and Ethnic Minority Psychology, 19,* 461–467. http://dx.doi.org/10.1037/a0032565

Yutrzenka, B. A. (1995). Making a case for training in ethnic and cultural diversity in increasing treatment efficacy. *Journal of Consulting and Clinical Psychology, 63,* 197–206. http://dx.doi.org/10.1037/0022-006X.63.2.197

Zane, N., & Ku, H. (2014). Effects of ethnic match, gender match, acculturation, cultural identity, and face concern on self-disclosure in counseling for Asian Americans. *Asian American Journal of Psychology, 5,* 66–74. http://dx.doi.org/10.1037/a0036078

Zárate, M. A., Quezada, S. A., Shenberger, J. M., & Lupo, A. K. (2014). Reducing racism and prejudice. In F. T. L. Leong, L. Comas-Díaz, G. C. Nagayama Hall, V. C. McLoyd, & J. E. Trimble, (Eds.), *APA handbook of multicultural psychology: Vol. 2. Applications and training* (pp. 593–606). Washington, DC: American Psychological Association. http://dx.doi.org/10.1037/14187-033

Zea, M. C., Asner-Self, K. K., Birman, D., & Buki, L. P. (2003). The abbreviated multidimensional acculturation scale: Empirical validation with two Latino/Latina samples. *Cultural Diversity & Ethnic Minority Psychology, 9,* 107–126.

INDEX

Accountability, in relational
    paradigm, 227
Acculturation, 9, 145–164
    current research on, 241
    enculturation vs., 147
    existing research literature on,
        153–155
    factors influencing research findings
        on, 156–160
    future research on, 161–163
    interpretation of research findings
        on, 160–161
    measurement of, 150–151
    and mental health service
        utilization, 85–86
    need for therapists to consider, 247
    previous research findings on,
        150–153
    recommendations for therapists
        on, 163
    relevant theory on, 147–150
    research findings on, 155–156
Acculturative stress, 145–146
Advocacy
    in multicultural psychology
        literature, 217
    role of, in social justice, 216
African Americans
    and ethnic identity, 189, 190
    increase in research on, 11–12
    mental health service utilization by,
        76–81, 83–87, 90–91
    mistrust of mental health services
        by, 70
    and racial/ethnic matching of clients
        and therapists, 117, 118,
        121, 126
    racism studies with, 171, 179
    treatment attendance by, 104, 108
    treatment completion by, 106, 109,
        241, 248
Age
    and acculturation, 158
    and culturally adapted treatments, 140
    and ethnic identity, 197
Agency, personal, 221

Alaska Natives
    cultural adaptations to treatment
        for, 130
    increase in research on, 12
Alegría, M., 110, 112
Ali, S. R., 23, 44
Allen, J., 190–191
Alvidrez, J., 72
American Indian and Alaska Native
    Mental Health Research, 6
American Psychological Association
    (APA), 6, 21, 25, 52, 127, 143
American Psychologist, 73
Ancis, J. R., 23, 44
Anxiety, 135
APA. See American Psychological
    Association
Aristotle, 220
Aron, A., 220
Arredondo, P., 51
Asian American Journal of Psychology, 6
Asian Americans
    acculturation of, 151
    conceptualization of mental health
        problems among, 68
    culturally adapted treatments with,
        140–141
    importance of ethnic identity to,
        197–198
    increase in research on, 12
    increasing treatment completion
        by, 127
    mental health service utilization by,
        76–81, 84–87, 94, 248
    and racial/ethnic matching of clients
        and therapists, 121, 124–126
    racism studies with, 171, 179
    treatment attendance by, 104, 108
    treatment completion by, 106,
        109, 241
Assumptions
    categorical, 242
    challenging of, 211–212
    embedded in social justice, 216–219
    in psychological research, 236
Austin, R., 21–22

Awareness, as multicultural counseling
    competency, 51

Barrett, M. S., 98
Barth, F., 184–185
Beauvais, F., 187
Becoming, process of, 222
Bernal, M. E., 186
Bernier, J. E., 53
Berry, John W., 148, 149, 213
Best practices, 41
Biases, 51, 63
Binning, K. R., 189
Biopsychosocial model, 169
Birz, S., 151
Bond, Michael, 189
Brislin, R. W., 22
Burns, B. J., 70

Cabassa, L. J., 148–149
Cachelin, F. M., 71, 85
Carter, Robert T., 45, 172, 184, 186
Categorical assumptions, 242
CCCI–R (Cross-Cultural Counseling
    Inventory—Revised), 58
Census estimates, 89
Chao, R. C., 24–25, 26
Chen, S., 71
Cheung, Y. W., 191
Chow, J. C., 71, 72, 93
Clancy, T., 111
Clarkson, P., 223
Client(s)
    access of, to mental health services,
        8–9
    expectations of, 96–98, 99, 113, 163
    as focus of therapy, 14–15
    language spoken by therapists and,
        123–124, 126, 127, 132
    racial heterogeneity of, 89–90
    therapist's multicultural competencies
        rated by, 40, 60–62
Client outcomes
    influenced by therapist's multicultural
        counseling competencies,
        59–60
    need for future research on, 238
Clinical practice, multicultural
    education in, 43–45
Cohen, J., 76, 79, 88, 108

Coleman, M. N., 26
Collectivism
    addressed in treatment, 130
    in relational paradigm, 226
Community, in multicultural
    psychology, 220
Community awareness initiatives, 93
Confucius, 220
Connectedness, in relational
    paradigm, 221
Constantine, M. G., 50
Contextualization, in relational
    paradigm, 221
Cookson, John, 146–147
Corne, S., 220
The Counseling Psychologist, 51
Counseling skills, 62
Critical race theory, 169
Cross-Cultural Counseling Inventory—
    Revised (CCCI–R), 58
Cultural diversity, 7
Cultural Diversity and Ethnic Minority
    Psychology, 6
Cultural Diversity and Mental Health, 6
Culturally adapted mental health
    services, 129–144
    as alternative to traditional
        treatments, 241
    conceptual issues relevant to,
        131–134
    existing research literature on,
        136–138
    future research on, 142–143
    interpretations of findings on,
        141–142
    previous research on, 134–135
    recommendations for therapists
        on, 143
    research findings on, 138–141
    traditional vs., 72, 247
    and treatment completion/
        attrition, 112
Cultural values, 226
Czopp, A. M., 167

Depression, 135
Diala, C., 93
Diener, E., 189, 190, 225
Diener, M., 189

Discrimination
    lack of access to mental health
        services as, 67–68
    as subjective, 170
Draper, M., 224
Durran, A., 53
Dynamic sizing, 132

EBPs. *See* Evidence-based practices
Ecological validity model, 133–134
Einstein, Albert, 243
Emergency mental health services, 72
Empirically supported treatments
    (ESTs), 13
Empowerment
    in multicultural psychology
        literature, 217
    in social justice, 216
    through social network
        integration, 227
Enculturation, 147
Escobar, J., 150
Espino, S. L., 223
ESTs (empirically supported
    treatments), 13
Ethical principles, 223
Ethnic gloss, 9n1, 201–202
Ethnic identity, 181–205
    and acculturation, 151
    complexity in development of, 14
    current research on, 239
    existing literature on, 192, 193
    factors influencing research findings
        on, 194–200
    future research on, 201–203
    interpretation of research findings
        on, 200–201
    measurement of, 185–188
    need for therapists to consider, 247
    origins of constructs of, 182–184
    recommendations for therapists
        on, 204
    relevant theory on, 184–185
    research findings on, 192, 194
    and well-being, 10, 188–191
Ethnicity, race vs., 183
Ethnic matching of clients and therapists.
    See Racial/ethnic matching of
    clients and therapists

Even the Rat Was White (Robert
    Guthrie), 17
Evidence-based practices (EBPs),
    235–248
    cultural adaptations to, 130–131
    focus on essential dependent
        variables in, 236–238
    improving research methods for,
        241–243
    and meta-analyses, 13
    and recommendations for therapists,
        246–248
    theory development for, 243–246
    use of research data in, 238–241
Expectations, in treatment, 96–98,
    113, 163
Expert opinion, 15
External validity, 13–14

Familismo, 52
Family
    including in culturally adapted
        treatment, 130
    mental health problems addressed
        in, 69–70
Feinberg, L., 53
Festinger, L., 168
First Nations peoples, 12
Flaherty, J. A., 151, 186
Flores, L. Y., 24–25
Freire, P., 219

Gans, Herbert, 184
Garland, A. F., 71
Gaviria, M., 151
Gaylord-Harden, N. K., 189
Gaztambide, D. J., 218–219
Geertz, Clifford, 181, 191
George, L. K., 70
Glass, G., 12
Good, G. E., 24–25
Gordon, M. M., 184
Graduate classes, on multiculturalism, 23
Grusec, J. E., 147
Guthrie, Robert, 17

Handbook of Multicultural Psychology, 167
Harrell, S. P., 169
Harris, P. M., 100, 112
Hastings, P. D., 147

Health insurance coverage, 71
Helms, Janet E., 183, 187
Hispanic Journal of Behavioral Sciences, 6
Hispanics and Latinos(as)
    acculturation of, 151
    cultural adaptations to treatment
        for, 130
    and ethnic identity, 190
    heterogeneity among, 116
    increase in research on, 12
    mental health service utilization by,
        76–79, 82, 84–87
    and racial/ethnic matching of clients
        and therapists, 117, 121
    treatment attendance by, 108
    treatment completion by, 106, 109
Holism, in relational paradigm, 221
Homophily, 117
Human behavior, theories
    explaining, 229
Human rights, 222–223
Huo, Y. J., 189

Identity
    continual development of, 222
    defined, 182
    and development of ethnic
        identity, 204
    and social interactions, 224
Identity Structure Analysis (ISA),
    187–188
Imagined ethnicity, 184
Immigration, 146–147
Immigration status, 71
Individualism
    in identity research, 224
    in mental health services, 11
    and social interactions, 226
    and subjective well-being, 189
    valued in Western psychology, 130
Instructors, recommendations for, 41–46
Interactive volition, 221
Internal validity, 13–14
International Association for
    Cross-Cultural Psychology, 6
Intersectionality, 226, 244
ISA (Identity Structure Analysis),
    187–188

Jaffee, K., 71
Jahoda, G., 5

Journal of Black Psychology, 6
Journal of Cross-Cultural Psychology, 6

Kashima, Y., 151
Kazdin, A. E., 111, 130
Kelly, S. M., 40
Keyes, C. L. M., 189
Kiev, Ari, 145
King, Martin Luther, Jr., 232
Knight, G. P., 186
Knowledge, as multicultural counseling
    competency, 51–52
Korean Americans, 190

Ladany, N., 37, 41, 50
Lambert, M. J., 113, 134
Language
    spoken by clients and therapists, 123,
        126, 127, 132
    use of culturally appropriate, 133,
        143
Latinos(as). *See* Hispanics and
    Latinos(as)
"Letter from Birmingham Jail" (Martin
    Luther King Jr.), 232
Local referral networks, 93
López, E. D. S., 190–191, 225

Mandara, J., 189
Mark, A. Y, 167
Martín-Baró, I. M., 220
Marx, Karl, 219
Materialism. *See* Philosophical
    materialism
MCC(s). *See* Multicultural counseling
    competency(-ies)
McLeod, J. D., 169, 170
Mead, Margaret, 209, 213
Measurement
    of acculturation, 150–151
    of ethnic identity, 185–188
    of racism/prejudice, in studies, 178
MEIM (Multigroup Ethnic Identity
    Measure), 187
Mendenhall, M., 149
Mendoza, R., 148
Mental health concerns
    multicultural conceptualizations of,
        68–69
    poverty as risk factor for, 71
    and relational paradigm, 225

Mental Health: Culture, Race, and Ethnicity in 2001, 73
Mental health insurance coverage, 71
Mental health services
    client access to, 8–9
    defined for meta-analyses, 250
    in different locations, 72
    emergency, 72
    improving, for minority populations, 214
    mistrust of, among people of color, 70
    multiculturalism in, 5–6
    private, 72
    public, 72, 86
    public payment of, 90
    studies on race/ethnicity and, 237–238
    theoretical aims of, 214–215
    voluntary vs. involuntary use of, 72
Mental health service utilization, 8–9, 67–94
    existing research literature on, 75–78
    future research on, 91–92
    interpretation of research findings on, 88
    issues of interpretation of findings on, 88
    participant characteristics influencing research on, 84–87
    previous research on, 72–74
    publication bias influencing research on, 79–80
    recommendations for therapists on, 93–94
    relevant theory on, 68–72
    research findings on, 76, 78–79
    secondary analyses of, 89–91
    study characteristics influencing research on, 80–84
Meta-analyses methods, 249–252
    data analyses, 252
    data collection processes, 251–252
    general eligibility criteria, 249–250
    information sources and search strategies, 250–251
Miami Youth Development Project, 223
Molina, L. E., 189
Mollen, D., 40, 42
Morality, problems in studying, 230

Moral sensibility, 222, 231
Moreno, M. V., 53
Moynihan, D. P., 182
Multicultural awareness, 25
Multicultural counseling competency (-ies) (MCC[s]), 49–64
    defined, 21
    evaluation of, 50, 60–62
    existing research literature on, 55, 56
    factors influencing research findings on, 57–60
    as focus of multicultural education, 42–43
    as foundation of multicultural education, 24
    future research on, 60–63
    high expectations for, 43–44
    importance of, 10–11
    previous research on, 53–54
    recommendations for therapists on, 63–64
    relevant theory on, 51–53
    research findings on, 55, 57, 59–60
Multicultural education and training, 21–47
    existing research literature on, 28–30
    factors influencing research findings on, 31–35
    future research on, 39–41
    interpretation of research findings on, 35–36
    previous research on, 23–25
    recommendations for instructors/ program directors on, 41–46
    recommendations for therapists on, 38
    relevant theory on, 22–23
    research findings on, 30–31
    secondary analyses of, 36–38
    trends in recent research on, 25–26
Multiculturalism as a Fourth Force (Paul Pedersen), 213
Multicultural psychology, 3–18, 209–234
    challenges in, 8–11
    conceptual analysis of, 232–234
    defining, 213–214
    importance of multicultural counseling competencies to, 50
    meta-analyses of, 11–15

Multicultural psychology, *continued*
    objectives of, 231
    overview of, 4–8
    philosophy of, 209–215
    and relational paradigm, 219–232
    and social justice, 215–219
    theoretical aims of, 214–215
Multicultural training. *See* Multicultural
        education and training
Multidimensional framework, for
        acculturation, 151
Multiethnic individuals, 202
Multigroup Ethnic Identity Measure
        (MEIM), 187
Mutual edification, 221, 227

Naïve transitivity, 219
National Association for Multicultural
        Education, 41
Native American Indians
    acculturation issues faced by, 162
    and ethnic gloss, 9n1
    importance of ethnic identity to,
        197–198
    increase in research on, 12
Neville, H. A., 169
North America, cultural diversity in, 7

Observer ratings
    of multicultural counseling
            competencies, 62–63
    of multicultural education
            effectiveness, 36–37
Oddou, G., 149
Oetting, E. R., 187
Olmedo, E., 150
Other-affirmation, 231
Other-engagement, 222
Outreach programs, 93

Padgett, D. K., 70, 92, 93
Padilla, A., 151
Participant characteristics, effects of
    acculturation studies, 158–159
    culturally adapted treatment studies,
        140–141
    ethnic identity studies, 196–199
    mental health service utilization
        studies, 84–87
    multicultural education studies, 33

racism studies, 176
    studies on racial/ethnic matching
            of clients and therapists,
            122–124
    treatment participation studies,
            106–107
Participatory action research, 217
Pascoe, A. E., 177
Paz, O., 234
Pedersen, Paul B., 3, 6, 22, 53, 213
Performance evaluations, 45
Philosophical materialism
    influence of, on psychology, 218–219
    relational paradigm vs., 228
Philosophy
    development of, for multicultural
            psychology, 220
    and foundations of multicultural
            psychology, 210–215
Phinney, Jean S., 183–184, 185, 187,
        190, 191
Pieterse, A. L., 177
Ponterotto, J. G., 21–22, 39, 53
Poverty
    and access to mental health
            services, 71
    increasing access to mental health
            services for those in, 214
    and mental health, 245–246
Power
    abuses of, in industrial
            revolution, 219
    and accountability, 227
    inequities in, and mental health,
            245–246
    in multicultural psychology
            literature, 217
    obfuscation of, 218
    sharing of, and multiculturalism, 43
    and social justice, 216
Pratt-Hyatt, J. S., 189
Prejudice. *See* Racism and prejudice
Private mental health services, 72
Program directors, recommendations
        for, 41–46
Pseudo-ethnicity, 184
PsychINFO, 11–12, 237
Psychological distress
    ethnic identity as buffer against, 202
    and racism, 178–179

Psycho-social conceptualism, of racism, 169
Publication bias
  correction of, 41
Publication bias, effects of
  acculturation studies, 160
  culturally adapted treatment studies, 140
  ethnic identity studies, 199–200
  mental health service utilization studies, 79–80
  multicultural counseling competency studies, 58–59
  multicultural education studies, 34–35
  racism studies, 174
  studies on racial/ethnic matching of clients and therapists, 124
  treatment participation studies, 106, 107–108
Public mental health services, 72, 86
Public payment, of mental health services, 90

Questions, value of asking, 210, 212

Race, ethnicity vs., 183
Race-based traumatic stress injury, 170
Racial battle fatigue, 170
Racial diversity, 33, 37–38
Racial/ethnic matching of clients and therapists, 9, 115–128
  as culturally adapted mental health service, 132
  existing research literature on, 119–121
  future research on, 125–126
  interpretation of research findings on, 124–125
  previous research on, 117–119
  recommendations for therapists on, 126–127
  relevant theory on, 117
  research findings across racial groups, 121–124
Racial groups
  differing mental illness rates among, 70
  heterogeneity in, 14
  socioeconomic differences among, 71

Racial identity, 183. *See also* Ethnic identity
Racism and prejudice, 167–180
  existing literature on, 172–174
  factors influencing research findings on, 174–176
  future research on, 178–179
  interpretations of research findings on, 176–177
  measurement of, in studies, 178
  need for therapists to consider, 247
  previous research on, 169–172
  recommendations for therapists on handling, 179–180
  relevant theory on, 168–169
  research findings on, 174
  secondary analyses of, 177
  and well-being, 10
Ragsdale, B. L., 189
Rawls, J., 215–216
Relational paradigm, 219–232
  assumptions and limitations of, 228–232
  benefits to multicultural psychology from, 223–228
  defining, 220–221
  philosophical materialism vs., 228
  social justice reconceptualized through, 219–223
Relationships
  importance of, in relational paradigm, 220
  influence of, on identity, 224
  and social change, 226
Relative deprivation theory, 168
Research data, 15
Research design, 242–243
Responsibility to others, 222, 227
Retrospective surveys, 40–41
Richards, M. H., 189
Richman, J. A., 151, 171, 176
Ridley, C. R., 22–23, 40, 42
Rights, human, 222–223
Rivkin, I. D., 190–191
Root, M. P. P., 188
Rural areas, mental health services in, 72
Ryff, C. D., 189

Saenz, D. S., 186
Salzman, M., 163

Saunderson, W., 188
Schmitt, M. T., 176–177
Schnittker, J., 169, 170
Self-affirmation, 231
Self-concept
    as a fluid pattern, 222
    and identity, 182
Self-esteem, 196, 202, 204
Self-in-relation, 222
Self-report surveys
    for evaluation of multicultural
        counseling competencies, 50
    in multicultural psychology
        research, 243
    used in multicultural education
        studies, 40–41
    validity of, 62
Seligman, M. E. P., 189
Sellers, R. M., 170
Settles, I. H., 189
Shelton, J. N., 170
Shimada, E., 151
Silva, L., 192, 210, 232
Simpson, J. A., 182
Skill development, 24
Skills, as multicultural counseling
    competency, 52–53
Smart Richman, L., 177
Smith, E. J., 53
Smith, T. B., 26, 192, 224
Snowden, L. R., 71, 111
Social change, 226
Social comparison theory, 168
Social identity theory, 186–187,
    202, 203
Social interactions
    and identity, 224
    and individualism, 226
Social justice, 215–223
    assumptions embedded in, 216–219
    as central to multicultural
        psychology, 215–216
    defining, 215–216
    and multicultural psychology,
        215–219
    as objective of therapists, 215
    real-world applications of, 232
    reconceptualization of, through
        relational paradigm, 219–223
    as value, 230

Social networks
    advances in research on, 229
    empowerment through integration
        of, 227
    negative outcomes due to lack of, 221
Social psychology, 117
Social science, 182–183
Social Science Research Council, 147
Socioeconomic factors
    in access to mental health services, 71
    in treatment completion/
        attrition, 111
Sociorace, 183
Soth-McNett, A. M., 53
Standardized approaches,
    in treatment, 11
Steele, C., 169
Stephan, C. W., 186
Stephan, W. G., 186
Stigma, associated with mental health
    service utilization, 70, 90–91
Storey, C., 111
Striegel-Moore, R. H., 71
Study characteristics, effects of
    acculturation studies, 156–158
    culturally adapted treatment studies,
        140–141
    ethnic identity studies, 194–196
    mental health service utilization
        studies, 80–84
    multicultural education studies,
        31–33
    racism studies, 174–176
    studies on racial/ethnic matching
        of clients and therapists,
        122–124
    treatment participation studies,
        106–107
Subjective well-being, 188
Suburban areas, mental health services
    in, 72
Sue, D. W., 51, 53
Sue, S., 94, 132
Swanson, J. W., 70
Swartz, M. S., 70

Tajfel, H., 186–187, 202
Teacher education, 41
Theoretical basis, of multicultural
    education, 37

Theory development, research on, 243–246
Therapeutic alliance
  and effectiveness of treatment, 223
  as factor in treatment completion/attrition, 98
Therapists
  acculturation recommendations for, 163
  cultural awareness of, 51
  cultural knowledge of, 51–52
  culturally adapted mental health services recommendations for, 143
  cultural resources available to, 134
  ethnic identity recommendations for, 204
  evidence-based practice recommendations for, 246–248
  implicit biases of, 51, 63
  language spoken by clients and, 123, 126, 127, 132
  mental health service utilization recommendations for, 93–94
  multicultural concerns of, 17–18
  multicultural counseling competencies of, 52–53, 63–64
  multicultural education of, 38
  racial/ethnic matching of clients and therapists, 126–127
  and racism/prejudice in clients, 179–180
  social justice as objective of, 215
  treatment participation recommendations for, 112–113
Tov, W., 190
Traditional mental health services
  addressing cultural factors in, 134
  contextual variables minimized in, 130
  culturally adapted vs., 72, 247
Trauma, 225
Treatment attendance, 97, 110. See also Treatment participation
Treatment completion/attrition, 97–99. See also Treatment participation
  measures of, 111
  and racial/ethnic matching of clients and therapists, 118
  treatment attendance vs., 110

Treatment goals, client-generated, 143
Treatment participation, 8–9, 95–114
  existing research literature on, 102, 103
  future research on, 110–112
  interpretation of research findings on, 108–110
  need to future research on, 238
  previous research on, 97–101
  recommendations for therapists on, 112–113
  relevant theory on, 96–97
  research findings across measures of, 102, 104–108
  and therapist's multicultural competence, 100
Triandis, H. C., 151
Trickett, E. J., 223
Trimble, J. E., 148
Tripartite model, of multicultural counseling competencies, 51

Universalism
  and culturally adapted mental health services, 130–131
  in mental health services, 5
  in multicultural education, 23
Unzueta, M. M, 189
Urban areas, mental health services in, 72

Value(s)
  promotion of, 231
  social justice as, 230
Van den Berghe, Pierre, 185
Vasquez-Nuttall, E., 53
Vega, W., 150
Villareal, M., 151
Volition, interactive, 221

Wagner, H. R., 70
Walzer, A. S., 167
Waters, M. C., 187
We-consciousness, 222
Wei, M., 24–25
Weiner, E. S., 182
Weinreich, P., 187–188
WEIRD (Western, educated, industrialized, rich, and democratic) populations, 17

Well-being
    and ethnic identity, 10, 188–191, 198
    and racism, 10, 170, 176–177
    and relational paradigm, 225
    subjective, 188
*White Cloud Journal of American Indian/
    Alaska Native Mental Health*, 6
White/European Americans and
    Canadians
    and ethnic identity, 190
    mental service utilization by, 76–79
    as normative reference group, 74, 101
    and racial/ethnic matching of clients
        and therapists, 127
Wintrob, R. M., 151

Wong, P. T. P., 190
Workplace programs, for multicultural
    education and training, 40
Worldviews
    and acculturation, 146
    culturally adapted treatments
        considering, 132–133, 143, 241
    and racial/ethnic matching of clients
        and therapists, 116, 125–126
    in relational paradigm, 226
Worthington, R. L., 53

Yap, S. C. Y., 189
Yip, T., 186–187, 188
Yoon, Eunju, 152

ABOUT THE AUTHORS

Timothy B. Smith, PhD, is a professor and department chair of the Department of Counseling Psychology at Brigham Young University in Provo, Utah. His research on multicultural psychology, spirituality, and quality relationships has received several national awards, including from Division 45 (Society for the Psychological Study of Culture, Ethnicity and Race) of the American Psychological Association (APA). He is a Fulbright Scholar and a Fellow of APA (Division 17, Society of Counseling Psychology).

Joseph E. Trimble, PhD, is a Distinguished University Professor and professor of psychology at Western Washington University and a President's Professor at the Center for Alaska Native Health Research at the University of Alaska Fairbanks. He has written over 140 publications on multicultural topics in psychology, including 20 books. His excellence in teaching and research awards for his work in the field of multicultural psychology include the Janet E. Helms Award for Mentoring and Scholarship in Professional Psychology; the Distinguished Elder Award from the National Multicultural Conference and Summit; the Henry Tomes Award for Distinguished Contributions to the

Advancement of Ethnic Minority Psychology; the International Lifetime Achievement Award for Multicultural and Diversity Counseling awarded by the University of Toronto's Ontario Institute for Studies in Education; the 2013 Francis J. Bonner, MD Award from the Department of Psychiatry at Massachusetts General Hospital; and the 2013 Elizabeth Hurlock Beckman Award.